Mr H Kemley
2 Bede Street
Sherborne
DT9 3SD

GW00372516

CATCHING GOD AT WORK

(THE UNFINISHED SYMPHONY)

A DOCTOR LOOKS AT THE GLORY OF GOD'S WORLD
AND HIS PLANS TO HEAL ITS SICKNESS

John Mitchell

Deo
Favente Supero

Copyright © John Mitchell 2010
ISBN Number   978-0-9565273-0-1

This book is published by Dr John Mitchell, Yeovil,
First Edition 2010

Printed by Creeds of Bridport.

The cover picture was obtained from The Science Photo Library.

It is an optical image of the Horsehead Nebula in the constellation of Orion, taken through the U.K. Schmidt telescope in Australia, owned by the Royal Observatory, Edinburgh.

Contents

PREFACE	**8**
INTRODUCTION	**11**
THE STRUCTURE OF THE BIBLE	19
THE BIG THEMES OF THE BIBLE MESSAGE	20
THE OLD TESTAMENT	**24**
CREATION AND THE FALL IN GENESIS	**24**
GOD'S MASTER PLAN	29
GOD'S VOCATIONAL TRAINING SCHEME	34
EXODUS	**39**
THE TEN COMMANDMENTS	42
THE COVENANTS	43
LEVITICUS	**44**
NUMBERS	**44**
DEUTERONOMY	**45**
JOSHUA	**47**
JUDGES	**48**
RUTH	**48**
1 SAMUEL	**49**
2 SAMUEL	**51**
1 KINGS	**52**
2 KINGS	**54**
1 CHRONICLES	**55**
2 CHRONICLES	**56**
EZRA	**58**
NEHEMIAH	**58**
ESTHER	**60**
JOB	**61**
THE PSALMS	**63**
PROVERBS	**65**
ECCLESIASTES	**67**
THE SONG OF SOLOMON	**68**
THE PROPHETS	**69**
ISAIAH	**75**
JEREMIAH	**83**
LAMENTATIONS	**86**
EZEKIEL	**86**
DANIEL	**90**
HOSEA TO MALACHI (Minor Prophets)	**92**
HOSEA	93
JOEL	94

AMOS	95
OBADIAH	97
JONAH	98
MICAH	98
NAHUM	101
HABBAKUK	102
ZEPHANIAH	103
HAGGAI	104
ZECHARIAH	105
MALACHI	107
THE TIME BETWEEN THE TESTAMENTS	**109**
THE NEW TESTAMENT	**114**
A SHORT INTRODUCTION.	**114**
A WAY INTO THE NEW TESTAMENT	115
THE NEW TESTAMENT RECORDS	117
THE GOSPELS	**118**
JESUS, THE TOWERING CENTRAL FIGURE	**121**
THE STORY OF JESUS	**128**
HIS BIRTH AND THE INCARNATION	128
JESUS' THREE YEARS OF MINISTRY AND HIS DEATH AND RESURRECTION AS TOLD BY ALL FOUR EVANGELISTS	132
JESUS BEGINS HIS MINISTRY	133
JESUS' PARABLES	134
JESUS' MIRACLES	135
PETER'S RECOGNITION OF JESUS AS THE CHRIST	136
JESUS' TRANSFIGURATION	137
THE OPPOSITION INCREASES	137
JESUS ENTERS JERUSALEM	138
THE LAST SUPPER	139
THE GARDEN OF GETHSEMANE	140
JESUS BEFORE THE SANHEDRIN	141
JESUS BEFORE PILATE	141
THE CRUCIFIXION	143
JESUS' BURIAL	145
THE RESURRECTION	146
THE POST-RESURRECTION APPEARANCES	146
A COMMENTARY ON THE CROSS AND RESURRECTION	**149**
THE LORD'S PRAYER	154
GOD THE FATHER	157
THE SPIRIT OF GOD IN THE OLD TESTAMENT	162
THE HOLY SPIRIT IN THE NEW TESTAMENT	164
THE TRINITY - GOD IN THREE PERSONS	167
A COMMENTARY ON THE TRINITY	168
THE KINGDOM OF GOD	**173**
A COMMENTARY ON THE KINGDOM	**178**

ST JOHN'S GOSPEL   **193**
  THE MYSTERY OF THE INCARNATION   193
  ST JOHN'S GOSPEL CONTINUES   194
    NEW BIRTH AND ETERNAL LIFE   195
  JOHN CONTINUES IN CHAPTER 4   198
    LIGHT   204
ACTS   **206**
PAUL'S EPISTLES AND HIS MISSIONARY ACTIVITY   **213**
  GRACE   216
ROMANS   **218**
  CREATION   223
  EVIL, THE DEVIL, AND HUMAN SIN   232
1 CORINTHIANS   **236**
  THE CHURCH   238
  THE CREEDS   242
  THE NICENE CREED   244
  CHAPTER 13. PAUL WRITES ABOUT LOVE.   245
  CHAPTER 13   246
  1 CORINTHIANS CONTINUES   246
2 CORINTHIANS   **247**
GALATIANS   **250**
EPHESIANS   **251**
  MARRIAGE   254
PHILIPPIANS   **258**
COLOSSIANS   **260**
1 AND 2 THESSALONIANS   **262**
1 TIMOTHY   **262**
2 TIMOTHY   **264**
  SCRIPTURE   265
TITUS   **266**
PHILEMON   **267**
HEBREWS   **267**
  FAITH   269
JAMES   **272**
1 AND 2 PETER   **273**
1, 2 AND 3 JOHN   **275**
JUDE   **277**
REVELATION   **278**
CONCLUDING COMMENTARY   **286**
POSTSCRIPT   **288**
  CHRISTIANITY AND COMMUNITY AND FAMILY LIFE   296
  CHRISTIANITY AND THE ARTS   298
  PHILOSOPHY AND POLITICS   299
  THE RELATIONSHIP OF FAITH AND SCIENCE   300
GOD'S UNFINISHED SYMPHONY   **312**

APPENDICES   **315**

   APPENDIX 1   **315**

      HOW ARE WE TO UNDERSTAND GENDER?   315

      THE SOCIOLOGY OF MARRIAGE   318

   APPENDIX 2   **321**

      PHILOSOPHY, SCIENCE AND THEOLOGY   321

      SCIENCE AND THEOLOGY COMPARED AND CONTRASTED   324

      THE SCIENTIFIC METHOD   326

      RELATIVITY, QUANTUM MECHANICS AND STRING THEORY   329

   APPENDIX 3   **331**

      MYTH AND HISTORY   331

   APPENDIX 4   **335**

      SIMILE, METAPHOR, SYMBOL, PARABLE AND ALLEGORY   335

      IMAGINATION   339

   APPENDIX 5   **340**

      SECULAR, SECULARISATION AND SECULARISM   340

   APPENDIX 6   **347**

      MUSIC   347

GLOSSARY OF WORDS AND TERMS   **351**

      DEFINITIONS AND DESCRIPTIONS   351

BIBLIOGRAPHY   **360**

MAPS   **366**

Dedication : This book is dedicated to the countless wonderful Christians who have helped me in my journey of faith; to 'Hadders' and her two friends, without whose expression of interest in learning more about the Christian faith it would never have been written, and above all to my wife Shirley who has shared my life and faith for fifty years. She has patiently tolerated the often severe disruption that the writing of the book has caused. She has been my severest critic throughout and greatly reduced the extent of the necessary proof-reading and editing.

I am especially grateful to David Upton, who has done the final proof reading and editing and the preparation for printing. My thanks are also due to Creeds of Bridport for their advice and help with the printing itself.

NB 1) Where woman, or she, appears in the text the meaning should be clear; where 'man' or 'he' is referred to in the text it may mean man as male or stand for mankind as both male and female. The reader is asked to sense what is intended rather than being irritated by necessarily frequent distracting acrobatic alternatives on the page.

2) Whereas God is very often referred to in the Old Testament as the Lord, in order to avoid using YHWH, the special, forbidden Hebrew name for God, I have in most cases used the term God in order to avoid confusion. For that reason it needs to be pointed out that when Jesus is called Lord in the New Testament it is because he is being given the status accorded to YHWH, the God Almighty of the Old Testament.

3) The Bible references are in almost every case taken from the New International Version.

PREFACE

Five years ago my wife and I spent a holiday with three friends. One day all three of them expressed a desire to know more about the Christian faith. My first thought was to try to give them a brief account of my understanding of it in the form of a letter but it gradually turned into something more ambitious and substantial. It seemed as though their expression of interest had led to the growth of a seed that had lain dormant for some long while, namely a desire to write about the faith that has been a vital part of my life for over fifty years.

The more I thought about it the more reasons occurred to me for making this bold attempt. It is obvious in talking to both Christians and non-Christians that few people know a great deal about the faith and even many of those who have a strong faith do not have a clear understanding of it or find it easy to think and talk about it. A number of regular worshippers have admitted that they have difficulties with certain parts of the Creed which is after all the definitive statement of what Christians believe. These problems will inevitably increase with the reduction of specifically Christian School Assemblies, the number of those attending Sunday Worship and the decreased number of young people attending Junior Church and Christian Youth Clubs. Added to this is the increased study of other faiths, each of which has a different view of the nature of God, and the fairly numerous fictional accounts of the Gospel story that may be interesting but are a distraction for both believers and unbelievers. There is also the influence of assertive atheists who do not believe that God exists, and of agnostics who claim that we cannot know about him.

Christians, on the other hand, boldly assert that God not only exists but also that he can be known. To be a Christian is to believe and trust in Jesus Christ as Lord and Saviour, and in God as Father, through his Holy Spirit. To be a practising Christian is to become involved, as members of his Church, in public worship and in serving and witnessing to others. The Church is the body of Christ and is responsible for carrying on his ministry of teaching and preaching, healing and serving that he began when he was on earth. Believers, however good they may become, are not so much paragons of virtue as sinners who are aware of having been forgiven and wish to share their experience with others.

There is no simple answer to the question of how much Christians need to know about their faith but if, as we believe, God has revealed to us something of himself and of his plans for us and for his world, then sense dictates that we listen to what he has to say. In a society that is increasingly full of specialists, with the consequent fragmentation of human knowledge, there is a need to be able to relate our understanding of the faith to other disciplines, such as science, literature, history and politics. This requires a sufficient knowledge of the faith and a willingness to try to listen to what those with other interests are saying and to use a good deal of imaginative thinking in an attempt to bridge the gaps. The conflict that is thought to exist between science and religion is still, for many people, a live issue and it presents in a number of different forms. This lack of mutual understanding is no doubt explained in part by the tendency of the Church, until recently at least, to neglect God's creation in its necessary focus on his programme of salvation, or redemption as it is otherwise called. The Old Testament is a wonderful antidote to this failing in its frequent expressions of amazement at the glory of his universe, especially in a number of the Psalms.

In many parts of the world today the Church is growing and undergoing persecution, with Christians paying a heavy price, even martyrdom, for witnessing to their faith. In our own country the chief problem is apathy and a failure to recognise the increasingly rapid erosion of Christian faith in our society. In the majority of towns and villages in the Western world the Christian faith is not at present gaining ground and it is hard to win hearts and minds for Christ in an increasingly secular and materialistic world. There appears, almost invariably, to be an inverse relationship between material and spiritual well-being. In the developed countries, there is an automatic tendency for affluence, and the materialism that naturally accompanies it, to stifle the development of spiritual life and growth. This leads inevitably to a selfish disregard for the needs of others and above all the needs of our children and young people. We are too often failing to set them an example in the way we treat each other in the home and in society and the way in which we conduct business and politics. We are exercising too little discipline in our intimate physical relationships and neglecting to uphold the safeguard of marriage, with both cohabitation and divorce on the increase.

We are also disregarding the welfare of the environment in which we live and of the several billion people with whom we share the planet. The scientists tell us that we are endangering the delicate balancing mechanisms of the earth and the life that it supports, including our own. We are inevitably damaging the whole complex system by our selfish use of the world's resources. This includes the earth and its forests, the sea, the atmosphere and also the animal kingdom over which we have been given rule, as we are told in the first chapter of Genesis. What is not so clear is how long the resources of our world can be expected to last and how we should view our stewardship of them. Our overriding priority should be, as Jesus taught us, the spiritual aspiration of seeking first the kingdom of God and discovering how this affects everything else. This involves obedience to his commandments not only in our close personal relationships and in our social and business dealings but also in our local, national and international political negotiations. The real challenge is to our morality and not only to achieving a reduction in our carbon emissions. Our treatment of the earth is but one symptom of our failure to obey God's commandment to love him and to love our neighbour as ourselves.

It is important for us to talk to each other across the gaps that divide our water-tight specialties and our narrow, parochial interests and to recognise our spiritual as well as our scientific and political responsibilities. The dialogue has already begun and as Christians we have a duty to contribute to it. It is because we are bound above all to share our experience of the love of God that I offer what follows. It is offered in the hope and prayer that it may be of help to some in increasing their faith and to others in moving them towards it – and towards becoming disciples of Jesus in a world that is in such evident need of the kingdom of heaven that he came to inaugurate. Christians today, in the Western World at least, need cheering up. I would like to think that this book might do this for them and help them to recognise the greatness of God and of the Christian Gospel that has been faithfully handed down to us.

INTRODUCTION

The Christian faith is not a religion in the sense of a body of belief and teaching about how we think of God. It is rather God's own revelation of himself to us through a series of individuals and events recorded in the Old Testament, culminating in his sending of his own Son, Jesus Christ, that is described in the New Testament. These historical facts constitute the Gospel – the Good News that God has visited his people. By means of the life, death and resurrection of Jesus he has done all that is required to reconcile us to himself and to renew the whole of his creation. This massive programme of redemption and renewal, which the Bible refers to as the kingdom of God, was foretold by the prophets in the Old Testament and inaugurated by Jesus at his coming. It will be completed when he comes again in glory and judgement at the end of the age. The Good News that the kingdom had at last begun to arrive was announced by Jesus at the start of his ministry. It has been proclaimed and demonstrated by his Church and has been evident wherever God's will is done ever since that time. Needless to say we do not always contribute to its coming but in spite of our failures the Christian conviction is that God will one day bring his kingdom to fruition.

My purpose is to present the Christian faith as Good News for the world today, and the Bible as its most important book. It is described in the preface to the King James Authorised Version as 'God's sacred Word', the preaching of which is an 'inestimable treasure, which excelleth all the riches of the earth.' The key to understanding the Bible is Jesus, the Son of God, who together with God the Father is made real to us by his Holy Spirit. His coming, like the kingdom that he comes to introduce, is foretold in the Old Testament. When he speaks of himself in the New Testament as the fulfilment of the Law and the Prophets, he floods the whole of the Old Testament with fresh significance. The Old Testament is like a candle that is only truly lit by the flame of the New Testament. It may appear to be a bold claim but until we know Jesus we cannot know the true meaning of either the Old or the New Testament. Reading the Bible without the light that only a knowledge of Christ can bring to it is in a real sense like trying to appreciate the beauty of a stained glass window at night.

Our own national identity and that of many other countries has been moulded by this biblical Christian faith. Victor Hugo rightly said that 'The Bible made England' and our salvation as a civilisation lies in rediscovering its message. In the Coronation Service the monarch is given a copy of the Bible with these words: "We present you with this Book, the most valuable thing this world affords." It will never be out of date; it speaks of our origin and our destiny, our beginning and our end, and we need to recover an interest in both. Deprived of its nourishment we are like a tree whose roots have been severed and whose branches are withering and without direction. Dr John Sentamu said in his inauguration sermon as Archbishop of York in 2005: "There is nothing more needed by humanity today than the recovery of a sense of 'beyondness' in the whole of life to revive the spring of wonder and adoration. Jesus says 'Follow me'. May his commanding voice capture our hearts and turn us into radical disciples."

If an explanation is needed for giving so much space to the Old Testament – which incidentally occupies nearly three quarters of our Bible – it is that it speaks of God's relationship with Israel as a nation, with whom he made covenants, based on promises and obligations. This in turn casts light on the New Testament and complements its focus on his new covenant relationship, through Christ, with individuals and communities of faith in the new Israel of his Church. He continues to be active in the life of nations as well as that of individuals, though we may not recognise it, and the Old Testament continues to be a source of spiritual instruction and nourishment to both Jews and Christians, and many others also. It is long and not always easy and in places frankly unattractive, as is so much of history, and it is unlikely to be read as closely as the New Testament. But we cannot neglect it without diminishing our understanding of the full message of the Bible.

Genesis begins with the story of creation and the Fall and goes on to tell the stories of the Flood and of the Tower of Babel. The beginning of what would seem to be a truly historical thread in God's dealings with man some four thousand years ago, was the call of Abraham. It was through him that God began the process of calling out and preparing a people for himself through whom he planned to introduce his own new life into his creation in Christ. In this process of preparation it is impossible to overestimate the importance of God's Old Testament prophets. They reminded the people of God's promises to them, and of their obligations to him, which of course they frequently failed to honour. They also encouraged them to look for God's constant, faithful activity on their behalf and spoke to them of things yet to take place, above all the coming of his chosen Redeemer, the Messiah or Christ, as he would come to be known.

This phenomenon of prophecy served a unique function for the people of God throughout the centuries. It increased their faith in his sovereign power and bound together the progressive revelation of his purposes in both the Old and New Testaments. It also served a unique function in relating his people's destiny to the secular history of the surrounding nations in the Old Testament. In revealing the frequently repeated pattern of their disobedience and their punishment, repentance and restoration, it draws attention to the fact that this pattern in the life of nations is still in operation everywhere today through the judgement that appears to be built into the structure of creation. God has not ceased to be the Lord and ruler of history, as the prophets were constantly proclaiming. They also, and this includes Jesus himself and the New Testament writers, spoke prophetically about God's plan for his creation beyond history when Jesus returns to complete his kingdom. We live in an expanding universe, we are told, and the Bible is an expanding revelation of its creator and his purposes. It is a thoroughly evolutionary book. Darwin need never have unsettled the Victorian Church, as Cardinal Newman and many other contemporary Christians recognised from the outset.

If an excuse is needed for writing yet another book about the Bible and its story it is that its aim is to whet the appetite for the reading of the Bible itself. The digests of each of the books of the Bible are designed as tasters to describe and also recommend them. The book is written for all those who wish to know more about Scripture and the Christian faith, whether believers or not, and who are prepared to spend some time in order to enlarge their understanding. It would be misleading to suggest that this understanding can be acquired rapidly or without effort. The Bible is after all the story of what God has already done, what he is doing and what he intends to do in order to bring his entire creation to completion.

When we come to the New Testament, if it is not already familiar territory, the reading of a Gospel will be recommended as an essential preliminary. There is almost too much literature available already, none of which can speak with the authority of Scripture, to which we need to return again and again. It has been said that one of the tragedies of the modern world is that reading has become a substitute for thinking. Though it is an incomparable source of instruction and inspiration for living, the Bible should be seen not so much as an invitation to learning as a challenge to belief and active commitment. It issues us with a challenge to be disciples and servants and to be involved in the coming of God's kingdom. But the Bible is a long and complex book, written by many authors over a period of a thousand years and it needs to be explained and interpreted. If it is asked why a lay person should presume to undertake such an enormous task, I can only take shelter behind C S Lewis who wrote in the introduction to his Reflections on the Psalms, 'It often happens that two schoolboys can solve difficulties in their work for one another better than the master can. The fellow pupil can help more because he knows less!' My only other excuse is that as a doctor I have been trained to find out what is the matter with people – to make a diagnosis and if possible to prescribe treatment. This may possibly be helpful in seeing how exquisitely God's provision for the fallen world of his creation would seem to provide, as far as we can understand it, a perfect solution to what appears to be the matter with it. Everything that he does, not only in creation but also in its redemption, can be viewed, with the aid of faith, as evidence that can be subjected to a truly scientific examination. If this sounds to be a far-fetched claim, I hope to able to make it appear more reasonable as time goes on.

I have made an attempt to 'reshape the data', to use a helpful phrase from Rowan Williams' book 'Grace and Necessity', and to try to present a fresh picture of the enormous canvas of Scripture. Part of this reshaping consists of isolating and tracing the development of the dominant themes that run throughout the Bible from beginning to end so that it can be seen as a seamless whole and as a vast unfinished symphony. The main body of the book is a series of accounts – sometimes quite brief – of each of the sixty six books, in order to see what each is about and what kind of material it contains. The exceptions to this are the Psalms and Proverbs that must arguably first be read and allowed to speak for themselves before being subjected to study and comment. They are therefore simply given a very short introduction. I have tried to do justice to the hugely important topic of prophecy in a separate section before looking at the sixteen prophets themselves. I had not originally intended to look at each of the prophets individually but they have gradually emerged as such a vital part of God's revelation of his plans for us that, at risk of undue length and imbalance, I have felt obliged to give some space to each one of them.

The book is interspersed with a number of essays on the major biblical themes and several other important topics. If these sometimes seem to be an interruption they can be read separately, but they are intended as an integral part of the reshaping of the data that I have attempted in order to clarify the message of the Bible. They are usually placed in relation to the book of the Bible where the topic concerned is referred to most fully. There is a good deal of sometimes quite lengthy quotation in order to reveal the brilliant quality of the language of Scripture and the richness of its truth. My chief reason for including these gems is to act as an encouragement to readers to quarry the source for themselves. Also included are a number of quotations from secular works of prose, poetry, philosophy and science where these relate to biblical truth or help to cast light on it. I have added a fairly extensive Postscript in order to do justice to the relationships between faith and these other disciplines and to the conflict so often seen to exist between faith and science that could hardly be dealt with in the main body of the book. The same applies to a discussion of the ways in which theology and science respectively investigate the truth about God and about his world and their similarities and differences. This, together with several short articles on other relevant topics, is included in a series of appendices. There is, in addition, a fairly comprehensive glossary in order to make as clear as possible the meaning of some of the most important terms, a number of which need to be described rather than simply defined. For this reason, and because there is an unusually extensive list of contents at the start, there is no index at the end.

The resulting book may sometimes appear to be a rather bumpy ride and involve a degree of repetition – as does the Bible itself. It cannot pretend to be more than a brief and incomplete account of the Christian Gospel that is proclaimed in the New Testament and the preparations for it that are described in the Old Testament. It is on both of these that each generation has to build its own understanding of the truth, with the aid of tradition and reason. It is no surprise that some aspects of this understanding have varied from one period to another in the past two thousand years. The Good News of the Gospel is that God the Father has been revealed by his Son Jesus, through his life and ministry, death and resurrection, and that both are revealed to us by the Holy Spirit who was poured out at Pentecost. The Christian belief is that through this we learn the truth about God and about ourselves, about the world we live in, and about where we come from and where we're going. When seen through the eyes of faith, this Christ Event, from which we measure time both forwards and backwards, AD and BC, towers in importance over every other event in history. If the God of creation was truly embodied in Christ, as Christians have the temerity to believe, there can be no other comparable happening. As Christians we can rejoice that our Lord and Saviour, Jesus Christ, is still capable of being seen as the One in whom the whole of the expanding universe, in all its evident immensity and complexity, 'holds together'. (Col 1:17). These are bold claims to make so early on. My hope and prayer is that those who are sceptical will read on and see how it is possible to hold such seemingly outrageous beliefs, and that some will even come to share them.

The chief reason for writing this book is a desire to share the conviction that the greatest discovery anyone can ever make is that the ultimate truth is not to be found in any intellectual proposition or any scientific discovery or formula but in the person of Christ. The Bible tells us that he is the God of creation made known to us in human flesh, to whom we relate as whole people in worship, praise and prayer. This ultimate truth is revealed not to reason alone, but to the whole spiritual being of man, and appeals also to his heart and will. The mind is only a part of our total make-up and cannot, unaided, reach the goal to which our whole personality aspires. For D.H. Lawrence thought itself was not a purely rational exercise but rather 'a man in his wholeness wholly attending.' Needless to say God demands our whole attention more surely than any other subject. The only still point from which all things can be understood is the God who made them, but like his universe he too is always on the move. In the words of T.S. Eliot in his Four Quartets, 'there is only the dance' – the constant evidence of the perpetual motion of God's creative activity – the dance of dolphins and swallows and of God himself. He keeps us all guessing; scientists, philosophers, artists and politicians, as well as worshippers. He is a God of surprises. Einstein is recorded as saying 'I have spent my whole life trying to catch him at his work'

16

– an expression that encompasses both theological and scientific aspiration. The theologian investigates God's nature, arguing from what he's done to what he's like, and the scientist what he's up to in creation – 'thinking his thoughts after him' in the words of Kepler, the seventeenth century astronomer.

Both theology and science are concerned with phenomena, literally things that reveal themselves to us. For the believing scientist, research becomes a kind of prayer and for all believers God and his revelation of himself are phenomena that invite our exploration as surely as the natural phenomena of his universe. It is becoming increasingly clear that the natural and the supernatural are not as distinct as we once imagined. It is simply that the phenomena and the methods by which we investigate them are different. Some would wish to say that creation is so wonderful that we have no need to interest ourselves in the idea of a creator. But what if he has expressed an interest in us? This book is the result of an irresistible compulsion to write about what God has done for us in Christ. What I have attempted has had a long process of incubation, and as T.S. Eliot said of the experience of writing some of his poetry, 'We do not know until the shell breaks what kind of egg we have been sitting on.'[1] Even now I'm not quite sure what sort of egg I have laid. It is clear that trying to catch God at his work involves not only theology, or the study of God himself, but a study of the world that he has made in all its variety and the ways in which we obtain our knowledge of it.

What I have written is not original, only an original arrangement of the data, and there are no doubt errors of fact, errors of reasoning and errors of understanding and interpretation of biblical truth. There can be few if any books on this complex subject of which this is not true. My hope and prayer is that this particular re-arrangement will help others to a fuller understanding of the Gospel of Christ and will thereby enrich their lives. One of my reasons for writing about the Gospel is my firm conviction that it is the way things are. Einstein said of the theory of relativity that it was too beautiful to be wrong and the same can be said of the Gospel. It is the only thing that makes sense of a world that was described by Jung as 'brutal and cruel, and at the same time of divine beauty.'[2] The Good News is that the God

---

[1] The Use of Poetry. Conclusion p144
[2] Memories, Dreams, Reflections p390.

of endless power and love has taken drastic and infinitely costly action to deal with the problem of sin and evil and suffering that in his wisdom he has allowed to exist. The Gospel is the story of this drastic and costly action. In spite of all the evidence to the contrary the world can be seen to make sense after all even if the truth, as might be expected, is frequently paradoxical and challenging. The only thing that ultimately makes sense is love, strong and unsentimental love. Reason is vital for our understanding but it is not the key that unlocks the deepest truths about our lives. We are all of us looking not so much for dogma and doctrine as for love, though none of us experience it as richly as we know we might. Philip Larkin wrote in his poem 'Faith Healing':

'In everyone there sleeps
A sense of life lived according to love.'

The Christian conviction is that the Cross of Christ provides us with the definitive shape of self-giving love. It is this love that we all of us seek and that we long to waken in us. 'This is how we know what love is: Jesus Christ laid down his life for us.' (1 John 3:16.) This revelation of the shape of love and all that Scripture tells us about God and about his plan for the redemption of his whole creation gives rise to Christian theology and the doctrines and creeds that are its essential accompaniments. Love is the universal language of communication by means of which creation is consummated. As the crowning demonstration of God himself acting in relation to everything he has made it provides us with the key to our understanding of the world. Love could be said to be the spiritual equivalent of the so-called single theory of everything by means of which scientists seek to unify all physical phenomena. Maybe it does duty for both. In Paul's words in 1 Cor 13 we shall not 'know fully', either about God himself or about his creation until we see him 'face to face'.

It might be argued that what Christians believe about the love of God should lead them to demonstrate more of it in their own lives. The trouble is, that as with everything that involves fallible human beings, our best intentions often end in failure. An ostensibly unbelieving friend once said to me, quite justifiably, in response to yet another failure on my part: 'If your faith is as good as I think it is, you would not complain.' Many who do not practise the faith in terms of public worship and witness have a very good idea of how it ought to work in the lives of those who do and are thereby able to keep us on our toes. There are fortunately many examples of the greatest of the saints who make up for the rest of us. They are the ones who truly listen to God and respond to his demands. This book is an attempt to follow their example and to focus on what God is thinking and doing and saying – rather than primarily on our own ideas and activities, which is our natural inclination.

The next short section is a brief look at the basic structure of the Bible in which, above all other books, we catch God himself at his work and discover what he is thinking and doing, and what he is saying to us.

THE STRUCTURE OF THE BIBLE

The Bible is a book containing many books – sixty-six in all – written during a period of over a thousand years. The earliest of the thirty nine books of the Old Testament were written almost three and a half thousand years ago, and the latest, the twenty seven books of the New Testament, almost two thousand years ago. There is a gap of five hundred years between Malachi in around 450 BC and the earliest of the New Testament books in around 50 AD. These very different books, written by a variety of authors, all have the same focus on God and on his plans for his people and for his creation.

The Old Testament is a record of the love and concern of God for the small nation of people through whom he has chosen to bring blessing to all nations and from whom, for this reason, he demands faithful love and obedience in return. It consists of four main sections with several different categories of material: History; Law; Poetry and Wisdom Literature, and Prophecy. The first five books of the Bible, known as the Pentateuch, literally 'five books', contain both history, and pre-history, and Law. They are Genesis, Exodus, Leviticus, Numbers and Deuteronomy and they are traditionally thought to have been written largely by Moses. The next twelve, from Joshua to Esther, are called the historical books; the following five, Job, Psalms, Proverbs, Ecclesiastes and The Song of Solomon are known as the

Poetry and Wisdom Literature. The remaining books, from Isaiah to Malachi, are referred to as the Prophets. There are four 'major' prophets, Isaiah, Jeremiah, Ezekiel and Daniel and twelve 'minor' prophets – so called simply because their books are shorter.

The New Testament consists of four Gospels, written by the four Evangelists, the Acts of the Apostles, twenty one Epistles and the Revelation. The focus of all these books is above all on the coming of Jesus Christ, the One through whom the blessings promised in the Old Testament have been, are being and will continue to be realised. The focus is also on the Church as the body of people through whom, in spite of all their failings, it is God's plan to proclaim and demonstrate these blessings. They are called to play their part in witnessing to the coming of God's kingdom which is the Good News foretold in the Old Testament and announced at the beginning of the Gospels.

THE BIG THEMES OF THE BIBLE MESSAGE

Every one of the books of the Bible speaks with the same voice because they are, each of them, to the eye of faith, clearly informed and inspired, but not dictated, by the same Spirit. The more closely we study the Scriptures the more remarkable and convincing they appear to be and the more impressive in their consistent message through the many different writers who contributed to them. They are as relevant as when they were written, and more so because their applications have been multiplying in the intervening years as our knowledge of the world to which they relate has increased.

The Bible is arranged more or less chronologically rather than systematically and is a consistent, progressive revelation with constantly recurring themes that are evident throughout its length. The story of God's majestic strategy in creation and redemption centres naturally on God himself. It tells us about who he is and what he has done and what he is doing, but also about what he will do in the future, as it is revealed to us through prophecy. One of the chief aims of this book is to try to show how these big themes fit together like the pieces of a jig-saw and eventually become combined and harmonised so that the vast and complex programme becomes more comprehensible. We shall naturally move forwards through the story of God's progressive self-revelation. We shall sometimes look back, however, in order to notice how the story has been unfolding and how the themes are being developed and are linked over time by the threads of prophetic communication.

The fundamental themes that run through the Bible from beginning to end can be seen as:

1. God himself, the Creator and overriding sovereign presence who reveals himself progressively as Lord and Saviour and eventually comes to be recognised as Father, Son and Holy Spirit in the New Testament. He is the God of love and, as his creation reveals, his power is beyond imagining.

2. The Creation, culminating in Man, created in God's image, and his fall that highlights the evil already present in creation. The mystery of evil and Man's sin and need of redemption are constantly recurring themes throughout the Bible.

3. God's people. In the Old Testament, the people of Israel with whom he established his original covenant relationship through Abraham. In the New Testament also the new Israel of the Church, by means of the new covenant, or testament, established through the sacrificial death of his Son Jesus.

4. The Law and the Prophets. These include not only the commandments given through Moses, but also the covenants between God and his people, and the prophets who constantly reminded them of both. It was through the prophets that he told them also of his future plans for them and for his creation.

5. The Sacrifices, and the Priests who were appointed to administer them, brought to perfection in the once-for-all sacrifice of Christ the Redeemer for the sins of the whole world.

6. The Kingdom of God, first announced to King David, to whom God promised that his throne would be established for ever as God's own everlasting kingdom. (2 Samuel 7:16.) This is a dominant theme in the New Testament, with the coming of the kingdom inaugurated by Jesus and to be completed when he comes again in glory and judgement at the end of the age.

These key themes and their varied manifestations can be seen as together making up the score of the monumental unfinished symphony of God's activity in creation and redemption. The dominant theme throughout Scripture, always and everywhere, is God and what he progressively reveals to us of himself as we are ready to hear it. The symphony begins with God and his creation of the heavens and the earth in Genesis and ends with the coda or finale of the envisaged renewal and consummation of his creation in the new heaven and the new earth in Revelation. This coda is the final movement that is yet to be performed when Jesus comes again and brings an end to history. The themes recur and are progressively developed, and varied in their expression, as in the musical model. They are revealed either singly or in combination through the huge variety of people and events and places that make up the stories by which the message of the Bible is conveyed. In the Old Testament, the first of the two huge movements of the symphony, we have, for example, God giving the Commandments to Moses on the mountain and Solomon building the Temple in Jerusalem. In the New Testament, the second huge movement, we have Jesus' birth in Bethlehem, his crucifixion on Calvary and the coming of the Holy Spirit at Pentecost when all the people were gathered together in 'one place'. There are many other important though less fundamental examples.

As with the musical model, each and every one of these variations of personality, event and place, and the development of the themes that they represent, have their own unique importance. Because God's salvation extends to the whole of his creation, without limits as to either space or time, the whole of human history and of eternity is included within the orbit of this all-encompassing programme. It is not only the finale that matters, though it will be the most glorious of all the movements, but also the rich pageant of all the countless individuals and nations and kingdoms throughout history that will be brought to their completion in it. All those who have gone before us, we ourselves and those who follow us are destined to be the material of which the final movement is to be composed, if we will only accept the invitation that God offers us. It has been said that every age is equidistant from eternity: in the words of TS Eliot, 'history is a pattern of timeless moments.'[3] Our ancestors and their communities were not mere precursors in a process of perpetual improvement but existed, as we now do ourselves, as definitive cultures within this unfolding history. Only science, in spite of inevitable errors, can be said to make continuing progress. Each and every individual exists to give glory to God, and as Rev 21: 22-27 indicates, when ultimately freed from all that offends, every community and nation has the possibility of being incorporated into the eternal city of his kingdom. This adds an entirely new meaning to our lives.

We can also envisage many of these themes in pictorial form as innumerable artists have done throughout the centuries. We can also project ourselves in our imagination into the stories of the people, events and places involved, but we must not lose sight of the progressive development of the themes over time and their variations in terms of these personalities, events and places. This is because it is in this evidently evolutionary way that God has revealed himself and his plans for his creation. His work of renewal and redemption in history is every bit as much a part of his creation and just as scientific if we can only see it, as the so-called natural world that it is his intention to renew and redeem. When he made the world he made it make itself and he has entrusted us, made in his own image, with the freedom and responsibility of co-operating with him in its completion. He has also given us the opportunity to co-operate with him in our own development and transformation so that we can become fit to live with him in eternity. The Bible tells the story of how he has set about making all these things possible. The big themes, and the huge variety of different forms in which they are embodied are the connecting strands that run throughout the story of this colossal undertaking.

We need now to go back to the beginning of the Bible where in the first verses of Genesis the origin of the universe is described as God's sovereign creative act.

---

[3] Four Quartets, Little Gidding V

THE OLD TESTAMENT

CREATION AND THE FALL IN GENESIS

Genesis, the first book of the Bible, begins with God and his creation of heaven and earth; of all that is. This is because, as it gradually emerges, God's subsequent activity, above all through the incarnation and saving work of Christ, is concerned with nothing less than everything that he has made. He is revealed in the first three verses as expressing himself through his Word – "Let there be light" – and acting through his Spirit who is said to have 'hovered over the waters'. There is thus a hint from the very outset of the threefold nature of the God whom it is the precious and unique experience of the Christian to recognise as three persons, as the 'Blessed Trinity' – as himself already a community. The writer is traditionally thought to be Moses. He begins with a progressive, positively evolutionary-sounding description of the creation – apart from its apparent compression into six days! He tells us that the earth that God created was initially formless, empty and dark. He next describes the creation of light, thus producing the separation of day and night, and he follows this with the creation of sea and sky and dry land. Next to appear are plants and living creatures in the sea and the sky and on land, and lastly Man.

The writer of Genesis can hardly have imagined that the Creation would one day come to be regarded by scientists as having started with the Big Bang more than thirteen billion years ago. Nor could he have guessed that the solar system and our earth would not appear for another five billion years and that it was not until a further billion years had elapsed that the earliest forms of life were able to develop. This had to await the synthesis of the carbon and the other elements of which all living things are made from the dust of dying stars. It took several more billion years for Man to emerge as the leading shoot of the evolutionary process. This is the time scale we are now told we

24

have to give to this colossal story. This seemingly endless passage of time has no doubt to elapse between God's dream and its fulfilling.

God created Man 'in his own image', as both male and female, 'breathing the breath of life into his nostrils' so that he became a 'living being'. This would appear to provide a recognition of our obvious differences from all God's other creatures, above all our ability to seek a relationship with him. These obvious differences are rendered even more remarkable by the recent scientific discovery that we share at least ninety eight percent of our DNA with our nearest primate relative, the chimpanzee. It has now emerged that we inherit not just the same number of genes as a mouse, for instance – fewer than 21,000 – but in most cases the very same genes. Just as different words are not required in order to write different books, so new genes are not required to make new species; it is apparently necessary only to change the order and pattern of their use and the length of time that they are given to operate. It is now known that a certain gene called FOX P2 is critical for the normal development of both speech in people and song in birds and that a mutation in this gene causes language defects in people.

It is no wonder that we feel such an affinity with our animal ancestors and spend so much time studying them, domesticating them where possible and trying to preserve them from harm or even extinction. Our renewed interest in them, with our knowledge so wonderfully increased by modern technology, becomes a kind of extended genealogy. The ways in which we differ from them and above all our precise evolutionary relationship with them, remain a mystery. In his 'Origin of Species' Darwin made no mention of this problem, returning to it some ten years later in his 'Descent of Man.' He wrote that 'Man with all his noble qualities still bears in his bodily frame the indelible stamp of his lowly origin.' The mystery has not yet been solved. If his noble qualities are truly distinct, and of a different order, then we must assume a separate creative act but the problem is likely to continue to frustrate our attempts to investigate it.

The Biblical story continues with the man and the woman being told to be fruitful and multiply and to fill the earth and subdue it. They are to rule over the other creatures and along with them to use the plants and the fruit of trees as food – not to exploit creation for our own selfish ends but to be good stewards, as we now speak of it. The woman given to Adam as a 'suitable helper' and companion, because 'it is not good for the man to be alone,' is graphically described as coming from his side. This is symbolic of the leaving and cleaving and the 'becoming one flesh' of marriage that we can see to be the divinely ordained arrangement for safeguarding our marital relationships and the offspring that result from our physical union.

We find them naked and unashamed in the garden but they disobey God almost immediately. The 'Fall' is pictured graphically as eating the forbidden fruit from the tree of the knowledge of good and evil that will lead to their spiritual death – that is to their separation from God. Their sin lies in their desire for knowledge and independence rather than relationship with him. The man blames the woman – a recognisable pattern! – and the woman blames the serpent, who has contradicted God and deceived her and led her into disobedience. Evil is both within and without, and the man and the woman are both guilty. They know immediately that they are 'naked'; they experience shame and fear. As a result of their disobedience they sacrifice the eternal life of fellowship with God for the 'knowledge of good and evil' that is so attractive to them. As a result, they are driven out of the garden to till the ground in hardship, through painful toil and sweat, and to experience pain in childbearing. Their relationship with the earth has also been damaged as a result of the change in their relationship with God.

Death and disease were clearly present in nature throughout its evolutionary development and the presence of pre-existing evil is indicated by the serpent that symbolises the devil who is already at enmity with God. By their own disobedience Adam and Eve, and all of us through them and through our own disobedience, are drawn into this enmity that is one of the constant themes of Scripture. At the same time the devil makes a new enemy in Man and seals his own fate: the serpent is cursed and promised continual conflict with humanity. He will 'strike man's heel' and the woman's offspring will 'crush his head'. Christians see this as teaching us a dual truth. The devil will continue to tempt and try to harm us but there is also the indication, right from the start, of his ultimate defeat through Christ's victory on the Cross. This victory alone will one day lead to the reversal of the Fall; to our reconciliation with God and our eventual, uninterrupted fellowship with him. From the very first pages of Scripture it is revealed that he has already sown the seed of our recovery and we catch an early glimpse of the perfection of his planning. The problem of good and evil has intrigued and baffled the finest minds in history. It is beyond us to understand but this extraordinary allegorical story gives us the clearest indication we have of how we should approach this impenetrable mystery.

The beautiful story of Adam and Eve's initial, innocent relationship with God in the garden of Eden is surely given to us to bring about a sense of nostalgia for this uninterrupted fellowship with God our creator that we can somehow sense, however deep-down, to be our destiny. 'In our beginning is our end.' Our lives are a journey from God into God. The myth of a lost paradise has been found to be an element in every culture: it would appear to be ingrained in our collective psyche.

Our fellowship with God is fractured by our individual rejection of him. This rejection takes the form of our misuse of the free will he has given us; of our self-centred pursuit of our own agenda, and of our determination to prove that we know best and that we can do without him. Nietzsche, the brilliant maverick philosopher with whom we associate the idea that 'God is dead', proved conclusively by all he said and did and all he tried to be that we cannot do without him, that we cannot overcome the dark side of our nature and save ourselves. All this struggling is somehow essential for our development however: it must be the way that God ordained it. It would appear that we did not become but were created mortal, with the spiritual gravity that causes each one of us to fall from the height that we can aspire to only through God's grace. He alone can finally rescue us and one day enable us to overcome this gravity through the final stage of our redemption and his gift of a spiritual as opposed to a purely physical body. The Good News of the biblical story is that the pain and suffering of this world will one day be done away with and that our endurance of them in this life will somehow render our experience of heaven so much more glorious by contrast. There is a long way to travel before we reach this goal however – in biblical terms we have to wait until the last three chapters of Revelation.

Genesis continues with a stark example of what sin brings with it. Tragedy ensues immediately: Adam and Eve's firstborn son Cain kills his younger brother Abel. The next story is of the flood. God sees the greatness of man's wickedness and is grieved that he has made him. He is described as sending the flood, saving only the righteous Noah and his family and the animals in the ark that Noah is instructed to make. God starts afresh with this remnant after the flood subsides and he makes a covenant with them never again to cut off all life by a flood, sealing it with the sign of the 'rainbow in the clouds'. Noah, though apparently uniquely worthy of being saved, is far from perfect and as a start to his life after the deluge he gets drunk. It was a no doubt an expression of his relief at no longer being incarcerated with a load of animals! If God were to attempt to choose only entirely satisfactory people for his work he would never find anyone to do it.

The trouble continues: men get above themselves. "Come let us build ourselves a city, with a tower that reaches to the heavens, so that we may make a name for ourselves and not be scattered over the face of the whole earth." (Gen 11:4). We are still at it. An Indian architect in Delhi has recently announced plans to build the world's tallest building to upstage competitors elsewhere and has said: "It is about status. It is about glorification. It is high time that people started realising that we too are a great nation." Civilisation and the building of cities are inevitable and necessary but they carry with them the danger that men will be less close to the earth and to God. In Genesis 11:6 the Lord is pictured coming down to see the city and the tower that the men are building and he says, "If as one people speaking the same language they have begun to do this, then nothing they plan to do will be impossible for them." They have to be confused with many languages and scattered over the earth to ensure a variety of peoples, each with their different cultures and languages, rather than their becoming one over-mighty nation – of which the European Union is determined to become an example. They also have to be taught that they cannot build the kingdom of heaven on their own. This is a lesson that we still have not learned, but in a strange way we have to keep on trying, by exercising the massive freedom that we have been given. It is a sobering fact that this variety of different peoples inevitably gives rise to conflict. This conflict is bound to accompany the negotiations on which the development of the world depends – negotiations about land and natural resources, about economics and the balance of power. Jesus tells us bluntly in Matt 24:6,7, and also in Mark and Luke, that there will be "wars and rumours of wars" and that "such things must happen. Nation will rise against nation, and kingdom against kingdom" until he comes again in glory at the end of the age.

But this is still in the future and we are as yet only at the start of history in our unfolding story of God's dealings with his world. He needs a master plan to deal with the problem posed by his wayward people. The rest of the Genesis story and a condensed account of the remainder of the Old Testament will now be related in this context.

GOD'S MASTER PLAN

The remainder of Genesis and the whole of the Old Testament is the story of how God begins to put this plan into action. There could be no better preparation for this story than a reading of Psalm 105 in which the writer gives thanks to the Lord for his gracious dealings with his people from their earliest days until their entry into the promised land. What follows is an attempt to give a continuous account of this story and all that results from it as it is recorded in the Old Testament, from Genesis to Malachi. When we then come to look at each of the Old Testament books in turn it may inevitably involve some repetition, as happens in Scripture itself.

It would appear from the account in the early chapters of Genesis that the time came when God judged that his people were ready for him to reveal himself to them. Their ability to receive this revelation must clearly have involved a number of factors. It must have depended on such things as the stage of their psychological maturity and of the development of their language and thought. It must also have depended on the existence of an alphabet and the means of creating written records for their own use and for the use of those who came after them. It seems that it was not until around 2000BC that all these things were beginning to come together and it was at this point in time that, as we read in Gen 12, God called out the patriarch Abraham. He made a covenant with him that he was to leave his own country for 'the land that I will show you' and a promise that he would make him into 'a great nation' and 'a father of many nations'. He would be a blessing to all peoples on earth through the 'everlasting covenant' that would extend to his descendants. Abraham believed God and was obedient to his call, thereby setting the pattern for God's dealings with man forever afterwards, reckoning him righteous on the basis of his faith in him and in his promises. It is through Abraham's line, issuing in the virgin Mary at the appointed time, and at the appointed place in that same promised land, that God would reveal himself in human flesh in the person of his only Son Jesus, the Christ.

Abraham further proved his faith and obedience by his willingness to sacrifice his only son Isaac. This was in spite of the fact that it was through him alone that the promises God had made to him could be fulfilled. God's sparing of Isaac is graphically described in his provision of an alternative sacrifice in the 'ram caught by its horns' in a thicket. As a result Isaac survived and some years later he married Rebekah. His younger son Jacob, later named Israel, had twelve sons. These twelve sons give their names to the twelve tribes of Israel who had a hugely important place throughout the whole extent of the biblical story. Israel is mentioned more than 2000 times in the Old Testament alone. One of these sons, the favourite youngest son Joseph, was sold into Egypt by his brothers because they were jealous of him. But the Lord was with him and Pharaoh, the Egyptian king, put him in charge of the whole land of Egypt. When a famine occurred in Canaan his brothers, hearing that there was corn in Egypt, went to buy some. They met Joseph who later revealed himself to them, and forgave them, telling them that it was really God who had sent him into Egypt, not them. Having obtained Pharaoah's permission, he invited them and Jacob his father and all the twelve tribes to join him in Egypt, in order to escape the famine. They remained in Egypt for about four hundred years and initially prospered greatly. But eventually other Pharaohs came to rule 'who did not know about Joseph' and from whom they no longer received favoured treatment. Privileges were withdrawn and they gradually became slaves. Genesis ends with the death of Jacob, and later the death of Joseph, but not until he had confirmed that he had truly forgiven his brothers and assured them that God would surely come to their aid and take them to the land he had promised to Abraham, Isaac and Jacob. They needed constant encouragement to keep alive their faith in God's promises.

It was at this time that God raised up Moses, the first and greatest of the prophets. Moses had been born in Egypt and was brought up in court circles. He is described in Acts 7:22 as having been 'educated in all the wisdom of the Egyptians and was powerful in speech and action.' Egyptian education was amongst the finest of the day and this training no doubt helped him to become an outstanding leader. He would eventually lead the people out of Egypt, probably around 1400 BC, after the ruling Pharaoh had been persuaded by the plagues to let them go. Only three months after they left Egypt God made a conditional covenant with them, through Moses at Mount Sinai, that if they obeyed him fully they would be his 'treasured possession' and that they would be for him a 'kingdom of priests and a holy nation.' (Ex 19:6). Moses met with God at the top of the mountain where he was given the Ten Commandments that he then delivered to the people. On his return from the mountain he told them, "Do not be afraid. God has come to test you, so that the fear of God will be with you to keep you from sinning." (Ex 20:20).

Moses held the people together with great difficulty during their forty years of wandering and testing in the desert, even though God was with him, inspiring and strengthening him. In spite of this special relationship and his long period of outstanding leadership even he was not always obedient however and he later paid a price for this. It was not Moses but his successor Joshua whom God chose to lead the people of Israel into the land that he had promised to Abraham hundreds of years before. When they eventually entered the promised land things went far from smoothly. Gaining control of the land of Canaan from the tribes who already lived there was no easy task and cost many lives. In addition to this the people of Israel intermarried with these tribes, against instructions, and were influenced by their barbaric religious beliefs and practices. Following the death of Joshua 'the Lord raised up Judges, who saved them out of the hand of raiders.' (Judg 2:16). These Judges were in the nature of deliverers for his people – leaders in battle and rulers in peace, as Joshua himself had been. The best known of them were Gideon, Samson and Samuel. They were not able to provide stable government, however, and we read in Judges 17:6 that 'in those days Israel had no king; everyone did as he saw fit.'

When the people later increased in numbers and became a nation they asked for a king to provide them with an identity and with security from unfriendly neighbouring nations, especially the Philistines. This request was eventually granted, in spite of concern that it might threaten God's own sovereignty over his people, and Saul was anointed as the first of the kings by the prophet Samuel. The kings were not without their problems as leaders either and the majority of them, even if they began promisingly, were failures. There are many lessons for the present day: the majority of leaders are liable to be a disappointment to those they govern and often to themselves as well. The notable exception, for all his faults, was King David who was promised that through his son Solomon, his kingdom and his throne would be established for ever as God's own everlasting kingdom. This was the kingdom that Jesus would come to inaugurate a thousand years later.

To provide for the spiritual welfare of his people God raised up prophets who reminded them of the commandments and the covenants that he had made with them, and also of his blessing and his judgement, depending on whether they were faithful or unfaithful to him. The prophets exerted their ministry and influence mainly during the period of these fallible kings and during the two captivities to which God's people were subjected, in Assyria and Babylon, as a punishment for their disobedience. He used other nations to teach them the lessons that they needed to learn, as he continues to do with the nations of the world today, though we tend not to see it in these terms.

During the time of Moses the people had also been given priests, who came initially from the family of his brother Aaron and later from the members of the tribe of Levi. They were to act as God's representatives, to mediate between God and Man in worship and to offer sacrifices, a function previously carried out by the head of each household. These sacrifices were offered initially in the tabernacle in the desert as prescribed by God through Moses and later, when the people were settled in the promised land, in the Temple built by king Solomon. The sacrifices took the form of unblemished animals that were offered to God in penitence and praise and thanksgiving. The unblemished animals symbolised God's holiness and reminded the people of their need of forgiveness and cleansing from sin. The priests provided tradition, stability and order and the prophets provided the element of challenge and inspiration. Both of these contributions are still needed in the Church today to give balance to its life and worship.

King David was succeeded by his son Solomon whose wisdom was legendary but who overspent on lavish buildings. Later he became disobedient, marrying many foreign women, against specific instructions, and thereby incurred God's anger and judgement. After Solomon's death the united kingdom divided into the ten northern tribes of Israel centred on Samaria and the two southern tribes, Judah and Benjamin centred on their capital Jerusalem, each with their own kings. Neither of these two kingdoms responded to the pleadings of God through his prophets. Their repeated disobedience and lack of faithfulness in their following of other gods was punished by their defeat and exile under foreign powers. In the case of the northern kingdom their divinely ordained captors were the Assyrians who, in 721 BC, took 27,000 of them into a captivity from which they never returned. There are rather surprisingly no known records of their subsequent history. They had presumably become fully integrated, or even more widely dispersed, by the time the Assyrians were defeated by the Babylonians over a hundred years later in 612 BC.The southern kingdom of Judah was defeated by the Babylonians under king Nebuchadnezzar who carried many of their people off to Babylon in 597 BC. Ten years later the Babylonians completely destroyed Jerusalem and took captive many of the remaining people in the city.

During their years of captivity in Babylon this small remnant of God's people, deprived of the Temple and of sacrifices, developed a more mature and spiritual style of worship. They met in synagogues where they experienced the preaching and teaching of the Law and the Prophets and they also developed a more personal style of spirituality and prayer and came to see themselves as individuals and not merely as members of the Jewish nation. It was not until 539BC when Cyrus the Persian in turn defeated the Babylonians and destroyed the city of Babylon that they were allowed home as foretold in Isaiah 44:24-28, 45:13 and Micah 5, and encouraged to rebuild their temple that had been razed to the ground some 60 years before. It is recorded in Ezra 1:1-11 that they returned under their governor Zerubbabel in 538 and finished the temple in 516. In 458 the community was strengthened by the arrival of Ezra the priest who was encouraged to develop the temple worship and ensure obedience to the Law.

The return of the Jews to their own land with Cyrus' blessing was of vital importance in re-establishing their identity as a nation and in reviving their spiritual life. Thirteen years later, in 445 BC, the then Persian king Artaxerxes allowed his cupbearer Nehemiah to return to rebuild the walls and tighten up the religious and social life. (Neh 6:15.) This was just two years after the Greeks began work on the Parthenon in Athens. When Nehemiah left Jerusalem in 433 and returned to the service of the Persian king the Jews fell into sin once more. Tithes were ignored, the Sabbath broken, foreign intermarriage took place and the priests became corrupt. These sins were condemned by the prophet Malachi in the last book of the Old Testament.

Following Malachi there were 400 years without further written prophecy. This period will be described in a later chapter on the time between the two Testaments. The Jews, as they became more generally known following their return from captivity, continued to be at the mercy of their powerful ruling neighbours. These included the Persians who were positively helpful to them, the Greeks who finally defeated the Persians in 333-331BC, and the Romans. These years without prophecy continued until John the Baptist, the last of the Old Testament prophets, came to herald the arrival of the Christ. This is described at the start of the New Testament.

GOD'S VOCATIONAL TRAINING SCHEME

The more we study the Old Testament account of God's dealings with his people Israel, the more it looks like the most remarkable and extensive vocational training scheme in history. His hand is clearly at work, not only in the call of Abraham but also in the Exodus from Egypt, the entry into the promised land and the captivity of Judah and their eventual return from Babylon. Apart from the spiritual lessons that they learned while they were in Egypt, they must have learned many others also. They must have seen and wondered at the great pyramids of Giza built almost a thousand years before they arrived. In the first chapter of Exodus it is recorded that the Egyptians 'put slave masters over them to oppress them with forced labour' and that they made bricks and 'built Pithom and Rameses as store cities for Pharaoh.' It is not possible to identify these cities with certainty but it may be that the people of Israel were also involved in the building that was carried out in the great palaces at Karnak and Luxor and the royal tombs in the Valley of the Kings from around 1550 BC onwards when they were still in Egypt.

The exact date of their departure is not known but is variously estimated as up to fifty years or more on one or other side of 1400BC. This period included the reigns of some of the greatest pharaohs of the 18th to 20th dynasties when Egypt was at the height of its political and cultural power and influence. The people of Israel must have gained immeasurably from their exposure to Egyptian culture including their expertise in administration, engineering, building and irrigation. They must also have been hugely influenced in terms of their own future creativity by Egyptian art – by their woodwork, metalwork and sculpture. It is interesting to note from biblical and archaeological evidence that the design of the tabernacle furniture bore remarkable similarities to some of that found in Tutankhamen's tomb. They will also have learned from Egypt's social organisation that involved strong, stable family life with an emphasis on respect for women and the care of children. We know that in the early years they enjoyed the luxurious Egyptian style of living; it was only later that they were treated as slaves. It is perhaps no surprise that there is so little mention of all these aspects of their life in Egypt: the scriptures naturally concentrate on other, more spiritual issues.

We get an insight into what the people missed when they were later wandering in the desert. It is predictable that only two months after they left Egypt in God's great saving act of the Exodus that they were never to forget, they were complaining about the food! We read in Exodus 16:3 that 'the whole community grumbled against Moses and Aaron.' They said to them, "If only we had died by the Lord's hand in Egypt! There we sat round pots of meat and ate all we wanted, but you have brought us out into this desert to starve this entire assembly to death." Later, in Numbers 11, they said, "If only we had meat to eat! We remember the fish we ate in Egypt at no cost – also the cucumbers, melons, leeks, onions and garlic. But now we have lost our appetite; we never see anything but this manna." Shortly after their departure, when they were being chased by the Egyptians, they had asked Moses, "Was it because there were no graves in Egypt that you brought us to the desert to die? What have you done to us by bringing us out of Egypt? Didn't we say to you in Egypt, Leave us alone; let us serve the Egyptians? It would have been better for us to serve the Egyptians than to die in the desert!" (Ex 14:11,12). In a moment of exasperation Moses cried out to the Lord, "What am I to do with these people? They are almost ready to stone me." He had to remind them that they were once "slaves in Egypt". (Deut. 6:12). It is surprising that he ever thought that they could be knocked into shape. It is all remarkably graphic. How would today's Church cope with such a rigorous wilderness experience? Maybe that is precisely what we are undergoing, in another form.

During this time Moses told them in Deut 8:2,5 that "God led you all the way in the desert these forty years to humble you and to test you in order to know what was in your heart, whether or not you would obey his commands" and "Know then in your heart that as a man disciplines his son so the Lord disciplines you." He also told them in 8:19 in even stronger words, "If you ever forget the Lord your God and follow other gods and worship and bow down to them, I testify against you today that you will surely be destroyed. Like the nations the Lord destroyed before you, so you will be destroyed for not obeying the Lord your God." Through his blessings and curses, his love of his people and his punishments; through their humiliation and defeat and exile, using both carrot and stick, God trained a people for his work and service and prepared them to be the cradle of his coming to earth in Jesus. He was and continues to be relentless in the pursuit of his loving purposes. It was the only way his master plan could ever have had any hope of coming to fruition.

When we come to the promised land which they entered under the leadership of Joshua, we can see that although their disobedience and punishment continued, it was the one place on earth that God needed to lead his people, for their own benefit and more especially for his purposes through them. The land of Canaan, a fertile land 'flowing with milk and honey' – what is now Israel – is a small strip of land, little more than a hundred miles long and fifty miles wide. It runs from Lebanon in the north to Gaza and the Negev desert in the south and is bounded by the Mediterranean in the West and the river Jordan in the East. Its outline has remained fairly constant throughout its stormy history but it has had various different names – Palestine under Roman rule at the time of Christ, often the Holy Land in the Middle Ages, and Israel today. It held and still continues to hold a strategic position on the western edge of the Fertile Crescent at the meeting of East and West. It was also situated on the routes used for trade and the movement of armies between the powerful nations of Egypt in the south and Assyria and Babylon in the north. In the Book of Ezekiel 5:5 God says of its capital city "This is Jerusalem, which I have set in the centre of the nations, with countries all around her." Even a brief study of the map of this area reveals the crucial position of Israel and its capital, Jerusalem as the focal point of the gigantic land mass of no less than three continents, Europe, Asia and Africa. This is further accentuated by the position of the five seas around it – the Mediterranean, Black Sea, Caspian Sea, Red Sea and the Persian Gulf – each of which helped to guide most of the traffic through this narrow isthmus. Furthermore the Sinai Peninsula to the south remained the essential land link for the great sea routes between the East and the Mediterranean, until the Suez Canal was completed in 1869.

Above all this Holy Land was to become the place chosen by God where he would eventually come to earth in his Son Jesus hundreds of years later. It was also the vantage point from which the Gospel would be spread by land and sea throughout the Roman Empire and later to all corners of the earth. This would be at a time when the Roman Empire, for all its pagan practices and the persecution that occurred later, provided the peace and security, the lines of communication and, in its Eastern half at least, used the common Greek language that made the spread of the Gospel possible. There was also a widespread and growing belief in one God and a spiritual hunger for a faith that could provide the people with meaning and hope. We cannot imagine a more perfect time and place for God to have revealed himself in this unique way. All well in advance of the coming of the media, of cameramen and newsmen who would undoubtedly have distorted the Good News and its reception – if they had considered it worthy of their attention!

To return to the people of Israel. After about seven hundred years in the promised land, marked by disobedience and unfaithfulness and the division of the previously united kingdom, the people of both the Northern and the Southern kingdoms were taken into captivity, in Assyria and Babylon respectively. With regard to the period of Judah's captivity we know that Babylon was at the height of her power and cultural influence and scientific achievement, as Assyria had been in the case of the northern kingdom, and as Egypt had been when the people of Israel were in captivity there over five hundred years before. As an instance of this influence, it appears that our division of hours and minutes into sixty units is a direct descendant of the ancient Babylonian system of counting and measurement. We could imagine that these three centres of excellence were carefully chosen, not so much for purposes of punishment and correction as for the education of God's people.

Both Assyria and Babylon, the two ancient kingdoms of Mesopotamia, were located in what is now Iraq. Assyria was in the north around present day Mosul, close to the old capital Nineveh. Babylon was in the southern plain, fifty miles south of present day Baghdad. They were both of them within the eastern limits of the fertile crescent with the Tigris river flowing through them. We can only guess at the influence on God's people of their exposure to these civilisations. We have already seen that Judah's period of exile in Babylon had an enormous influence on the development of the spiritual lives of her people. During their time in captivity they learned to do without the Temple, coming to rely on spiritual sacrifices such as prayer and fasting rather than physical, animal sacrifices. They began to meet for worship in the synagogue where their scriptures – what is now our Old Testament – were read and taught and the Psalms, either said or sung, were used as aids to their worship. Personal piety and praise and prayer became the practice not only in the synagogues that are thought by some to have originated during the captivity, but also in their homes. They also began to develop an interest in teachings about the end things and in life after death. They were no doubt guided by the very few suggestive Old Testament references to the idea of resurrection. These appear in the Psalms and in Isaiah and also in Daniel 12:2 where we read that 'Multitudes who sleep in the dust of the earth will awake: some to everlasting life, others to shame and everlasting contempt.'

A hundred years after Judah's return from exile in Babylon further written prophecy ceased in Israel with Malachi, around 430 BC, but the people will have continued to profit from the interpretation of all that had already been written. During the following four hundred years of prophetic silence until the coming of John the Baptist their newly developed spiritual maturity must have played a huge part in enabling them to continue to believe that God had not forgotten them. When we come to the New Testament it will be apparent how important all these changes in spiritual outlook were in preparation for the Christian spirituality and worship of those who would come to believe in Jesus. The issue of life after death was a cause of division between the Pharisees, and the Sadducees who accepted only the first five books of the Old Testament in which there are no references to the resurrection. It was also the cause of an interesting clash between Jesus and the Sadducees recorded in all of the first three Gospels. This particular issue and the whole subject of God's prolonged and patient preparation of his people provides an indication of the need to avoid seeing the Old and New Testaments as totally separate books, as they are so often made out to be. It is also of interest that the notion of immortality was surfacing in Greek and Roman thought during this period. We can imagine that the Spirit was preparing the Gentiles also for the Good News of the gift of eternal life through the Gospel that was soon to burst upon the Roman world.

We now return to the beginning to look in greater detail at the books of the Old Testament from which the story told in the last two chapters has been taken. We begin with Exodus because we have already spent some time on the material contained in Genesis, which ended with the death of Jacob and of Joseph.

EXODUS

At the start of Exodus, after Joseph's death, the Israelites continued to increase in numbers 'so that the land was filled with them' and they became a threat to the Egyptians. A new Pharaoh came to power who apparently knew nothing of Joseph. The people of Israel began to be oppressed and subjected to slave labour by the Egyptians and they turned to God for help. Remembering his promise to Abraham, God called out Moses who was initially very reluctant to respond to his call to lead the people out of Egypt. In chapter 3 God speaks to him from the burning bush and counters Moses' excuses one after another in one of the most striking dialogues in Scripture. "Who am I to do this?" Moses asks, and God promises him, "I will be with you." Moses then asks how he is to answer the people's questions about who has sent him. God's answer is: "I AM WHO I AM. This is what you are to say to the Israelites: 'I AM has sent me to you.' Say to the Israelites, 'The LORD, the God of your fathers – the God of Abraham, the God of Isaac and the God of Jacob – has sent me to you.' This is my name for ever, the name by which I am to be remembered from generation to generation." God is telling Moses that he is not only Elohim the God of all the earth, the world-wide, cosmic God. He is also Yahweh, which in Hebrew, that had no vowels, was YHWH, the name that was too sacred to utter. This is sometimes translated Jehovah but more usually the LORD or 'I AM', meaning that 'He is' or 'He will be'. Yahweh is the personal name of the One true God who is progressively revealing himself to Israel and who will later reveal himself in Jesus to the whole of mankind, including the Gentiles. It has been said that Yahweh is the Trinity incognito. When Jesus is called Lord he becomes identified with Yahweh, with the self-revealing God of the Old Testament. Moses can hardly have been expected to understand the significance of God's momentous statement about who he really is and he continues with his questions.

"What if they do not believe me or listen to me?" Moses asks. God turns his staff into a snake as a sign, but Moses continues to try to excuse himself: "Lord, I have never been eloquent, I am slow of speech and tongue." At this God begins to become impatient. "Who gave man his mouth? Now go; I will help you speak and will teach you what to say." But Moses continues to back-pedal: "O Lord, please send someone else to do it." At this point God becomes even more angry and talks of enlisting the aid of Moses' brother Aaron who can "speak well ... and will speak to the people for you, and it will be as if he were your mouth and as if you were God to him." God repeats his promise of his help for them both and ends the interview. "But take this staff in your hand so that you can perform miraculous signs with it." Moses is not given the choice of refusing God's call – as Saul of Tarsus, later St Paul, was to discover even more dramatically over a thousand years later.

Moses then begins a long dialogue with Pharaoh who is initially unwilling to allow the people of Israel to leave Egypt. He eventually changes his mind, however, on account of the plagues that God brings on the land. Before the last of these the Israelites are told to sprinkle the blood of the lambs that they eat in their last meal in Egypt on the door frames of their houses so that their firstborn will be 'passed over' and not be killed along with the Egyptian firstborn. This striking down of the firstborn in Egypt, including the firstborn of Pharaoh himself, is what finally changes his mind and he says to Moses and Aaron "Up! Leave my people, you and the Israelites! Go, worship the

Lord as you have requested. Take your flocks and herds, as you have said, and go. And also bless me."

In this way they escape from bondage in Egypt, an event that continues to be celebrated by Jews to this day as the Passover, the great festival of the Lord and symbol of God's deliverance of his people. No sooner are they free however than they see the Egyptians following them and complain to Moses that they would have preferred to serve the Egyptians rather than to die in the desert. But God divides the waters of the Red Sea for them and causes it to flow back as the Egyptians cross over so that apparently all of them are drowned. Things go well for a short while but the people then begin to grumble about the lack of the water and the good food they enjoyed in Egypt. God provides water and manna and later quail. Three months after they have left Egypt they come to the Desert of Sinai and camp in front of the mountain. God comes down in a cloud with fire and smoke in the sight of all the people. Moses then goes up the mountain with Aaron and returns with the Ten Commandments. Later, Moses receives instructions about making the Tabernacle in which the omnipotent, unchanging and transcendent God of the universe will come to dwell or 'tabernacle' with his people, thereby revealing his nearness to them as well. Such was his own unique and intimate relationship with God that we read in Ex 33:11 'The Lord would speak to Moses face to face, as a man speaks with his friend.' Only a few verses later, however, the Lord says to him: "You cannot see my face, for no-one may see me and live." We have to wait until the final chapter of Revelation before we read of God's servants in the Holy City being enabled to see God's face. There is a limit even to Moses' intimacy with God. Moses was leader, law-giver, judge, prophet and priest. He fulfilled all possible roles but king. He was Israel's greatest leader, in spite of his initial reticence about accepting the challenge and responsibility of leadership. With God's help he finally overcame his initial timidity.

The tabernacle, with the ark that contained the tablets of the covenant, where the worship of God was focused, was a 'church' building and furniture for a people on the move. It is set up and God is pleased and 'the cloud covered the Tent of Meeting, and the glory of the Lord filled the tabernacle' so that even Moses could not enter. Priests are consecrated, initially only Aaron and his sons, and detailed instructions are given with regard to their sacred garments. Exodus ends with emphasis on the central importance of the tabernacle. 'In all the travels of the Israelites, whenever the cloud lifted from above the tabernacle, they would set out; but if the cloud did not lift, they did not set out. So the cloud of the Lord was over the tabernacle by day, and the fire was in the cloud by night, in the sight of all the house of Israel during all their travels.' (Ex 40:38).

THE TEN COMMANDMENTS

"I am the Lord your God, who brought you out of Egypt …
You shall have no other gods before me.
"You shall not make for yourself an idol … and bow down in worship.
"You shall not misuse the name of the Lord your God.
"Remember the Sabbath day by keeping it holy.
"Honour your Father and your mother.
"You shall not murder.
"You shall not commit adultery.
"You shall not steal.
"You shall not give false testimony against your neighbour.
"You shall not covet your neighbour's house … or his wife … or anything that belongs to him."
                    Exodus 20:2-17 (Abridged)

The Lord gives Moses further laws for the people in Leviticus and in 19:18 he adds the instruction to them to "love your neighbour as yourself."

When we come to the New Testament Jesus is asked which of the commandments is the most important and he provides us with a new formula that is recorded in almost identical words in all of the first three Gospels:
"'Love the Lord your God with all your heart and with all your soul and with all your mind and with all your strength.' This is the greatest commandment. And the second is like it: 'Love your neighbour as

yourself.' All the law and the Prophets hang on these two commandments." (Mt 22:37-39).

THE COVENANTS

When God made covenants with his people they were similar to those that were in use in the near east to govern relationships between kings and their people and between nations, either as equals or as greater and lesser nations. God's covenants with his people were of necessity in the latter category but they were naturally richer, more spiritual agreements. By means of these covenants he bound his people to himself in order to use them to bring blessing to others. Some of the covenants were unconditional and involved only promises and others were conditional in that they also specified obligations on the part of the people and penalties for their disloyalty to him and their failure to obey the Law. The Law was summed up in the commandments and they provided the covenant framework within which they needed to keep in order to maintain their relationship with God. The covenant he made with Noah was unconditional and a guarantee to him and to his descendants and to every living creature that was with him in the ark that there would never again be a flood to destroy the earth. This covenant was sealed and symbolised by the sign of the rainbow. The covenant that God made with Abraham was also unconditional. He promised to give him the land of Canaan, to make him into a great nation and to bless 'all peoples on earth' through him. He later promised him a son through whom he would have an uncountable number of offspring through whom these blessings would come.

The conditional covenant that God made with Moses at Mt Sinai to be Israel's God provided they obeyed his commandments was an extension of the unconditional promises that he made to Noah and to Abraham. The people would be his 'treasured possession' but only if they obeyed him fully, as Moses later spelt out in Deut 30:11-20. Several hundred years after this God made another unconditional covenant with king David, recorded in 2 Sam 7:5-16, that his kingdom would be everlasting. This was because it was truly God's own kingdom in which he himself would ultimately reign over all the nations and over all creation. This kingdom, when it is finally completed, will be the ultimate blessing that he promised Abraham would come through his descendants. It will be made possible by Jesus' sacrifice on the Cross that will establish the wholly new covenant or testament for which all the preceding covenants have been a preparation.

LEVITICUS

The book of Leviticus provides detailed instructions about the religious ritual, the laws and regulations governing worship, and the precise method of offering sacrifices. The sacrifices were controlled and explained to the people by the priests and were kept absolutely pure so that they symbolised both God's holiness and his compassion. Whatever their superficial resemblance to pagan sacrifices they were very different from them. They received their meaning from the Lord's covenant relationship with Israel and served several distinct functions, depending on the occasion. The sacrifices of the various unblemished animals were an offering of worship, praise and thanksgiving to God in his holiness. They could also symbolise the people's communion with him and with each other as well as their repentance and God's forgiveness of their sins and the restoration of their relationship with him. They were not always offerings for sin. The regulations laid down for the offering of the sacrifices were extremely complex and detailed. When the priests and people ate portions of the meat offering in a sacrificial meal it clearly foreshadowed the bread that symbolisesChrist's body in the Christian sacrament of the Eucharist.

NUMBERS

Numbers derives its name from the census carried out by Moses. It takes the story on from Mt Sinai to the borders of the promised land.

It also portrays Israel's identity as the Lord's redeemed covenant people and her vocation as the servant people of God, charged with establishing his kingdom on earth. But the grumbling and disobedience continued. His people Israel were denied entry to the promised land of Canaan for a generation and spent 40 years wandering in the desert. Only their children were to inherit the land, but God proclaims his continued faithfulness to his purpose for his people despite their unfaithfulness to him. The Lord says to Moses, "Tell Aaron and his sons, 'This is how you are to bless the Israelites.' Say to them: "The Lord bless you and keep you; the Lord make his face shine upon you and be gracious to you; the Lord turn his face towards you and give you peace." God's love for his people is revealed from one end of the Bible to the other, as is his discipline and his judgement.

DEUTERONOMY

This book consists of a series of addresses given by Moses in warm personal terms, as a leader and as a father to his children whom he is about to leave after many years. He has led them out of Egypt and through the desert for forty years before handing over the leadership to Joshua who will lead them into the promised land. He surveys the journey from Egypt, the people's rebellion and God's patient loyalty. "What other nation is so great as to have their gods near to them the way the Lord our God is near us whenever we pray to him?" he asks. (4:7). He restates and underlines some of the laws of Exodus, Leviticus and Numbers and stresses the need for obedience after they have settled in the promised land. In chapter 11:26-28 Moses gives them a promise and a warning: "See, I am setting before you today a blessing and a curse – the blessing if you obey the commands of the Lord your God that I am giving you today; the curse if you disobey the commands of the Lord your God and turn from the way that I command you today by following other gods, which you have not known." In 18:15 Moses tells the people that "The Lord your God will raise up for you a prophet like me from among your own brothers. You must listen to him." This promise no doubt referred most immediately to Joshua which in Hebrew meant "The Lord saves" but also prophetically to the ultimate Saviour over a thousand years later, to Jesus, whose name was the Greek form of Joshua. He will be not only a king but also a prophet; a new Moses for a new and even greater Exodus, not releasing the people of Israel from bondage in Egypt, but all people everywhere from the bondage of sin.

In Chapter 31 Moses tells the people that he is no longer able to lead them. The Lord has told him "You shall not cross the Jordan because you broke faith with me ... and did not uphold my holiness among the Israelites." He had disobeyed God on an important occasion in the past and forfeited his right to lead the people into the promised land. Moses says to Joshua in the presence of all Israel "Be strong and courageous, for you must go with this people into the land that the Lord swore to their forefathers to give them, and you must divide it among them for their inheritance. The Lord himself goes before you and will be with you; he will never leave you nor forsake you. Do not be afraid; do not be discouraged." (31:7,8). There follows a solemn prediction by the Lord of Moses' death on Mount Nebo that overlooked the promised land. There is an even more solemn prediction of the future disobedience of God's people and this is repeated in a song of praise and of warning that Moses recites in the hearing of the whole assembly of Israel. "They are not just idle words for you – they are your life." he tells them. "By them you will live long in the land you are crossing the Jordan to possess." Following this he pronounces individual blessings on the twelve tribes and after climbing Mount Nebo to be shown the whole of the promised land by the Lord, he dies and is buried in Moab. As befitted the death of Israel's greatest Old Testament statesman, 'The Israelites grieved in the plains of Moab thirty days, until the time of weeping and mourning was over.' Finally in the very last verses of Deuteronomy we read of him: 'Since then, no prophet has risen in Israel like Moses, whom the Lord knew face to face, who did all those miraculous signs and wonders the Lord sent him to do in Egypt – to Pharaoh and to all his officials and to his whole land. For no-one has ever shown the mighty power or performed the awesome deeds that Moses did in the sight of all Israel.'

JOSHUA

This book describes the establishment of Israel in the promised land, led by Joshua who was a military strategist and statesman but above all God's servant and a particularly spiritual man. God promises him that "As I was with Moses, so will I be with you; I will never leave you or forsake you" and he exhorts him to "be strong and very courageous". It is a history written probably many years later, from a spiritual standpoint. It shows how God deals with his people and how he remains true to his promises in spite of their disobedience. It tells a story of God preparing a faithful people and insisting that they do not become tainted by the religion and the evil of the Canaanites, the people already in the land. By breaking into the world of nations who went after other gods, God was signalling his intention of one day gaining authority over the whole of his creation. This is the only possible explanation for the bloody battles fought by Israel to conquer Canaan for their own land so that his long-term purposes could be carried out through them. It was God's land, as are all other lands, of which his people are stewards on his behalf. If Israel were to be unfaithful she would lose this land as she nearly did under the Judges and as she eventually did for a number of years during the exile in Babylon. The God of the first Joshua is also the God of the second Joshua, Jesus, who will also wield the sword of judgement as well as being the definitive Saviour. After all the struggles he had endured in fighting God's holy war Joshua says in his final words to the people who had shared them with him: "But if serving the Lord seems undesirable to you, then choose for yourselves this day whom you will serve ... but as for me and my household, we will serve the Lord." (24:15). He issues a final warning that God is a holy and jealous God who will not forgive their rebellion and their sins and will bring disaster on them if they serve foreign gods. The book ends with the death and burial of Joshua.

JUDGES

Judges describes the life of Israel in the promised land during the period of around 300 years between the death of Joshua and the rise of the monarchy. This was a time characterised by recurring cycles of disobedience, oppression, cries of distress and gracious divine deliverance that reveal the covenant faithfulness of God and demonstrate his almost unbelievable patience and long-suffering. In two separate verses, 17:6 and the very last verse, 21:25, we read: 'In those days Israel had no king; everyone did as he saw fit'. Judges are strictly dispensers of justice but the judges described here are more like heroic leaders, the best known of whom are Deborah, Gideon, Samson and Samuel who anointed Saul the first of the kings. In 2:16 we read 'Then the Lord raised up judges who saved them out of the hands of raiders'. The book teaches us that God in his providence recompenses a nation in direct relation to the obedience and faithfulness of its people. Our welfare and our salvation lie in doing the will of God because in the end it is the only thing that works. It is no different nowadays but we are not accustomed to thinking in these terms.

RUTH

Ruth is a tender, sensitively told story of a young widow from Moab who returns to Bethlehem with Naomi, her widowed mother-in-law, to whom she says in 1:16, "Where you go I will go, your people will be my people and your God my God." Following a touching account of the manner of their meeting, she marries Boaz in whose field she has been gleaning the grains of barley and wheat. She had the great distinction that one of her grandsons was king David. The story provides a wonderful example of people whose unselfish lives reflect the love of God himself. Such lives are blessed and are a blessing to others, in this case to Naomi who is moved from sadness and bitterness to fullness and praise and who finds fulfilment in caring for the son born to Ruth and Boaz. The story is reminiscent of the moving stories in Genesis of Abraham's servant finding Rebekah as a wife for his son Isaac in Ch 24 and Jacob falling in love with Rachel in Ch 29. It may be a surprise to find such a book in the Bible but it is a wonderful illustration of God's intimate, personal love and concern for individuals, even in the sometimes rather harsh climate of the Old Testament. It is a master-class in story-telling.

1 SAMUEL

Samuel was the last and greatest of the judges, and the first, after Moses, of the great prophets. He was used by God to anoint both of Israel's first two kings, Saul and David and he continued to be their spiritual guide, in what was for Israel a totally new experience. A people on the move need a leader; a nation with territory and cities to defend feels the need of a king. A king provides a nation with a sense of identity and unity and a degree of protection from its often unfriendly neighbours; in the case of Israel chiefly the Philistines.

There was a danger however that the appointment of a human king would interfere with Israel's exclusive covenant relationship with God as their true spiritual king and protector. In the end Samuel is given permission to accede to the people's request in spite of their failure to value this exclusive relationship. "Listen to them and give them a king," he is told in 8:22 and later he is told of God's choice of Saul as king. But he is also told to warn the people of the demands the king will make on them, taking their sons to serve with his chariots and horses, for example, and taking the best of their fields and vineyards and olive groves and giving them to his attendants. Samuel anoints Saul as king privately and prophesies that the Spirit of the Lord will come upon him in power. Saul is later confirmed as king in the presence of the Lord and of all the people. At the inauguration ceremony Samuel calls the people to repentance and renewal of their covenant allegiance to the Lord and thus places kingship on a radically different footing from that in the surrounding nations.

It is clear that the granting of kings to Israel was a risky experiment. Moses had recognised five hundred years before this when the people were still in the desert that they would later ask for a king when they entered the promised land. In Deuteronomy 17:14-20 he laid down conditions that would govern such an appointment. "Be sure to appoint over you the king the Lord chooses ... He must be from among your own brothers ... He must not take many wives ... He must not accumulate large amounts of gold and silver." In addition to this he is to "write for himself on a scroll a copy of the law, taken from that of the priests ... and to read it all the days of his life so that he may revere the Lord his God ... and not consider himself better than his brothers and turn from the law to the right or to the left." This was a tall order: it is no wonder that all the kings were a disappointment in one way or another. It was clearly God's intention, however, that in spite of the risks and the strict rules that were required to minimise them, there should be kings in Israel. This was because it was his method of providing a visible human model of his own kingship and the throne from which he himself would eventually reign over the whole creation in his own everlasting kingdom.

On this understanding of the arrangement the Lord continued to be Israel's ultimate sovereign and the king was subject to the law of the Lord and the word of the prophet. This remains a vital truth for us 3000 years later and it is yet another illustration of the continuing importance of the Old Testament. In this case it enables us to understand the spiritual principles involved in God's vision of government and kingship – and the related principles underlying the coronation service of our own kings and queens that are in essence derived from it. The Lord himself chooses from among the people the one who is to rule on his behalf and he is anointed by his priestly representative. The king is accepted and acclaimed by the people and offers his allegiance to the Lord in ruling and serving them in his name.

This is the ideal prescription. Saul's honeymoon period as king is unfortunately short-lived. He fails to abide by the terms of his delegated kingship in disobeying God's instructions. The Lord is grieved that he has made Saul king over Israel and instructs Samuel to anoint David as king. Though previously only a shepherd he emerges at once as a mighty warrior and triumphs over the Philistine giant Goliath in the well-known and well-loved story of their remarkable encounter. Saul is eventually defeated in the battle of Gilboa against the Philistines and at the end of 1 Samuel, he takes his own life on the field of battle.

2 SAMUEL

At the start of 2 Samuel David laments for Saul and his great friend Jonathan, one of Saul's three sons, all of whom died at the battle of Gilboa. He is anointed by the men of Judah as king over the house of Judah and later the elders of Israel anoint him as their king also. David eventually conquers Jerusalem, making it the capital of his kingdom and he brings the ark of the covenant with him. He is at first successful, prospering and winning many battles. God promises him: "Now I will make your name great, like the names of the greatest men of the earth." (7:9). He promises that his son Solomon will succeed him and that he is the one who will build the Temple as a permanent centre of worship, where the ark will be housed. He also promises that he will "establish the throne of his kingdom for ever." God says of Solomon: "I will be his father, and he shall be my Son." (7:14). Two verses later he confirms his promise to David that "Your house and your kingdom shall endure for ever before me; your throne shall be established for ever."

The main responsibility of the king was the maintenance of righteousness, with the duty not only to act as judge but to preserve justice and to proclaim the law. David assumed the role of both king and priest, and was also a shepherd and a servant to his people. He had his weaknesses and he committed grievous sins that included taking Bathsheba, the wife of Uriah the Hittite, by having him killed in battle. But he was forgiven, no doubt because he was profoundly spiritual and willing to acknowledge his sin and to repent. A large number of the Psalms are attributed to him and they include some of the greatest spiritual literature ever written. It is no wonder that, in spite of his sins, he remained God's favourite of all the kings.

1 KINGS

The two books of the Kings describe the history of Israel's monarchy from the closing days of the rule of David until the time of the Babylonian exile of the southern kingdom of Judah. After an extensive account of Solomon's reign the narrator records the division of the kingdom and then, by means of parallel accounts, presents an interrelated picture of developments within the two kingdoms. This makes for a very complicated read and there is not room here to attempt to clarify it. At the start David is still alive, but old and frail. One of his sons, Adonijah, puts himself forward as king but Solomon inherits the Kingdom as promised. Before he dies David charges Solomon to keep God's laws so that he will honour his promise to David that there will always be a man on the throne of Israel. The emphasis in these books is not so much on strict historical recording as on pointing out that obedience and fidelity are the key to success in the unfolding of Israel's historical destiny. They are under the guidance of Israel's covenant Lord who rules all history in accordance with his sovereign purposes. The emphasis is also on prophecy and its fulfilment that stitches the whole fabric of the story together. (1Ki 8:56). A succession of prophets are sent by God to warn and exhort his people, but their messages fall mainly on deaf ears.

Solomon makes a good start; he asks for wisdom, for a wise and discerning heart, and he is promised that, and also riches and honour. The people are happy and Solomon's wisdom is sought by many foreign kings. He builds the temple of the Lord in seven years and brings the ark of the Lord and all the sacred furnishings into it. His own palace – which was larger – took thirteen years to build! He addresses the people, and praises God and dedicates the temple to him saying, "The heavens, even the highest heavens, cannot contain you. How much less this temple I have built!" (1Ki 8:27). His prayer includes the request that visitors and foreigners may recognise the greatness of their God 'so that all the peoples of the earth may know that the Lord is God and that there is no other.' (1Ki 8:60). Already there is mention of God's claim to universal authority. The Lord appears to Solomon and promises him that "I will establish your royal throne over Israel for ever, as I promised David your father. But if you or your sons turn away from me ... then I will cut off Israel from the land I have given them and will reject this temple I have consecrated for my name." (1Ki 9:5,6,7). The Queen of Sheba visits Solomon and is overwhelmed by his riches and splendour. She 'talked with him about all that she had on her mind ... and he answered all her questions.'

Trouble is on the way however. He takes foreign wives against God's express commands and 'his wives led him astray,' and he 'did evil in the sight of the Lord,' and followed other gods. The Lord 'was angry with him' and vowed to tear the kingdom away from him, but for David's sake not in his lifetime, and not the whole kingdom. The ten northern tribes are given to Jeroboam leaving Judah and Benjamin with Solomon's son Rehoboam in the south so that "my servant David may always have a lamp before me in Jerusalem." (11:36) Solomon dies after reigning for 40 years. In the end the wise and favoured Solomon, son of his great father, David, is yet another disappointment.

The kings of both Israel in the north and Judah in the south did evil, notably the northern king, Ahab, during whose reign Elijah exercised his prophetic ministry. There is a memorable story in 1 Kings 17 in which Elijah raises a widow's son to life. In the following chapter he is enabled by God to win a notable contest with the 450 prophets of Baal on Mount Carmel. This story is a demonstration of Elijah's courage and unshakeable faith in God. Elijah's greatness is indicated by his mysterious identification with John the Baptist as Jesus' forerunner, and by his presence, along with Moses, at Jesus' transfiguration nearly nine hundred years after his death! This is recorded in Matthew 17: 1-13 and in Mark 9:2-13. The remainder of 1Kings is a catalogue of the failure and judgement of the kings of both Israel and Judah, notably of Ahab and his wife Jezebel who had Naboth the Jezreelite killed so that they could steal his vineyard, for which they both paid with their lives.

2 KINGS

2 Kings begins with a number of prophecies and miracles of Elijah, who is then taken up into heaven in a chariot of fire in a whirlwind, leaving Elisha, whom he had anointed as his successor, to carry on his ministry. Elisha's early ministry includes the raising to life of a young boy, the Shunammite's son, and the healing of Naaman, the commander of a foreign king's army, of his leprosy. The story of Kings continues with a further catalogue of failures and judgements of the kings of both Israel and Judah, all of whom 'did evil in the eyes of the Lord'. This evil consisted in their serving other Gods and worshipping idols, which they had been expressly forbidden to do by the prophets. Chapter 7 reveals that 'They followed worthless idols and themselves became worthless,' and further that 'The Lord was angry with Israel and removed them from his presence' and 'tore Israel away from the house of David.' The story of the defeat and deportation of the northern kingdom by Assyria in 721 BC and that of the southern kingdom by Babylon in two stages, in 597 and later in 586, has already been told in a previous chapter. This second deportation is the last event described in 2 Kings – apart from the final, fascinating detail that Judah's king Jehoiachin was later allowed by Evil-Merodach, the new king of Babylon, thirty seven years after he had been taken captive, to 'put aside his prison clothes and for the rest of his life ate regularly at the king's table.' He was also given 'a regular allowance as long as he lived.' It is an interesting reflection on the merciful treatment of at least one of Babylon's captives.

It is clear that all the kings failed in different ways to live up to the ideal of kingship, including even David, who was regarded as the standard by which the other kings were judged. As a result the hope for a righteous ruler was thrust further into the future. This continuing expectation gradually crystallised into the 'messianic hope' of the One who would 'reign on David's throne … with justice and righteousness … forever.' (Isaiah 9:7). But it would be more than six hundred years before Isaiah's prophecy would be fulfilled in Jesus.

1 CHRONICLES

1 and 2 Chronicles are annals of the sacred history of Israel from Adam to the freeing of Judah from exile in Babylon by Cyrus, king of Persia. The material is selected, arranged and integrated from many sources to compose a narrative sermon for the Jews, as the southern tribes of Judah and Benjamin were known following their return from exile in Babylon. It covers the same period of history as Samuel and the two books of Kings that had been written for the rather different needs of the community while they were still in exile. As Israel struggled to find her bearings as God's people in a new situation they needed to know that God's covenants were still in force. They also needed to know that the promises to David were still valid after the break in the line of earthly kings, the defeat of the nation, the destruction of Jerusalem and of the Temple, and the exile to Babylon. Their reassurance was the rebuilding of the Temple and the re-establishing of worship. The Law and the prophets remained the focus of the covenant life of the people and were always more important than their human kings.

1 Chronicles begins with lengthy genealogies followed by the death of Saul. David becomes king over all Israel and very significantly the Ark is brought to Jerusalem. David composes a psalm of thanks to the Lord. 'Give thanks to the Lord, call on his name; make known among the nations what he has done.' 'He is the Lord, his judgements are in all the earth. He remembers his covenant for ever.' These extracts come from David's outpouring of praise and thanks to God that covers nearly thirty verses from 16: 8-36. It is too long to be quoted in full but too good to be missed. David is told by Nathan the prophet that he is not the one to build the temple 'because he has shed blood'. This will be done by his son Solomon whose kingdom will be 'established for ever'. The message is that the promise still stands.

David praises the Lord: "Who is like your people Israel – the one nation on earth whose God went out to redeem a people for himself." (17:21). Some of David's victories are described and later his preparation of materials to build the temple and his instructions to Solomon to get on with it. He plans for Solomon to be king and tells him that if he forsakes God he will reject him for ever. "Be strong and courageous and do the work. Do not be afraid or discouraged, for the Lord God, my God, is with you." (28:20). Gifts are given for the building of the temple and David prays the prayer of praise below in the presence of the whole assembly. This glorious song of praise in chapter 29 is David's last recorded word. Solomon is acknowledged as king a second time and David dies, 'at a good old age', having enjoyed long life, wealth and honour.

> "Praise be to you, O Lord,
>   God of our Father Israel,
>   from everlasting to everlasting.
> Yours , O Lord is the greatness and the power
>   and the glory and the majesty and the splendour,
>   for everything in heaven and on earth is yours.
> Yours, O Lord is the kingdom;
>   you are exalted as head over all.
> Wealth and honour come from you;
>   you are the ruler of all things.
> In your hands are strength and power
>   to exalt and give strength to all.
> Now, our God, we give you thanks,
>   and praise your glorious name."

2 CHRONICLES

2 Chronicles begins with Solomon establishing himself as king 'for the Lord was with him and made him exceedingly great'. The temple is built and furnished and the Ark is brought into the inner sanctuary, 'and the glory of the Lord filled the temple'. (5:14). Solomon says a prayer of dedication: "The heavens, even the highest heavens, cannot contain you. How much less this temple that I have built!" (6:18). "Now arise, O Lord God, and come to your resting place." Solomon finishes praying, fire comes down from heaven and the glory of the Lord fills the temple and he answers Solomon's prayer:

> "If my people, who are called by my name, will humble
> themselves and pray and seek my face and turn from their

wicked ways, then I will hear from heaven and will forgive their sin and will heal their land." (7:14). "But if you turn away and forsake the decrees and commands I have given you and go off and serve other gods and worship them, then I will uproot Israel from my land, which I have given them, and will reject this temple which I have consecrated for my Name." (7:19,20.)

This he later did when they were disobedient. These promises and warnings are still relevant for us today.

Solomon is visited by the Queen of Sheba who tells him that "not even half the greatness of your wisdom was told me" and his splendour is described. But abruptly, only a few verses later, it is recorded that after reigning in Jerusalem over all Israel he dies and is buried in the city of David his father. His fairly sudden loss of favour with God at the end of his life was explained in 1 Kings.

What follows is the story of the disobedience of both the northern and the southern kingdoms and their captivity and exile in Assyria and Babylon respectively. There is no record of the northern kingdom ever returning to their land but the southern kingdom of Judah is released after fifty years by Cyrus the Persian when he defeats the Babylonians in 538BC. The book closes with this edict from Cyrus: "The Lord, the God of heaven, has given me all the kingdoms of the earth and has appointed me to build a temple for him at Jerusalem in Judah. Anyone of his people among you – may the Lord his God be with him, and let him go up." This release from captivity was foretold by Isaiah in 44:26-28 and 45:1-13. These and all other prophecies provide an example of the way in which prophecy stitches together the narrative, converting it from a series of separate events into a continuous unfolding drama that is clearly overseen by a guiding hand.

EZRA

Ezra, Nehemiah and Esther cover the last century of Old Testament Jewish history. The first two books describe the three-stage return of Judah to Jerusalem under Zerubbabel, Ezra and Nehemiah, stretched out over almost that whole period, from 538 to 445 BC. The Book of Ezra lists those who return and describes the rebuilding of the altar and of the temple, albeit a humbler construction than Solomon's. There is opposition however and Ataxerxes, now king of Persia, receives a letter from local trouble-makers and orders them to stop building. Work comes to a standstill until the second year of the reign of Darius who forbids interference and gives them what they need for the work. The temple is completed and dedicated with appropriate celebration, and the priests are installed for the service of God according to the book of Moses. They celebrate the Passover and, for seven days, the feast of unleavened bread. Ezra, 'a teacher well versed in the Law of Moses' then comes to Jerusalem from Babylon and 'devoted himself to the study and observance of the Law of the Lord, and to teaching its decrees and laws in Israel'. Ataxerxes writes him an encouraging letter offering him all the help he needs and Ezra praises the Lord because his hand is on him. He prays about the people's intermarriage with neighbouring tribes and they confess and repent and make a covenant to separate from the peoples around and from their foreign wives.

NEHEMIAH

The Book of Nehemiah begins with him hearing that those who have returned to Jerusalem are in great trouble and disgrace and that 'the wall of Jerusalem is broken down, and its gates have been burned with fire'. He weeps and prays for his people and repents for himself and for them and asks Artaxerxes the king of Persia, for whom he is acting as cup-bearer, to allow him to go back to Jerusalem as governor and rebuild the city. His request is granted and he arrives, probably in or around 445 BC. He tells the people about his gratitude to God for the support he has received from king Ataxerxes and his plan to rebuild the walls, whereupon they reply, "Let us start rebuilding." But they meet with opposition and have to post guards so that half the men do the work and half are armed for their defence. 'Those who carried materials did their work with one hand and held a weapon in the other' and each man repaired the part of the wall nearest to his home.

In spite of opposition from Nehemiah's enemies the wall is completed in 52 days. The people settle in their towns but they return for Ezra the priest to read aloud the Law. The people understand it and they then all bow down and worship the Lord. They recite his wonderful works as creator, and describe his goodness to them and how he has guided them throughout their history. They repent and admit to the Lord that "In all that has happened to us, you have been just; you have acted faithfully, while we did wrong". The people make a binding agreement that they put in writing, to follow the Law of God given through Moses and not to intermarry, in order to maintain the purity of their worship. They promise to observe the Sabbath and to bring to the house of the Lord each year 'the first fruits of our crops and of every tree … and the firstborn of our sons and of our cattle, of our herds and of our flocks'. (10:36). They celebrate the dedication of the wall 'with songs of thanksgiving and with the music of cymbals, harps and lyres'.

In spite of all these good intentions, however, Nehemiah has only to be away visiting king Artaxerxes in Babylon for the people to fail to bring the portions assigned to the Levites, and to begin treading winepresses on the Sabbath, selling merchandise in Jerusalem and marrying foreign wives. On his return to Jerusalem Nehemiah rebukes them and reminds them of God's judgement on wrongdoing in the past and the book ends with his prayer. "Remember me for this, O my God, and do not blot out what I have so faithfully done for the house of my God and its services … and show mercy to me according to your great love." If Judah, the only continuing remnant of Israel, do not remain faithful to their God they will not survive as a nation to welcome the Messiah when he comes a full four hundred years later.

We have the prophets yet to look at but there is no more history of God's people recorded in the Bible beyond their return to Jerusalem – apart from the story told in the book of Esther that comes next.

ESTHER

The small book of Esther is an absorbing story from the period following Judah's exile to Babylon when Xerxes was king of Persia from 486-465BC. It is of unknown provenance and with many inconsistencies, and tells of a Jewish girl whom the king made his queen. He thereby enabled her to save her family and people from a massacre planned by Haman, a high-ranking Persian official. This story might appear to be the stuff of opera or a historical novel and a rather surprising book to find as a part of Scripture but it provides a vital link in the triumph of God's purposes, so often reliant on the remnant of faithful people, and almost frustrated by man's wickedness. The events described in the Persian city of Susa threatened the continuity of God's purposes in redemptive history. The future existence of God's chosen people, and ultimately therefore the appearance of the Messiah, were jeopardised by Haman's edict to destroy the Jews. The Jews triumph, however, and they continue to celebrate this deliverance from Haman every year in the festival of Purim when the book of Esther is read and traditionally the congregation in the synagogue shouts and boos whenever the name of Haman is mentioned!

It might seem strange that this book, with no overt reference to God, should appear in the scriptural canon. In spite of this, it bears the stamp of God's dealings with Esther and everyone else in the story. He frequently uses unlikely people and events to safeguard his plans for his people and for the world and his sovereign rule is assumed at every point. Because of its apparently secular nature the story conveys all the more powerfully its message of God's working through individuals who are often unaware that they are involved in the furtherance of his purposes. His kingdom is not advanced only by those who are consciously working and praying for its coming. Story-telling has a central place in conveying spiritual truth and this book provides another master class in the art.

JOB

Job is a unique and fascinating book. It is written almost exclusively in the form of poetry, as are the Psalms and the majority of the prophets. It tells the story of Job, a godly man whom Satan is allowed by God to deprive of all his great riches, his children, and his health in the hope that he can thereby destroy Job's faith and godliness. Job laments his position – "Why did I not perish at birth? ... I have no rest but only turmoil," – and three of his friends try to advise him. In describing the destitution and suffering of an apparently righteous man the book explores the problem of the justice of a good, all-powerful God in the light of human suffering. If God is both good and also almighty why does he permit evil and disease and natural disasters and suffering?

If, as the Bible everywhere maintains, God is almighty and perfectly just and no man is wholly innocent then it looks as though we each of us deserve every disaster that afflicts us. But we complain, of course, because we cannot understand and accept misfortune when we are at the receiving end and others no better than we are – or worse – appear to be more fortunate. The God to whom we are accustomed to turn in times of need becomes himself the overwhelming enigma and problem. As the writer of Lamentations describes it, 'The Lord is like an enemy' (2:5) and Isaiah expresses the same idea in 63:10. We invoke his help in delivering us from trouble for which he is ultimately responsible. This is a paradox that is powerfully expressed by T.S. Eliot in his 'Four Quartets':

> Who then devised the torment? Love.
> Love is the unfamiliar name
> Behind the hands that wove
> The intolerable shirt of flame
> That human hands cannot remove.

We are asking love to defend us against love. It is the God who has woven the intolerable shirt of flame to whom we go for help with its removal. It is a paradox that is resolved only by the mystery of God's love, that is beyond our understanding. Job's friends are not aware of such subtleties. They subscribe to the idea that we deserve all the trouble we get and they are naturally always a source of irritation to him. Job's own words are, to them, full of irritating self-pity and self-justification. There is no meeting of minds. Even young Elihu appears self-righteous and too proud by half of his own wisdom, in spite of his protested humility. He asks his friend Job, "Do you know how God controls the clouds and makes his lightning flash?"

The overall impression is that his counsellors talk too much, as we all do, and make judgements without any real authority. When God speaks to Job 'out of the storm' in Chapter 38 he says some of the same things as Elihu but they sound different when he utters them because he speaks with the authority that belongs only to him. Only the One who 'makes his lightning flash' can ask us if we know how he does it. We encounter the same authority when we come to the ministry of Jesus. Our own authority is derived but we are unable to avoid giving ourselves the credit for it and thus becoming part of the problem. Job also usurps God's place and needs to learn humility. In chapter 38 God asks him "Where were you when I laid the earth's foundation?" and "Who endowed the heart with wisdom or gave understanding to the mind?" He has more than met his match and is silenced and unable to argue as he did with his friends.

Job has tried all ways and God's answer to him is that he knows what he is doing! Love is the key; love and trust. Job makes a remarkable statement of faith when he says: "Though he slay me, yet will I hope in him." (3l:15). He makes an even more remarkable expression of his faith when he says: "I know that my redeemer lives and in the end he will stand upon the earth ... in my flesh will I see God." Only with the coming of Jesus the sinless redeemer does God provide us with a demonstration of his perfect love and the nearest he can give to an answer to the problem of suffering. If you're prepared to be crucified you can't be expected to explain it. This must be enough for us: we have to continue to struggle with the mystery.

God's final words to Job are: "Will the one who contends with the Almighty correct him? Let him who accuses God answer him!" God does not answer the question of why the relatively innocent suffer but merely states that things are as he ordained them and Job must simply accept them as they are. Job's response is: "I am unworthy – how can I reply to you?" He is confronted with reality. "Surely I spoke of things I did not understand, things too wonderful for me to know." "My ears had heard of you but now my eyes have seen you. Therefore

I despise myself and repent in dust and ashes." Finally, the Lord ticks off Job's friends but Job forgives them and prays for them and his prayer is accepted. Our last news of Job is that 'the Lord made him prosperous again and gave him twice as much as before' and 'blessed the latter part of his life more than the first'. His faith and trust in God was rewarded to an unusual degree. We could wish that all misfortune and all life's stories ended as happily!

The harsh truth is that we need to be tried and tested in order to grow and mature. In the words of GK Chesterton the 'core of ethics' is that 'peace and happiness can only exist on some condition.' He was speaking of the essence of fairy tales and Job could almost be seen as an example of this tradition. But it is much more than this. In its account of an extraordinary, miraculous and well-deserved reversal of fortune it resembles the stories of Ruth and Esther and like them it is keyed into the developing Judeo-Christian revelation of God. It looks forward to the One who alone will, in the end, enable this 'condition' to be met for all men everywhere by his saving, sacrificial death. If the story of Job can also be called a myth it is not only an explanatory story to do with reconciling a God of infinite goodness and power with the reality of evil and suffering but a myth that is acted out for us in the setting of Israel's spiritual history, whoever Job himself and his advisers may have been. There can be no other book quite like it in the whole of literature.

THE PSALMS

The origin and authorship of the psalms is uncertain, though some are traditionally regarded as the work of king David. They were used in public and private worship, both said and sung, and collected together in their final form, probably in the third century BC, as a book of religious instruction and of prayer and praise and lament. The psalms are full of praise and thanksgiving to God and of such profound spiritual experience that even the coming of Jesus and the Holy Spirit has not made them obsolete. They are a priceless dialogue between the soul and God and they include, as honesty demands, questioning and complaint and anger that are essential elements in our response to him. The psalms express the whole range of human religious experience, from dark depression similar to that in Job's suffering, to joy, as in his restoration. They contain some matchless poetry. They are of complex structure and full of rich imagery, simile and metaphor and of repetition, as befits their poetic style. They were frequently quoted by Jesus himself and they continue to be a source of comfort, spiritual nourishment and inspiration to present day Jews and Christians and no doubt many others also.

Psalm 16

You have made known to me the path
   of life;
You will fill me with joy in your presence...

Psalm 46

There is a river whose streams make
   Glad the city of God,
The holy place where the Most High dwells.

Psalm 23

The Lord is my shepherd, I shall not be in want.
He makes me lie down in green pastures,
   he leads me beside quiet waters,
   he restores my soul.
He guides me in paths of righteousness
   For his name's sake.
Even though I walk through the valley
   of the shadow of death,
I will fear no evil, for you are with me;
   your rod and your staff, they comfort me.
You prepare a table before me
   in the presence of my enemies.
You anoint my head with oil;
   my cup overflows.
Surely goodness and love will follow me
   all the days of my life,
and I will dwell in the house of the Lord for ever.

Psalm 98

Sing to the Lord a new song,
  for he has done marvellous things;
his right hand and his holy arm
  have worked salvation for him.

The Lord has made his salvation known
  and revealed his righteousness to the nations.
He has remembered his love
  and his faithfulness to the house of Israel;
all the ends of the earth have seen
  the salvation of our God.

Shout for joy to the Lord, all the earth,
  burst into jubilant song with music;
make music to the Lord with the harp,
  with the harp and the sound of singing,
With trumpets and the blast of the ram's horn –
  shout for joy before the Lord, the King.

Let the sea resound, and everything in it,
  the world, and all who live in it.
Let the rivers clap their hands,
  let the mountains sing together for joy;
let them sing before the Lord,
  for he comes to judge the earth.
He will judge the world in righteousness
  and the peoples with equity.

PROVERBS

The Proverbs were ascribed to Solomon but it is clear from later chapters that he was not the only author of the book. They are for 'attaining wisdom and discipline; ... for doing what is right and just and fair'. There are a number of themes, chief of which are wisdom and folly; the righteous and the wicked; the rich and the poor; words and the tongue; the family and relationships, and laziness and hard work. The basis of wisdom is the fear of the Lord and from this spiritual starting point the Proverbs continue through sound general precepts for a good life and personal relationships, to practical daily matters and politics, but in no special order. Tasters could include the following:

Trust in the Lord with all your heart and lean not on your own understanding; in all your ways acknowledge him and he will make your paths straight (3:5,6)

The Lord abhors dishonest scales, but accurate weights are his delight. (11:1)

The teaching of the wise is a fountain of life. (13:14)

A gentle answer turns away wrath but a harsh word stirs up anger. (15:1)

Starting a quarrel is like breaching a dam; so drop the matter before a dispute breaks out. (17:14)

He who guards his mouth and his tongue keeps himself from calamity. (21:23)

There is no wisdom, no insight, no plan that can succeed against the Lord. (21:30)

Don't wear yourself out to get rich. (23:4)

Let another praise you , not your own mouth. (27:2)

Keep falsehood and lies far from me; give me neither poverty nor riches, but give me only my daily bread. (30:8)

Proverbs ends with an epilogue about the 'wife of noble character'. Browsing is the order of the day!

ECCLESIASTES

"I am determined to be wise" –
but this was beyond me.
Whatever wisdom may be,
it is far off and most profound –
who can discover it? "

Ecclesiastes is the Greek word for teacher, preacher, speaker or philosopher. The book declares itself as the words of the Teacher, son of David, king of Jerusalem and may be in part at least the work of Solomon. Although an unfamiliar form to us, it is typical of the Wisdom Literature of Old Testament times and wonderfully written. The writer is now old and looks back on his life as a king, as a man of action and a man of wisdom. He is disillusioned about his achievements in all these capacities, which are 'like chasing after the wind' and 'meaningless'. He is wearied by wickedness and the lack of justice and of judgement, and by the oppression and the loneliness that he sees around him. Even faith cannot resolve the problem of evil. But he has some good advice for other old men. 'Do not say, "Why were the old days better than these?" for it is not wise to ask such questions. When times are good, be happy; but when times are bad, consider: God has made the one as well as the other.'

He is aware of the uselessness of advancement and riches, unless they are seen as a gift from God, though even then he has to leave them behind when he dies. Otherwise these too are meaningless and a chasing after the wind. Like Proverbs, it is all very up-to-date. Without God life is futile; everything is 'in his hands'. He has lost confidence in work, in his 'great projects' and in his power, his luxuries and pleasures and even in knowledge and wisdom, though it is 'better than folly'. 'There is nothing new under the sun.' God has 'set eternity in the hearts of men; yet they cannot fathom what he has done from beginning to end.' 'Who knows if the spirit of man rises upwards' and 'who can tell him under the sun after he is gone?' he asks. In a moment of insight and inspiration he says in 12:7 'the dust returns to the ground it came from , and the spirit returns to God who gave it.' These strivings after the idea of immortality will be given substance only by the bodily resurrection of Jesus in which we are told we too will one day share. In 5:7 the Teacher tells us that we should 'Stand in awe of God' and he ends with 'the conclusion of the matter' which is: 'Fear God, and keep his commandments, for this is the whole duty of man. For God will bring every deed into judgement, including every hidden thing, whether it be good or evil.' The fundamentals of life and death and judgement do not change, even over thousands of years.

THE SONG OF SOLOMON

This may be yet another example of Solomon's work and is a series of poems on the theme of love. They are full of the passion and joy and wonder of human love between man and woman and they speak of its spontaneity and beauty, and its power and exclusiveness. 'My lover is mine and I am his.' Love is experienced in its varied moments of separation and intimacy, anguish and ecstasy, tension and contentment. The book is in the form of a conversation between lover and beloved and their friends, the voice of the woman being dominant. It might seem a strange book to have in the Bible but physical love when it is enjoyed with gratitude can be celebrated as a gift of God. So glorious is this provision that its language can even contribute to our understanding of the love that we share with him. Two Hebrew words are used for love in this book. The first of them is used to indicate the physical, sexual love between man and woman and is equivalent to the Greek word Eros. The second points to the love that involves a more general and genuine concern for the whole person of the other. This comes closer to the meaning of the Greek word Agape that means loving the other dearly and is the word almost invariably used for love in the New Testament.

The Song shares its use of subtle but highly sensuous and suggestive imagery drawn from nature with the love poetry of many cultures. "All beautiful you are, my darling; there is no flaw in you." "How much more pleasing is your love than wine, and the fragrance of your perfume than any spice!" It is unashamedly erotic. The presence of this extraordinary book in the canon of Scripture surely tells us something of the depth and range of the gifts and joys that we receive as children of our generous and loving heavenly Father. Our recognition that they all of them come in the end from him is a powerful incentive to praise and thanksgiving.

THE PROPHETS

'Surely the Sovereign Lord does nothing without revealing his plan to his servants the prophets.' (Amos 3;7).
'Prophecy never had its origin in the will of man, but men spoke from God as they were carried along by the Holy Spirit.' (2 Pet 1;19-21).

There had been Old Testament prophets in Israel from Moses onwards through Joshua, Samuel and David, to Elijah and Elisha, from the 15th to the 9th century BC. They were followed by the writing prophets, Isaiah to Malachi, from the 8th to the 5th century. We have already encountered the greatest of all the prophets, Moses and Elijah; Moses in Exodus and Deuteronomy, and Elijah in 1 and 2 Kings. As early in the Bible as Deut 18:15 Moses' made an extraordinary prophecy that "God will raise up for you a prophet like me from among your own brothers. You must listen to him." This is to our ears an unmistakable reference to Jesus – to the Messiah, as the One who is promised later comes to be known. But it is referring to him not as the king who will sit on the throne of David for ever, but as a prophet, of necessity the greatest of all the prophets. He is the fulfilment of the Prophets and the Law to which they constantly drew attention, of kingship, and of the priesthood and the sacrifices as well. He is the One to whom the whole of the Old Testament looks forward, as we shall see more clearly when we get to the New Testament and look backwards. The last of the Old Testament prophets, four hundred years after Malachi, will be John the Baptist, Jesus' contemporary herald, God's messenger sent ahead to 'prepare the way for the Lord'. Prophecy did not cease at this point however and following Jesus himself there have continued to be prophets, amongst the apostles who wrote the Gospels and epistles, and throughout the past two thousand years of Church history.

The prophets were literally those who 'spoke for God'. They were called out by him from various walks of life: it was a vocation, not a profession. Along with the priests, who were appointed to mediate between God and man in worship and in the administration of the sacrifices for sin, they were God's chief means of maintaining his relationship with his people Israel. The prophet's commission was to deliver the messages that the kings and priests and the people needed to hear in their particular time and circumstances. As with human parents, God needed to remind his children of the guidelines he had laid down for their relationship with him, with their families and neighbours and with the rest of the community. He also wanted them to know the plans he had for their future. In these two ways he established his authority and gave them confidence that in spite of the freedom he had given them, including the freedom to try to frustrate his plans, he was ultimately in control. This helped to make him worthy of their belief and trust, and of their worship. At the very start of Isaiah God gives them this message:

> "Hear, O heavens! Listen, O earth!
> For the Lord has spoken:
> I reared children and brought them up,
> but they have rebelled against me."

Later in Isaiah 65:2 God says to them:

> "All day long I have held out my hands
> to an obstinate people."

God's children have always been a trouble to him: it appears that he is prepared to be continually disappointed in them, especially in his kings and leaders. The prophets of Israel spoke to the people of their need to be obedient to what God had already revealed but also of their need to enlarge their understanding of what he required of them next and to move forward. They were for this reason men of vision and originality, and therefore sometimes excitable and impatient. The priests, in their responsibility for the sacrifices, were at home with administration, with tradition and ritual, and with orderly worship and thus provided a steadying influence. The Church of today continues to need both kinds of people to perform these same roles in order to ensure a balanced ministry, even if they inevitably infuriate each other on occasion.

The surrounding nations had seers, or wise men, but no other nation had the unique, miraculous provision of the God-given prophets of Israel. They played the key role in reminding them of what it meant to be God's people. The prophets spoke to them as preachers of right living in accordance with the commandments and covenants that God had already made with them and of their need of repentance for their disobedience. A part of their vocation was to ensure that the priests remained faithful and that the kings were not allowed to consider themselves above the Law. They were also God's chief means of warning his people of judgement and punishment for their sins and even more important of telling them of his promises of their eventual restoration. But they also spoke of things yet to happen in the even more distant future: proclamation and prediction were both of them essential elements in their message. Chief among these future events were the coming of the Messiah and the kingdom of God, and the outpouring of the Holy Spirit that took place at Pentecost. When man unaided predicts anything he is almost invariably wrong. When the prophets speak of God's future plans for his people, and they turn out to have been fulfilled, we are bound to sit up and take notice. Like the miracles in the New Testament prophecy adds a new dimension to the story.

The prophets spoke in down to earth but frequently highly creative poetic language, with liberal use of metaphor and symbols and imaginative pictorial images. They were true artists in their approach to their ministry. Their individual personalities and styles of speaking and writing were not submerged in any way in the delivery of their message: quite the reverse. The truth that God conveyed through them was a whole that no single one of them could have adequately expressed on his own. In the case of the priests and ministers of the Christian Church today, who act both as prophets in preaching the Word and as priests in administering the sacraments, it takes the efforts of many individuals, including lay people, each using their own gifts, to attempt to do justice to the fullness of the Gospel.

The importance of the prophets is suggested by the fact that the writing prophets, Isaiah to Malachi, take up a fifth of the pages of our Bible; almost the same space as the whole of the New Testament. Unless they occupy a great deal more space than they warrant, they deserve a great deal more attention than we give them. The prophetic books, some written by the prophets themselves, others compiled, are like a collection of powerful, inspirational published sermons. They were addressed during the three hundred years from around 750 to 450 BC to various different congregations. Some of the prophets spoke to the northern and some to the southern kingdom at various times during these three eventful centuries in which both of them were taken into captivity. Some also referred in their 'oracles' or communications to other nations including Egypt, Assyria and Babylon, as well as a number of Israel's smaller and closer neighbours, all of whom would also, in the end, be subject to God's judgement and punishment.

The prophets' warnings of judgement frequently made them unpopular and led to a great deal of hostility and to their being regarded as 'fools and maniacs', as Hosea complained. This hostility sometimes led to persecution and even to death. We might wonder why they were prepared to do the job. They were clearly men of great courage and integrity but the real answer lay in their conviction that they had been called by God. This calling had nevertheless to be tested by the quality of their words and prophecies and of the lives they lived, in order to distinguish between true and false prophets. The false prophets said what people wanted to hear: "Tell us pleasant things, prophesy illusions!" (Is 30:10). The authentic calling of the true prophets was what made them willing to speak the frequently unpopular truth to kings and priests and people, whatever the consequences. They described their calling in various graphic terms as God's hand upon them, and of his word being put into their mouths. It was this conviction of their calling that above all gave them the authority with which they delivered their message as from God. It was this authority and the spiritual leadership they gave that explained their influence on the life of the nation. They enabled Israel to continue to believe that they were God's people and that he would never abandon them. It was not for Israel's benefit only however, as Isaiah tells us in 49:6, but in order that they might be "a light for the Gentiles, that you may bring my salvation to the ends of the earth." It was not favouritism but the conferring of responsibility and a call to serve, just as it is with the Church today.

Without the prophets it is hard to imagine that the people of Israel would have been able to maintain their national identity and that their unique religious faith and mission would have survived. The powerful, antagonistic nations and empires that surrounded them were a constant threat to their safety as they are to modern-day Israel but in the end they have outlasted them all. It has been said that the persisting presence of the Jewish people is the most powerful evidence for the existence of God. He had repeatedly promised them that he would one day bless them and bring all mankind to recognise their special status as those through whom he had especially worked out his purposes in the world. "As the new heavens and the new earth that I make will endure before me, so will your name and descendents endure," he told them at the very end of Isaiah, in 66:22. In spite of their being defeated and exiled by these other nations as punishment for their sins they recognised God's powerful and faithful hand upon them throughout their history. The supreme demonstration of this faithfulness was their deliverance from Egypt in the Exodus which they still continue to celebrate more than three thousand years later.

It was this sense of continuity and coherence that the prophets did so much to establish and foster in making the people aware of God's lordship, not only over the affairs of their own nation but of every other nation on earth as well. God is the Lord of all history. Without prophecy they could not have made sense of the unfolding revelation of God's constant activity in redemptive history as a massive connected programme of his love at work in the world, and nor could we. Prophecy and the prophets provided a line of continuity between the Old and New Testaments for the people of the time and for future generations, including ourselves. The link is beautifully expressed in the first verse of the book of Hebrews: 'God, who at sundry times and in divers places has spoken to us through the prophets, has in these last days spoken to us through his Son.'

When Jesus came he made it plain that he had not come to do away with the Law and the Prophets but to fulfil them and to reveal their true significance, thus further binding the story together and confirming and strengthening this continuity. He frequently spoke of the Old Testament prophecies that were clearly referring to himself. The prophets had prepared the way for him and he in his turn made plain that he was the One they had been looking forward to, thus flooding them with light and interpreting their words for us. Jesus himself also prophesied, notably in telling the disciples of his impending death and resurrection and of the coming of the Holy Spirit. He also spoke to them in Jn 14:29 about the crucial importance of prophecy: "I have told you now before it happens, so that when it does happen you will believe." He is making it plain that prophecy is not given to satisfy curiosity but to inform in advance and thereby increase faith.

Prophecy, in its fullest sense of God reminding his people of their covenant relationship with him and telling them about his plans for the future, is thus the chief method of biblical revelation and of his communication with his people. It continues to be so today: the same principles still apply. We have the same need to acknowledge God as he has revealed himself in both the Old and the New Testaments and the same need of prophets to interpret the Scriptures and point the way ahead for us. Our failures and our disobedience are still subject to his judgement and to inevitable punishment, but equally, through repentance, we still have a way back to him, to forgiveness and restoration. Whether we regard judgement as the direct, sovereign action of God as it is presented to us in the Old Testament or as an inexorable reality built into his creation, our recognition of its reality helps us to interpret what has happened in history and what we see happening in the world all around us today.

It is because of this element of judgement that the God of the Old Testament is frequently depicted as harsh and unfeeling, capricious and vengeful and as One to be approached only in fear and not in the spirit of love that he commanded us to show for him and for each other. There is what we are bound to see as harshness, of course: God is to be loved but must also be feared. Judgement is an inevitable aspect of God's dealings with us. He is not to be thwarted in his plans for his people and for their ultimate good, whatever the cost to their comfort, even their lives sometimes, as with his own Son. There is a real sense in which God is responsible for all suffering, but he must consider it to be justified by the destiny he has in mind for us and for his whole creation. And who are we to argue with him? He tells us in Isaiah 46:11:

> "What I have said; that will I bring about;
> what I have planned, that will I do."

There is also, and above all, the yearning of a father for a close relationship with his children. Through both Zechariah, in 1:3, and Malachi, in 3:7, he pleads with them "Return to me and I will return to you." In Jeremiah 3:14 he tries another approach, "Return, faithless people, for I am your husband." Later in the same chapter of Jeremiah the family metaphor is extended:

"How gladly would I treat you like sons
and give you a desirable land,
the most beautiful inheritance of any nation.
I thought you would call me 'Father'
and not turn away from following me.
But like a woman unfaithful to her husband,
so you have been unfaithful to me, O house of Israel."

In Jeremiah 31:3, he tells his people that "I have loved you with an everlasting love." If we study Scripture and make full use of our imagination, the discrepancy between the God of the Old and New Testaments begins to recede. If he had not given Israel and the surrounding nations a hard time his plans would never have got off the ground. We have already seen that one of the remarkable truths the prophets revealed was that the principles of God's dealings with his own people Israel applied equally to all the other nations on earth, and throughout history. He is the same God of mercy and compassion, and also, inevitably, of judgement, in every age. His love and gracious goodness have really been apparent from the very beginning and the prophets make this clear, just as his judgement is apparent in both the Old and the New Testament. Jesus has many harsh words to say in the Gospels, to the corrupt religious leaders in particular. The dialogue between God and his people never ceases and the prophets are his chief communicators in every age.

ISAIAH

Isaiah is a prince among the prophets and extensively quoted in the New Testament, especially in Matthew's gospel. The account of his call and commissioning in chapter 6, which occurred 'in the year that king Uzziah died', probably 740 BC, is unique in its lofty vision of God. "My eyes have seen the King, the Lord Almighty." He describes him as 'seated on a throne, high and exalted' with angels singing his

praises: "Holy, holy, holy is the Lord Almighty; the whole earth is full
of his glory." Isaiah's experience is of being 'a man of unclean lips'
and of living among a people of unclean lips, whose deeds are evil
and whose prayers and ritual sacrifices and offerings have become
meaningless and detestable to God. His mouth is touched with a live
coal from the altar and he is told "your guilt is taken away and your
sin atoned for." When he hears the Lord asking "Whom shall I send"
he says, without apparent hesitation, "Here am I. Send me," – quite
unlike Moses' initially reluctant response to God's call. He carried out
his prophetic ministry during the unsettled and dangerous period of
increasing power and expansion of the Assyrian empire and the
decline of both the northern and southern kingdoms of Israel and
Judah.

The book of Isaiah is written almost exclusively in poetic form,
with frequent repetition. It contains over 2000 different words and this
contributes to the complexity and richness of its ideas and images. It
is also a long book, the longest in the Bible. It is clearly not written as
a continuous text, though the style is remarkably consistent, but reads
more like a collection of spoken sermons or written messages,
delivered over many years on numerous different occasions, possibly
by more than one prophet. For this reason the arrangement of the book
is not logical or chronological and appears somewhat arbitrary, which
can make it confusing, especially on first encounter. There are various
kinds of material; woes and warnings of judgement, and promises of
eventual blessing to Israel and Judah, and through them to the world.
There is also advice given to kings about unwise alliances,
judgements of surrounding nations, bursts of spontaneous praise and
specific prophetic predictions of future events.

Much of it is presented in the form of dialogue, some of it being
passages spoken by Isaiah and some that he attributes to God himself,
which can be confusing. But our ignorance of its precise construction,
of who wrote and edited it and of the details of its complex historical
background, need not detract in any way from our appreciation of its
spiritual depth. It stands as a whole, and as a glorious testimony to the
power and artistic beauty of the prophetic tradition of Israel. None of
the other prophets had as great a vision as Isaiah of the holiness and
sovereignty of their God Yahweh, the God of creation and the ruler of
all the nations on earth. He contrasts Israel's God with the impotent

idols and gods of other nations. God says again and again "I am God and there is no other."

Isaiah is in the centre of the Bible and at the centre of Old Testament history. From this centre it looks back, as did all the prophets, to the people's previous rebellion and their breaking of the commandments and covenants. God's disappointment with them is graphically conveyed by Isaiah in his description of them in 5:2 as God's vineyard from which he 'looked for a crop of good grapes' but 'it yielded only bad fruit.' The book of Isaiah also looks forward to their inevitable judgement and punishment, but even more importantly, following this, to their eventual blessing and glory. Then, as he writes in 61:9, 'All who see them will acknowledge that they are a people the Lord has blessed.'

The book of Isaiah is painted on a huge canvas and depicts the spiritual, social and political issues facing the small nation of Israel. They live in the midst of a series of mighty empires who are used to defeat them and take them captive as punishment for their disobedience, and who in their turn will be judged and punished by the same Lord of all history. It was a profound and challenging message for the nation in her relationship with her neighbours, as it is for the Church of God today in her relationships with the world in which it seeks to serve the self-same God. It is full of lessons not only for the Church but also for the western nations nurtured on the Christian faith, and through them for the whole world in the present day.

Isaiah graphically describes his understanding of his calling in the notable passage in chapter 61:1,2 in which he speaks of the truly comprehensive nature of his ministry:

"The Spirit of the Sovereign Lord is on me,
because the Lord has anointed me to preach good news to the poor.
He has sent me to bind up the broken-hearted,
to proclaim freedom to the captives
and release from darkness for the prisoners,
To proclaim the year of the Lord's favour
and the day of vengeance of our God,
to comfort all who mourn."

Jesus read these same words aloud, but without the last two lines, in the synagogue at Nazareth as recorded in Luke 4. He made it clear that they applied above all to his own ministry, and by implication to the ministry of his body the Church. Many of its members have made remarkable contributions in the past 2000 years to the 'freeing of captives', but few to equal that of the great Christian prophet William Wilberforce and his supporters some 2500 years after Isaiah made his statement. He wrote in his diary on a Sunday in 1787: 'God Almighty has placed before me two great objects, the suppression of the slave trade and the reformation of manners.' The latter referred no doubt to child labour and working hours in factories and other issues that he also tackled later. When he addressed the House of Commons in 1789 to recommend the 'total abolition of slavery', tragically still with us in various forms, he spoke of the same feelings of inadequacy as Isaiah had done: "It is impossible for me not to feel both terrified and concerned at my inadequacy to such a task." As an evangelical Christian who was no doubt steeped in the Scriptures, he must surely have been aware of following in the footsteps of Isaiah, and above all those of Jesus himself.

None of the other prophets were given to anticipate such a huge number of future events in God's programme of redemption. A number of Isaiah's prophecies were of local, fairly contemporary reference. Some were fulfilled in the New Testament; others still remain to be fulfilled and both of these will be looked at later. In the first of these categories are his prophecies in 8:4 about the imminent exile of the northern kingdom to Assyria that took place in 722 BC and in 39:5 the subsequent exile of the southern kingdom to Babylon that eventually took place in 587 BC. In the case of Judah he tells them that Cyrus the Persian will allow a remnant of them to return to their own land in order to rebuild the Temple in Jerusalem that had been destroyed by the Babylonians. This looks forward to the time when Cyrus will conquer Babylon in 539 BC. (40:2, 44:28-45:13). 'In that day', as Isaiah tells us in 10:20,21, 'the remnant of Israel, the survivors of the house of Jacob, will return'. God works, as always, with those few who are faithful to him. It would appear to be a case of the survival of those who are fittest for his work. Maybe this can be seen as a form of natural selection working in the spiritual sphere!

The second half of Isaiah, from chapter 40 onwards, is concerned with the latter part of the exile of Judah to Babylon and the years after the return of this remnant. It begins with words of reassurance and the promise of an apparently fairly imminent freedom from captivity: 'Comfort, comfort my people, says your God.' This is immediately followed in the same chapter by a reference that is quoted by Mark and Luke in the New Testament as referring to John the Baptist. He will 'prepare the way of the Lord', referring to Jesus who will bring them an even more extensive freedom from the burden and bondage of sin. The rest of this remarkable chapter and the following fifteen chapters consist of a mixture of a huge range of different kinds of communication, including the words of Isaiah and those that he indicates as coming from the mouth of God himself. Whether the people are still in Babylon or recently returned they need to have their relationship with God strengthened. Isaiah tells them in 54:5 that "Your Maker is your husband – the Holy One of Israel is your Redeemer" and he reminds them, in 63;16, of God's previous goodness to them and that he is still their Father. They need to be encouraged to continue to trust him in spite of their recent experience of being apparently abandoned in exile. To this end he demands their attention – "Listen to me" – and reminds them of what he has done for them in their past history, that he is their God, the only God of all the earth. "I am the first and the last ... I will not yield my glory to another." (48:12).

He instructs and questions them, reasons with them, challenges them and warns them of the dangers of idolatry. Above all he repeats his promises of future blessing. Some of these promises are ones they have already heard, others are new to them: "See the former things have taken place, and new things I declare: before they spring into being I announce them to you." (42:9). He contrasts himself with idols and other gods who cannot foretell future events and thereby confirms his sovereignty over them and other nations. Throughout all this Isaiah is often so overcome with God's greatness and goodness that he gets carried away, like St Paul in some of his New Testament epistles, and in 49:13 he breaks out into a burst of praise:

> "Shout for joy, O heavens;
> rejoice, O earth;
> burst into song, O mountains!
> For the Lord comforts his people
> and will have compassion on his afflicted ones."

In spite of all the attention that God has lavished on them however, his people still have not learned to do what is pleasing to him, as we learn from chapter 56 onwards: "I, the Lord, love justice; I hate robbery and iniquity", but "They all turn their own way, each seeks his own gain." "On the day of your fasting, you do as you please and exploit all your workers. Your fasting ends in quarrelling and strife and in striking each other with wicked fists." Isaiah continues his account of God spelling out his message to the people in the form of a powerful and challenging rhetorical question:

> "Is not this the kind of fasting I have chosen:
> to loose the chains of injustice
>   and untie the cords of the yoke,
> to set the oppressed free and break every yoke?
> Is it not to share your food with the hungry
>   and to provide the poor wanderer with shelter –
> when you see the naked, to clothe him,
>   and not to turn away from your own flesh and blood?
> Then your light will break forth as the dawn,
>   and your healing will quickly appear;
> then your righteousness will go before you
>   and the glory of the Lord will be your rearguard.
> Then you will call, and the Lord will answer;
>   you will cry for help, and he will say: Here am I." (58:6-9).

As other prophets had also told them, God is looking for his people to "keep your feet from breaking the Sabbath and from doing what you please on my holy day." (58:13). They have to recognise, yet again, their need of repentance; to see, as Isaiah expresses it in 64:6 that 'all our righteous acts are like filthy rags'. They must repent in order to enable God to bless them once more through the faithful remnant and confirm his unchangeable covenant with them.

Throughout his book Isaiah also foretells events that are yet to take place, above all the coming of the Messiah, another six hundred years in the future. He refers to him as the 'Prince of Peace' in 9:6 and in 53:7 as the 'man of sorrows, familiar with suffering'. In 9:1,2 he speaks graphically of how God will in the future 'honour Galilee of the Gentiles, by the way of the sea, along the Jordan' and how through this coming of the Messiah, 'the people walking in darkness have seen a great light.' He also foretells the coming of his herald, John the Baptist. He speaks, in 44:3, of the coming of the Holy Spirit: "I will pour out my Spirit on your offspring, and my blessing on your descendents."

God has promised to 'make known the end from the beginning' and Isaiah also refers prophetically to an event yet further in the future which even now has still not taken place. When he speaks in 61:2 of 'the day of vengeance of our God' it would appear that unknowingly he is making prophetic reference to what we now speak of as Jesus the Messiah's second coming in glory and judgement. When that day comes the Lord will then emerge as the one universal, unifying God of all the earth before whom Isaiah tells us in chapter 45:23 'every knee will bow'. It is only then that there will be peace and justice. Isaiah is given to see that 'They will beat their swords into ploughshares and their spears into pruning hooks. Nation will not take up sword against nation, nor will they train for war any more,' (2:4) and he foresees that 'the wolf will live with the lamb ... and the lion will eat straw like the ox.' (11:6,7). We can have no real understanding of the reality of this twofold vision but it is a glorious expression of the message of Scripture that things will one day be different and that there will eventually be an end to war and violence.

This universal, worldwide outcome will have been made possible by God's calling not only of Israel but also of the Gentiles and their inclusion in his Church, whose members will continue his work during the present Church age between Jesus' first and second coming. In 49:6 God says to Isaiah, "It is too small a thing for you to be my servant to restore the tribes of Jacob and bring back those of Israel I have kept. I will also make you a light for the Gentiles, that you may bring my salvation to the ends of the earth." Christ, the light of the world, was sent not only to God's people Israel, but through them to the world, for the redemption of his whole creation.

Earlier, in chapter 26:19, Isaiah gives one of the few unmistakable hints in the Old Testament of the resurrection of the body that will be central to our experience of this redemption: 'But your dead will live: their bodies will rise.' Another of Isaiah's visions, in 65:17, is of God creating 'new heavens and a new earth', an image that is echoed in John's vision of the Holy City, the New Jerusalem, in chapter 21 of Revelation. He has a vision, in 60:19, of the Lord being their 'everlasting light' and this too appears in Rev 22:5 where we read that in the heavenly city 'they have no need of a lamp or the light of the sun, for the Lord will give them light.' He foresees in 25:8 that God 'will swallow up death for ever ... and wipe away the tears from all faces,' which again is repeated in Rev 21. The range and penetration of Isaiah's inspired prophetic imagination and thinking and the quality of the ideas through which he conveys his message are extraordinary. It is remarkable that the writer of Revelation, some seven hundred years later, should have had no higher vision and no better words than his to provide us with the most exalted imagery of heaven that we have in the whole of Scripture. There are a number of passages in his book that effortlessly deserve a place in any anthology of the world's greatest literature, quite apart from their key place in the spiritual heritage of the Old Testament. We can surely be forgiven for returning again and again to some of these favourite passages:

'For unto us a child is born,
  to us a son is given,
  and the government will be upon his shoulders.
And he will be called
  Wonderful Counsellor, Mighty God,
  Everlasting Father, Prince of Peace.
Of the increase of his government and peace
  there will be no end.
He will reign on David's throne
  and over his kingdom,
establishing and upholding it
  with justice and righteousness
  from that time forth for ever.' (9:6,7)

'Those who hope in the Lord
  will renew their strength.
They will soar on wings like eagles;
  they will run and not grow weary,
  they will walk and not be faint.' (40:31)

'Surely he took up our infirmities
  and carried our sorrows,
yet we considered him stricken by God,
  smitten by him and afflicted.
But he was pierced for our transgressions,
  he was crushed for our iniquities;
the punishment that brought us peace was upon him,
  and by his wounds we are healed.' (53:4,5)

'You will go out in joy
  and be led forth in peace;
the mountains and hills
  will burst into song before you
and all the trees of the fields
  will clap their hands.' (55:12)

It is impossible to read these verses without being encouraged and uplifted. It is hardly necessary in many instances to have even an inkling of their true meaning to enjoy them as language, and as spiritual nourishment. The book of Isaiah can speak powerfully to those without faith as well as those who have it. Those with the greatest possible faith and knowledge cannot claim to understand fully what he is saying and what he is looking forward to. Even Isaiah himself could not, of necessity, have known the reality of the things he was given to foretell. The more we read Isaiah the more clear it becomes that no commentary can do justice to this book. As with the rest of Scripture we need to read the book itself so that the outstanding passages can be encountered and savoured in context.

JEREMIAH

Jeremiah, who was a priest as well as being called as a prophet, lived and prophesied in Jerusalem during the reigns of the last five kings of Judah between 626 and 586 BC. In this latter year Judah was defeated by Nebuchadnezzar, Jerusalem and the Temple were destroyed and several thousands of the people were taken into captivity in Babylon, as Jeremiah had told them would happen. He spoke graphically of his call: 'Then the Lord reached out his hand and touched my mouth and said to me, "Now I have put my words in your mouth." ' Throughout his ministry he made use of vivid images and symbols. On one occasion he was instructed by God to buy a clay jar from a potter and break it in order to show what God would do to the nation.

Jeremiah was a gentle and sensitive man but also strong and determined, with an unswerving loyalty and obedience to God and a profound love and concern for his people. As a result he spoke with great authority but also with a deep anguish at his recognition at what was to happen to them on account of their sins. 'Since my people are crushed, I am crushed.' (8:7). This anguish combined with the persecution he endured led him to despair of his ministry and even of life itself – he was ignored, mocked and ridiculed, beaten, put in prison and on one occasion thrown into a cistern. But God's word was 'in his heart like a fire' (20:9), so that he could not ignore it and give up his ministry, in spite of the struggles within him and the opposition all around him. His life bore witness to the truth that, in Jung's words, 'only the wounded healer heals', as Jesus' life and death were to reveal in a truly definitive way.

Jeremiah's message centred on God's sovereignty over all nations and on the sins of the people. These included idolatry, in their case worshipping false and foreign gods, immorality and, above all, the lack of integrity and sincerity of the priests. They included also the worthless words of comfort of the false prophets, who 'dress the wound of my people as though it were not serious.' (6:14). A large part of the book is made up of anguished statements about their sins; in 9:7 Jeremiah tells them that 'they do not know the requirements of the Lord.' These are followed by his reporting of words of judgement from God, who complains in 2:27 that his people "have turned their backs to me and not their faces." In 7:11 he asks: "Has this house, which bears my Name, become a den of robbers to you?" – a question that Jesus would later ask when he entered the Temple in Jerusalem. God would punish the people in various ways, by 'sword, plague and famine' but ultimately by defeat and exile for seventy years in Babylon. The Babylonians had already deported a number of them, including the prophet Daniel, in 605, and others including Ezekiel in 597. They were still threatening them and would destroy Jerusalem and the Temple in 586 and deport yet more of them.

To their surprise and anger, Jeremiah advised them not to resist an overwhelmingly more powerful enemy. In a letter to those already in captivity in Babylon his advice was to live as normal a life as possible, to build houses and settle down, to marry and have children and to pray for the country to which they had gone 'because if it prospers, you too will prosper'. He also promised them that they would one day be released and return home with great rejoicing, when Babylon would be defeated in its turn by the Persians under Cyrus in 539 BC.

His dominant theme, as with all the prophets, was hope for the future. So clear was his spiritual vision that he was able to view the destruction of Jerusalem with equanimity, even the destruction of the Temple itself and the sacrificial system, because he saw that what mattered was the people's obedience to the law and their love of God and of their neighbour. In 31:33 he was given to reveal God's promise that the law would be written not on stone tablets but on people's hearts. In this way their obedience would be spontaneous, having arisen from within and resulting from their relationship with God, rather than imposed from without as a commandment.

> "I will put my law in their minds
> and write it on their hearts.
> I will be their God,
> and they will be my people." (31:33)

This promise must have been an enormous encouragement to the people and have helped them to develop a sense of individual worth and to increase the depth of their spiritual lives. It would ultimately be fulfilled in the coming of the Holy Spirit at Pentecost some six hundred years later. There was also an emerging interest at this time in personal identity and destiny and hence in a concern with a life after death. This change of emphasis in effect added an element of psychology to what had previously been almost exclusively theology, or a concern with God and his requirements. There was now a place also for human needs and for maturing as individuals, but this was not without its dangers in that God might cease to be the chief focus in the lives of his people. Jeremiah's part in God's plan to introduce this potentially risky change is a measure of his greatness as a prophet and a man of God.

LAMENTATIONS

Lamentations, possibly also attributable to Jeremiah, describes in studied poetic language and in great detail, the destruction of Jerusalem brought about by the Lord through the agency of the Babylonians. Thus we read in 2:5 that 'The Lord is like an enemy; he has swallowed up Israel.' This prompts the writer to ask in 3:38: 'Is it not from the Most High that both calamities and good things come?' But once again hope is the final note, especially in this third chapter: 'Great is your faithfulness' and 'Men are not cast off by the Lord forever.' This is the miraculous, paradoxical hope and confidence that only those who trust in a God of infinite and everlasting love can begin to imagine as a possibility. But even Jesus, when he was dying on the Cross was recorded by Mark as crying out to his Father "My God, my God, why have you forsaken me?" If Jesus himself had this experience of abandonment it makes the faith and spiritual vision of these Old Testament men of God more remarkable still. How were they able to express this extraordinary trust in God in spite of knowing nothing of the Cross and Resurrection that is our definitive evidence of his endless love and his triumph over death and evil? Only God's even more extraordinary gift of revelation and prophecy can possibly explain it.

EZEKIEL

Ezekiel, who was also a priest, and like Jeremiah from a priestly family, received his prophetic calling in 593 BC whilst already an exile in Babylon. He had been taken from Judah by Nebuchadnezzar four years earlier, in 597, along with about 10,000 others, in the second of three waves of deportation. In the very first verse he tells us that 'the heavens were opened and I saw visions of God.' In the second chapter he describes how God spoke to him and 'the Spirit came into me and raised me to my feet, and I heard him speaking to me. He said: "Son of man, I am sending you to the Israelites, to a rebellious nation that has rebelled against me." ' He is to speak "whether they listen or fail to listen" and not to be afraid, and he then graphically describes being given a scroll to eat, as a sign that he must make God's message his own and deliver it as his human agent. What makes Ezekiel unique among the prophets is the sheer wealth and individuality of the symbols, pictorial images and visions that fill his writing, some of which appear very strange.

It appears that he lived in Babylon as a married man in his own house and had enjoyed a relatively normal life, as Jeremiah had advised the exiles to do in a letter that he addressed to them from Jerusalem. His ministry was naturally to his fellow exiles but it was initially addressed in the form of warnings of coming judgement and exile to those who were still in Judah and its capital, Jerusalem. Like Jeremiah and others of the prophets he could clearly see their coming defeat and destruction and captivity on account of their many sins. He was a man of great intelligence, with a broad knowledge and grasp of human affairs and of spiritual issues. As a result, his prophecies were influential in helping the people to understand where God was leading them through this time of upheaval. In particular he was led to make clear the responsibility of every individual for their own sins, a teaching that is in line with the emphasis on personal spirituality in Jeremiah. This marked a change from the previous Old Testament tendency to view the nation as one body rather than a community of individuals. It can be seen as a preparation for the greater emphasis on individual believers in the New Testament, albeit drawn together in the spiritual body of the Church.

Referring to himself in many places as 'Son of man', almost a hundred times in fact, Ezekiel delivers the prophetic message of God's holiness and his sovereignty over all creation, his judgement, and his eventual redemption of his people. The first twenty four chapters, covering the first seven years of his ministry, from 593 BC until the fall of Jerusalem in 586, are taken up with harsh judgements of Judah on account of their idolatry, in the form of their reliance on foreign gods and other nations rather than on God, and their moral corruption. The news of the catastrophic fall of Jerusalem, when it happens, is brought to him by a man who has escaped from the city. More exiles are then brought to Babylon and much of the remainder of Ezekiel is devoted to a different message, of hope and encouragement and promises of eventual restoration. But this is not before he has delivered some harsh words of prophecy directed against Egypt and some of the smaller nations surrounding Israel. God's judgement is upon them as well as on Israel. He is seen by Ezekiel, and by the other prophets, as having a decisive hand in the destiny of every nation and the whole of history.

The final chapters, from 36 to 48, are concerned with Ezekiel's central theme of God's holiness and his sovereignty over Israel and all other nations and with the restoration of God's people following the judgement and punishment that will come upon them both. Ezekiel is told by the 'Sovereign Lord' to say to Israel:

> "I will show the holiness of my great name, which has been profaned among the nations, the name that you have profaned among them. Then the nations will know that I am the Lord, when I show myself holy through you before their eyes. For I will take you out of the nations; I will gather you from all the countries and bring you back into your own land. I will sprinkle clean water on you, and you will be clean; I will cleanse you from all your impurities and from all your idols. I will give you a new heart and put a new spirit in you; I will remove from you your heart of stone and give you a heart of flesh. And I will put my Spirit in you and move you to follow my decrees and be careful to keep my laws. You will live in the land I gave your forefathers; you will be my people, and I will be your God." (36:23-28).

Then comes Ezekiel's most startling and memorable vision of the valley full of dry bones in chapter 37. He sees them being brought together, clothed with muscle and flesh and finally having life breathed into them, symbolising what will eventually happen to the whole house of Israel. Both Judah and the northern house of Israel will one day be brought together under one king. 'And they will have one shepherd'. This is a reference that to us can mean only one person, Christ himself, the Messiah to whom the prophets ultimately point.

Ezekiel, complex and visionary to the last, still trying to describe the indescribable, ends his book with a vision of a restored Temple. In this he is given a powerful experience of the glory of the Lord returning to his Temple, following its departure when Jerusalem was under judgement. Ezekiel then continues with precise instructions about the construction of the Temple and about the ritual to be followed within it, thus emphasising the need for the people to recognise the holiness and sovereignty of God in their approach to him in worship. He also emphasises the need for the apportioning of land for a 'sacred district' for the Lord, as a space for the sanctuary and the priests, and another adjoining area for the city that will 'belong to the whole house of Israel' – perhaps their equivalent of Hyde Park! Ezekiel also emphasises the need for a restriction of the power of the 'princes', for fair-trading and for offerings to pay for the sacrifices. It all sounds like a very well thought out scheme. These messages no doubt came naturally to him as a priest and they must have exerted an enormous influence on those who later returned to Jerusalem in 538 BC to rebuild the Temple. This focus of worship had been denied them for almost seventy years in captivity but would continue to be at the centre of the life of the Jews for more than six hundred years until its destruction by the Romans in AD 70.

In his final vision Ezekiel describes how he is brought back to the entrance of the temple in the city and sees water coming out from under the threshold. It is coming from its south side and becoming an ever wider and deeper river and flowing into the sea and providing nourishment for 'swarms of living creatures.' He sees also 'a great number of trees on each side of the river' and 'fruit trees of all kinds' whose 'leaves will not wither, nor will their fruit fail.' They will bear fruit every month and 'it will serve for food and their leaves for healing.' Speaking of the city and its twelve gates, named after the twelve tribes of Israel, Ezekiel ends his book with these words: 'And the name of the city from that time on will be: "THE LORD IS THERE." '

Ezekiel provides, as did Isaiah, vital material for the final vision of the Holy City in Revelation, a book that was not written for another six hundred years. In spite of this no finer imagery was available to the writer to convey its glory. For this and other reasons Ezekiel cannot be denied a place among the spiritual giants.

DANIEL

If Ezekiel is a complex book Daniel is in some ways even more so. In addition to the complexity of its contents there is the question of who Daniel was, who wrote the book and when it was written. There are some inexplicable historical inaccuracies but it survives these difficulties as do other parts of Scripture. It is a rich store of unusual and fascinating stories, dreams and prophecies. It also provides the origin of a number of well-known phrases. These include the 'lion's den', 'the writing on the wall' and 'Belshazzar's feast' during which the writing appeared.

The book starts with Daniel's arrival in Babylon in about 605 BC in the first deportation from Judah by king Nebuchadnezzar. It describes his training, along with Shadrach, Meshach and Abednego, as a promising candidate for service in the king's palace. Following a successful battle to avoid compromising their dietary laws and their principles by accepting the royal food and wine, and insisting rather on vegetables and water, they gain favour for their wisdom and understanding. As a result Daniel is soon in the limelight. Nebuchadnezzar has a dream, which he has forgotten, and which his wise men are naturally unable to describe, let alone interpret. Daniel offers to tell him what it means and urges his three friends to ask for God's help with the mystery, to which he receives the answer in a vision. This first dream was of a large statue made of gold, silver and bronze and a mixture of iron and clay, all of which were destroyed by a rock, 'not cut by human hands' that became 'a huge mountain and filled the whole earth.' Daniel tells Nebuchadnezzar that he is that 'head of gold' and the other elements represent future kingdoms. These are thought to be the Medes, the Persians and the Greeks or their Syrian successors, or possibly the Romans. All of these are destroyed, but they will be followed by a kingdom set up by the God of heaven 'that will never be destroyed'. (2:44).

Nebuchadnezzar has another dream, also interpreted by Daniel, in which he is warned of coming judgement if he does not repent. Between these two dreams Daniel's three friends are thrown into a blazing furnace because they refuse to worship the king's ninety foot high 'image of gold'. They miraculously survive this ordeal, being apparently joined by a fourth man whom the king describes as looking like a 'son of the gods'. (3:25). The king then issues a decree that the God of Shadrach, Meshach and Abednego is to be honoured by the people of all nations.

The next thing we hear is that Daniel interprets some writing on the wall for a later king, referred to as Belshazzar, during a great banquet. The words that the hand writes are 'Mene, Mene, Tekel, Parsin' whose meaning is that the king has been 'weighed on the scales and found wanting' and that his kingdom will be 'given to the Medes and Persians'. (5:28). On the very evening of the feast, at the time of the defeat of the Babylonians by Cyrus the Persian in 539 BC, he is slain! In the next chapter Daniel is thrown into the lions' den by the new king because he refuses to cease saying his prayers to God. Much to the king's joy he is unharmed 'because he had trusted in his God'. Those who had falsely accused him are then thrown into the lions' den, along with their wives and children, and they are not so fortunate! The king then issues a decree, similar to that issued by his predecessor, Nebuchadnezzar, that people in every part of his kingdom 'must fear and reverence the God of Daniel'. To this decree he rather surprisingly adds a prophecy: 'For he is the living God and he endures for ever; his kingdom will not be destroyed, his dominion will never end.'

From chapter 7 on the book is exclusively apocalyptic, like the book of Revelation, and takes the form of visions about the end times. Daniel sees the 'Ancient of days' on his throne in judgement, attended by 'ten thousand times ten thousand'. In the remaining chapters Daniel receives further complex revelations. He sees in a vision 'one like a son of man, coming with the clouds of heaven. He approached the Ancient of days, and was led into his presence. He was given authority, glory and sovereign power; all peoples nations and men of every language worshipped him. His dominion is an everlasting dominion that will not pass away, and his kingdom is one that will never be destroyed.' (7:13,14).

This is clearly, as we can now see, a reference to the promised Messiah. It is hard for us to appreciate just how encouraging this prophecy of the ultimate triumph of their God must have been to the Jewish people in the second century BC. During this time the Syrian king, Antiochus Epiphanes, desecrated the Temple and attempted to destroy the Jewish faith. They were barely managing to hold on to their unique religious tradition against enormous odds. This fragile thread could, humanly speaking, have been severed by such ferocious opposition, with incalculable consequences for the world. This book must have been one of their most powerful sources of inspiration. It helped them to know that they were not fighting the battle on their own: their Messiah would come to vindicate their faith and Daniel indicates that they have not long to wait. The fact that Jesus did not fulfil their earthly, military expectations and that the majority of Jews would not, and still do not recognise and accept him, is the next part of the story that is told in the New Testament.

HOSEA TO MALACHI (Minor Prophets)

Following these four major OT prophets there are 12 'minor' prophets, – so called because their books are shorter. They cover the same period of three to four hundred years. The majority of these prophets, like Isaiah, were sent to the southern kingdom of Judah. Of the others, Hosea and Amos had a special mission to the northern kingdom before it fell to Assyria in 722 BC; Jonah and Nahum's concern was with the Assyrian capital Nineveh, and Obadiah denounced Israel's long-standing enemy and unpopular neighbour, Edom.

The prophets spoke as well as wrote so that these books were both addresses and letters for their contemporaries and records for posterity and each of them expressed his own individuality and concerns. Amos concentrated on law and justice, and Hosea on God's love, as Isaiah had spoken of his sovereignty and holiness. The four major prophets have been considered at some length, the remaining twelve minor prophets will be looked at rather more briefly. The justification for such a large number of individual portraits of the twelve 'minor' prophets is that they brought added life and reality to the same basic message by their own personality, as every preacher needs to do, as well as focusing on different issues. There were no doubt others who spoke for God during this time whose words are not included in Scripture. It would seem likely that the ones who are included were those who communicated the message most effectively and challengingly and they continue to speak powerfully to us today.

HOSEA

Hosea, the only one of the writing prophets to come from the northern kingdom of Israel, prophesied primarily to them for some thirty eight years from about the middle of the 8th century BC. These were the last troubled years of the northern kingdom in which they had no less than six kings in twenty five years. Hosea's message, symbolised by his unfaithful wife, Gomer, was that the people of Israel had been unfaithful to God by failing to acknowledge him in their national life. They were worshipping Canaanite deities, notably Baal, and this amounted to spiritual adultery. Their leaders, the kings, priests and merchants, were the chief offenders. They set up idols, lawlessness and injustice reigned and there was burglary, highway robbery, murder and drunkenness. They offered sacrifices and observed the ritual but saw no need of forgiveness and their worship made no difference to the way they lived their lives. God said to them "I desire mercy, not sacrifice, and acknowledgement of God rather than burnt offerings." He continued to love them nevertheless, in spite of their behaviour: "How can I give you up? My heart is changed within me; all my compassion is aroused" – and he encouraged Hosea to continue loving his wife. Faithfulness, both sexual and spiritual are the themes of this book and 4:14 has an important and perhaps surprising message for us, that the men will be judged more harshly than the women. "I will not punish your daughters when they turn to prostitution, nor your daughters-in-law when they commit adultery, because the men themselves consort with harlots and sacrifice with shrine-prostitutes - a people without understanding will come to ruin!"

The northern kingdom would be judged and punished by their defeat and exile at the hands of the Assyrians, which happened in 722 BC. They did not return from this exile to await the Messiah as did Judah from her later captivity at the hands of the Babylonians but would be 'wanderers among the nations'. This is not the last word, however; God's love for his people is such that he will never forsake them: "I will betroth you to me for ever", and Hosea pleads with them to come back to him. 'Return O Israel, to the Lord your God. Your sins have been your downfall. Take words with you and return to the Lord. Say to him: "Forgive all our sins and receive us graciously, that we may offer the fruit of our lips." ' His covenant with them ensures that they will never cease to be his people. "I will say to those called Not my people, 'You are my people'; and they will say, 'You are my God.' " It is inconceivable that God would ultimately abandon the people through whom, from the beginning, in spite of their sins and shortcomings, he had planned to achieve his purposes for the world.

JOEL

Joel's identity is not known and his dates cannot be ascertained; neither can any historical events be identified in his prophecy. It is possible, but is considered unlikely, that the fearsome plague of locusts and the severe drought that he foresaw, and so graphically described as coming upon Judah, represented the Babylonians, or any subsequent threatening nations. Rather it is presented as a reason for all the people to repent: farmers, whose crops and cattle and granaries will be affected, vine growers and priests whose grain and drink offerings will no longer be available. Joel sees that the 'day of the Lord is coming ... like dawn spreading across the mountains a large and mighty army comes' leaving behind them a 'desert waste'. 'The day of the Lord is great; it is dreadful. Who can endure it?' God pleads through the prophet for all of his people to return to him with all their heart, 'with fasting and weeping and mourning'. The prophet envisages the possibility that the Lord would then change his mind but it appears that the people were unrepentant. The Lord needed to save them from the catastrophe and to restore the pastures and the fruit trees and enable the granaries to be refilled and the vats to overflow with new wine and oil. They would then praise the name of the Lord their God:

> "And afterwards,
>   I will pour out my Spirit on all people.
> Your sons and daughters will prophesy,
>   your old men will dream dreams,
>   your young men will see visions."

This prophecy in chapter 2 goes on to speak of the coming of the 'great and dreadful day of the Lord. And everyone who calls on the name of the Lord will be saved.' This unique Old Testament prophecy is quoted by Peter in his sermon on the day of Pentecost and he interprets the first part as being fulfilled by the coming of the Holy Spirit on that day several hundred years later. The second part will not be fulfilled until Jesus comes again at the end of the present age. In the third and last chapter Joel speaks of God's oft-repeated message, common to all the prophets, of the promised restoration of Judah and Jerusalem and the judgement of the nations for their treatment of God's people.

AMOS

Amos, who was a near contemporary of Hosea in the middle of the 8th century BC and came from a village near Bethlehem in the southern kingdom, was nevertheless sent to prophesy to the people of the northern kingdom. They were prosperous and powerful at that time, but corrupt in every aspect of their lives, as were all the surrounding nations who also belonged to God and for whom Amos also had a message of judgement. The leaders in Israel were 'trampling on the heads of the poor and denying justice to the oppressed ... boosting the price, and cheating with dishonest scales.' They were guilty of bribery, indulging in sexual immorality, and 'lounging on their couches and drinking wine by the bowlful.' It is no surprise to hear that their worship was not acceptable to God: "I hate, I despise your religious feasts."

Though highly intelligent and articulate, Amos was a relatively humble man, a shepherd and a fig farmer, and he could not have been a more suitable messenger to send to the over-affluent northerners. His description of his calling, as with other prophets, involved the use of a number of symbols. The Lord said to him "Look, I am setting a plumb-line among my people; I will spare them no longer." They were to undergo a test of uprightness that they would clearly fail. This made them very angry and Amaziah the priest of Bethel told Jeroboam the king that "the land cannot bear all his words." He says to Amos "Get out you seer", which needless to say he ignored.

As a countryman he would perhaps naturally scorn their elaborate 'stone mansions' and their luxurious living and he quite possibly enjoyed reporting that the Lord would 'tear down the winter house along with the summer house.' This would appear at least to be a critical reference to 'second homes' even in those times. If so it is very interesting and also highly topical: these words are challenging for us in the West in the 21st century. Amos explains in 3:2 that God will judge Israel harshly for a very good reason:

> "You only have I chosen
> of all the families of the earth;
> therefore I will punish you
> for all your sins."

He had a job for them to do: he gave them a hard time so that they would become more worthy servants in setting an example to others. But the people had not repented; they had ignored the invitation to 'seek the Lord and live' and they would be judged and punished. Amos tells them that 'the Sovereign Lord does nothing without revealing his plan to his prophets.' In 8:11 he says:

> "The days are coming" declares the Sovereign Lord
> when I will send a famine through the land –
> not a famine of food or a thirst for water,
> but a famine of hearing the words of the Lord."

These are also sobering words for us, in a day when the Word of God is being so widely neglected. Their punishment would also be that "I will stir up a nation against you ... an enemy will overrun the land ... and I will send you into exile beyond Damascus." (5:27) "Israel will certainly go into exile." (7:17) This enemy was identified by Hosea as Assyria and their defeat and exile to Assyria took place in 722 BC.

As always with the message of the prophets this is not the end of the story. "I will not totally destroy the house of Jacob, I will shake the house of Israel among the nations." This is what happened in the dispersion, in which they were either obliged to move by their captors or moved voluntarily throughout the middle east and beyond. But in the last verse of Amos the Lord says: "I will plant Israel in their own land, never again to be uprooted from the land I have given them." As is so often the case the interpretation and the timing of the fulfilment of prophecy cannot be established with certainty. The overriding impression of this book of Amos is its astonishing relevance to us in our own situation today. The range of nearly three thousand years from which it speaks to us can only increase our confidence in God's progressive revelation of himself to us and the continuing value of the Old Testament. The prophetic books are bound to raise the question of the place of prophecy in the Church today and the congregation to whom Christian prophets can presume to speak. Is it only to our own Church members, to the nation, or to the whole world, as maybe only the Church of Rome and the Pope can claim the right and the authority to do? The overriding message of the Old Testament prophets was, and is, that the whole earth and all creation belongs to the one true God for whom they had the privilege to speak.

OBADIAH

Obadiah's origins and dates are not known and his book, with only a single chapter, is the shortest in the Old Testament. It is nevertheless an interesting document in revealing God's strong denunciation of Edom for the way they have treated God's people. Edom is regarded as being the country of Jacob's brother Esau and was situated south and east of Judah. Its capital city of Petra, now frequently visited in tours of the Holy Land, is about fifty miles south of the Dead Sea in present day Jordan. Its people are graphically addressed as 'you who live in the clefts of the rocks and make your home on the heights.' Their pride is denounced, as is their obvious pleasure in Israel's misfortunes – to the extent of co-operating with their enemies, seizing her wealth and even killing their people when they had been under attack from other nations. "Because of the violence against your brother Jacob, you will be covered with shame; you will be destroyed for ever" – which happened many years later. The last verse of this single, short chapter is: 'Deliverers will govern the mountains of Esau And the kingdom will be the Lord's.'

JONAH

Jonah was a recognisable person, son of Amittai as he tells us, to whom the word of the Lord came to "Go to the great city of Nineveh and preach against it, because its wickedness has come up before me." All we can know for certain is that this must have been at some time before the judgement and defeat of Assyria and its capital city of Nineveh that took place at the hands of the Babylonians in 612 BC. It is not certain exactly when Jonah lived and when the book was written and whether or not he wrote it. These are not the important issues. It is essential that neither they, nor the question of what kind of book it is, whether history or story, spoil our enjoyment and profit in reading this gripping and spiritually enriching book. Whatever view Jesus himself took of it he is recorded as quoting it in both Matthew 12 and Luke 11 where he told those who were seeking for a sign that they would be given none except the sign of Jonah. "For as Jonah was three days and three nights in the belly of a huge fish, so the Son of Man will be three days and three nights in the heart of the earth." He goes on to challenge them with the fact that "The men of Nineveh will stand up at the judgement with this generation and condemn it; for they repented at the preaching of Jonah, and now one greater than Jonah is here."

The story of Jonah is brilliantly told, with an economy of words that makes it impossible to summarise, and it demands to be read in full.

MICAH

Micah was a contemporary of Isaiah, Amos and Hosea in the middle of the 8th century BC and prophesied between 750 and 686. He came from Moresheth, a town in southern Judah and one of his chief concerns was the injustices suffered by those who lived in the surrounding country. His book begins with the 'word of the Lord' that came to him and the vision he saw 'concerning Samaria and Judah'. He proceeds with a graphic description of the Lord coming in judgement on both these kingdoms, northern and southern. He rebukes 'those who plan iniquity' and who have the power to 'covet and seize fields' and 'defraud a man of his home, a fellow-man of his inheritance.' He goes on to rebuke the leaders who 'despise justice and distort all that is right' and who 'hate good and love evil and tear the skin from my people.' He also rebukes the false prophets who 'lead people astray' and deny that judgement is coming. There is no end to their wrongdoing and wickedness. Later he tells them that 'the ruler demands gifts, the judge accepts bribes' and he asks how he can exonerate 'those who use dishonest scales with a bag of false weights.' Very practical and down to earth complaints that are also relevant for our present-day society.

"But as for me, I am filled with power and with the Spirit of the Lord, and with justice and might, to declare to Jacob his transgression, to Israel his sin." His book is like a quarry with gems of insight and prediction apparently randomly distributed, which may well be in part a result of its having been assembled from a series of short messages delivered at different times. Having rebuked the people for their treatment of each other he reveals God's anger at their response to him in worship. He asks them: "And what does the Lord require of you? To act justly and to love mercy and to walk humbly with your God." He foresees that 'Zion will be like a ploughed field, Jerusalem will become a heap of rubble, the temple hill a mound overgrown with thickets.' This prophecy was very effectively quoted a hundred years later by Jeremiah in 26:18 in support of his own prediction, which was strongly rejected, but fulfilled in 586 BC. Micah had also told the people that "You will go into Babylon," which happened in that year. He goes on to say however that "There the Lord will redeem you out of the hand of your enemies" who "do not know the thoughts of the Lord; they do not understand his plan."

The supreme event in God's plan is then revealed in Micah's unique, inspired reference to the birth place of the Messiah:

"But you, Bethlehem Ephrathah, though you are small among the clans of Judah, out of you will come for me one who will be ruler over Israel, whose origins are from of old, from ancient times. He will stand and shepherd his flock in the strength of the Lord, in the majesty of the name of the Lord his God. And they will live securely, for then his greatness will reach to the ends of the earth. And he will be their peace."

Who else but the Spirit of God himself could have enabled Micah to reveal this news to Israel and have enabled our faith to be strengthened, over two thousand years later, by our recognition of this divinely ordained gift of prophecy?

Looking even further ahead to yet more distant future blessings for Israel and the nations Micah delivers a remarkable and reassuring vision in 4:1-5, in large part a quotation from Isaiah, of God's plan for the fulfilment of his purpose:

> In the last days
> the mountain of the Lord's temple will be established
>   as chief among the mountains;
> it will be raised above the hills,
>   and people will stream to it.
>
> Many nations will come and say,
> "Come, let us go up to the mountain of the Lord,
>   to the house of the God of Jacob.
> He will teach us his ways,
>   so that we may walk in his paths.
> The law will go out from Zion,
>   the word of the Lord from Jerusalem.
> He will judge between many peoples
>   and will settle disputes for strong nations far and wide.
> They will beat their swords into ploughshares
>   and their spears into pruning hooks.
> Nation will not take up sword against nation,
>   nor will they train for war any more.
> Every man will sit under his own vine
>   and under his own fig-tree,
> and no-one will make them afraid,
>   for the Lord Almighty has spoken.
> All the nations may walk
>   in the name of their gods;
> we will walk in the name of the Lord
>   our God for ever and ever."

NAHUM

Nahum was a prophet from Judah and his vision was of God's intention to destroy Nineveh, the capital city of Assyria, an event that took place at the hands of the Babylonians in 612 BC. This destruction had been predicted by Jonah but the inhabitants repented at that time and were granted stay of execution. Nahum looks back to a similar event, namely the destruction of Thebes by the Assyrians themselves in 663 BC. Thebes was the site of present day Karnak and Luxor and once Egypt's most magnificent capital, situated on both banks of the Nile. His book must therefore have been written at some time between these two dates. The tone of his book is one of vengeance directed towards Assyria and her kings for their past cruelty to Judah and their butchery of those they had conquered. Nahum's language is full of expression and vivid word pictures. His message is that 'the Lord will not leave the guilty unpunished,' which refers to Assyria, and he relays God's promise to Judah that "I will break their yoke from your neck." He gives a graphic account of the destruction of the city of Nineveh that is full of rich poetic imagery, with 'galloping horses, flashing swords and glittering spears'. He really goes to town!

Nineveh 'will have no descendants' and 'fire will devour you', a prophecy vindicated by history and by archaeological evidence. Nahum ends by telling the men of Nineveh that 'Everyone that hears the news about you claps his hands at your fall, for who has not felt your endless cruelty?' The fall of the Berlin Wall between two and three thousand years later was greeted with similar jubilation. This book, as with so much of the Old Testament, may sound barbarous but we can imagine that as with so many of the words of the prophets it was a huge encouragement for the small vulnerable nation of Judah to know that her God was sovereign over all the nations of the earth. We derive the same encouragement from the words of both the New and the Old Testament today.

HABBAKUK

Habbakuk lived in Judah, probably towards the end of the 7th century BC, during the period of the Babylonian threat to Judah and their subsequent invasion and destruction of Jerusalem in 586 BC. The oracle, or prophetic message, that he received was not directed against Israel or the surrounding nations, as with most of the prophets, but was rather in the form of a dialogue with the Lord, prompted by his complaint at his delay in coming to his aid. "How long, O Lord, must I call for help, but you do not listen? Or cry out to you 'Violence!' but you do not save?" He complains – speaking on behalf of others also – that God tolerates wrongdoing and the injustice of the wicked 'hemming in' the righteous. It is reminiscent of Job and the Psalms in its expression of personal, questioning response to God and his often inexplicable ways.

Parts of this book at least were used in worship, as we use psalms and hymns today, because it ended, as always, on a note of praise and of hope and trust in God. The Lord's unexpected answer to Habbakuk's question is that "I am going to do something in your days that you would not believe, even if you were told. I am raising up the Babylonians." Habbakuk knows about the Babylonians whom God has 'appointed to execute judgement' and he cannot believe it. "Why are you, whose eyes are too pure to look on evil, silent while the wicked swallow up those more righteous than themselves?" The Lord replies "Write down the revelation and make it plain on tablets so that a herald may run with it." Then, speaking, it would appear, about the Babylonian king: "See, he is puffed up; his desires are not upright – but the righteous will live by his faith." This last phrase appears again in Paul's epistles to the Romans and Galatians.

The Lord goes on to say that the one who is used in judgement on Judah will himself be judged and destroyed:

> "Because you have plundered many nations, the peoples
> who are left will plunder you. Woe to him who builds a
> city with bloodshed and establishes a town by crime! Has
> not the Lord Almighty determined that the people's

labour is only fuel for the fire, that nations exhaust themselves for nothing? For the earth will be filled with the knowledge of the glory of God as the waters cover the sea."

Habbakuk, like Job, is silenced and in his third and last chapter reflects on God's greatness and what he has done. "I stand in awe of your deeds, O Lord." He lists a number of them and bows to God's judgement on Judah, expressing his determination to 'wait patiently for the day of calamity to come on the nation invading us.' Those who trust in God must take the long view. His near-final words are: "Yet I will rejoice in the Lord, I will be joyful in God my Saviour." They are as fresh and relevant as though they had been written yesterday and not over two and a half thousand years ago.

ZEPHANIAH

Zephaniah also prophesied in Judah in the second half of the 7th century BC. He was quite possibly a descendant of king Hezekiah and for that reason familiar with court circles and politics. He denounces both Judah and the surrounding nations and paints a dark picture of the rapidly approaching 'great day of the Lord' in which all will experience his anger. He comes across as sarcastic and humourless, as an archetypal hell-fire preacher, delivering his message with apparent vindictiveness and relish. Unlike the other prophets he has very little human insight and warmth and not a great deal of poetic imagination. But as always the final note is of optimism and blessing for God's people: 'Be glad and rejoice with all your heart, O Daughter of Jerusalem! The Lord, the king of Israel is with you; never again will you fear any harm.' The Lord says: "I will give you honour and praise among all the peoples of the earth when I restore your fortunes before your very eyes." It is one of the numerous paradoxes that even quite unappealing people can be inspired to say wonderful things.

HAGGAI

Haggai preached three sermons, all very precisely dated, in September, October and December in 520 BC, the second year of the reign of the Persian king, Darius. They were sermons of encouragement to those who had returned to Jerusalem, following their exile in Babylon, to help rebuild the Temple. The word of the Lord came through Haggai to their leader, Zerubbabel and to Joshua the high priest and to those doing the work. Things had not been going well in the years since their return and the Lord told them to "give careful thought to your ways. Go up into the mountains and bring down timber and build the house, so that I may take pleasure in it and be honoured." He complained that "my house remains a ruin, while each of you is busy with his own house." This is reminiscent of king Solomon, and true also of some modern day leaders, and he told them that he had brought a drought on them as punishment. The response was dramatic. They obeyed the word of the prophet 'because the Lord their God had sent him. And the people feared the Lord.' The Lord 'stirred up the spirit of Zerubbabel, Joshua and the whole remnant of the people,' and within just over three weeks the work was under way once more.

In the second of his two short chapters the next word of the Lord came once again through Haggai, a word of powerful encouragement that their work on God's house would not be in vain. This was to counter their fears that it would not be as magnificent as the original Temple built by Solomon. "Be strong . For I am with you. Do not fear. I will shake all nations, and the desired of all nations will come and I will fill this house with glory." Its glory will be even greater than that of Solomon's because of the future coming of the Messiah. Haggai's third word was concerning the need for adopting a right spirit towards the whole enterprise. It was no good rebuilding the Temple if the heart of the people was not right and they were not obedient.

A second message came through Haggai on the same day to Zerubbabel from the Lord that "I will shake the heavens and the earth. I will overturn royal thrones and shatter the power of the foreign kingdoms." This promise must have helped to enable Zerubbabel to hold on and to complete the building in spite of the powerful and threatening surrounding nations and it has no doubt encouraged many others also in threatening times. It must have saved them from despair when they needed to believe and trust that God would ultimately triumph over their enemies. The Old Testament prophets continue to exercise a ministry today, over two thousand years later, because God called them and gave them a message that is of continuing relevance and a model and encouragement for prophets, pastors and people in our own time.

ZECHARIAH

Zechariah, like Haggai, returned to Jerusalem from Babylon and began to prophesy at the same time, in 520 BC. The immediate scene is Jerusalem and Zechariah's message is primarily one of encouragement to all those who are involved in the rebuilding of the Temple. It is also an encouragement to them above all to remember their primary allegiance to the Lord for whom they are doing this great work and to recognise the plans that he has for their future and through them for the future of all the nations on earth. Without this vision they are bound to falter. In one of the Lord's first words to Zechariah he says: "I will return to Jerusalem with mercy, and there my house will be rebuilt. Jerusalem will be a city without walls. And I myself will be a wall of fire around it, and I will be its glory within." It is to be open to those outside and does not require physical walls of protection that can provoke antagonism as the wall recently erected by the Israelis has so obviously done, and as did the Berlin Wall before it. God himself is its circumference and its centre – a wonderful image for the Church of today.

Zechariah is asked a question about fasting and the word of the Lord comes to him again, indicating that fasting can be an empty exercise. They should rather "Administer true justice; show mercy and compassion to one another. Do not oppress the widow or the fatherless, the alien or the poor. In your hearts do not think evil of each other." On another occasion the Lord Almighty says: "Once again men and women of ripe old age will sit in the streets of Jerusalem, each with his cane in hand because of his age." And in an unusual reference to children: "The city streets will be filled with boys and girls playing there."

In the last six chapters of Zechariah there is a series of prophecies that are familiar to readers of the New Testament. Zechariah is alone in being given, in 9:9, the prophetic vision of Christ's triumphal entry into Jerusalem:

> Rejoice greatly, O Daughter of Zion!
> Shout, Daughter of Jerusalem!
> See, your king comes to you,
>   righteous and having salvation,
>   gentle and riding on a donkey,
>   on a colt, the foal of a donkey.

This is quoted by both Matthew and John in their account of this event. In chapter twelve, echoing a similar idea in the Psalms and in Isaiah, Zechariah reports the word of the Lord to him saying: "They will look on me, the one they have pierced," which is quoted in John's gospel with reference to Jesus' crucifixion. Later, in the following chapter, the Lord Almighty declares: "Strike the shepherd and the sheep will be scattered." Both Matthew and Mark record Jesus as quoting this with reference to himself when he tells his disciples during the last supper: "This very night you will all fall away on account of me." (Mt 26:31).

Finally, in the last chapter, Zechariah is given the word of the Lord that "A day of the Lord is coming when the nations will be gathered to fight against Jerusalem" which "will be captured". 'Then the Lord will go out and fight against those nations, as he fights on the day of battle. On that day his feet will stand on the mount of Olives.' Several verses later Zechariah tells us: 'The Lord will be king over the whole earth. On that day there will be one Lord and his name the only name ... Then the survivors from all the nations that have attacked Jerusalem will go up year after year to worship the king, the Lord Almighty.' He is attempting, as the prophets frequently do, to describe the indescribable but all of these words echo with other passages in Scripture about the destiny of his people Israel.

The prophets serve a unique function in connecting the Old and New Testaments and in strengthening our trust in God and in his faithful, progressive communication with his people. It is an extraordinary example of this communication that Zechariah should have been given these pictures of events that either would not take place for at least another five hundred years or that are yet to happen.

MALACHI

When Malachi delivered 'the word of the Lord to Israel' – and when his book was written in around 433 BC – nearly a hundred years had elapsed since the rebuilding of the Temple had been completed. Some years before Malachi began to prophesy the Persian king had allowed Ezra, a Jewish priest, to return to Jerusalem to raise the standard of Temple worship. Several years later Nehemiah returned as governor to introduce social reforms and to oversee the rebuilding of the walls of the city. But all was not well in spite of their efforts. Malachi delivers his challenging message in the form of questions and answers exchanged between the Lord and his people that vividly highlight the problems. He has shown his love for them but they have not acknowledged him. "If I am a father, where is the honour due to me? If I am a master, where is the respect due to me?" He accuses the priests in particular of showing contempt for his name, for which they will pay by being "despised and humiliated before all the people".

They were defiling his altar by offering him blind and blemished animals rather than the pure offering demanded by the Law. "Will a man rob God? Yet you rob me – in tithes and offerings." The people had made a binding, written agreement with Nehemiah to bring the firstborn of their cattle and flocks and a tithe, or tenth of their crops and fruit to the house of God. They had also made an agreement to keep the Sabbath holy and not to intermarry with the surrounding nations but they were leaving their own wives in favour of foreign women. 'Has not the Lord made them one? In flesh and spirit they are his. And why one? Because he was seeking godly offspring. So guard yourself in your spirit and do not break faith with the wife of your youth.' "I hate divorce," says the Lord God of Israel. (2:15,16). All this would be merely a tiresome catalogue of the failings of a small, obscure middle-eastern nation if they had not been God's own people and especially if it were not all so absolutely up to date and relevant to our own present-day failings. We do not always give our best to God in worship and we are not always generous in our giving. As a nation we are treating the seventh day of the week like any other, and we have a uniquely high rate of marriage breakdown and divorce and all the social problems it brings with it. God's chief requirement is faithfulness, both to him and to each other, as he is faithful to us..

"See, I will send my messenger, who will prepare the way before me. Then suddenly the Lord you are seeking will come to his temple; the messenger of the covenant, whom you desire, will come." These prophecies were fulfilled by the coming of John the Baptist and of Jesus the Messiah respectively. 'But who can survive the day of his coming? For he will be like a refiner's fire or a launderer's soap.' God has not changed however; his desire is to be merciful and he says to the people: "Return to me, and I will return to you. Bring the whole tithe into the storehouse. Test me in this," says the Lord Almighty, "and see if I will not throw open the floodgates of heaven and pour out so much blessing that you will not have enough room for it. Yet you have said harsh things against me. You have said 'It is futile to serve God.' " He will spare them nevertheless. 'And you will again see the distinction between the righteous and the wicked, between those who serve God and those who do not.'

At the very end of Malachi, in the last words of our Old Testament, there is a reiteration of God's promise to send Elijah – meaning John the Baptist, as we now know. "See, I will send you the prophet Elijah before the great and dreadful day of the Lord comes. He will turn the hearts of the fathers to their children, and the hearts of the children to their fathers; or else I will come and strike the land with a curse." The coming of the Messiah, the great and dreadful day, will bring not only salvation but also judgement. It is as though Malachi foresees prophetically that the Jews will reject him and that the land will indeed be cursed – which happened when the Temple was destroyed by the Romans in AD 70.

There were no doubt many men of God who continued to minister to the Jewish people and remind them of God's message and teachings but Malachi was the last of the writing prophets in the scriptural canon of the Old Testament. It would seem that God must have told his people all that was necessary for them to hear for their instruction and encouragement and given their teachers sufficient material to last them for four hundred years.

THE TIME BETWEEN THE TESTAMENTS

A period of four hundred years elapsed from Malachi to the coming of John the Baptist and then of Jesus, the long-awaited Christ, in around 5BC. This is equivalent to the time between the accession of Elizabeth 1 and the coronation of our present Queen Elizabeth 2 in 1953. During this time we have no scriptural record of events or of prophecy but this was a time of enormous significance for the Jews and for the world into which Christ eventually came and we have other sources of information about it. There were plenty of men, rather like modern-day preachers, who interpreted prophecy and like the prophets continually spoke to the people of their need of repentance and also provided them with encouragement. They did this by reminding them of the commandments and the covenants and of God's sovereignty over all nations and of his promises for their future.

This was the period in which Greek culture reached its height. During the 8th century BC the Greeks had invented their alphabet by adapting a Phoenecian version of the Semitic alphabet that had only consonants. The Hebrew of the Old Testament was an example of this simple form of language. The Aramaic spoken by Jesus in the New Testament was a Syrian version of the same Semitic language. The addition of vowels by the Greeks rendered the alphabet suitable for an Indo-European language. This combination of a rich and complex language, and an alphabet by means of which it could be more faithfully expressed in writing, was what enabled the New Testament writers to convey subtle abstract ideas in Greek that they could never have conveyed in Hebrew. The outstanding example of this is John's use of the Greek Logos to denote the eternal Word of God made flesh in Jesus in the first chapter of his Gospel. This combination was naturally also the chief factor in making possible the flowering of Greek philosophy and culture in the Classical age in Greece in the fifth and fourth centuries BC. During this time, following Homer in the 8th and Heraclitus in the 6th century BC, there lived a number of men of enduring stature and reputation. Among these were Herodotus the historian, Hippocrates the physician and the Greek dramatists:

Aeschylus, Sophocles and Euripides. Above all there were the great philosophers: Socrates, Plato and Aristotle. Pericles and Demosthenes the orators and Pythagoras, Euclid and Archimedes the mathematicians also lived during this period. The centuries before Christ's coming were thus characterised by unprecedented creativity and questioning and were an ideal preparation for the Gospel.

Plato sought knowledge only by means of reason but he was the most spiritually-minded of the philosophers and spoke in 'The Republic' of the search for absolute Good and of the perfection of the divine. It was he who provided the philosophical grounding for the theology of St Augustine in the fourth century AD. Aristotle initiated thinking about logic that clarified the rules governing the use of reasoning and the methods employed in it. He contributed to ethics and politics, psychology and biology, and even to the idea of development and evolution in nature. He also laid the ground rules for learning the truth about the world not only by reason but also by means of the scientific method of empirical observation and experiment. It was no doubt this independent investigation of the natural world that made Aristotle appear as a threat to the early Church and what had been revealed to it through faith. It was most likely for this reason that the full extent of his contribution to our knowledge of philosophy and science was only slowly appreciated.

It was not until the thirteenth century that St Thomas Aquinas was able to use Aristotle's teachings in the formulating of his own theology, as Augustine had done with Plato eight hundred years before, and to argue for the recognition of the scientific observation of the natural world as a legitimate pursuit. In spite of this, a further four hundred years later, in the seventeenth century, Galileo could still be persecuted and spend the last eight years of his life under house arrest for claiming that the earth revolved around the sun! Another two hundred years after this, as late as the middle of the nineteenth century, Darwin aroused the furious opposition of many in the Church against his theory of evolution, and the controversy still continues to rage in some quarters. To those who have properly understood the biblical teaching of an ordered creation, however, it has always been seen to encourage scientific investigation.

During the years between the Old and New Testaments the Greek language was fully developed. Especially with the coming of Alexander in 330 BC it became the commonly accepted language of the whole of the Middle East, and later of the eastern half of the Roman Empire including Asia Minor, Syria and Egypt. It was even used, along with Latin, in the western part of the Empire. The Jews no longer spoke and wrote Hebrew, especially those who had dispersed widely to Alexandria and elsewhere and what we now know as the Old Testament was translated into Greek in Alexandria from around 250 BC. This was of enormous importance to the Jews, especially to those who had left the Holy Land and those to whom they recommended their faith. It was the only Scripture available to the early church until the New Testament came to be written, also in Greek, though some of it was probably written originally in Aramaic. When this happened, during the first century AD, the whole of what is now our Bible was in the one common, universal language. Without this development of the Greek language and their alphabet, and the associated Greek philosophy with all its depth and range, it would never have been possible to describe and record what God revealed to us of himself in Jesus the Messiah. Even two thousand years later we do not have the capacity to think more clearly and the words to express more accurately what we struggle to understand about our faith. This rich flowering of Greek culture was happening only seven hundred miles to the West of Palestine across the north eastern corner of the Mediterranean. It was during the later years of this period, at the end of the third century BC, between 221and 206, and several thousand miles to the East, that the Qin dynasty was building the first unified Chinese empire and was responsible for the Terracotta Warriors and for starting work on the Great Wall of China.

An additional Greek contribution was their study of rhetoric. This was continued by the Romans, most notably Cicero, and was a valuable discipline for the proclamation of the Christian Gospel. Yet another contribution was the teaching of the Stoics that was a major influence in the development of Christian asceticism. The positive Greek influence was thus very great but it was also a threat to the faith if the use of reason became overemphasised. Paul in particular saw the need to warn in his letters, especially 1Corinthians, against too great a reliance on purely human wisdom and reason in understanding the Gospel. This powerful influence of Greek thinking on the early Church may have side-lined the less educated amongst the Jewish Christians. It has also been suggested that the emergence of Islam in the 7th century may have resulted in part from the need to provide a simpler religion because the Gospel had become too intellectual and too westernised for Arab followers.

Thus in spite of all the benefits it conferred on the development of thought, Greek philosophy continued to be a potential threat to religious faith, especially in the form of the heresy of gnosticism, a spurious form of enlightenment through secret knowledge. The Greeks were also a political threat as well from 330 BC, under Alexander. After his death his followers posed an even greater threat and attempted to deprive the Jews of religious and political freedom, destroying copies of their Jewish Scriptures – what is now our Old Testament. They required offerings to be made to the Greek God Zeus and under Antiochus Epiphanes, the king of Syria, erected a statue of Zeus and insultingly sacrificed a pig in the Temple in Jerusalem. This led to the revolt of the Maccabees between 166 and 144BC. They were a large and courageous Jewish family, of whom Judas was the most famous, and they aimed at securing political freedom. This campaign is well documented in 'The History of the Jewish War' by the Jewish historian, Josephus, and in the first and second book of Maccabees in the Apocrypha.

The revolt was joined by the Hasidim, the predecessors of the Pharisees, who were seeking religious freedom and who abandoned the struggle and left when this was gained. Eventually, after a heroic campaign without which the Jewish faith might well have been extinguished, political freedom was also achieved. But infighting, including disagreement between the Pharisees who were the teachers, and the Sadducees, the aristocratic, politically-minded priests, detracted from the victory. Further outside interference was also on the way and in 63BC the Romans, under Pompey, captured Jerusalem and murdered priests performing their duties in the Temple.

This was an inauspicious start to the Roman rule that provided the historical setting of the events of the New Testament but it cannot be allowed to blind us to Rome's massive achievements. These included the stability that enabled the Gospel to be spread throughout the empire. They also included the writing of their poets, amongst whom Virgil was a towering figure. He was chosen by Dante as his guide through Hell and Purgatory in The Divine Comedy and he is sometimes referred to as the prophet of the Gentiles on account of his fancied prediction of the coming of Christ in the fourth of his Eclogues. His crowning work was the Aeneid that describes the

112

legendary origin of the Roman nation. It is both an Iliad and an Odyssey, a battle and a journey. It is in the tradition of the epics of Homer and of the much older Babylonian Epic of Gilgamesh, in which human affairs are subject to supernatural influence. In its exploration of life as both a battle and a journey the story of the Aeneid accords in a deep sense both with Christian experience and with the experience of every human being.

THE NEW TESTAMENT

A SHORT INTRODUCTION.

Against this turbulent political background the Good News of the long-awaited Messiah burst suddenly upon the world of the Roman Empire – albeit initially only upon the few who witnessed his unbelievably humble beginnings. The preparations for this unique event were resumed with two separate announcements, both of them recorded in Luke's Gospel. The first was by an angel of the Lord to Zechariah, of the coming birth of his son John the Baptist. The second was by the angel Gabriel to Mary, of the coming birth of her Son Jesus. This was followed by the recording of the births, first of John the Baptist, and then of Jesus. We hear nothing of the next thirty years, apart from Luke's references to Jesus' presentation to the Lord in the Temple as a 6-week old baby, and his later visit to Jerusalem for the Passover at the age of twelve. On the first of these visits Simeon, who had been promised by the Holy Spirit that he would see the Lord's Christ before he died, uttered these memorable words when he saw him in the Temple:

> "For my eyes have seen your salvation,
>   which you have prepared in the sight of all people,
> a light for revelation to the Gentiles
> and glory for your people Israel."

Thirty years later, out of nowhere as it must have seemed to those who were unaware of these preparations, came John the Baptist, the last and greatest of the Old Testament prophets. He came, in the words of Isaiah in chapter 40, as a voice of one calling in the desert: "Prepare the way for the Lord; make straight in the wilderness a highway for our God." John preached a 'baptism of repentance for the forgiveness of sins' and announced that the Kingdom of God was near at hand. Suddenly everything had changed: God was on the move once more.

John spoke of Jesus as the greater one who was to come who would baptise, not with water but with the Holy Spirit and with fire, whose sandals he was not worthy to stoop down and untie. When Jesus joined him at the river Jordan he insisted on being baptised with the water of John's baptism. Jesus was then led by the Spirit into the desert where he was tempted three times by Satan, whose aim was to destroy his future ministry. These temptations had to be resisted before Jesus could set out fully prepared and empowered by the Holy Spirit for the work that God his Father had for him to do.

Only then did he begin his ministry of preaching, teaching and healing. This led him, after three years of increasing opposition from the religious authorities, to his death on the Cross. But on the third day he was raised to life as he had frequently promised his disciples would happen. This story and the accounts of Jesus' post-resurrection appearances are told in all four gospels. The story of his final Ascension, the coming of the Holy Spirit and the first thirty years of the history of the Church, is told in Acts. During these years the epistles were written by Paul and others to instruct and encourage the young churches in Palestine and in Greece and Asia Minor. Some years later Revelation was added to give further hope and encouragement for the Church throughout the present age. This age would bring terrible suffering before the return of Christ and the coming of the new heaven and the new earth of God's kingdom as the destiny of his whole creation.

A WAY INTO THE NEW TESTAMENT

If the Scriptures are not already familiar reading then there could be no better preparation than to read one of the Gospels at this stage – perhaps Luke and ideally his book of Acts as well. The reading of the New Testament itself is the definitive way to approach Christian truth. This will provide an introduction without which the themes that have been identified and the way in which the New Testament is presented will be less easy to follow. These themes are, at risk of repetition:

1. God himself, progressively revealed in the Old Testament, and experienced by the disciples and by the early Church as Father, Son and Holy Spirit in the New Testament.
2. The Creation and God's plan to overcome all sin and evil and the devil by Jesus' death and resurrection.
3. God's people; now including Jesus' disciples and his first followers, and after the coming of the Holy Spirit at Pentecost, the new Israel of the New Testament Church.
4. The continuing phenomenon of prophecy, with Jesus as the fulfilment of the Law and the prophets.
5. Sacrifice, in its ultimate expression in the Cross of Christ.
6. The kingdom of God, inaugurated by Christ's coming to earth, and to be completed when he comes again in glory and judgement at the end of the age.

In addition to the attempt to do justice to the Gospels, the Acts and each of the epistles individually, there is also a separate essay-type section on each of these major themes. In the case of God himself there is one on the Father, one on Jesus, one on the Holy Spirit and another on the Holy Trinity. Creation, the phenomenon of evil, the Church and the Cross and the Kingdom have each of them been separately considered at some length. Prophecy has already been considered in the Old Testament but it remains as a major theme in the New Testament. There are also additional sections on a number of other important topics, such as Marriage, Grace and the Creeds

In an attempt to provide a helpful presentation of the rich and complex story told in the New Testament I have 'reshaped the data,' as every preacher has to do in his preaching of a sermon. In the case of the Gospels, instead of treating each one in turn, or considering them all together, I have provided two separate accounts:

1. The basic story told by all four gospel writers, the first three of whom, the synoptic or same-view writers, present it in a relatively similar way and frequently share sections of material that are common to all three.
2. The story told by John who tells it in a rather different way, with a considerable amount of material that is not included in Matthew, Mark or Luke.

Prior to this there is a section on the New Testament records themselves. Particularly in the case of the Gospels it is important to understand what sort of books they are; when they were written; who wrote them and why, and to try to use some imagination on what was involved in their construction. None of these are immediately obvious.

THE NEW TESTAMENT RECORDS

The four Gospels, the Acts of the Apostles, the twenty-one epistles and the Revelation, together take up roughly the same space as the Old Testament prophets. This collection of books, designed to instruct and inspire believers and win converts, is thus quite surprisingly brief. The authorised body of literature that we have today, the so-called canon, was not finally chosen by the Early Church until the fourth century. The wonder is that this small body of literature, written two thousand years ago by practical men engaged in the heat of often dangerous ministry, should have survived the critical scrutiny and challenge of scholars and scoffers from that time on. It continues to be the definitive source of orthodox belief and practice but there is a need for reason and for the traditional understanding of the Church to help with its interpretation.

These New Testament records were written during the second half of the first century AD, a number of the epistles being probably earlier than Acts and some of the Gospels. The authors of these books had encountered the most remarkable and enigmatic man who has ever lived. It took them many years of reflection to come to terms with who he really was and to begin to understand his colossal significance. It was a task that could not be rushed. Even now, 2000 years later, we are still struggling with the startling conclusion to which these writers came, that he was both man and God.

The records reveal differences of emphasis and detail depending on the minds and personalities of the New Testament writers. As was the case with the Old Testament prophets, their individuality is not submerged as a result of their common source of inspiration. Their experience of the truth appears to have been remarkably similar but they present the story in their own characteristic style of writing. There must, on the other hand, have been a great deal of sharing of memories and insights in the fellowship enjoyed by the members of the early Church. In the case of the synoptic Gospels they contain a certain amount of more or less identical material. They would all have relied heavily on the oral tradition and the preaching of the apostles, as well as on other available documents of the sayings of Jesus, and all been guided by the same Holy Spirit, as Jesus had promised they would be. It was because the risen Christ lived in them through His spirit that their experiences of him remained fresh in their hearts and minds for so many years before they wrote about them.

THE GOSPELS

The Gospels are unique pieces of inspired creative writing with no precise parallel in the whole of the rest of literature. They are unique because they portray a unique person in a unique way. Jesus had a unique conception, a unique life and a unique death and, uniquely, he was raised to new life three days later. It is this unique and extraordinary story that the Gospels tell. As Gospels they are literally Good News – and properly understood, the best news that the world has ever heard. None of them is much more than twenty thousand words in length. They describe his birth of a virgin, or in the case of Mark and John, emphasise his divine nature and origin. They give us no record of Jesus' early years, apart from two tantalising fragments in Luke. After a gap of nearly thirty years, they resume the story with an account of the three years of his public ministry, followed by his death and resurrection and his post-resurrection appearances. Jesus' existence as a preacher and teacher and his crucifixion are well-attested facts of secular history. They are recorded by the Jewish historian Josephus who also records his resurrection but contemporary secular historians tell us very little else about him. We therefore rely heavily on the Gospel records. They were probably all written up to thirty or more years after he died, by which time his continuing impact was well recognised. His followers must have felt the need and were no doubt prompted by the Spirit to make written records available for posterity.

The more these gospel records are read and studied the more perfectly they appear to fulfil their purpose. The only possible excuse for this particular experiment of reshaping the data is that by presenting them in a shortened, digested and re-ordered form their essence and the glorious story they tell may be revealed and the appetite whetted for reading the originals. They are the only books that, like the rest of Scripture, have the same quality of inspiration and evident authority and coherence. Their composition was evidently a task of extraordinary subtlety and complexity and they could not have been written without this element of inspiration. They could not all of them mention everything or even mention the things they do in precisely the same words or precisely the same order. The wonder of it is that they complement each other in such a way as to present a balanced picture that no single account could possibly have done. Who knows what part the Holy Spirit may have had in the orchestration of this wonderful co-operative effort? They cover the most important events of the three years of Jesus' ministry and commentary as well and we cannot expect always to find strict chronological accuracy. There has been some reshaping of the data already. They are each of them a complex holding together of narrative with an interpretation of its significance as the evangelists had come to understand the truth about Jesus at least thirty years after his resurrection.

The gospel writers were men who had come to know Jesus, either during his earthly life or following his resurrection. The writers were generally thought by the early church to have been Matthew and John who had been Jesus' disciples, and Mark and Luke who were prominent in Acts. Mark was a close associate of Peter, and Luke worked closely with Paul who had met the risen Christ on the road to Damascus. John describes graphically in his first epistle how the disciples had 'heard and seen and touched' the eternal Word of life, the Son of God. Luke writes at the start of his Gospel of how he is giving an account of things 'just as they were handed down to us by those who from the first were eye-witnesses and servants of the Word.' Thus the Gospel writers were no mere recorders or biographers; they were truly Evangelists, or announcers of news. They were writing about what was to them Gospel or Good News, to be shared and proclaimed, so that others would come to believe and trust in Jesus.

John describes his Gospel, in 20: 31, as having been written 'that you may believe that Jesus is the Christ, the Son of God and that by believing you may have life in his name.' He says that Jesus did 'many other things' that there was no room for the evangelists to record. The Gospels needed to be relatively brief and were written with great economy of words. They all of them describe, in their own terms, Jesus' divine origin; his baptism by John the Baptist; the feeding of the five thousand; Peter's profession of faith and his later denial of Jesus, and the anointing of Jesus by Mary. They all of them also record Jesus' triumphal entry into Jerusalem, the cleansing of the Temple, the Last Supper, his betrayal by Judas and his trial, crucifixion, burial and resurrection. Not surprisingly these would seem to be the things that they regarded as of greatest importance. All of them provide us with a varying selection of his healings and other miracles, his frequent forgiveness of sins and a record of his teachings. They also all of them emphasise the mounting opposition of the religious leaders from an early stage in Jesus' ministry, his brilliant answers to their awkward questions and his increasingly frequent predictions of his crucifixion and resurrection.

The four Evangelists, inspired by the same Spirit, tell the same basic story about the same instantly recognisable figure and his life, death and resurrection. But apart from the differences in their personalities and styles there are other differences between the Gospels written by the first three writers and the fourth. The first three synoptic or 'same view' Gospels, Matthew, Mark and Luke, confine themselves more closely to the story, though there is commentary as well. Mark is thought to have been written first and Matthew and Luke to have used the same basic framework and contents, along with material from another source. John offers more reflection and interpretation, both in his prologue, with his reference to Jesus as the Greek Logos, God's eternal 'Word', and in the selection of Jesus' teaching that he records. This is often in the form of metaphor rather than in parables, eg: "I am the bread of Life" (6:35), and extended metaphors such as the Good Shepherd (10:11-16) and the True Vine. (15:1-8).

Whilst Mark and Luke and John appear to have been written mainly for Gentiles, Matthew wrote chiefly for Jewish readers. His emphasis is on Jesus as Messiah and he includes more frequent Old Testament quotations than any of the other writers in order to emphasise the frequent fulfilment of prophecy. For all that, however, or maybe for that very reason, he gives the fullest sustained account, in chapter 23, of Jesus' harsh words to the Jewish teachers, the Pharisees. Whilst Mark emphasises the suffering and humanity of Jesus, John emphasises rather his authority and his divinity. He records him as using the divine name, "I am," when he tells the Jews in Jn 8:58, "Before Abraham was born, I am."

With regard to their varying selection of material, only Matthew and Luke include the Sermon on the Mount, only Mark and Luke the Lord's prayer. Only Luke records the two remarkable parables of the Good Samaritan and the Prodigal Son, in chapters 10 and 15 of his Gospel. These are both of them unforgettable stories and like all stories they must be read rather than described. The story of the Prodigal is Jesus' definitive treatment of the subject of forgiveness and reconciliation and, as we would expect, is a master class in human psychology as well as revealing the love of God the Father for his children. John records a large number of events and encounters not mentioned by the other Evangelists, including the wedding at Cana, the meetings with Nicodemus and with the woman at the well, and the raising of Lazarus. All this adds immeasurably to the variety and richness of the biblical record. It should not be seen as evidence of a discrepancy often argued to exist between the four Gospels. They cannot all mention everything without risk of being merely clones – and of too great length.

JESUS, THE TOWERING CENTRAL FIGURE

Most people who know anything at all about Jesus hold him in high esteem. What many of them are not so keen on are some of his followers – and the challenge that the Cross inevitably presents to our human pride and self sufficiency. At the very start of the Gospels we are alerted to the fact that Jesus was no ordinary man by the story of his unusual birth. Jesus' herald, John the Baptist, was the first to recognise his unique status when he said, in Jn 1:34, "I have seen and testify that this is the Son of God." He went on to say that he was not worthy even to untie or to carry his sandals.

Jesus' three years of public ministry began with his baptism by John, followed by his temptation by the devil in the desert, before he set out on his mission of preaching, teaching and healing. His words and miracles led to the crowds exclaiming that "nothing like this has ever been seen in Israel." He is recorded in Mt 7:29 as teaching with authority, unlike the teachers of the law, and when he taught in the synagogue at his home town of Nazareth in Luke 4 they were amazed and asked "Where did this man get his wisdom and his miraculous powers?" But because they thought they recognised him as a mere 'carpenter's son', they took offence at him, which prompted him to say to them that "Only in his home town and in his own house is a prophet without honour."

Jesus spoke starkly about the reasons for his coming. It was not only to "seek and save what was lost," (Lk 19:10), and as John tells us in his first epistle to 'destroy the devil's work'. In Lk 10:57 he asked: "Do you think that I came to bring peace on earth? No, I tell you, but division." The kingdom he had come to usher in was not what people had expected and he provided us with a good example of what he meant. Thus all four Evangelists record his anger at the misuse of his Father's house, the Temple, for dishonest trading, when he scattered the coins of the money-changers in the temple area and overturned their tables. To those who sold doves he said, "Get these out of here! How dare you turn my Father's house into a market?" (Jn 2:15,16). He also had some harsh words for the Pharisees on a number of occasions. He was, and continues to be, the divine spiritual revolutionary who brings judgement as well as salvation.

He was also gentle, however, especially with children, and matchless in his searching encounters with individuals as diverse as Nicodemus and the woman taken in adultery. His conversation with the Samaritan woman at the well in John 4 must surely be the most subtle and challenging encounter anywhere in literature. Jesus' treatment of women in general was also revolutionary, and although they were not members of his band of twelve apostles, they were included amongst his disciples and played a large part in his life and ministry. They were present at Jesus' burial by Joseph of Arimathea and Nicodemus, and the first to discover that the tomb was empty on the first day of the week. Apart from John, whom Jesus chose to look after his mother Mary, they were the only ones amongst his followers to be present at the foot of the Cross. It is clear from Acts that women also played a large part in the work and witness of the Early Church. The Gospels make it clear that women were not the only unexpected friends that Jesus made and the Pharisees and teachers of the law could not understand why he and his disciples ate and drank with 'tax collectors and sinners'. (Mt 9:10). Only the One who played a part in creation could understand human nature and individuals of all kinds as he did.

The gospel-writers record that the disciples struggled, as we still do, to understand him and to resolve the mystery of his being. It is a measure of the enigma of his person and the variety and complexity of our individual responses to him that Einstein, who was a Jew and did not believe in a personal God but only a 'cosmic spirit', could yet say that "No-one can read the Gospels without feeling the actual presence of Jesus." Maybe not all Christians could speak with such conviction. Who did he think this 'luminous figure' as he described him, really was? And, more importantly, what do we make of him? It remained for the post-Resurrection, post-Pentecost Church, enlightened by the Holy Spirit, to become increasingly aware of who he really was and to describe in Acts and the epistles what was revealed to them about him. It is surprising, nevertheless, that it took several hundred years for the early Church to formulate the doctrine of the Trinity and to agree about his divinity and his inclusion in the Godhead, together with the Father and the Holy Spirit. But whatever argument there may have been in the early Church, and since, about the status of Jesus and his relationship with the Father and the Holy Spirit, it has been the experience of believers throughout the centuries that he evokes our worship as only God himself can do. John describes how Thomas, having seen and touched the wounds of the resurrected Jesus, said to him "My Lord and my God." The Church still struggles with the apparently contradictory truth that he is both wholly God and wholly man. It is a dilemma that Scripture never attempts to resolve for us. It is only possible because his incarnation through the virgin Mary was a completely new and mysterious creative act of God by his Holy Spirit.

As befits the complexity of his being, Jesus has a number of different names and titles, several dozen in fact, and he performs a number of different roles on our behalf. Jesus, meaning Saviour, denotes his supremely important function as well as being his given name: he is inseparable from the office that he holds. Messiah, or Christ in the Greek, denotes the One chosen and anointed by God as the Saviour foretold in the Old Testament. He is also described and addressed as Lord in recognition of his divinity. In 'being from God' he is known as the Son of God and in being also human he refers to himself most often as the Son of Man. Peter's recognition of Jesus at Caesarea Philippi as the Christ, the Son of the living God, his royal, public title, was a momentous and decisive insight that, as Jesus told him in Mt 16:15, only the Father could have revealed to him. This was an understanding confined at that time to the disciples. Jesus almost always used the humbler title, Son of Man, which is perhaps puzzling. He is recorded as using it no less than forty times and in all four Gospels. Its origins are in Daniel and Ezekiel and its significance is somewhat obscure and ambiguous in that, appropriately, it has both divine and human connotations. But it was safe, which might explain this preference. Safe because not understood as claiming special status as God's chosen One, or more explicitly as his Son. On the one hand it avoided the risk of his role as Messiah or Christ being misunderstood and on the other it avoided his making himself equal with God, as his one and only Son, and thereby causing too-early confrontation with the religious authorities. It was provocation enough that he frequently had challenging, always brilliant things to say to these authorities, above all the Pharisees, and his words inevitably increased their opposition to him. He also enraged them by his not infrequent, provocative healings on the Sabbath. But the time had not yet come for him to allow them to have their way and to kill him. Until then he needed to avoid too decisive a confrontation. When he came to the time of his trial he made no effort to deny his divinity.

It is interesting that in addition to the several names and titles already referred to Jesus also used another – 'the Son' on its own, without qualification. This is recorded on only very few occasions and only in John's Gospel, notably 5:25-27, a passage in which Jesus used all three names, not only Son but also Son of God and Son of Man. He used this other name when he was speaking of himself in his intimate family relationship with his Father. The importance of this for us is that we too are invited to be God's sons and daughters in this intimate way. This is made possible only by the presence of the Spirit in our hearts whereby we are enabled to cry "Abba, Father", as Paul tells us in Romans 8:15 and Galatians 4:6.

One of the most remarkable facts about Jesus' life and mission was his clear indication that he came, above all, to die. All four gospel writers, three of them in almost identical words, record his warning to the disciples that he would be betrayed to the chief priests and the teachers of the law and would be turned over to the Gentiles to be mocked and flogged and that he would be crucified. In each case this is followed by the promise that on the third day he would be raised to life. He told Nicodemus in John 3:16 that God so loved the world that he "gave his one and only Son." Jesus must surely have been a willing volunteer, however, and indeed he makes this clear in John 10:18 where he says that he lays down his life of his own accord.

Another remarkable feature of Jesus' life and ministry was his deference to his Father whose will he described, in Jn 4:34, as his food. This sense of dependence no doubt explains his frequent, prolonged periods of prayer to his Father, often alone in the wilderness or in a solitary place, (Mk 1:35), on a mountain, (Mt14:23), and frequently at night. The most powerful and moving example is his agonised prayer to his Father on the last night of his earthly life in the garden of Gethsemane, while his disciples slept. (Mk 14:32-39). It appears that he needed the guidance and strength that only his communication with his Father could give him. Mark's account of this prayer records him using the intimate name of "Abba, Father" in his plea that "this cup" of suffering might be taken away, before he finally agreed to shoulder his terrifying burden: "Yet not what I will, but what you will." (Mk 14:36). His prayers to his Father also include his cry of desolation from the Cross when he quoted Psalm 22 to express his experience of abandonment only moments before his death: "My God, my God, why have you forsaken me?" We can only see this terrible, agonised cry as evidence of his experience of the separation and rejection that he was suffering on our behalf before his relationship with his Father was re-established. It is the definitive expression of human despair; a cry that many millions have echoed down the ages in their own experience of abandonment and desolation.

Jesus is a man like no other. The writers of the gospels and epistles give us a description of the One in whom all the strands we have been following unmistakably converge and are perfectly combined and fulfilled. He is the Son of God who has revealed the Father and left us with the Spirit after he ascended into heaven. He is the One who has conquered evil and defeated the devil through his death and resurrection. He is the One who through the Spirit calls out his people, the New Israel of the Church, through whom he continues his work in the world. He is the supreme Prophet in whom all prophecy is fulfilled. He is the One whose one perfect once-for-all sacrifice of himself brings salvation and replaces all previous sacrifices that could only point forwards to him. Finally he is the One who will come again, or reappear, and will reign forever on the throne of David in the everlasting kingdom of his Father.

Jesus is quite simply the most colossal figure in history. He has made a greater impact, in spite of his lack of worldly pomp and power, than any other man or woman who has ever lived. It is a tragic fact that Western civilisation, built so largely on Christian foundations, is neglecting to honour and worship him and is decaying and making it difficult to discern his image in its culture. Faith in him is now growing and flourishing in some other parts of the world while we are in turmoil and turning so often to alternative and less nourishing forms of spirituality. When Jesus entered Jerusalem on Palm Sunday he is recorded in Luke 19:42 as weeping over it and saying: "If you ... had only known ... what would bring you peace – but now it is hidden from your eyes." He is surely weeping over us today.

For each one of us and for communities that continue to look to him, he fulfils every essential role and function that we can identify because he is also God, the One from whom all human roles and everything else as well derive their true significance. We all of us need people to fill these roles for us. We need leaders to guide and shepherds to care for us, brothers to identify with and to share our roots and companions to confide in and to be with us in the good times and the bad. We also need prophets to speak to us of God and priests or pastors to minister to us in his name. Above all we need a saviour and a king to serve and worship and to put on the throne of our lives in order to avoid enthroning ourselves. Human relationships and friendships, especially marriage, can fulfil some of these needs but not all of them. Only in the person of Jesus, at the very centre of our lives, at the deepest, spiritual level and in the fellowship of his Church can all these needs begin to be met. It is sad that even more people cannot rejoice with John Newton in the words of his inspiring hymn:

"Jesus my Shepherd, Saviour, Friend,
My Prophet, Priest and King,
My Lord, my Life, my Way, my End,
Accept the praise I bring."

He was not only born in our likeness as a man for our salvation but is truly, with the Father and the Holy Spirit, the Alpha and the Omega, the First and the Last, the Beginning and the End. Paul tells us in Col 1:15 that 'He is the image of the invisible God.' His coming to earth two thousand years ago, from which we record time both backwards and forwards, BC and AD, is the pivotal, defining moment in world history. Every time we see the date on a newspaper or write it on a letter we are accosted by it, and Easter Day, as well as every other Sunday of the year, is a reminder of his resurrection. This first day of the week on which he rose from the dead was the day with which the early Church replaced the Jewish Saturday or Sabbath, their day of rest. As the supremely important event in the history of the earth on which we live, his coming must also be the supreme event in the history of the entire universe. If the God of all creation has sent his Son Jesus to any part of his universe to suffer a necessarily once-for-all death at the hands of his own creatures and raised him to life, then this redemptive event can have no equal anywhere or ever. It must be decisive not only for our earth but for the whole of creation in its thirteen billion year existence. It is an inescapable truth, albeit perceived as such only by the eye of faith.

One day, Jesus tells us, we shall "see the Son of Man sitting at the right hand of the Mighty One and coming on the clouds of heaven, with power and great glory." (Mt 26:64, Mk 14:62, Lk 21:25-28) It is the scandalous claim of the Christian faith that a seemingly parochial event in Palestine two thousand years ago continues to be decisive for the salvation not of the Church only, but of all men and of all creation, forever. So clearly does Jesus stand out from the pages of the New Testament that to the eye of faith the Bible appears as a portrait of him, or even more substantially, if we can envisage it, a three-dimensional, composite sculptural image. In the world and in the whole of creation, in all its beauty and grandeur, we also recognise his sustaining presence and the shape of his love. In the words of Teilhard de Chardin: 'Jesus is known as a person; he compels recognition as a world.'

THE STORY OF JESUS

HIS BIRTH AND THE INCARNATION

The New Testament starts with the birth of Jesus. If he was so out of the ordinary as to be both man and God, as he was gradually recognised to be, then his birth is likely to have been out of the ordinary also. John writes at the start of his Gospel, in his inspired statement of Christian truth, that the Word was with God and was God; that through him all things were made, and that he was himself made flesh and made his dwelling among us. Luke introduces the news about his birth more literally, in 1:26-38, with Mary's visit from the angel Gabriel. He tells her that "You will be with child and give birth to a son, and you are to give him the name Jesus. He will be great and will be called the Son of the Most High. The Lord God will give him the throne of his Father David, and he will reign over the house of Jacob for ever; his kingdom will never end." "How will this be," Mary asks the angel, "since I am a virgin?" The angel answers: "The Holy Spirit will come upon you, and the power of the Most High will overshadow you. So the holy one to be born will be called the Son of God." "I am the Lord's servant," Mary answers: "May it be to me as you have said." The angel also tells her that her cousin Elizabeth is six months pregnant and we now know that her offspring would be John the Baptist. Luke then describes her hurrying to visit her as well as Elizabeth's joy at seeing her and Mary's spontaneous outburst of praise:

> "My soul glorifies the Lord
>   and my spirit rejoices in God my Saviour,
>   for he has been mindful of the humble state of his servant.
> From now on all generations will call me blessed,
>   for the Mighty One has done great things for me –
>   holy is his name."

Matthew gives us Joseph's side of the story. In 1:18-25 he tells us: 'This is how the birth of Jesus Christ came about: His Mother Mary was pledged to be married to Joseph, but before they came together, she was found to be with child through the Holy Spirit. Because Joseph her husband was a righteous man and did not want to expose her to public disgrace, he had in mind to divorce her quietly.' This is hardly surprising in that he had not been involved – or it seems as yet even consulted. The term husband here really means what we would call fiancée and the relationship involved was so strong and binding an engagement that it could be broken only by what was referred to as divorce. Matthew goes on: 'But after he had considered this, an angel of the Lord appeared to him in a dream and said: "Joseph son of David, do not be afraid to take Mary home as your wife, because what is conceived in her is from the Holy Spirit. She will give birth to a son, and you are to give him the name Jesus, because he will save his people from their sins." 'When Joseph woke up, he did what the angel of the Lord had commanded him and took Mary home as his wife. But he had no union with her until she gave birth to a son. And he gave him the name Jesus.'

The Christian doctrine of the virgin birth – more accurately the virginal conception – cannot, as is sometimes suggested, stand or fall on a particular translation of the Hebrew word used by Isaiah and translated either virgin or young woman. It has to depend rather, in part at least, on these authentic-sounding stories of Mary and Joseph facing quite separately the dilemma presented by her unusual pregnancy and the reassurance given in each case by the angel of God. If we prefer to believe, as some do, that these stories have been constructed by the gospel writers to fit in with their understanding of prophecy, how can we believe anything else they tell us? Apart from this the virginal conception is a necessity demanded by the massive requirements of the incarnation in which, as we believe, God enters his universe in Jesus. This is an event that must involve a completely new, unique creative act.

The Christian belief that Jesus was conceived of a virgin is not an optional extra but the very foundation of the incarnation, and without the incarnation there is no Gospel – no Good News to tell. If Jesus the Christ was not conceived and born of a virgin there is no salvation: it is hard to see how he could have otherwise been divine as well as human, and we cannot save ourselves. If he was also divine he must have been so from the very outset, from the moment of his conception, thus requiring a break with normal reproductive procedure. He cannot have changed his essential nature and become so later, after his birth. Even God cannot allow himself to change something into something else: there is no point. Only a sovereign act of God himself by his Spirit could have brought about this unique conception and its outcome in the dual nature of Jesus. Maybe the eternal Word could be made in human likeness only because we had first been made in the image or likeness of God. It was perhaps this affinity that God first implanted in man that enabled the eternal Word to become miraculously fused with flesh in Mary's womb. In this way he began a totally new chapter in the history of his creation.

Thus it is essential that, as we believe, Jesus was conceived as both completely man and completely God. If Jesus was not man we are not involved and therefore not represented; if he was not also God he cannot save us. If we choose not to believe in this miraculous conception of the Redeemer because it is too great a thing for God to do then he is not great enough to be of the slightest use to us: he is not able to save us, and who can doubt we need that? Anything less than this unique intervention would have resulted in a purely human child, subject to the limitations inherent in the purely human genes of both parents. This miraculous conception can perhaps be seen as the grafting of the divine into human stock, the introduction of 'divine DNA', we could argue. It is God's entry into his creation through Mary with his own divine presence; not a mutation to affect successive generations also, but a provision for this single unique birth. If the seed that is involved brings the creator himself into his creation in a once-for-all visit at one point in time then this astonishing event must of necessity be decisive for the whole of that creation.

It would appear from Paul's words in Romans 8 that only the co-creator, Christ himself, could be the seed for the new crop of the kingdom of heaven. Only he could reverse the decay to which God had subjected his universe in the colossal process of life and growth and death and renewal that he built into it from the very beginning. The eternal life of God must somehow have had to penetrate not only the spiritual realm for our salvation, but the physical realm as well. In some way that is incomprehensible to us, God had himself to enter, in

Christ, into the human reproductive process and appear in the form of a man and undergo death at our hands in order to make incorruptible life available for all that he has created. He alone in his perfect divinity could provide the one thing required: the new element of divine life without which the new creation, the new heaven and the new earth could not, in the end, be fashioned from the old. The incarnation is an impenetrable mystery that has puzzled the greatest minds in the Church for two thousand years. The remarkable thing is that we can understand anything of what God reveals to us about himself.

If it appears to be an irreconcilable contradiction even to envisage, let alone believe, that Jesus is both completely God and completely man – one or the other but surely not both – it is not unreasonable to point to equivalent contradictions in the natural world. The dual nature of light as both wave and particle was once an example of an irreconcilable contradiction, and Relativity and Quantum Physics remain so. Both work perfectly, we are told, in the sphere of the very large and of the almost infinitesimally small respectively, but they cannot apparently be made to agree together. They are contradictory theories, much as Jesus' dual nature is apparently contradictory. Jung graphically expressed his bafflement that God can 'reduce his totality to the infinitesimal human scale' and went on to say that in spite of his 'incredible emptying', 'it is hard to see why the human frame is not shattered by the incarnation.'[4] It could be said that we need an equivalent of the string theory, or whatever more elegant and accurate unified theory may eventually come to resolve the scientific dilemma, in order to resolve the mystery of the incarnation. We are confronted by the creative genius of God working in both these spheres. Even he cannot, at present, enable us to understand what he has done because of our inevitable limitations.

All that we can or need to understand about Jesus' birth and incarnation, and all that follows from it, is that by means of this glorious event we have been given the opportunity to enter into a new life with God. When Jesus ascends to his Father he is seen not only to have brought the Godhead into human flesh but also to be taking humanity into the Godhead and enabling us to share, to an extent already, in his divine life, here and now on earth. Who can doubt that

---

[4] Memories Dreams and Reflections p370

when he ascended into heaven still bearing the scars of crucifixion in his 'dazzling body' that he changed everything there as well? If the eternal Son of God can be seen in Revelation 22 as the Lamb on the throne with God maybe, with trepidation, we can allow of Jung's startling assertion that the incarnation 'means nothing less than a world-shaking transformation of God'.[5] If this is heresy it prompts us to ponder on the enormity of what God has done in becoming incarnate in Christ. We shall not know until by God's grace we experience the new heaven and the new earth – the ultimate triumph that his birth and incarnation were designed to bring about. We are at present completely and gloriously out of our depth.

JESUS' THREE YEARS OF MINISTRY AND HIS DEATH AND RESURRECTION AS TOLD BY ALL FOUR EVANGELISTS

The Evangelists begin their Gospels with either Jesus' miraculous conception in Matthew and Luke or with a statement of his divine origin as the Son of God in Mark and as the eternal Word made flesh in John. They continue, each in his own individual style, to describe Jesus' three years of ministry and his death and resurrection. All four gospel writers record the important event of his baptism by John the Baptist. In this we see Jesus emerging from the privacy of his early years into the increasing glare of his public ministry. John was naturally reticent about baptising him but Jesus insisted that it was necessary for him to identify with those he had come to save, in order to 'fulfil all righteousness'. It was clearly his definitive anointing and empowering for his ministry. The Holy Spirit descended on him in bodily form like a dove and a voice from heaven said "This is my Son, whom I love; with him I am well pleased." Following this the synoptic Gospels tell us that Jesus was led by the Spirit into the desert to be tempted by the devil. After forty days of fasting the devil tempted him to satisfy his bodily hunger by turning stones into bread. He also tempted him to misuse his supernatural power by throwing

---

[5] 'Answer to Job' p63

himself from the highest point of the temple and tried to persuade him to destroy his vocation by claiming his kingdom without enduring the suffering that alone could enable him to bring it about. The reality of this encounter is beyond our understanding. By his determination to do his Father's will, and by his use of the weapon of scriptural truth in the power of the Spirit, Jesus resisted all three of these temptations and 'the devil left him'. He no doubt returned on many occasions during the three years of Jesus' ministry in the course of which he must frequently have counted the cost of what he had set out to do.

JESUS BEGINS HIS MINISTRY

From that time on Jesus began to preach and to tell people to "Repent for the kingdom of heaven is near." He began also to call his twelve disciples and to teach them and the people and to heal the sick. His calling of twelve disciples and the close relationship that he established with them, although they persistently failed to understand him, was quite clearly a crucial, strategic element in the planning of his ministry. Simon Peter and his brother Andrew and James and John the sons of Zebedee, were the first to be called and Peter, James and John remained the most prominent. This meant that on some of the most important occasions, such as the healing of Jairus' daughter and the Transfiguration, he was accompanied only by these three so that together they formed a team of four. The others, including Philip and Nathaniel are mentioned but much less often, though all of them are named in all three synoptic Gospels.

In his fourth chapter Luke provides us with a unique insight into Jesus' comprehensive vision of his ministry. He records Jesus reading in the synagogue at Nazareth from Isaiah 61, in which the prophet speaks of his anointing for his own ministry:

"The Spirit of the Lord is on me,
   because he has anointed me
   to preach good news to the poor.
He has sent me to proclaim freedom for the prisoners
   And recovery of sight for the blind,
To release the oppressed,
   To proclaim the year of the Lord's favour."

Jesus told his hearers that it was his ministry and that of his Church to which these words ultimately referred and in which they would finally be fulfilled. Jesus also told them that "no prophet is accepted in his home town" and quoted again from the Old Testament to remind them of God's interest in the Gentiles as well as the Jews. This made them furious and they tried to throw him down a cliff.

This is only chapter 4 and it is obvious that the conflict that is such a prominent feature of the Gospels evidently began almost at once. As early as chapter 3 of Mark the Pharisees began to plot with the Herodians how they might kill him because he had healed a man with a shrivelled hand on the Sabbath. John writes as early as chapter 5 that 'the Jews tried all the harder to kill him' for 'not only was he breaking the Sabbath, but he was even calling God his own Father, making himself equal with God.' Throughout the Gospel stories, in addition to teaching and performing miracles, Jesus was constantly referring to this conflict and to the fact that he had come to die at the hands of his own people.

JESUS' PARABLES

Jesus teaching ministry was divided between his disciples whom he taught mainly in the form of plain speaking and dialogue and the crowds to whom he spoke almost exclusively in parables. These were stories that he told in order to help them to understand the kingdom of God that he had come to introduce. In that the kingdom is our total spiritual environment, both within us and without, all his teachings can be seen as instruction about what we should know and do as subjects of this kingdom, in order that God's will may be done. When he taught about adultery and divorce, giving to the needy, prayer and fasting, and forgiving or judging others, he was really teaching about how God's kingdom could more nearly come – if only we would let it. Hence Jesus' emphasis on the first two commandments to love God and our neighbour as ourselves. In Luke 14:13 he issued the uncomfortable challenge that when we give a lunch or a dinner we should not invite our family or friends but the poor and the lame and the blind, without thought of repayment. This is in line with his strict, seemingly impossible demands, that we should love not only our friends but our enemies as well and treat them as we would wish them to treat us. The majority of us tend to live by the pecking order values of the world that drive us forward on a selfish course that is ultimately unsustainable. The Beatitudes, recorded in Matthew 5: 3-10 are an uncomfortable reminder of the principles underlying Jesus' vision of the kingdom:

> "Blessed are the poor in spirit,
>   for theirs is the kingdom of heaven.
> Blessed are those who mourn,
>   for they will be comforted.
> Blessed are the meek,
>   for they will inherit the earth.
> Blessed are those who hunger and thirst for righteousness,
>   for they will be filled.
> Blessed are the merciful,
>   for they will be shown mercy.
> Blessed are the pure in heart,
>   for they will see God.
> Blessed are the peacemakers,
>   for they will be called sons of God.
> Blessed are those who are persecuted because of righteousness,
>   for theirs is the kingdom of heaven."

These Beatitudes, like the parables, were a method of instruction that only Jesus could use. This was because he was teaching about things that only the One who was involved in creating us could know. The Psalms have over a dozen similar statements beginning with the same introduction: 'Blessed is he who fears and trusts the Lord' and 'Blessed are those who seek him with all their hearts.' What made the Beatitudes of Jesus unique was the element of prophecy through which he told his disciples of the outcome of being "poor in spirit" and "peacemakers," and being "persecuted because of righteousness": "Blessed are the pure in heart, for they will see God." Who else could know that the pure in heart would truly see God but God himself?

JESUS' MIRACLES

Jesus' teaching and preaching were everywhere accompanied by miracles, in all four of the Gospels. A number of them appear in all three of the Synoptic gospels; only one, the feeding of the five thousand appears in all four gospels. Several appear in only one or two; for example only John records the turning of water into wine at the wedding at Cana. Jesus revealed his sovereignty over the realm of nature by his calming of the storm and his walking on the water. He demonstrated his power over disease in his numerous healing miracles and above all he demonstrated his power over death itself. All three synoptic gospel writers record the raising of Jairus' daughter; only Luke records the raising of the widow's son at Nain and only John records the story of the raising of Lazarus.

For those to whom Jesus is a mere man his miracles are bound to be a problem. Miracles are impossible to accept unless we believe and trust in a God who gives us confidence that he is able to perform them. If we believe that Jesus is the Son of God and co-creator of the universe then there must surely have been few limits to the authority that his Father gave him over his creation when he was on earth. There can be no limits to the power of God the Father who performed the greatest miracle of all when he raised Jesus from the dead three days after he had been crucified. The crucifixion is an established fact of secular as well as Gospel history and the resurrection has defied repeated attempts to disprove it. Whilst some might understandably see miracles as contrary to nature, as a breaking of natural law, they can otherwise be seen as God doing what is natural to him and as revealing the spiritual reality underlying the whole of his creation. They are the unveiling of the fundamental truth to which all other truth is subordinate. Miracles are bound to be unattractive to the scientist who does not have faith in an all-powerful God. He quite understandably needs to believe that the world that he investigates will always behave in a totally predictable fashion, thus leaving no room for the exercise of God's sovereignty.

PETER'S RECOGNITION OF JESUS AS THE CHRIST

The opposition to Jesus was present from the very start and the later chapters of all four gospels show this net of opposition closing around him ever more tightly. This was a fact that he recognised and accepted as the inevitable conclusion of his earthly ministry. It was something that the disciples naturally found it hard to understand and even harder to accept. It would appear that a turning point in their gradual understanding of his destiny was reached when Peter recognised Jesus as 'the Christ, the Son of the living God' – an event recorded by all four of the evangelists. This recognition did not prevent Peter from questioning Jesus' need to die and being told: "Get behind me Satan." This fierce rebuke from Jesus, recorded in chapter 16 of Matthew`s Gospel, was because Peter had presented him with exactly the same temptation as Satan had used in the wilderness. He had, in effect, tempted him to claim the kingdom without undergoing his death on the Cross that alone could make it possible.

JESUS' TRANSFIGURATION

The first three evangelists go on to tell us that this recognition of the truth about Jesus was followed a week or so later by the Transfiguration, thus presumably establishing a connection between them. On a high mountain, witnessed by Peter, James and John, Jesus' face 'shone like the sun' and as at his baptism, a voice from heaven said: "This is my Son, whom I love: with him I am well pleased." This time there was the added instruction to "Listen to him." Moses, the great leader and law-giver, and Elijah, the greatest of the Old Testament prophets, appeared with him 'in glorious splendour'. Luke tells us that they spoke about 'his departure, which he was about to bring to fulfilment at Jerusalem'. This crucial event of the transfiguration was a confirmation for Moses and Elijah and for the three disciples, that Jesus was not only the fulfilment of the Law and the Prophets but the One who would bring in a totally new order by his sacrificial death. This revelation was only for them and for the disciples, who were told not to speak of it until after the resurrection. It must have been a crucial experience in preparing them for all that was to come. It was no doubt also a crucially important and encouraging experience for Jesus himself who was to face crucifixion less than a year later.

THE OPPOSITION INCREASES

From this time on, the opposition was even more marked; the attitude of the teachers of the law was increasingly confrontational and Jesus was increasingly scornful and critical of them. He told the twelve disciples that "the Son of Man will be betrayed to the chief priests and the teachers of the law. They will condemn him to death and turn him over to the Gentiles to be mocked and flogged and crucified." But Luke records in 18:34 that 'the disciples did not understand any of this. Its meaning was hidden from them, and they did not know what he was talking about.'

JESUS ENTERS JERUSALEM

At Passover, when Jesus rode triumphantly into Jerusalem on a donkey, as foretold by Zechariah, in order to reveal the nature of his kingship to the world, he proceeded to drive out those who were buying and selling and exchanging money in the temple area. The opposition naturally intensified even more. During this last week Jesus worsted the chief priests and teachers of the law in a number of encounters. They hoped, as Luke tells us in 20:20 'to catch Jesus in something he said so that they might hand him over to the power and authority of the governor.' They asked him: "Is it right for us to pay taxes to Caesar or not?" He responded by telling them to bring him a denarius and asked them whose portrait was on the coin. "Caesar's", they replied. "Then give to Caesar what is Caesar's, and to God what is God's," Jesus told them, which reduced them to silence. It is interesting that in thus sanctioning our dual loyalty to the State as well as to God he is giving his blessing to the process of secularisation that we now recognise as a threat to our primary allegiance to God himself. This dual loyalty involves a balance that we are seldom able to achieve. (For a further discussion of this topic see Appendix 5.)

The Sadducees also tried to catch him out with a complicated question about the resurrection. Once again his answer silenced them and in all three synoptic gospels it is recorded that from that day 'no-one dared to ask him any more questions.' This is followed in Matthew by a series of devastating 'woes' addressed to the teachers of the law and the Pharisees because of their hypocrisy and their arrogance and blindness to truth. Luke also records, in 19:42, Jesus' anguish at the blindness of the people and their failure to recognise the day of their salvation. As he approached Jerusalem and saw the city, he wept over it and said, "If you, even you, had only known on this day what would bring you peace – but it is now hidden from your eyes."

All three synoptic gospels then have a very similar lengthy passage of parallel, intertwined teaching on the destruction of Jerusalem that was to take place in AD 70, and on the signs of the end of the age. After this "all the nations of the earth will mourn. They will see the Son of Man coming on the clouds of the sky, with power and great glory" and "the angels will gather his people from the four winds, from one end of heaven to the other." (Mt 24; Mk 13, Lk 21).

From here on all four gospels move in step to describe the last few days of Jesus' earthly ministry, albeit with the usual variations in order and timing and detail. At some stage Judas had gone to the chief priests to betray him. He had been paid his thirty pieces of silver and he thereafter 'watched for an opportunity to hand him over.' The chief priests for their part were plotting 'to arrest Jesus in some sly way and kill him', but not during the Passover Feast in case there was a riot among the people. This was not God's plan, however: Jesus had other ideas and he remained in control. At some time during the week he had been anointed for burial with expensive alabaster ointment by a woman, mentioned in all four gospels, whose loving act Jesus told us would be remembered 'wherever this gospel is preached throughout the world'. God's time for the crucifixion was the day of the Passover Feast, the day of salvation for the Jews.

THE LAST SUPPER

On the Thursday night before his death Jesus ate his last supper with his disciples. During the course of the meal John tells us that Jesus washed his disciples' feet and told them that they should do the same for each other. In the synoptic gospels Jesus gave them bread and wine that symbolised his body and blood that he would sacrifice for them, and told them to continue to do this in remembrance of him. (See Paul's account in 1Corinthians). After this he spoke to them of his impending betrayal and said to Judas: "What you are about to do, do quickly." He accelerated the pace and ensured that he would be arrested and tried that night and crucified next day, the Friday of the Passover, in spite of the reluctance of the chief priests. After this they sang a hymn and left the upper room in which they had eaten the meal. They then went to the Mount of Olives where Jesus predicted that before the cock crowed Peter would deny him three times. He and all the other disciples protested that even if they had to die with him they would never disown him. As it turned out when they went with Jesus to the garden of Gethsemane they all fell asleep while he faced his hideous ordeal alone in prayer to his Father.

THE GARDEN OF GETHSEMANE

Jesus' time of prayer in Gethsemane was the start of the passion story. It was here that he finally demonstrated his recognition of the enormity of the burden that he was bearing on behalf of the world. He experienced the chilling impact of the darkness of hell and all the hideous forces of evil that he was confronting and that he had to overcome by his impending sacrificial death. He told his disciples that it was more than he could bear to contemplate: "My soul is overwhelmed with sorrow to the point of death." He moved away from them, knelt down, fell with his face to the ground and prayed: "Father, if you are willing, take this cup from me; yet not my will, but yours be done." Only Luke records that at this terrible moment 'an angel from heaven appeared to him and strengthened him.' Matthew and Mark both record that three times he repeated this prayer and returned to his disciples and three times he found them asleep and thus failing to recognise his need of their support in his time of greatest agony. He told them that "the hour is near" and that "the Son of Man has been betrayed into the hands of sinners." Soon afterwards Judas arrived with a large crowd armed with swords and clubs, sent from the chief priests and elders. He kissed Jesus, which was his signal that they should arrest him. Jesus offered no resistance, saying to them: "this is your hour – when darkness reigns." They bound him and took him to the house of the high priest where the teachers of the law and the elders were already assembled in readiness for his arrival – at a night-time court that was illegal.

In spite of all the disciples' protestations of loyalty when Jesus was arrested 'they all deserted him and fled'. When he was taken to the house of Caiaphas the high priest, Peter sat in the courtyard and denied that he knew him, firstly to two separate servant girls, and thirdly to some bystanders. When the cock crowed 'he went outside and wept bitterly'. Judas was seized with remorse, returned the coins to the chief priests confessing that he had "betrayed innocent blood" and then went away and hanged himself.

JESUS BEFORE THE SANHEDRIN

Each of the gospel writers tells the story as he has come to understand it and by piecing together their individual versions we can get the fullest possible picture of what took place during these next crucial days. Matthew and Mark tell us that the chief priests and the whole of the Sanhedrin, the official Jewish religious court, were looking for false evidence against Jesus so that they could put him to death, but they could not find any. Many testified falsely against him but 'their statements did not agree'. Finally two witnesses came forward with conflicting versions of Jesus' reference to the temple of his body that the Jews would destroy and that would be rebuilt in three days. They twisted this into a reference to the temple at Jerusalem that they claimed Jesus had said he would destroy and rebuild. When they brought false accusations against him that they knew themselves to be wilful misunderstandings, he remained silent. When Pilate later asked: "What is truth?", it was a rhetorical question to which he did not wait for an answer. When, on the other hand, the high priest challenged him: "I charge you under oath by the living God: Tell us if you are the Christ, the Son of God," Jesus said: "Yes, it is as you say." In order to further strengthen his claim, he went on to quote a reference to the Messiah in Daniel 7 as the Son of Man whom he would see "sitting at the right hand of God and coming on the clouds of heaven." At this the high priest 'tore his clothes', which it was illegal for a priest to do. "He has spoken blasphemy! Why do we need any more witnesses? What do you think?" "He is worthy of death", they answered. Then they spat in his face and struck him with their fists and blindfolded him, challenging him to say who had hit him. The terrible reality of the treatment of the Messiah at the hands of his own people was prophetically envisaged by Isaiah in his haunting fifty third chapter. He spoke of the servant whose 'appearance was so disfigured' and whose 'form was marred beyond human likeness.'

JESUS BEFORE PILATE

They then bound Jesus and brought him before Pilate, the Roman governor of Judea, in the early morning. He asked them what charges they were bringing against him and advised them to take him and judge him by their own law. "But we have no right to execute anyone," the Jews objected. Pilate then went back inside the palace – which the Jews would not enter because it would render them unclean and unable to eat the Passover – and he asked Jesus "Are you the king of the Jews?" "I am," Jesus replied. Much to Pilate's amazement, when the chief priests made further false accusations about 'stirring up people all over Judea by his teaching', and 'subverting our nation and opposing payment of taxes to Caesar and claiming to be Christ, a king', Jesus refused to reply. Pilate questioned him further and went out to tell the Jews: "I find no basis for a charge against him" but hearing that Jesus was a Galilean and under Herod's jurisdiction he sent him to Herod who was in Jerusalem at the time. Herod was 'greatly pleased, because for a long time he had been wanting to see him, hoping he would perform some miracle.'

Herod 'plied Jesus with many questions but Jesus gave him no answer' and after his soldiers had ridiculed and mocked him he sent him back to Pilate. Luke tells us: 'That day Herod and Pilate became friends – before this they had been enemies.' Pilate repeated that Jesus had done nothing worthy of death and said that he would punish him and release him. He asked the people whether they wished him to release Jesus or a notorious prisoner called Barabbas, as he was entitled to do. Matthew records that 'the chief priests and elders persuaded the crowd to ask for Barabbas and to have Jesus executed.' They chose Barabbas and when Pilate asked what he should do with Jesus they shouted: "Crucify him." When Pilate asked what crime he had committed they shouted all the louder: "Crucify him." So Pilate, 'seeing that he was getting nowhere and an uproar was starting', took water and washed his hands in front of the crowd and said: "I am innocent of this man's blood. It is your responsibility." All the people answered: "Let his blood be on us and on our children!" Then Pilate released Barabbas to them and had Jesus flogged and handed him over to be crucified.

At this point all four gospels record Jesus' harsh treatment at the hands of the soldiers who put a crown of thorns on his head and clothed him for a time in a purple robe to mock his royalty, saying "Hail, king of the Jews" and striking him in the face and spitting on him. John tells us that seeing all this Pilate came out once more to protest that he had found him innocent, in a vain attempt to diminish his own responsibility for what was happening to an innocent man. When he heard the Jews insisting that according to their law he must die because he claimed to be the Son of God, he was even more afraid. Pilate tried yet again to question Jesus. "Where do you come from?" he asked, but Jesus refused to answer. "Don't you realise I have power either to free you or to crucify you?" Jesus answered, "You would have no power over me if it were not given to you from above." On hearing this Pilate tried even harder to set Jesus free but the Jews kept on shouting: "If you let this man go, you are no friend of Caesar." After a further attempt by Pilate to present Jesus to them as their king they shouted: "Take him away! Take him away! Crucify him." When he asked them: "Shall I crucify your king?", the chief priests answered: "We have no king but Caesar" and 'finally Pilate handed him over to them to be crucified.'

No more terrible surrender of all that the Jewish nation should have been upholding can be imagined. If they had only known it they were attempting to destroy the God who had saved them in their Exodus from Egypt – and on the very day of Passover itself. He was their only true king but they wanted him on their own terms, not his, and were determined to be rid of him. The tenants of Jesus' parable were trying to get rid of the landlord's Son so that they could steal his inheritance. Throughout this terrible miscarriage of justice it was not Jesus who was on trial but the chief priests and Pilate and Herod and the crowds and the disciples and all who have ever lived or will live. They condemned themselves at the bar of truth as they sought to condemn him with lies that he allowed them to use against him. They played into his hands, not he into theirs, and he was to turn the tables on us all to our eternal advantage. Who can claim to be sure that any others, including ourselves, would have done differently under the same circumstances? Maybe we too would have thought that he deserved to die and would have been consenting when his executioners 'led him away to crucify him'.

THE CRUCIFIXION

There is no possible definitive account of this unique event. It is only by combining the four brief, individual Gospel fragments that we are able to paint something like a composite picture. No single one of them, or even all of them together, can begin to tell the whole story.

This is the holiest ground of all and demands a lighter tread than it is possible to achieve. As the soldiers led him away a large number of people followed him, agonising and beating their breasts for him but he turned and said to them, "Daughters of Jerusalem, do not weep for me; weep for yourselves and for your children." The Roman soldiers took him outside the city walls to Golgotha, the 'Place of the Skull' where they crucified him at the third hour, 'with two others – one on each side and Jesus in the middle'. Even as they inflicted this most terrible of deaths on him and he hung between two criminals, Luke tells us that he said, "Father, forgive them, for they do not know what they are doing." Fastened to his cross was a notice prepared by Pilate that read JESUS OF NAZARETH, KING OF THE JEWS and was written in Aramaic, Latin and Greek. The chief priests objected to this, saying that it should have read that he claimed to be king of the Jews. But they were overruled. Pilate told them, "What I have written I have written" and it stayed for all the world to see.

The soldiers, casting lots for his clothes, and those who passed by, including the chief priests, the teachers of the law and the elders, hurled insults at him. "Let this Christ, this king of Israel come down now from the cross and we will believe in him. He trusts in God. Let God rescue him now if he wants him, for he said I am the Son of God." Matthew tells us that 'in the same way the robbers who were crucified with him also heaped insults on him.' Luke's account suggests that one of them had a change of heart, however, and he records him asking his fellow-robber a remarkable question: "Don't you fear God, since you are under the same sentence? We are punished justly, for we are getting what our deeds deserve. But this man has done no wrong." Then he turned to Jesus: "Remember me when you come into your kingdom." Jesus answered him, "I tell you the truth, today you will be with me in paradise." This must be the most extraordinary encounter in history and the most extraordinary memory that anyone could be given to savour throughout eternity.

John tells us that near the cross of Jesus stood his mother, his mother's sister, Mary the wife of Clopas, and Mary Magdalene. When Jesus saw his mother there, and 'the disciple whom he loved' standing nearby, he said to his mother, "Dear woman, here is your son, and to the disciple, "Here is your mother." We are told that 'From that time on, this disciple took her into his home.' It was now about the sixth hour and darkness came over the whole land until the ninth hour, for the sun stopped shining. Jesus cried out in a loud voice, "Eloi, Eloi, lama sabachthani?" – words from Psalm 22, meaning "My God, my God, why have you forsaken me?" When those who were standing by heard him say "I am thirsty," a man immediately ran and filled a sponge with wine vinegar, put it on a stalk of hyssop and lifted it to Jesus' lips. After he had received the drink, knowing that all was now completed, he said: "It is finished." Then he called out in a loud voice, "Father, into your hands I commit my spirit." With that he bowed his head and gave up his spirit. At that moment, according to Matthew, the curtain of the temple was torn in two from top to bottom and the earth shook and the rocks split. Mark tells us that when the centurion who stood there in front of Jesus heard his cry and saw how he died, he said: "Surely this man was the Son of God." Since that time countless millions have come to the same conclusion.

JESUS' BURIAL

Because the Jews did not want the bodies left on the crosses during the Sabbath, they asked Pilate to have the legs broken and the bodies taken down. But when they came to Jesus and found that he was already dead, they did not break his legs. Later Joseph of Arimathea, a secret disciple of Jesus, asked Pilate for his body. His request was granted and he took the body, accompanied by Nicodemus, another secret disciple. In Matthew's account he wrapped it in a clean linen cloth, and watched by the women, placed it in his own new tomb in which no-one had ever been laid and rolled a large stone against the entrance. Matthew tells us that the next day the chief priests and Pharisees went to see Pilate and asked him to ensure that the tomb was made secure until the third day, when Jesus said that he would rise again. This was in case the disciples came and stole the body and then told the people that he had been raised from the dead. Pilate agreed to this and gave them a guard of Roman soldiers and they went and made the tomb secure by putting a seal on the stone and posting the guard. After the resurrection the soldiers described their terror when an angel of the Lord rolled back the stone. The chief priests gave them a large sum of money to say that Jesus' disciples came during the night and stole him away while they were still asleep. They also promised to keep the guards out of trouble with the governor. We are told that this story was still being circulated by the Jews at the time the Gospel was written.

THE RESURRECTION

Mark tells us that when the Sabbath was over, early in the morning on the first day of the week, just after sunrise, the women went to the tomb to anoint Jesus' body. They found that the stone had been rolled away from the entrance. As they entered the tomb they saw an angel who said to them:

> "Do not be afraid. I know that you are looking for Jesus who was crucified. He is not here; he has risen, just as he said. Come and see the place where he lay. Then go quickly and tell his disciples that he has risen from the dead and is going ahead of you into Galilee. There you will see him, just as he told you."

When they came back from the tomb, they told all these things to the disciples. Luke tells us that they did not believe the women 'because their words seemed to them like nonsense.' Peter and John, however, got up and ran to the tomb. They bent over and looked into the tomb and saw the strips of linen lying there, as well as the burial cloth that had been around Jesus' head, folded up separately. John tells us in his gospel that he went inside and that he saw and believed. But he says also that even after all that Jesus had told them they still did not understand that he had to rise from the dead.

THE POST-RESURRECTION APPEARANCES

Matthew ends his gospel with the eleven disciples going to Galilee, 'to the mountain where Jesus had told them to go'. He commanded them:

> "Go and make disciples of all nations, baptising them in the name of the Father and of the Son and of the Holy Spirit, and teaching them to obey everything I have

commanded you. And surely I am with you always, to the very end of the age."

For his part Luke gives us a wonderful account in chapter 24 of Jesus' appearance to one named Cleopas and a companion on the road to Emmaus, when they initially failed to recognise him. Jesus feigned not to know what had been happening in Jerusalem and if there is any story about him that proves he had a sense of humour, this is surely it. They talked with him at length and Jesus explained to them 'what was said in all the Scriptures concerning himself' but they did not recognise him until he later broke bread in their house. They said to each other afterwards, "Were not our hearts burning within us while he talked with us on the road and opened the Scriptures to us?" How good it would be to know which of the numerous relevant Old Testament passages he referred to during their time together. This is yet another story that should be read in its entirety.

After this Luke describes Jesus' appearance to the disciples when they thought at first that he was a ghost. But he invited them to look at his hands and his feet: "It is I myself! Touch me and see" – and he ate some fish in their presence. He then 'opened their minds so that they could understand the Scriptures' and recognise that the Christ had to suffer and rise from the dead on the third day. They were to be his witnesses but were to "stay in the city until you have been clothed with power from on high." Luke describes his final appearance in the first chapter of Acts that ends with his Ascension when 'he was taken up before their very eyes, and a cloud hid him from their sight.'

The last two chapters of John's gospel devote the most space of all to Jesus' post-resurrection appearances. He is described as appearing first to Mary Magdalene outside the tomb, where she mistook him for the gardener and recognised him only when he spoke her name. He told her to go and inform the disciples, to whom he appeared the same evening. He showed them his hands and his side and they were overjoyed to see him. He said to them: "Peace be with you. As the Father has sent me, I am sending you." He breathed on them and said to them: "Receive the Holy Spirit" and he gave them authority to grant pardon or to withhold it. A week later he appeared to them again when Thomas was also with them. When Jesus invited him to touch his hands and his side and to "stop doubting and believe", Thomas said to him "My Lord and my God." Jesus told him how much more blessed are "those who have not seen and yet have believed".

Lastly he appeared to some of the disciples a third time, standing on the shore in the early morning after they had been fishing unsuccessfully all night. He enabled them to catch a record number of fish but again they did not realise that it was Jesus until he invited them to come and have breakfast. When they had finished eating Jesus asked Peter three times "Do you love me?" Three times Peter responded: "You know that I love you" and three times Jesus told him: "Feed my sheep." He told Peter that he would undergo a painful death and then said to him "Follow me." Peter had been reinstated by this threefold exchange, after denying Jesus three times during his trial, and was made ready for his critically important ministry.

It is clear from all these descriptions that Jesus was the same person but also somehow different; apparently more recognisable by his voice and his familiar actions than simply by his appearance. His resurrection body evidently still carried the scars of his crucifixion but it was a new body – a body that could appear and disappear, and that is described in Jn 20:19 as passing through a locked door. It was not a matter of resuscitation because Jesus had truly died. It was not a physical body raised like that of Lazarus to its former life, nor a transfigured physical body, as Jesus' human body had been for a short while on the mountain. It was a new, spiritual body, formed from the seed of his previous physical body that had 'fallen into the ground and died' and been raised to an eternal life, never to die again. Paul tells us in Romans 6:9 that 'He cannot die again; death no longer has mastery over him.' It was, and is, an incorruptible, imperishable body in which we shall also be similarly clothed when Jesus comes again. Paul tells us in Phil 3:21 that he will 'transform our lowly bodies so that they will be like his glorious body.' The reality of it is beyond our understanding but our inclusion in his glorious resurrection is both implicit and explicit in many passages in Scripture. Chapter 15 of Paul's first epistle to the Corinthians is entirely devoted to the resurrection.

A COMMENTARY ON THE CROSS AND RESURRECTION

One day God said:
"We made man in our own image
but able to reject us. We must let him do it
and show him that it isn't possible."
"I will go and live as man," said his Son.
"We will live in him by our Spirit,"
they agreed together.
So they did.

When the triune God of Father, Son and Holy Spirit conceived the idea of making us as men and women in his own image to live with him in eternity, he had first to prepare us for this spiritual life by giving us an apprenticeship in the physical world without which we could never possibly have been ready for it. He had then to send his Son to fetch us: we could never have found the way by ourselves. He had to enter this physical world by coming in the likeness of man, in Jesus. He had to reveal himself and the nature of this spiritual life in order to show us the way to it through him and to equip us to live it with him, if we chose to do so. On account of the Fall and of our disobedience and alienation from God, this fetching would involve his dying at our hands and rising again as the only possible means of achieving our reconciliation and leading us into the new life that he planned for us. His Spirit had then to come to us as our indwelling Comforter when Jesus finally ascended to his Father, to live this new life in us and prepare us for an even fuller life with him in heaven.

There must have been a Council of the Trinity at which our salvation was arranged; Jesus must have been involved in the discussion and have had the right to refuse to play his part. Indeed he tells us as much in John 10:18, where he speaks of his laying down his life "of my own accord". He goes on to tell us: "I have authority to lay it down and authority to take it up again. This command I received from my Father." If there had been any other way for God to reconcile us to himself he would surely have taken it. It is unthinkable that he

149

would have made this infinitely costly sacrifice if it could have been avoided. Only perfect love could contemplate, let alone act, on such a necessity. 'This is how we know what love is: Jesus laid down his life for us.' (1 Jn 3:16). The only way to deal with a rebellious child is to master him – to let him do his worst and show him that he cannot get away with it. The only way that God could do this with us as his rebellious children was by coming to earth to reveal himself to us in human form and in the end allowing us to kill him.

If this had been the end of the story it would have been the supreme tragedy, a tragedy that even the Greek myth makers and dramatists could not have conceived, though Plato hinted at man's inability to tolerate perfection in Book 2 of 'The Republic'. It would have been no less than the uniquely criminal murder of the one perfectly innocent man who ever lived. Instead the world's most terrible miscarriage of justice was converted three days later into the greatest triumph in history and the means of our redemption. God the Father's response to the murder of his only Son at our hands was the Resurrection. This was the definitive demonstration that he is in control, that he is able to check-mate us and stop us in our tracks. It demonstrates, above all, his endless, perfect love.

The cross and resurrection and the pouring out of his Spirit are God's crucial strategy for dealing with the greatest problem both in the heavens and on earth, the problem of evil that must be abolished before his creation can reach its perfect destiny. These three events in God's programme of redemption are less tangible but in a real sense just as precise and scientific as everything else in the creation that it is his purpose to redeem. They are his provision for the extension of the evolutionary development of mankind and of his universe, without which neither of them could ever be brought to fruition. They are also his definitive response to the related problem of suffering in that he has entered his fallen world and given his own life in order, eventually, to abolish suffering along with death and all vestiges of evil. This means that it is possible to reconcile his omnipotence and his perfect love with the existence of this terrible reality of suffering. He has taken the burden of it on his own shoulders on the cross. Even this cannot silence the queries and the cries of those who are obliged to endure almost endless suffering and pain but it would seem to be the most that God could do to meet them in their need. His other precious provision is his promise of the Comforter to be with us and with them in their own suffering – suffering that must surely also contribute in its turn to the coming of the kingdom. The Cross and Resurrection are also crucial for our interpretation and understanding of history. This is because the kingdom that Jesus has thereby opened up for us is the ultimate destiny of all of us and all that we achieve throughout that history and everything else in all creation that eventually survives God's scorching final judgement. The cross is God's unique method of enabling his purposes for his whole creation to be achieved.

Paradoxically, the matchless love revealed by the cross is a stumbling block for many. Its challenge is somehow more fearsome and more uncomfortable than the thunder of the commandments that we cannot obey and whose impossible demands made it necessary for God to save us in this way. This is because it reveals the sin that is the root cause of our disobedience and the terrible suffering that Jesus had to undergo in order to cancel it on our behalf. Those who hear this good news have to humble themselves to accept the salvation that he has won for us at such great cost. This cost is clearly indicated in Jesus' statement in Mt 20:28 that "the Son of Man did not come to be served, but to serve, and to give his life as a ransom for many." The word translated as ransom that Jesus used was most commonly used for the price paid to redeem a slave. He thus emphasised the cost of his sharing in our human life and liberating the world from sin with his own life so that we might be drawn into the everlasting life of God himself. This is the Good News that the Bible reveals of what an infinitely merciful, suffering God has been prepared to do in order to ensure our salvation.

The cross appears to us to be irrelevant, however, until we have been convicted of sin by the Holy Spirit: the initiative is with God himself. To the eyes of faith the Cross reveals God's endless, incomprehensible love and the resurrection demonstrates his irresistible power. Love never fails: our salvation depends on God's indestructibility. By becoming incarnate in Christ and dying at our hands and rising again he turned the tables on us to our eternal advantage. When Jesus ascended to the Father he enabled the Holy Spirit to become incarnate in all those who would ask for this extraordinary privilege. Only when Jesus had revealed God the Father to us could the Holy Spirit reveal the Father and the Son to us in our own hearts. This was the next stage in our evolutionary development and in the furthering of the kingdom that is his ultimate aim.

This may appear too fantastic to believe and to come from too far in the past. But suppose it really is the way things are and always will be and we have taken no interest in these things. The Gospel has to be believed, by the exercise of faith. But equally this extraordinary story has to be convincingly dismissed as nonsense by those who do not believe it if they are to feel entirely secure in their unbelief – and the resurrection has defied all attempts to disprove it. George Orwell spoke of believers being 'mentally unfree' but there is an insecurity in unbelief as there is of necessity an element of doubt in faith. Jesus told us that he is himself the truth that makes us truly free. Paul speaking to the Athenians in Acts 17:20, and seeing the city full of idols, tells them that "In the past God overlooked such ignorance, but now he commands all men everywhere to repent." The majority of those people who choose to ignore the Gospel altogether appear to be able to get away with it but as the writer of Hebrews asks in 2:3: "How shall we escape if we ignore such a great salvation."

The place and time of this supreme event are clear evidence of God's planning. Jesus came to earth in Palestine, a tiny country surrounded by the great middle eastern empires and civilisations of the past – Egypt, Babylon, Assyria and Greece. He came at a time when the Roman Empire had established relative political stability and efficient lines of communication and Greek was the single main language, at least in the eastern half of the Empire. All the necessary conditions were in place for God to be able to reveal himself to his people and for them to be able to express and record and spread the Good News. And there was no press and no media to distort the truth and people's responses to it. It was the definitive place and time to stage the most momentous event in history.

In addition to this, crucifixion was the form of execution practised by the Romans, the cruellest and most degrading and barbarous and painful of all punishments, and only they could use it. The Jewish authorities who wished to kill Jesus were therefore obliged to collude with the hated Roman oppressors to achieve their aim, thus incriminating them both. When we consider all other forms of execution throughout history, such as stoning, beheading, shooting, hanging and burning, it is clear that they would none of them have been possible ways for the king of glory to sacrifice himself for his creation. His body needed to be intact for purposes of resurrection, though it was evidently scarred, and above all it was necessary for him to be able to speak while he was dying. He had to be able to broadcast to the world in order to reveal his love and his forgiveness and his divinity to those present at the time and through the biblical record to every generation since. Jesus used the Cross as a pulpit from which to deliver the most powerful sermon ever preached, though it contained only a very few words. His outstretched arms are the ultimate body language of love and acceptance for all men and for all time. The cross to which he was nailed, with its vertical and horizontal components, is the perfect symbol of his sacrifice for us and of the reconciliation it achieved. The vertical element speaks of our restored relationship with God above and with the earth below and the horizontal of our restored relationships with our neighbours.

Only this barbarous Roman crucifixion could have been the instrument of God's saving act of intervention on behalf of his people and nothing demonstrates more clearly the perfection of his planning. It involved the Jews who engineered it; the hated Romans without whom they could not have carried it out; the disciples who deserted Jesus and fled and, by implication, all of us and all men everywhere who would no doubt have failed him just as miserably. As a sovereign act of God the Cross is both in and out of time and is effective for all those who lived on earth before Christ's coming as well as those of us who have lived and will live, since he came. The sinfulness of every single one of us is a demonstration of our own involvement in it and of its continuing relevance and necessity. 'For all have sinned and come short of the glory of God,' as Paul tells us in Rom 3:23. The Cross is not simply a demonstration of God's love for us but his one definitive saving act for all time and forever on behalf of all that he has brought into being.

If there are creatures on other earths they can scarcely have been created in God's image, possessed of free will, and be fallen as we are. Unless God has decided to abandon them, they would also be in need of redemption in this supremely costly way and it is impossible to imagine that this sacrifice could be made more than once. Indeed Paul tells us categorically in Romans 6: 9 that 'since Christ was raised from the dead he cannot die again' and it is difficult to see how his death on this earth could be effective for those elsewhere in the universe who could not have heard about it in the same way that we have. Christ's redeeming death and resurrection is and must be unique in time and in eternity. He cannot have died and risen before and can never do so in the future. If his death is effective in redeeming not just us and our earth but the whole of his creation then there can be no need for him to die again. 'God was pleased to have all his fullness dwell in him, and through him to reconcile to himself all things, whether things on earth or in heaven, by making peace through his blood, shed on the cross.' (Col 1:19,20). It is beyond our limited understanding but this is what Scripture clearly reveals. The Cross is a demonstration of blazing, costly love poured out from the heart of God as the only means by which he could achieve this glorious reconciliation.

THE LORD'S PRAYER

Our Father, who art in heaven,
hallowed be thy name;
thy kingdom come;
thy will be done;
   on earth as it is in heaven.
Give us this day our daily bread.
And forgive us our trespasses,
   as we forgive those who trespass against us.
And lead us not into temptation;
but deliver us from evil.
For thine is the kingdom, the power and the glory,
   for ever and ever. Amen

This prayer, printed here in its traditional form, is recorded in Matthew 6 and Luke 11 as Jesus' answer to a request from his disciples to know how they should pray. In Matthew he prefaces his specific advice with a warning not to be like the hypocrites who love to be seen praying. When we pray we are to go into our room, close the door and pray to our Father who is unseen and who sees what is done in secret. We are not to bombard him with words, to "keep babbling like pagans", for he knows what we need before we ask him. As in all relationships there is a need for silence and this is especially so in our relationship with God. The simplicity of the pattern of this prayer is startling. We are to address our prayer to God as our heavenly Father. Our chief desire should be that his name is glorified, that his kingdom should come and that his will be done on earth as it is in heaven – beginning with ourselves. It would appear that all our prayers, including our intercession for individuals, should be a reflecting in God's presence on the overriding priority of his perfect will in all things. This means that they assume the form of worship.

All prayer, especially corporate prayer – and we are taught to say "Our Father", not "My Father" – is a meeting with God, however many are present. Prayer is the greatest of all exercises in extended imagination, in which we allow God to lead us to see his world through his eyes and not simply through our own. In our meeting and our fellowship with him we become aware not only of him but also of each other in relation to him. We are encouraged to see things in the context of God and of eternity and not simply of our own unaided experience. We also allow him to enlarge not only our time-frame but our knowledge, our vision and our sympathies so that we can begin to share with him in the extension of his kingdom. It is not a matter, as we can so easily imagine, of making our requests known to him because, as Jesus tells us, he knows them already.

We are, however, to ask for our daily bread – not for our bodies only but also for our souls and spirits. Jesus is clearly directing us to ask for and seek to ensure the necessities of life not only for ourselves but for all others as well. Our concern inevitably extends therefore, in terms of our physical nourishment, to questions of production and distribution and thence to politics and the use and the misuse of authority and power. This is a colossally challenging prayer and there are no limits to its implications. We can easily be misled by the fact that it is so familiar and that it appears to be so simple.

We are also to ask for forgiveness for our sins, with the clear teaching in Matthew's version that this will be dependent on our forgiving others. It has been said that when a deep injury is done to us we never truly recover until we have been able to forgive – theology and psychology, as usual, teach the same lesson. We cannot pretend that as Christians we have a monopoly on forgiveness – it is rather that we constantly fail – but we can safely claim that Jesus demonstrated it definitively and forever on the Cross.

Our last request is to be that we should be kept from temptation and delivered from evil. The Authorised Version includes an additional clause in Matthew that gives a powerful reason for asking for this deliverance: "For thine is the kingdom, and the power, and the glory, for ever." The strong inference is that the importance of our good conduct lies in its contribution to the coming of God's Kingdom. This is, for the Christian, the only ultimate foundation and motivation of all ethics and morality. Jesus does not tell us to offer this prayer in his name or mention the Holy Spirit, because there is no need to. As Christians we naturally offer all our prayers in Jesus' name and as Studdert Kennedy, the First World War padre, expressed it, the prayer is 'drenched with the Spirit'. The beauty of its openness is that it can be used by those on the way to faith as well as by those who have already found it.

If worship is built into our prayer then praise and thanksgiving and repentance are implicit, as responses to God's greatness and his grace and generosity, and to his holiness. Our adoration and our gratitude to him and our confession of our sins are not merely arbitrary duties or demands laid upon us but the key and secret of our spiritual health and welfare. If Jesus needed to spend so much time in prayer, how much more do we? Our communion with our heavenly Father in Jesus' name and through the Holy Spirit, is our spiritual food. We can exercise our bodies, look after our diet and our physical and mental health and education, and take elaborate care of our housing and clothing, but these alone are not enough to do justice to the full range of our needs as human beings. 'Man does not live on bread alone but on every word that comes from the mouth of the Lord'. (Dt 8:3). In the words of Victor Hugo: 'Truth is as much a source of nourishment as corn.'

Worship and prayer and praise and thanksgiving are good for us. They are essential for our growth and development, for the quality of our relationships with others, and above all our relationship with our heavenly Father. This is true not only for individuals but for communities and nations. We need to rescue the Gospel from the periphery of national life and seek to have it once more at the centre so that a prayerful awareness of God is seen as a natural and not simply a minority activity, whether it be in a church or in the fields or in the streets and homes of our land. "Our Father in heaven, hallowed be your name, your kingdom come, your will be done on earth as it is in heaven."

GOD THE FATHER

The idea of God as Father, as our Father in heaven, is unique to the Judaeo-Christian tradition. The term father has been used in other religious traditions but only in a much more restricted sense. The word father appears more than a thousand times in the Old Testament and on only ten occasions does it refer to God as our Father. But he is everywhere acting as Father to his people. He is their creator and the One who cares for them and who disciplines them to do his will so that thy can receive his blessing. The first specific reference to God as Father is in Deuteronomy 32:6, where Moses asks the people: "Is he not your Father, your Creator?" The next is in God's words to king David in 2 Sam 7:14 referring to his son Solomon when he tells him that "I will be his Father and he will be my son." There are several other references in the Psalms and in Isaiah and Jeremiah. The last is in Malachi 2:10 where the prophet asks: "Have we not all one Father? Did not one God create us?" He is here clearly recognised both as creator and as Father in his relationship with his people Israel.

Apart from these few early indications, we have to wait for the fuller truth to be disclosed in the New Testament, in which three quarters of over three hundred references to father are to God himself. The majority of these are made by Jesus, the remainder by the writers of the epistles. It becomes clear that any real understanding of God as our Father depends exclusively on his revelation of himself in his Son Jesus Christ. John writes, in 1:18, that 'God the One and Only, who is at the Father's side, has made him known.' Only God can make God known. It is only through Jesus, who is himself God, that by the work of the Holy Spirit his Father is truly made known to us as our Father also. (Rom 8:15,16; Gal 4:6). It is not until Jesus comes that the fog lifts and we see the direction in which God's revelation of himself has been moving. But in speaking of him as "my Father and your Father" in Jn 20:17, Jesus makes clear the distinction between his own unique sonship from eternity and our sonship by adoption into God's family through his saving work for us.

Jesus tells us in Mt 6:6 that the Father is unseen and sees what is done in secret, and in Jn 6:46 that "no-one has seen the Father except

157

the one who is from God." He tells us also that "no-one knows the Father except the Son and those to whom the Son chooses to reveal him." (Matt 11:27). We can come to the Father only through the Son, as Jesus tells us plainly in John 14:6. He tells us equally plainly and somewhat surprisingly three verses later, that "anyone who has seen me has seen the Father," which is a truly extraordinary claim. There is clearly more to God the creator of all things than we can see in the humanity of Jesus. It must be that as we come to recognise him in his pre-existing divinity as the One through whom and for whom all things were created, that he truly reveals the Father to us. In Philippians 2:7 Paul writes of Jesus laying aside the glory that he shared on equal terms with his Father in eternity before he 'made himself nothing' in coming to earth in 'human likeness'. Only in Jesus' communion with his Father can we begin to see him as he really is and only in the Father's oneness with Jesus can we begin to see God the Father as he really is.

There are many verses in Scripture that emphasise that Jesus and his Father are one – and one with us, if we will allow it. He says in John 14:11,20: "I am in the Father and the Father is in me ... and you are in me and I in you." Jesus speaks in John 16:32 of his never being alone, in spite of knowing that his disciples would desert him, "for my Father is with me". He goes further when he says in Jn 16:15 that "all that belongs to the Father is mine." They are clearly inseparable and long to include us in their close and loving relationship, through the Holy Spirit whom they have sent to be with us. Jesus tells us in Jn 15:15 that "I have called you friends, for everything that I learned from my Father I have made known to you."

One of the names that God gave himself, when speaking to Moses, was "the God of your fathers, the God of Abraham, the God of Isaac and the God of Jacob." (Exod 3:15). This was no doubt to make him, as the awesome Yahweh, "I am who I am," more real and immediate to his people Israel. When we come to the New Testament the same God is referred to by Paul in particular, in Rom 15:6 and elsewhere, as 'the God and Father of our Lord Jesus Christ', thus making him even more real and immediate to us. This title adds to his name all the depth and richness that Jesus brings in revealing him in his redeeming fatherly love for us. This makes him even more worthy of the worship that we are now to offer to him in the new Israel of the Church.

Jesus addresses his Father as Righteous and Holy and tells us that he is perfect, and that we are to be perfect also. (Matt 6:48). He describes him in Jn 6:32 as generous; as giving us "the true bread from heaven", Jesus himself. He also describes him as giving eternal life to those who believe in his Son, (Jn 6:40), and also, in Lk 11:13, as willing to give the Holy Spirit to all who ask him. Above all he has 'sent his Son to be the Saviour of the world.' (1 John 4:14). Jesus tells us in Mt 18:14 that the Father, being like Jesus the Good Shepherd, knows his sheep and that he is not willing that any should be lost or perish. For those who have no good experience of a loving earthly father we have no other term to use but only the possibility of showing them the love that they have so far been denied and praying that they may come to know and love their heavenly Father.

Jesus teaches us to address our prayers to our heavenly Father. He tells us also, in Mt 6:8, that he knows what we need before we ask him and that we are not to be anxious but to trust him, learning lessons from the birds of the air that he feeds and the lilies of the field that he clothes. We are to seek first his kingdom and his righteousness, so that "all these things will be given you as well." (Matt 6:25-34). He says on a number of occasions that whatever we ask the Father in his name he will give us. (Matt 18:19, John 14:14). The Father is always at his work, Jesus tells us in John 15:17, as is Jesus himself to whom the Father has 'committed all things'. (Matt 11:27). Their responsibility for the universe is bound to keep them busy! He tells us in Jn 10:32 that his work includes doing 'many great miracles' in his Father's name that witness also to his own authority.

Jesus tells us in Jn 14:2 that there are many rooms in his Father's house and that he is going to prepare a place for us. He also tells us in Jn 15:13 that his Father is the Gardener and that only what he plants will thrive and not be 'pulled up by the roots'. (Matt15:13). Jesus himself is the vine and we are the branches that the Father prunes in order to encourage more fruit – or cuts off if they bear no fruit. The imagery is rich and varied, as befits the Father's greatness. Jesus frequently refers to his greatness, telling us that he does only what his Father does, what he has learned from him and what he commands him to say and do, (Jn 14:24, 31, 15:10), and that "he is greater than I." (John 14:28). Jesus also tells us in Mt 24:36 that the Father alone knows the day and the hour when the Son of Man will return. "It is not for you to know the times or dates the Father has set by his own authority." (Acts 1:7.)

The Father's own words are recorded on two chief occasions in the Gospels: at Jesus' Baptism and at his Transfiguration, and just one other in Jn 12:28. At Jesus' baptism he is recorded, in each of the first three Gospels, as saying: "This is my Son, whom I love; with him I am well pleased." At the Transfiguration he adds the words: "Listen to him!" These additional words indicate clearly, to the ear of faith, that Jesus is the fulfilment of the Law and the Prophets who are represented by the symbolic appearance of Moses and Elijah with him and the three disciples on the mountain. These are key events in Jesus' life and ministry and it is clear that on each occasion the Father's seal of approval is a vital element in emphasising their importance to those who were present – and to us.

Jesus' words about his Father are much more numerous and many have already been quoted. The words that he addresses to his Father are also fairly numerous. It is clear from Luke's Gospel in particular that even Jesus needed to spend a great deal of time in prayer, conversing with his Father. This was often at night or early in the morning and notably almost always alone, and especially prior to making big decisions such as choosing his disciples. (Luke 9:12,13). In a number of cases, for example prior to the raising of Lazarus, and on two other occasions in particular, we have his very words. In the garden of Gethsemane he prays in anguish, "Father, if you are willing, take this cup from me; yet not my will, but yours be done." (Luke 22:42). His dialogue with his Father continues even on the Cross where he asks the Father to forgive those who are crucifying him: "Father, forgive them, for they do not know what they are doing." (Luke 23:34). He commits his spirit into his Father's hands and at the last utters the terrible cry of desolation. We can only suppose that he is overwhelmed by a devastating experience of total abandonment by his Father that he undergoes on our behalf, in his total identification with those he came to save: "My God, my God, why have you forsaken me?" (Matt 27:46, quoting Psalm 22:1). The communication between Father and Son is never interrupted until this terrifying moment, whose true nature and duration we cannot know. All we know is that it passed: that Jesus died, and that he was raised to life. He was not allowed to 'see decay', (Ps 16:10), as Peter tells his listeners in his first sermon at Pentecost in Acts 2:27.10.

Our own response to God the Father should be to pray to him as Jesus taught us, to praise and glorify him, and to submit to him as the One who 'disciplines us for our good that we may share in his holiness.' (Heb12:9). Jesus tells us in Matt 12:50 that "whoever does the will of my Father in heaven is my brother and sister and mother," and will enter the kingdom. It is his will that we are to be forgiving as a condition of our being forgiven ourselves. It is also his will that we should bear fruit in this and other ways to his glory, thus showing ourselves to be disciples of Jesus. (John 15:8). We cannot keep our discipleship to ourselves. Jesus warns us that "Whoever acknowledges me before men, I will acknowledge him before my Father in heaven. But whoever disowns me before men, I will disown him before my Father in heaven." (Matt 10:32,33). Equally, Jesus tells us in Jn 12:26 that "The Father will honour the one who serves me," thus once more emphasising their complete accord.

Some of Jesus' last words to his disciples about his relationship with his Father come in the sixteenth chapter of St John's Gospel. Here, at last, they experience him speaking to them no longer in 'figures of speech', as he had often appeared to them to do in the past, but 'clearly'. He tells them in Jn 16:28 that "I came from the Father and entered the world; now I am leaving the world and going back to the Father." Later, following his resurrection he makes the truth even clearer and more intimate when he says to them in John 20:17 that he is returning to "my Father and your Father, to my God and your God." Only four verses later he tells them: "As the Father has sent me, I am sending you," and at the end of Matthew's Gospel, he adds the reason for their being sent: "Therefore go and make disciples of all nations, baptising them in the name of the Father and of the Son and of the Holy Spirit." Enabled by the Spirit, following his coming at Pentecost, the Church began the mission that the Father, the Son and the Holy Spirit had planned before the foundation of the world.

When Jesus, the Son of Man returns "in his Father's glory with his angels" at the end of the age, 'every tongue will confess that Jesus Christ is Lord, to the glory of God the Father.' (Phil 2:11). Finally, as Paul writes in 1 Cor 15:24:

'Then the end will come, when he hands over the kingdom to God the Father after he has destroyed all dominion, authority and power. For he must reign until he has put all enemies under his feet. ... When he has done this, then the Son himself will be made subject to him who put everything under him, so that God may be all in all.'

It appears that the Father is in some way the first among equals in the Trinity of the Godhead, each member of which plays his own essential role in the colossal programme of creation and redemption.

THE SPIRIT OF GOD IN THE OLD TESTAMENT

The word spirit, used for God's Spirit in the Old Testament, and for the Holy Spirit as he is called in the New Testament, are translations of the Hebrew word ruach and the Greek word pneuma respectively. Their original meaning was wind and breath, as well as spirit. The Latin spiritus is less ambiguous, but also less rich in its metaphorical associations. The Spirit of God first appears as early as the second verse of the first chapter of Genesis, 'hovering over the waters` of the dark and formless earth. He appears once more as the 'breath of life' that the Lord God later 'breathed into the nostrils' of the man whom he had created in his own image, thus making him a 'living soul'. (Gen 2:7). Job says in Ch 33:4: "The Spirit of God has made me; and the breath of the Almighty gives me life." God's Spirit continues to 'hover', being his executive agent in all he does. From this early point on the Spirit is everywhere. Dante, in his Divine Comedy, speaks graphically of 'the down-pouring of the Holy Spirit which is diffused over the pages of the old and new testaments.' [6]

In the Old Testament he is often described as being given chiefly to individuals and often for specific but very varied tasks, sometimes prophecy and sometimes activities of a practical nature. For example, God tells Moses in Ex 31:3 that "I have filled Bezalel ... with the Spirit of God, with skill, ability and knowledge in all kinds of crafts –

---

[6] Paradiso xxlv 91-93.

to make artistic designs for work in gold, silver and bronze, to cut and set stones, to work in wood, and to engage in all kinds of craftsmanship." These skills are given in order to carry out the work of constructing the sanctuary. This was the movable tent or tabernacle set apart for the worship of God in the desert, with prescribed furniture and furnishings including the sacred wooden ark of the covenant, that was later replaced by the permanent Temple in Jerusalem built by Solomon. We are bound to wonder about the source of the inspiration of Bach and Handel, Mozart and Beethoven and all the great artists and craftsmen and writers. It is not easy for us to recognise the ultimate source of all our gifts and talents – and the secret of those who reach the heights of genius – but Jesus tells us in Jn 15:5 that "Apart from me you can do nothing." This arresting statement surely cannot refer only to certain of our activities and not to all.

There are just two references to the 'Holy Spirit' in the Old Testament, the first is in Psalm 51:11 and the second in Isaiah 63: 10-11. There are many instances of the 'Spirit of God' or the 'Spirit of the Lord' 'coming upon' individual great men of the Old Testament. Examples are Baalam in Num 24:2, Gideon in Judges 6:34, Saul in 1Sam 10:10 and David in 1Sam 16;13. On other occasions the Spirit 'stirred' in Samson in Judges 13:25, 'instructed' the people of Israel in Neh 9:20 and 'led' the psalmist in Ps 143:10. The prophet Ezekiel speaks frequently of the Spirit 'coming into him', (Ezek 2:2, 3:24), and also into the people of Israel. (Ezek 37:14). Both Ezekiel and Isaiah speak of the Spirit being one day 'poured out on the people of Israel'. (Ezek 39:29, Is 32:15, 44:3).

There are also clear references linking the Spirit's activity with the Messiah, the anointed and promised One who is to come. 'The Spirit of the Lord will rest on him – the Spirit of wisdom and understanding, the Spirit of counsel and of power, the Spirit of knowledge and of the fear of the Lord' (Is 11:2). Following Jesus' coming the Spirit would be even more active and this too was foretold. In Joel 2:28 there is the promise that God will one day pour out his Spirit, not on individuals, not even on his people of Israel, but on all people. It is this promise that Peter quotes, several hundred years later, as being fulfilled while he is speaking, in the first of all Christian sermons, on the day of Pentecost: "In the last days, God says, I will pour out my Spirit on all people. Your sons and daughters will prophesy, your young men will see visions, your old men will dream dreams." We shall have to wait until the second chapter of Acts for the fulfilment of this amazing prophecy.

THE HOLY SPIRIT IN THE NEW TESTAMENT

There are four fairly distinct clusters of references to God's Spirit in Scripture, the first two of which we have already looked at:

1) The first is diffused over the pages of the Old Testament.
2) The second is at the start of the gospels, and four separate instances are recorded, especially in Luke. These are the announcements of the births of John the Baptist and of Jesus, the baptism of Jesus by John, and the temptation of Jesus in the desert. Some of what appears below in connection with this second cluster has already been included elsewhere but some repetition is inevitable.
3) The third special focus on the Holy Spirit occurs at the end of John's gospel when Jesus speaks of the promise of the Spirit coming as a Counsellor or Comforter for us when Jesus himself has returned to the Father.
4) The fourth and final cluster of references to the Holy Spirit is a positive Milky Way, where the down-pouring of the Holy Spirit is diffused over almost every page of Acts, of the epistles and of Revelation.

When the Church lacks power and conviction it is likely to be due to a neglect of teaching on the Holy Spirit and a consequent failure of its members to experience his presence in their lives. The first evidence of this is in Acts 19:2 where we read that a group of believers in the church at Ephesus had 'not even heard that there is a Holy spirit.' When Paul laid hands on them they then 'spoke in tongues and prophesied.' The Christian faith involves not only belief but also vitality and action. This empowering is an essential ingredient in preaching the gospel and in all Christian service. There are numerous references to the activity of the Holy Spirit both before Jesus is born and also before he begins his public ministry. In the first chapter of Luke an angel of the Lord announces to Zechariah that his prayer has been heard and his wife Elizabeth will have a son, John – later to be called the Baptist – and that he will be 'filled with the Holy Spirit from birth.' Soon after this the angel Gabriel tells Mary that though she is a virgin she will be with child because the Holy Spirit will come upon her and the power of the Most high will overshadow her. (Luke 1:35). Some three months later Zechariah is also 'filled with the Holy Spirit' when his son John the Baptist is born and prophesies that "he will be called a prophet of the Most High and that he will go before the Lord to prepare the way for him". (Luke1:76) .

Thirty years later, at Jesus' insistence, John baptised him and the Holy Spirit 'descended on Jesus in bodily form like a dove. (Lk 3:22). Jesus was 'full of the Holy Spirit' as he returned from the Jordan and was 'led by the Spirit' in the desert, where for forty days he was tempted by the devil. After this, as Luke records in 4:18,19, Jesus returned 'in the power of the Spirit' and later went to the synagogue at Nazareth on the Sabbath day and read from chapter 61 of the prophet Isaiah:

"The Spirit of the Lord is on me
because he has anointed me
   to preach good news to the poor.
He has sent me to proclaim freedom for the prisoners
   and recovery of sight for the blind,
to release the oppressed,
   to proclaim the year of the Lord's favour".

He then told the people "Today this scripture is fulfilled in your hearing." Jesus' ministry had begun and the agenda was set for the ministry of his body the Church from then on. The age of the Holy Spirit came with the birth and the ministry of Jesus and would come more universally and more dramatically still when he was poured out some three years later and inaugurated the New Testament Church in the 'Big Bang' of Pentecost. The Spirit remained active in Jesus and in his teaching ministry, and most dramatically in the healings and the other miracles. He was not often specifically mentioned in the Gospels, except where Jesus spoke of his coming at the end of John's Gospel, because Jesus himself was there in person and the focus was naturally on him. Jesus told them in John 14 to 16 that when he returned to the Father and was no longer with his disciples in the flesh the Spirit would be sent to remind his followers of him and to be the very presence of the risen Christ living in the members of his Church. "I will not leave you as orphans; I will come to you." Jesus told the disciples that when the Spirit came he would "guide you into all truth. He will not speak on his own; he will speak only what he hears, and he will tell you what is yet to come." We do not need to learn Scripture as we learn history, for instance, because we have an indwelling, personal tutor. The Holy Spirit who inspired the writers of Scripture is present with us to guide us into the truth that it contains, if we are truly attentive to his voice.

During the period between his resurrection and ascension Jesus appeared on a number of occasions to his disciples. Only John describes one of these occasions when they were 'together with the doors locked for fear of the Jews' and when Jesus breathed on them and said, "Receive the Holy Spirit. If you forgive anyone his sins, they are forgiven; if you do not forgive them, they are not forgiven." (Jn 20:19-23). This appears to have been Jesus' special gift of the Spirit to the disciples for this priestly commission. The full pouring out of his Spirit on all believers was to come only later, at Pentecost. On this same occasion, or maybe on another separate one, Luke records Jesus telling the disciples to "stay in the city until you have been clothed with power from on high." (Lk 24:49). This is an instruction that Luke records Jesus giving them again at the beginning of Acts.

The disciples only began to understand Jesus' words when the Holy Spirit was poured out at Pentecost and even then the element of mystery remained as it has done for every generation of Christians since that time. God's presence with us and his work in us must always be a mystery but we know from Scripture and from personal experience that it is the Holy Spirit who enables us to know Jesus as Lord and God as our Father. It is this experience that provides the grounds for our recognition of God as three in one. The next chapter is an attempt to explore this extraordinary Christian understanding of God. The next part of the story of the Spirit's activity and his presence with us will be continued when we come to Acts and the epistles and Revelation where his down-pouring is everywhere diffused and no special treatment and description will be required. He is on every page.

THE TRINITY - GOD IN THREE PERSONS

God beyond our understanding; Christ within our reach; Spirit present at all times.

God is One, but he is also three in One. This is the precious Christian experience of God, clearly conveyed to us in Scripture, though not explicitly spelt out as a specific doctrine. This experience and understanding of God was only formulated as the doctrine of the Trinity and included in the creeds some three hundred years after Jesus' death and resurrection. The first hint of God as three in one comes, nevertheless, at the very beginning of Genesis, in the account of creation, where the writer makes use not of the singular word for God, El, but of the plural Elohim. He further makes reference to God, and to his Spirit 'hovering over the waters' and to his Word in pronouncing "Let there be light." In the next chapter God says: "Let us make man in our image," thus explicitly indicating his nature as plurality. It was perhaps because of the vital need to preserve the idea of one God in the Old Testament, in order to counteract the many gods of the surrounding nations, that this was not at first emphasised. Or maybe, more simply, it was because until Jesus came it would have been a totally incomprehensible idea. God is referred to as Father in the Old Testament on only a few occasions and in only five of its thirty nine books.

When we come to the New Testament however we see God emerging clearly as three persons. At Jesus' baptism in the Jordan in Luke 3:22 all three persons are clearly described as being involved and there is a clear separation of roles and functions. The Son is baptised by John, the Holy Spirit descends on him in bodily form like a dove and a voice comes from heaven saying, "You are my Son, whom I love; with you I am well pleased." In many places throughout the New Testament Jesus refers to God and prays to him as his Father, clearly therefore to a separate person. He tells his disciples, in John 14:26, that the Comforter or Counsellor, "the Holy Spirit, whom the

Father will send in my name will teach you all things and will remind you of everything that I have said to you." He tells them further, in 16:13, that "when he, the Spirit of truth comes, he will guide you into all truth. He will not speak on his own; he will speak only what he hears, and he will tell you what is yet to come." It is clear that he is yet another person; God's agent in creation, enabling us to have a personal experience of him. Only a person can inform and influence in all these ways, not an impersonal power.

When we come to Acts Luke records the coming in power of the Holy Spirit who gave the frightened disciples the courage to preach about their experience of the risen Christ and of his significance to the world. From then on the disciples speak and write of their experience of God as Father, Son and Holy Spirit. Our last glimpse of the Spirit in the Bible is in the final chapter of Revelation: "Then the angel showed me the river of the water of life, as clear as crystal, flowing from the throne of God and of the lamb down the middle of the great street of the city." All three members of the Godhead are finally revealed together: the Father and the eternal Son – 'the lamb slain from the foundation of the world' (Rev 13:8) – and the Holy Spirit, for whom the symbol of water is often used in Scripture, and who is here seen to be continuing his ceaseless healing and cleansing activity.

A COMMENTARY ON THE TRINITY

If God is Love
He must be three;
Love must be shared,
It must say "We".
Love is Good News
That must be heard –
So Love demands
At least a third.

God is, and must be, three in one; plurality as well as undivided unity. This is so not only as we experience him in his revelation of himself to us as Father, Son and Holy Spirit. He must also be so in himself, in his essential being as perfect love, and by virtue of what he does in creation. Both of these demand his threefold nature. Real, unselfish love, let alone perfect love, is too great a thing to be experienced by only one or even two participants; it must of necessity be poured out and shared with another – that is with a third at least.

We are created as male and female, by and in the image of this One God who is three persons. It is from him that we inherit our urge to share in creating, or procreating in our case, by expressing our own love in the desire to bring others into existence. God in his pre-existing relational nature is the origin and model for us as human beings; for our love, for marriage and for community. He must be the model also for our animal ancestors in their relationships. No-one who has seen the evidence of the care lavished even by the crocodile on her young can say that it is not an expression of an early, rudimentary form of love – albeit not widely shared with other species! After all, we too need to be tamed. He is also the model even for the very matter of the material universe itself that is increasingly being found by scientists to possess a measure of this same relational quality.

The God who is love and who created us to live in relationship with others and with him must have himself experienced relationships before he made us. He cannot bring into existence beings to live in relationship unless relationships already exist within his own being and experience. If God were to be only one person and to create other persons in his own image for company, then he would be exploring the territory of relationships of which he had no experience. There would be no model for our own relationships and for our capacity for communication. He is also the model and inspiration for everything that we do together in the Church, in politics and government, in science, and in art, literature and music and in every other human activity. It is our nature to talk and to be communicators because God was already talking and communicating when he made us. Creation was conceived and will be consummated in communication. 'Now the dwelling of God is with men, he will live with them. They will be his people and God himself will be with them and be their God.' (Rev 21:3).

God's ability to reveal himself to us also demands plurality because it requires corroboration, the testimony of one or more witnesses, which clearly no single person can provide for himself. "The words I say to you are not just my own," as Jesus tells us in Jn 14: 10. The Son reveals the Father and speaks the words that his

Father has given him. (Jn 8:26-29). The Father confirms him, as he did explicitly at his baptism; he also confirms him in and through the work that he has given him to do, (John 5:36), and in the final vindication revealed by his resurrection. Though Jesus makes it plain that he is, uniquely, "one who testifies for myself" he yet says, in Jn 8:18 that "my other witness is the Father, who sent me." Even he needed this confirmation from his Father while he was on earth. There have been many examples throughout history of spurious self-authenticating messiahs.

The Holy Spirit who is sent to live in us is known to us precisely because he has been sent to "speak only what he hears." (Jn 16:13). He comes as the Comforter to make the risen Christ and his teaching real to us in our hearts; only he can enable us to know God as our Father, (Gal 4:6), and Jesus as our Lord. (1Cor 12:3). God cannot be rightly known and approached as Father except through the Son, and by his Spirit, the agent through whom we direct our prayers to the Father. Jesus is not only our destination but the true and living way to the Father. 'Through Christ in one Spirit we have access to the Father' (Eph 2:8). We are prayed for by the ascended Christ, (Rom 8:34), and the Holy Spirit prays in us. (Rom 8:26). Being a Christian is not only having a personal relationship with Jesus but through him with the Father also, by the Spirit.

This is a fact that governs our approach to God and requires an awareness of each person of the Trinity; of Father, Son and Holy Spirit, without which our worship and praying and our thinking about him are unbalanced. The Trinity has been described as the anchor of all the lines of Christian thought. To focus on the Father alone is to ignore the love he has shown in sending his Son and in pouring out his Spirit. To focus on Jesus alone is to ignore the Father on whom he so clearly depended and the Spirit whom he promised to send us. To focus too strongly on the Spirit is to risk relating too loosely to both the Father and the Son and to risk exercising too great a degree of undisciplined freedom in our expression of the faith. The Father, Son and Holy Spirit are so at one with each other that we cannot rightly relate to God without relating rightly to all three divine persons of the Godhead. To recognise God as one and yet engaging in this three-way dialogue helps us to reinforce the priority of persons and relationships over theories and concepts, and of people and community over all grandiose plans and projects in our own human affairs.

For all the reasons outlined above the Trinity could be said to be a necessity. As a doctrine it is inevitably only a partially successful attempt to capture the nature of God, our creator, sustainer and redeemer, in a form of words. The God we worship, the One whom we are bound to recognise as the author of the Big Bang, resulting, as it must have done, from the energy of creative love flowing from within his Trinity, is not to be so easily pinned down. Words 'strain, crack and sometimes break, under the burden.'[7] They can take us only to the verge of spiritual truth; the reality of God is experienced only in an inexplicable encounter with love. We cannot understand him, let alone describe him, or know why he has made us. This is an example of what Pope Benedict refers to in his 'Introduction to Christianity' as 'baffled theology'. Maybe Jung was right when he said that a Trinity will always seek to become a quadernity and that God's creation is not only his will but somehow a necessity for him. Perhaps we can say of him that in his nature as love he chooses not to be self-sufficient. If he didn't need us why did he bring us into being? John Donne said in 'Devotions' that 'No man is an island.' If it is not good for a man to be alone maybe it's not good even for God and in spite of his own companionship within the Trinity he longs for others to share in his own glorious company. How else can we explain what he has done?

God himself and everything throughout his creation involves relationships. He is a God of prepositions: from and with and in; through, by, to and for. Without forcing the issue, we can say that the Son of God is eternally begotten from the Father and lives with him and in him; that through the Holy Spirit they both of them live with us and in us, and that by the same Holy Spirit they together bring to us redemption and restoration that is not for us only but for the whole of his creation. "May the grace of our Lord Jesus Christ and the love of God, the fellowship of the Holy Spirit, be with us all evermore." (2 Cor 13:14).

---

[7] Four Quartets, Burnt Norton V

DAVID'S PRAYER

"Praise be to you, O Lord,
God of our Father Israel,
from everlasting to everlasting.
Yours, O Lord, is the greatness and the power
and the glory and the majesty and the splendour,
for everything in heaven and earth is yours.
Yours, O Lord, is the kingdom;
you are exalted as head over all.
Wealth and honour come from you;
You are the ruler of all things.
In your hands are strength and power
to exalt and give strength to all.
Now, our God, we give you thanks,
And praise your glorious name." (1 Chron 29:10-13)

ISAIAH'S PROPHECY

For to us a child is born,
to us a son is given,
and the government will be on his shoulders.
And he will be called
Wonderful Counsellor, Mighty God,
Everlasting Father, Prince of Peace.
Of the increase of his government and peace
there will be no end.
He will reign on David's throne
and over his kingdom,
establishing and upholding it
with justice and righteousness
from that time on and for ever. (Is 9:6,7)

THE KINGDOM OF GOD

Until John, it was the law and the prophets: since then there is the good news of the kingdom of God. (Luke 16:16)

The story of the Kingdom began early in the Old Testament. Israel was finally allowed a king and Saul was anointed by Samuel. Saul was followed by king David to whom God promised, through the prophet Nathan, that his kingdom would endure for ever. Speaking to David of his son Solomon, he tells him: "I will set him over my house and my kingdom for ever; his throne will be established for ever." (1Chron 7:14). We are thus provided with an earthly model of the everlasting kingdom that belongs to God himself. (2 Sam 7:16, 1Chron 17:14). Isaiah tells us in 9:7 that it belongs also to the One who will come in his name, the Prince of Peace who will reign on David's throne for ever. The kingdom is referred to again a number of times in the Old Testament, in Daniel and in the Psalms.

When we come to the New Testament, the kingdom of God, or the kingdom of heaven as Matthew more often refers to it, is a central theme. It is arguably the central theme. It is everywhere and is mentioned more than a hundred and fifty times. It becomes the definitive term used by the first three gospel writers to describe God's sovereign presence and his relationship with his people. When Jesus begins his ministry he announces, as his herald John the Baptist did before him, that the Kingdom is "near", or even "within you", and he calls his people to repent and to believe the Good News of its arrival. (Mt 4:17). The long-awaited new order, looked forward to by "many kings and prophets", as Jesus tells us in Lk 10:24, is being inaugurated and the time for decision has come. Something completely new is happening that is decisive not only for the history of this world but of the age to come and for the whole of creation.

When his disciples ask Jesus how to pray he begins by telling them to address God as Father and to make the coming of his kingdom the chief object of their longings and their petitions. In what follows in the Lord's prayer it is apparent that the kingdom is wherever God's name is glorified and his will is done. Its coming amongst us could be

173

described as happening wherever we get things right as opposed to getting them wrong, whenever we manage to love each other. It would also appear to include wherever his people look to him to meet their deepest needs; wherever they ask him for their daily bread and for forgiveness, and wherever they ask not to be led into temptation but to be delivered from the evil one. The whole of this prayer that Jesus' has given us is about the coming of God's kingdom. Jesus' teaching is always and everywhere directed to the end that we might increasingly see our salvation, in the first instance, in the realisation of God's kingdom on earth. This will come about only as we do his will as it is done in heaven so that earth and heaven are progressively united.

When Jesus teaches his disciples about the kingdom he speaks to them clearly and directly of its membership and the conditions of entry, and of the knowledge of its secrets that he does not reveal to the crowds. (Mt 13:11). In order to enter the kingdom, he tells them, it is necessary to be 'be converted' and to 'do the will of God', (Matt 7:21), to be 'born again', (Jn 3:5), and 'become like little children.' (Matt 18:3). It is 'hard for a rich man to enter the kingdom of heaven' and Jesus tells the Pharisees that 'prostitutes and the hated tax-gatherers' will go into the kingdom before them. Neither wealth nor religious orthodoxy give us any advantage. (Mt 19:23). He tells us in Mt 6:33 that if we seek first God's kingdom and his righteousness everything else will be given to us as well. The kingdom is given to his children by the Father and is to be 'received', (Lk 18:17), and 'inherited'. (Matt 25:34.)

When Jesus speaks to the crowds about the kingdom, chiefly in the first three gospels, he is recorded as using mainly parables. He tells them many things in parables, and only in parables it seems: Matthew records in 13:34 that 'he did not say anything to them without using a parable.' The parables are mostly very short, easily remembered stories or powerful, suggestive images and comparisons requiring reflection, without which their meaning cannot be understood. Jesus' parables are unique vehicles for his teaching that only the One who has had a part in creating us can use in the way that he does. "Where did this man get his wisdom?" they ask in Matt 13:54. He is speaking prophetically, as only he can do, of how things are and how they will be in the new order of God's kingdom. The rule of God is both a present reality and a future hope; how it will operate in the age to come even he cannot reveal to us.

God's kingdom has no limits; it is everlasting, (1Chron 17:14, Is 9:7, Dan 4:3, Luke 1:33, 2 Pet 1:11) and is unlimited not only in time, but also in space. (Phil 2: 9,10) and it 'will never be destroyed'. (Dan 6: 26, 7:14, Heb 12:28). It is a spiritual kingdom; it belongs to God and as Jesus tells us in Jn 18:36, is 'not of this world.' There are for this reason few limits to the imagery that Jesus needs to use in order to bring it to life for us. The parables, similes, metaphors, symbols and allegories are drawn from every aspect of nature and our everyday lives. Because the kingdom is a new, living and growing reality and radically different from the old order, he speaks of it as seed sown, and as new wine that cannot be contained in old wine-skins for fear of bursting them. (Mt 13:3-8). The clear inference is that the mould of Judaism could never have expanded in order to contain the new wine of the kingdom. The kingdom is to be an influence for change and is likened to yeast that will work invisibly 'through all the dough' – through the whole lump of creation. (Mt 13:33). The kingdom is also valuable above all else and is referred to as treasure hidden in a field and as a pearl of great value that is worth selling all other possessions to obtain. (Mt 13:44,45).

Because the kingdom is about Jesus himself he tells a story about a landowner who plants a vineyard and goes away on a journey and who during his absence sends his servants to collect the fruits of the harvest from his tenants. But they mistreat them and even kill one of them and later kill his son also, thinking that they will take his inheritance. (Mt 21:33-46, Mk 12:1-12, Luke 20:9-19). Jesus is speaking of the Jews who are plotting to kill him, and will eventually have him crucified. As a result they will be punished and the vineyard will be rented out to others. He tells them in Mt 21:43, by way of interpretation, that "the kingdom will be taken away from you and given to a people who will produce its fruit." He is referring to the Church, which will include not only the Jews but also the Gentiles whom they so much despised. This is the clearest indication of God's intention to punish his people for rejecting Jesus and to include the Gentiles in the kingdom. Needless to say the Church, in its turn, frequently fails in its task of proclaiming the kingdom and needs to repent, as the Jews often needed to repent in the Old Testament and still do today.

If the Jews had accepted Jesus as their saviour and king as a nation, it is hard to see how they could ever have seen that the Gospel was not for them only but a universal message for the whole world. To this day they do not accept him as the Messiah and without their continuing existence as a nation practising Judaism, as the root from which Christianity arose, it would be difficult for us to understand the origins of our faith. By the same token it is becoming increasingly difficult to recognise our Christian roots without a more vibrant practice of the Christian faith in our own country today. In addition, without the continuing presence of the Jewish nation it is hard to see how God could honour his still unfulfilled promises to them as the people that he chose to serve him over three thousand years ago. It has been said, and this is referred to elsewhere, that the continued existence of the Jewish nation is one of the most compelling pieces of evidence of the existence of God.

Because the kingdom is God's invitation and 'rich welcome' to us, as it is described in 2 Pet 1:11, it is also a celebration. Jesus talks of it in Luke 14:16-24 as a great feast. And further, because he is himself the bridegroom, and the Church his bride, it is also likened, in Mt 22:2-14, to a wedding banquet, prepared by a king for his son. These images of feast and banquet suggest that the kingdom will be full of fun and laughter. Martin Luther said that 'If you're not allowed to laugh in heaven, I don't want to go there!' But in both these instances those who are invited do not respond, at which the king is enraged and destroys them and burns their city. This can be interpreted as referring to the destruction of Jerusalem in AD 70 as a consequence of the Jews' rejection of their Messiah. Because the fullness of the already inaugurated kingdom awaits the return of Jesus the bridegroom at the end of the age, we need to be ready and keep watch for his coming. In Matthew 25:1-13 he speaks of ten virgins, only five of whom have oil in their lamps and are able to go in to the banquet, the remainder being refused admission because, as he tells them: "I don't know you".

Luke is alone in recording a number of additional parables about the truths of the kingdom; about God's dealings with us and our own dealings with each other. These include the well-known parables of the Good Samaritan, and of the Prodigal Son in chapters 10 and 15 of his Gospel and they are surely the most remarkable stories that anyone has ever told. It is one of the apparent paradoxes of the Gospel that the prodigal appears to come off better in the end than his well-behaved elder brother. The greatness of this story and all of Jesus' teaching lies in its blend of theology and psychology.

When Luke comes to write Acts he records that after his resurrection Jesus appeared to his disciples over a period of forty days and he tells us in Acts 1:3 that he used this precious time to speak to them about the kingdom. He also records Philip preaching the good news of the kingdom in Samaria in Acts 8:12 and of Paul 'arguing persuasively about the kingdom of God' in the synagogue at Ephesus in Acts 19:8. At the very end of Acts when Paul is in prison in Rome he is once more described in 28:23,30 as explaining and declaring the kingdom of God and teaching about the Lord Jesus Christ. The kingdom was clearly a high priority on the agenda of the New Testament Church. Almost all the epistles contain one or more references to it, most notably in Romans 14:17 where Paul describes the kingdom as consisting of 'righteousness, peace and joy in the Holy Spirit'.

A specific reference to the kingdom appears lastly in Revelation 11:15 where, in expressing the final triumph of God, loud voices in heaven declare that "The kingdom of the world has become the kingdom of our Lord and of his Christ, and he will reign for ever and ever." There are other equally uplifting passages in Revelation describing the praise of the heavenly hosts in the completed kingdom. In 21:24-26 John envisages the bringing of the 'splendour of the kings of the earth' and the 'glory and honour of the nations' into the heavenly city. We have arrived at the final fulfilment of God's promise to David and we have seen how the kingdom is the central theme in the Bible's account of God's plan for his creation. There is simply no other plan available. If this one sounds too preposterous to be true what other programme do we have to offer as an alternative to what the Bible clearly tells us God has ordained?

A COMMENTARY ON THE KINGDOM

In view of the terrifying, persisting evil in the world a study of the kingdom is bound to raise a number of questions: "How does all this work; how is this kingdom to come, and why is it so slow in coming? What should it mean to us now, after all these years of waiting, when we pray: 'Your kingdom come, your will to be done on earth as in heaven' and what part should we be playing in its coming?"

The kingdom of God is revealed as the central reality of God's divine providence that has already been inaugurated and in which all things will ultimately find fulfilment. Everything that God has to give to his people and to his creation comes through his Son, Jesus Christ. In his grace he uses the Church as Christ's body in the world, enabled by his Holy Spirit, to assist him in completing the work that he began. It has been said that when God made the world he 'made it make itself' and in seeking us as volunteers he is continuing to use this same method. It is hard to see how else he could have planned it and how else he could have ensured that we shall be able to enjoy it together with him in eternity, because we have also worked and suffered for it in our earthly lives.

The evidence of God's abiding presence in his creation and his personal entry into it in the coming of his Son Jesus Christ has enabled us to recognise him as the pervading and enveloping environment – the divine milieu – in which we 'live and move and have our being'. (Acts 17:28). No satellite tracking can be more effective than his knowledge of our whereabouts and our activities. We may take numerous wrong turnings but as long as we are willing to recognise our error he can always pick us up and put us back on track. We cannot stray outside the limits of his sovereignty. 'Where can I flee from your presence?' the Psalmist asks in 139:7. God's kingdom is the limitless sphere of his everlasting dominion and his rule in the lives of his people. In Psalm 22:28 he is described as 'ruling over the nations' and in Daniel 4:17 as 'sovereign over the kingdoms of men'.

It is not surprising, in view of its complexity and the obvious, incomprehensible powers of evil ranged against it, that the coming of the kingdom is so long delayed. In the words of Teilhard de Chardin

178

in the Epilogue of his 'Milieu Divin', 'Our faith in the kingdom of God has been disconcerted by the resistance of the world to good.' We no longer have the fresh vision of the early church or the same encouragement of imagining that the kingdom might come soon. It was never envisaged, however, that Jesus' first coming would usher in the kingdom in its fullness; he needs to come again in order to realise the fruits of the victory that he won through his death and resurrection.

What the early church could never have envisaged was the delay – now extending to over two thousand years – that would separate these two events. Nor could it have envisaged the complex relationship that it would have with secular power and politics throughout its long history and the constant negotiations that this would necessitate. The yeast of the kingdom has been required to exert its influence over an inconceivably and increasingly large and complex lump of dough over this whole period. The delay does not appeal to our short-term Faustian impatience and appears to have been too long for us to keep our enthusiasm and expectancy alive. Jesus tells us in his parable in Matt 25:5 that half the virgins tired of waiting for the bridegroom and fell asleep. He also tells us in Matthew 24:14 that the gospel has to be preached 'in the whole world as a testimony to all nations' before the coming of the end and this has not yet happened. There are still languages into which even a part of the Scriptures has not yet been translated.

The Bible nowhere leads us to imagine that we can bring about the kingdom on our own as we are prone to imagine and as the long delay has encouraged us to try to do, most notably under Constantine, when Church and State were too closely linked. To be effective we need to accept God's rule in our own personal lives and to seek to aid its coming in the lives of those around us and in the communities in which we live. We are to do this by worshipping God, by studying his Word, by praying and breaking bread and by serving and witnessing to our faith, together with other Christians. The treasure that we have is much too good to keep to ourselves but we have to show the kingdom in action before we are justified in telling others about it. This action is demonstrated by the vast number of charitable works that have characterised the history of the Church for the past two thousand years and have been carried out by organisations and by individual Christians. Needless to say the Church has also done many things for which it has had cause to be ashamed and many acts of love and forgiveness have come from those outside it. There is evidence of God's work throughout his creation.

In order to obey God's command to love one another we need to cherish our intimate relationships and families, to foster our friendships, to build relationships with our neighbours, both close and distant, and to care for them. We also need to take an active part in the life of our community including an interest in politics, both local and national. We are also bound, depending on our abilities and opportunities, to take an appropriate interest in the wider international scene and the welfare of the earth that is our present home. This last responsibility is becoming more and more necessary, with warnings from many quarters of our part in damaging the earth system on which our physical welfare depends. Even if 'global warming' is only partly due to the way we are behaving we are obliged to mend our ways. It has been said that nature does not exist simply to be humanity's larder but that is how we are treating it.

All that we do in all these ways as Christians, in both our private and public life, should be done as servants and as mediators between God and those who are not consciously in touch with him themselves. The kingdom belongs to God himself and not to the Church, whose job is to proclaim it and to co-operate with him in its extension. Christ's followers, in whatever walk of life, are the "salt of the earth" and the "light of the world" as he tells us in Matthew 5:13,14. They bring out its true flavour, the flavour of Christ himself. They also help to preserve what is good in the world, and to shine the light of truth into its dark corners. The kingdom grows through the witness of individuals and of the whole body of the Church and through the work of the Holy Spirit in ways that it is not possible or necessary for us to know. God used other nations as well as Israel in the Old Testament and we cannot think that he is only working through his Church today. We are like bees making honey and the honeycomb, in ignorance of the fullness of what we are together helping to construct. The reality of the kingdom must be more wonderful than we can possibly imagine. It is a great mystery which, like all other mysteries, will one day be made plain when the king returns, an event for which Jesus told us we must always be prepared. We need to contribute to bringing the kingdom about and not merely wait passively for it to happen. Jesus gave us every encouragement to use our talents and we cannot fully enjoy what we have taken no part in building.

The further we get from our own individual relationships and begin to think of the kingdom in terms of societies and nations, the more difficult it is to see how it works. Oscar Cullmann wrote that 'the gospel does not begin by formulating a social policy.'[8] It operates rather by means of the example and influence of changed lives and in the words of T.S. Eliot, by 'interfering with the world.'[9] This interference brings about changes in the society of which we are a part by the work of the Holy Spirit; not merely by gaining converts but also by means of what he calls a 'conversion of social consciousness'.[10] He does not explain what he means by this or how it might come about but it could be seen as the spiritual equivalent of a change in the climate of opinion. It is an interesting idea that needs to be examined. There appears at least to be very little of this influence in our own society at present, with a wide gulf between the Church and the world outside.

Those who hold positions of great power and responsibility and live their lives in the glare of publicity must of necessity act as salt and light in highly influential ways that are not open to the majority of Christians. One of the finest examples in recent times of a changed life interfering with the world was that of the Polish Pope, John Paul, a towering Christian figure both before and after becoming Pope. Another was Cardinal Mindszenty, the Archbishop of Hungary, who was tried and imprisoned for a number of years before being eventually freed. They both played a vital role in the downfall of European Communism, along with a great number of courageous dissidents such as the Russian writer Alexander Solzhenitsyn and the scientist Andrei Sakharov. An outstanding member of the large company of persecuted saints was Richard Wurmbrand the Romanian Lutheran pastor, born a Jew, who was imprisoned and tortured for fourteen years before being released in 1964.

A vitally important part was also played by the Polish trade union Solidarity led by Lech Walesa, a devout Catholic. This protest movement involved not only the workers but an influential group of

---

[8] 'The Early Church' p202,
[9] The Idea of a Christian Society, Appendix
[10] Towards a Christian Britain, Broadcast Talk 1941

intellectuals of whom Professor Gemerek was a leading light. It was he who said that Solidarity, a model of non-violent revolution, had shown that Communism was 'powerless in the face of a re-awakening society' and that it had helped to bring the Warsaw Pact to an end. (This idea of a reawakening sounds very similar to Eliot's conversion of social consciousness). Another remarkable member of Solidarity was Marek Edelman. He was a polish Jew, who nearly fifty years before had been the leader of the Warsaw ghetto uprising against the Nazis in 1942. All of these, and many thousands of other less well-known men and women, worked and fought courageously against the evil that stood in the way of the coming of the Kingdom.

Politicians were also major contributors, notably the Russian President Gorbachev, and later Boris Yeltsin in the East, and Margaret Thatcher and Ronald Reagan in the West. It was Gorbachev who introduced Glasnost and Perestroika, the openness and restructuring that were the distinctive features of his presidency and that paved the way for even more radical reform and for the end of communism. Another outstanding figure was Vaclav Havel, the much-jailed, dissident playwright-philosopher and human rights activist who became President of Czechoslovakia in 1989 after the fall of the Berlin Wall.

In addition there were countless numbers of people of faith all over the world who prayed and wrote articles and letters and many who visited the countries behind the Iron Curtain taking Bibles and other Christian literature, along with their support and encouragement. All these men and women and many thousands of others, aided by powerful social, economic and political factors, combined to bring about the collapse of the atheistic regime of Russian and East German Marxist Communism.

Another interesting factor was the failure of the communist authorities, when they attempted to get rid of the Scriptures, also to ban the novels of Tolstoy and Dostoyevsky that contain so much Christian conviction and instruction. Like all defective regimes Russian Communism was 'broken to pieces' in the end by 'the stone that its builders had rejected', that is, in truth, by Christ himself, whom they had attempted unsuccessfully to banish. (Luke 20:17-18). The 'Iron Curtain' of the Berlin Wall was pulled down as a symbol of this collapse, as Hitler and Nazi Germany had been brought down and crushed more than forty years previously. The eventual defeat of Nazi

Germany in Europe and of Japanese militarism in the Far East were both clearly due to the Allied war effort but it is possible with the eye of faith to see judgement at work as well, and to detect the hand of God in the eventual destruction of these evil regimes. A vital part was also played by courageous individuals in Germany including the martyred pastor, Dietrich Bonhoeffer.

Other shining examples of pressure exerted peacefully in the cause of human freedom were Mahatma Gandhi in India and Martin Luther King who led the opposition to Segregation in the United States. Nelson Mandela, Archbishop Desmond Tutu and President De Clerk, amongst others, contributed to the downfall of Apartheid in South Africa. Desmond Tutu also followed up his initial contribution with the establishing of the Commission for Truth and Reconciliation that did so much to lessen the anger and bitterness in the years that followed.

It is a mistake, however, to see the fall of Communism, or any other regime that we recognise as evil, or somehow inferior, as a vindication of our own culture. Capitalism may succeed in avoiding, at least to some degree, the spiritual desolation of Communism and its inefficiency and lack of economic incentives and of spiritual hope. But the freedom involved in private enterprise also lays it open to the human failings of greed and exploitation and the West has made terrible mistakes. Democracy, as it is exercised in the European Union, with six hundred MEPs representing almost a million constituents each, and accountable to no-one because no-one votes for them personally, is a depressing alternative to a totalitarian regime. The concentration of bureaucratic political power involved, combined with the absence of a spiritual vision, is interfering with the personal freedom and responsibility of the people of the member nations in a way that is reminiscent of the suffocating bureaucracy of the Soviet Union. We should expect our own United Kingdom politicians to curb this bureaucracy rather than contributing to it with more of their own. The leaders are collectively, for a variety of reasons, driving us towards the unattractive and dangerous goal of a world civilisation.

It would appear that we have a Hobson's choice: we can either have nation states that occasionally get at each other's throats or build empires that inevitably fall to pieces in the end, some more quickly than others. In Roger Scruton's book 'The Need for Nations', their advantages are described and the case for them is powerfully argued.

We have been given seemingly unlimited freedom to make political and financial decisions with tragic consequences that are frequently foreseeable. No progress can be made without having the confidence to take risks. The trouble is we don't know when to stop and failures are inevitable, but our lives and memories are too short to remember our past experience of them and determine to avoid them in the future. It is not the failures of those in positions of power in government and finance but the arrogance and lack of concern for the resulting hardship of others and the hunger for power and riches that should cause shame and to which blame attaches. It is here that spiritual and not simply political and economic principles are at stake.

There is much in our own individual moral and social behaviour of which we need to be deeply ashamed and for which we need to repent and ask forgiveness. Our own political institutions and practices are also susceptible to decay and to the inexorable judgement that is built into the historical process and into the very fabric of creation. Lord May said, in his Presidential Address to British Association of Science in Sept 2009, in connection with our attempts to counter climate change, that 'a supernatural punisher may be part of the solution.' He sees the need for us to be penalised for our wrongdoing and our inability to call ourselves and others to account. He is making a powerful case for reinventing the Old Testament God whom we have forgotten, though it must be said that he is much else besides a supernatural punisher and that faith provides no simple solutions to our treatment of the planet.

As history has shown, the Church itself, let alone so-called Christian countries, must have opponents in order to prevent it becoming over-powerful and proud and thus denying its mission, as it has done so often in the past. It can contribute to bringing about antagonism and enmity by its own failings and in its turn is obliged to listen to the comments of those who are outside it. The world needs the Church but the Church cannot do without the world.

We in Britain are increasingly described as a 'broken society'. If our civilisation has been so largely built upon the foundations of the Christian faith, how can we think that it can be mended by anything less than a return to this faith as a vital element in our recovery? Everything in our present day society cries out for repentance and a return to God and to a consciousness of inevitable judgement. Our Christian heritage is becoming increasingly hard to recognise and we cannot invent another story for ourselves. To quote T.S. Eliot again: 'It is only by returning to the eternal source of truth that we can hope for a social organisation which will not, to its ultimate destruction, ignore some essential aspect of reality.'[11] Human leaders at best only attempt to lead us towards interim goals and even they are never fully attained so that disappointment both for them and for those who elect them is almost inevitable.

It is only God's kingdom, yet to be fully revealed at the end of the age, that can provide a framework in which all aspects of reality are included: no political agenda can presume to do this. There have been numerous attempts to impose political solutions based on revolutionary philosophical concepts, and various visions of a utopian community, but they have all failed. What we need is not simply a political programme but a way of life for society that works for all its members. Only God himself can point and work towards his kingdom by operating through his Spirit in the lives of his people and enabling them to act more effectively as salt and light in their own communities. He also works by sending them as missionaries to other lands, though they do not always avoid bringing an alien culture along with the Gospel. We now have the experience of missionaries from elsewhere reminding us of what we have taught them about the Gospel in the past and of people all over the world praying for this country. Archbishop John Sentamu is an outstanding example. From time to time God provides an added impetus to this process by raising up prophets and evangelists and by granting us a fresh out-pouring of his Holy Spirit. The best-known of these prophets in our own country have been George Whitefield and John Wesley who were God's agents in the Evangelical Revival in the eighteenth century but there have been others both before and since that time.

The Church in the United Kingdom and in the rest of Europe is an increasingly small remnant and we should be looking to God in repentance and in prayer for his power to be revealed in our midst once again. There are remarkable examples of a return to God in other parts of the world, however, in Africa, Asia and South America. They reveal, as always, the need of a spirit of prayerful repentance and a desire for God's blessing, as the Old Testament prophets constantly emphasised. But above all they reveal the need of the indispensable

---

[11] The Idea of a Christian Society, p63

element of God's own sovereign action. In the words of Martyn Lloyd-Jones in his book 'Authority', 'Revival is altogether in the hands of God.' There have been numerous demonstrations of the inadequacy of our purely human initiatives and programmes without the empowering of his Holy Spirit.

There is for all these reasons a limit to what political leaders can achieve, though by no means all of them recognise it. By the same token no political party can properly presume to use the label Christian in its title. The kingdom of God is a spiritual and not a political kingdom, with a cosmic dimension that extends far beyond our limited horizon. This is not to say that government plays no part in its growth and development. Government plays a vital role in ensuring the safety of the realm, and in establishing law and order and guarding essential freedoms. It also provides for justice, not only through the courts but also in the workplace and the social sphere. Where it attempts to operate in the area of personal relationships, for instance in divorce, it is a great deal less successful. These provisions are all of them necessary in bringing about a stable society in which worship is unhindered, where faith can flourish and where others may be brought into the kingdom. Paradoxically, however, there are many examples throughout the history of the Church where it has flourished even more strongly under persecution.

It is our privilege and duty as responsible citizens to play some part in politics and at the very least to cast our vote when we have the opportunity to do so. Failure to do this even if we have only a very sketchy understanding of the issues is an invitation to the various forms of dictatorship that millions of men and women have given their lives to stamp out. For Christians, involvement in politics, as candidates or voters, can be a powerful way of giving substance to our prayers for the coming of the kingdom. This is especially so where efforts are made to reduce dishonest practices. Needless to say our faith will not necessarily determine which party we stand or vote for. Nor, to all outward appearances, will a lively Christian faith necessarily make a massive difference to the way that politicians govern. It is not easy for them to express their faith in drawing up their policies or in exercising their responsibilities. Legislation should ideally be framed and decisions made on Christian principles, where these need to be invoked, but politics is the art of the possible. It depends on the horizons of the electorate as well as of the politicians.

Christians in government cannot often succeed in translating their faith into dramatic action as Sir William Wilberforce was enabled to do.

Jesus, in his stunning answer in Mark 12:17 to the question about paying taxes to Caesar, designed by the Pharisees to catch him out – "Give to Caesar what is Caesar's, and to God what is God's" – made it clear that we have a dual loyalty, to God and to the State. We live in two worlds, though one is evidently enough for most people. We owe loyalty, as Paul emphasises in Rom 13:1-7, both to God and to the governing authorities that have been established by him in order to avoid anarchy. How Christians react to persecution from a godless state must surely remain a personal decision, however. Jesus' reply, which astonished and silenced his questioners, put his seal on the necessary distinction between the spiritual and political realms, between the sacred and the secular. They both need to be able to develop independently and cannot safely be locked into a single rigid system, as in Islam. Their relationship is discussed in the section on Secularisation in Appendix 5

The democratic process, the best we have for ensuring 'government of the people, by the people, for the people', is by no means perfect but as Churchill said, 'everything else is worse.' Like every human endeavour it is vulnerable to the failings of our human nature. These failings can destroy the benefits even of this apparently unarguable necessity. Democracy, like everything else in human affairs, must operate within a moral framework. It has been cynically said by the psychologist Oliver James, in his book 'Affluenza', that democracy in the English-speaking nations today has come to mean the 'handing over of a vast number of decisions and powers to others in return for the freedom to pursue egotistical, hedonistic choices'. Ideally, involvement and appropriate comment and criticism are necessary activities for a proportion of the citizens in every society. It is hard to justify trying to oblige other nations to adopt democracy when we value it so little ourselves. A percentage of people fail to vote at all and there is the ever-present risk of electoral fraud, in our own country as well as elsewhere, whatever electoral system is in operation – and no system is perfect. There is also the added problem that politicians often need to make undeliverable promises in order to get elected and are likely to disappoint their supporters. At its best democracy is more likely than not to leave up to fifty percent or more of the electorate disappointed and saddled with a government they did not vote for. In addition to all this conservatives may conserve what should be discarded, liberals may abandon essential principles and disciplines and socialists may overestimate what central government can achieve. Revolutionaries are likely to destroy much of what must be preserved as permanent truth.

George Orwell wrote in a personal letter: 'The real division is not between conservatives and revolutionaries but between authoritarians and libertarians'. God has given us a frightening degree of freedom that is misused by dictators to exercise hideous power over their citizens. The only truly great leaders are those who do not seek personal aggrandisement and power. A remarkable example is Queen Elizabeth 1 who in 1601, towards the end of her reign, spoke the following words to the members in the House of Commons in what was afterwards called the 'Golden Speech':

> "To be a king and wear a crown, is a thing more glorious
> to them that see it than it's pleasant to them that bear it:
> for myself, I was never so much enticed with the glorious
> name of a king, or the royal authority of a queen, as
> delighted that God hath made me his instrument to
> maintain his truth and glory, and to defend this kingdom
> from dishonour, damage , tyranny, and oppression."

True statesmanship is not possible without this element of spiritual discernment. Our present Queen, Elizabeth II, is a Christian sovereign who is similarly devoted to the service of her people and helps us to understand the working of God's own kingdom.

Dictatorships are alien to the way that God treats the members of his own everlasting kingdom, and will always therefore, sooner or later, be subject to his judgement. There is nothing quite so dangerous as the illusion of invincibility: the greatest error that dictators can make is to have themselves seen as gods, thus usurping the sovereignty that belongs to God alone. The king of ancient Babylon, as a type of tyrants of all ages, is recorded in Isaiah 14:13 as saying to himself, "I will ascend to heaven; I will raise my throne above the stars of God ... I will make myself like the Most High." There have been many powerful leaders in history of whom it has been asked in amazement when they have gone, as Isaiah asked of this Babylonian king only a few verses later, "Is this the man who shook the earth and made kingdoms tremble?" The late President Ceausescu of Romania was a more recent example of a dictator who experienced a precipitate departure from power.

The only people who can be trusted with power are those who are not seeking it for their own ends and whose aim is rather to be servants and healers. Whether a leader presides over a city state or a nation state, an empire or a federal union, neither he nor the system of government is immune from the potentially fatal flaws in human nature that may lead to a failure to obey God's laws and help to bring about their downfall. In the words of Isaiah in 2:17 'The arrogance of man will be brought low and the pride of men humbled' – though it may take a very long time.

It was man's arrogance that made God's servant Samuel hesitate to anoint a king over Israel and risk jeopardising their primary loyalty to God himself. It brought about the need for Magna Carta to curb the power and corruption of King John and gives rise to the need to oppose dictatorships, by whatever means are necessary. We have had a number of recent examples of this dilemma. Jesus told us in Matthew 24:4 that there would be 'wars and rumours of wars'. God's kingdom is 'not of this world' so that we cannot fight to impose it, as Jesus told his disciples in John 18:36. The majority would nevertheless agree that we may sometimes need to fight and even to kill, once all diplomatic efforts have failed, in order to destroy evil regimes that pose a threat to the territory or the safety of other countries and murder innocent people:

It is the Soldier

It is the Soldier, not the minister
Who has given us the freedom of religion.

It is the Soldier, not the reporter
Who has given us the freedom of the press.

It is the Soldier, not the poet
Who has given us freedom of speech.

It is the Soldier, not the campus organiser
Who has given us freedom to protest.

It is the Soldier, not the lawyer
Who has given us the right to a fair trial.

It is the Soldier, not the politician
Who has given us the right to vote.

It is the Soldier who salutes the flag,
Who serves beneath the flag,
Whose coffin is draped by the flag,
Who allows the protester to burn the flag. [12]

It is above all, to those who have given the 'last full measure of devotion'[13] that we owe our hard won rights and freedoms. In the dark days before the 'Battle of Britain' in June 1940 Winston Churchill told the House of Commons that "Upon this battle depends the survival of Christian civilisation." These words were unusually explicit and a decision to take up arms is not in most cases consciously made in these terms. There are time-honoured criteria for making a decision on what can be claimed as a 'just war'. Each situation has to be considered on its own merits according to these criteria but they are not always easy to interpret. The majority accept that never to take up arms, attractive option though it may be, is tantamount to condoning evil and allowing it to triumph. None of us can neglect our duties to our own community and to other communities. Conflict is inevitable and we cannot turn the other cheek collectively. Teilhard de Chardin wrote, also in the Epilogue of his Milieu Divin: 'One day the Gospel tells us, the tension gradually accumulating between humanity and God will touch the limits prescribed by the possibilities of the world. And then will come the end.' It would seem that the earth cannot endlessly survive the pressure to which we are subjecting it and there will be no lasting peace until Jesus returns.

---

[12] A Reflection Charles M Province
[13] Lincoln, A. Gettysburg Address

The Good News, as Jesus constantly emphasised, is that the kingdom is 'at hand'. In spite of all appearances to the contrary it has been gradually developing throughout history as God continues to work out his often inscrutable purposes. In spite of all opposition it will one day be established in order to put an end to these tribulations, whether we look and work for it individually or not. The bad news, for those who are not interested in what they hear about it, is that there would appear to be, in the end, nowhere else to go. God does not prescribe any specific culture: it would not be consistent with the freedom he has given us. He does not provide a specific agenda but rather invites us to co-operate with him in the building of his kingdom in our own individual ways. He offers us salvation in Christ; the one thing that we cannot achieve for ourselves, and leaves the rest to us. "Work out your own salvation with fear and trembling, for it is God who works in you to will and to act according to his good purpose," as Paul tells us in Phil 2:12. President Kennedy was expressing this same truth when he spoke in his Inaugural Address in 1961 of 'asking his blessing and his help but knowing that here on earth God's work must truly be our own.'

There are other religions that have arisen both before and after Jesus' time on which a number of rich and varied cultures have been founded, as our own has been established so largely on Judaeo-Christian foundations. What the Bible reveals, implicitly throughout the Old and New Testaments and explicitly in Rev 21:24-26, is that all these cultures will in the end, where they survive the judgement, find their definitive destiny in the kingdom of God. Isaiah speaks in 9:6 of the child who is born and the Son who is given and says of him that 'the government will be upon his shoulders.' He alone can be relied on to govern with authority and justice. In Jesus' own words in Mk 10: 42-44, "You know that those who are regarded as rulers of the Gentiles lord it over them. Not so with you. Instead, whoever wants to be great among you must be your servant, and whoever wants to be first must be slave of all." In order to forward our human endeavours a certain spirit of competitiveness is required without which no progress is possible. What is also needed is a people who, without loss of an essential vigour, see beyond the bid for power and demonstrate the values of the kingdom that are necessary in order to point the way towards the destiny that God has for his whole creation.

Christians are bound to believe that whatever shape the Kingdom of Heaven finally assumes, it will be the Kingdom of the God and Father of our Lord and Saviour Jesus Christ, whatever surprises it may have in store for them. The colossal variety of peoples who are made in God's image and who colour his world with their many different languages, cultures, religions and histories must, in the end, find their fulfilment and destiny in him. It is not that all men must become Christians so that the Church will come to dominate the world, but that those who do should influence it with the flavour of Christ and light the way towards the goal that God has for it and for his people.

He will not compel us to enter his kingdom but there is no other coherent programme that has ever been envisaged for the world. Those who have the opportunity would do well to start looking and working and praying for it now. Jesus spoke in one of his parables, in Luke 14:23, of a certain man who sent his servants out into the roads and country lanes to issue powerful invitations to the people to come to his banquet. This was "so that my house may be full" and the invitations had to be issued because the Jews who were originally invited had failed to respond. It had always been God's intention to include the Gentiles in his kingdom. This is made plain in Isaiah 49:6, in the teaching of Jesus and in the ministry of Paul, and it has been confirmed throughout the past two thousand years of history. The invitation remains open but many are continuing to ignore it. Jesus tells us in John 14:2 that his house has ample accommodation and it is not yet full. He longs to welcome us at the banquet of his kingdom.

George Herbert writes about his individual, Christian experience of this invitation, in more intimate terms, in his beautiful poem entitled 'Love':

"You must sit down," says Love, "and taste my meat."

He is describing an extraordinary provision.

ST JOHN'S GOSPEL

John wrote his gospel, possibly as late as 90 AD, with the express purpose that 'you may believe that Jesus is the Christ, the Son of God, and that by believing you may have life in his name.' Like the synoptic gospels it is a statement of faith in Jesus as God's Son and an encouragement to believe in him, not simply a biography. It is a brilliant piece of creative writing with a similar overall construction to the other gospels but often describing different events and personal encounters in Jesus' ministry and providing a different selection of his teachings. John's record concentrates more on Jesus' teaching about eternal life than about the kingdom in which this eternal life is lived with God, which is the emphasis in the other Gospels. He also records those occasions when Jesus uses metaphors to reveal the nature and significance of his own person, rather than parables to reveal the nature of the kingdom that he came to inaugurate. But there is no contradiction between his account and that of the other Evangelists. Jesus and his message are instantly recognisable in both and the two different emphases demonstrate clearly that Jesus himself is the Good News that all four of them are at pains to present. They complement rather than contradict each other.

THE MYSTERY OF THE INCARNATION

'In the beginning was the Word, and the Word was with God, and the Word was God. He was with God in the beginning.'

In the idea of the eternal Word becoming flesh, John has given us an inspired expression of the central message of the Christian faith. It is this idea above all that is of such extraordinary quality that humanly speaking it must have taken many years to germinate. The depth of John's thinking alone could explain the fact that this Gospel was written later than the others. At the start of the Gospel, in place of the birth story, John has a reflective, imaginative prologue that gives the most sustained and profound presentation of Jesus anywhere in scripture, except perhaps that of St Paul in Philippians 2:5-11. It is introduced by a striking and powerful metaphor that is reminiscent of the start of Genesis: 'In the beginning was the Word, and the Word was with God, and the Word was God. He was with God in the beginning.' John makes use of the Greek word Logos in order to reveal Jesus the eternal Son as the exact image and expression of God the Father. John goes on to say: 'Through him all things were made; without him nothing was made that was made.' John presents Jesus as somehow both the co-creator and the blueprint of the universe. Dabar, the Hebrew equivalent of the Greek Logos, was used for God's word spoken through Moses and the other prophets in the Old Testament. Logos had a rich and varied meaning, from human reason and its expression, to the divine, creative, sustaining wisdom and power of God and his self-revelation. This self-revelation was ultimately expressed in his appearing in human likeness in the incarnation of his Son Jesus Christ who 'became flesh and made his dwelling among us … full of grace and truth,' thus extending the meaning of Logos even further. So much so that the Word comes to be used of the Gospel itself. This enfleshment of the Word is the essence of the miracle of the incarnation: if we believe this then everything else follows. It is the central truth of God's revelation of himself and the supreme mystery with which the early Church struggled in the formulation of the creeds. Paul talks in the passage in Philippians of Jesus being 'made in human likeness', and being 'found in appearance as a man'. How he can have emptied himself in order to do this is a question that we cannot answer.

ST JOHN'S GOSPEL CONTINUES

John's gospel contains many treasures that are not found in the other gospels. In the second chapter he describes the presence of Jesus at the marriage at Cana, where the One who is himself the bridegroom in relation to his bride the Church, performs his first miracle of changing water into wine. It remains true that if you invite Jesus you are assured of a good party: he makes a difference wherever he goes, though not necessarily in this particular way! There is no record of the names of the uniquely privileged couple, and no record of his attending any other wedding. The Gospels tell us of a number of meals that Jesus shared with friends, not all of them considered suitable companions by the self-righteous religious authorities, and on several occasions he referred to the kingdom as a feast.

In the third chapter John records a night-time visit paid to Jesus by Nicodemus, a Pharisee and a member of the Jewish ruling council, or Sanhedrin. Jesus told him that he could not see or enter the kingdom of God unless he was born again, which perplexed him – as it has perplexed many people in the church ever since. We need first to understand the truth about our natural birth into this familiar life before we can attempt to understand what Jesus was saying to Nicodemus about our rebirth into the less familiar eternal life. Nicodemus clearly thought he had come for a cosy chat. "Rabbi," he began, "we know you are a teacher who has come from God. For no-one could perform the miraculous signs you are doing if God were not with him." But he was corrected rather than congratulated. Jesus told him bluntly: "This is the verdict: Light is come into the world, but men loved darkness instead of light because their deeds were evil." He was not deterred however, and we read later, in John 20:39, that he came back to help Joseph of Arimathea with Jesus' burial. His meeting with Jesus must have made an indelible impression on him.

NEW BIRTH AND ETERNAL LIFE

Jesus expresses surprise that an educated man like Nicodemus cannot readily understand the idea of being born again but it is unfamiliar and we can sympathise with him. To be born physically is to enter, and hence to become alive, to a new environment; in our case to be expelled from the fluid environment of the womb and begin to breathe in the air of the outside world from which we thereafter obtain our oxygen. To be born again is to enter a new spiritual environment that is no less than God himself and thereby to become alive to him. We die to our old way of life without him in the same way that we died to our life in the womb when we were born: death and new life are inseparably linked.

Jesus makes it clear that this death and spiritual rebirth is an essential element in the Christian experience of conversion and not an option as is sometimes implied. If you are alive to God as a Christian you must have been born again: if you are not born again you cannot be said to be alive to God, and as Jesus told Nicodemus, you cannot enter the kingdom of God. "This is eternal life" Jesus tells us later, in 17:3, "that they may know you, the only true God, and Jesus Christ whom you have sent."

This life is the way that John uses to describe our membership of God's kingdom. It has been made possible by Christ's death for us on the Cross and through the operation of the Holy Spirit living in us. Jesus says in 10:10: "I have come that they may have life, and have it to the full." Our birth into this 'full' eternal life with God can quite legitimately be seen as a further stage in our evolutionary development. It is the means whereby we achieve a foretaste of our destiny as human beings and is analogous to the gradual change of certain species from an aquatic to an air-breathing terrestrial environment at an earlier stage in the history of evolution.

The chief characteristic of this new life is not its endlessness but the quality of the relationship that is involved, without which an eternal life in heaven, or anywhere else, would be intolerable! It will be not only tolerable but endlessly enriching. This will be because God's infinite and eternal nature and our increasing knowledge and love of him and all that he has made, in company with others, will be an unceasing source of joy. To be known and loved by God in this life is to be already in an altogether new sphere of living in which communion with him in prayer should be as natural as breathing. It is also to be immune from ultimate spiritual death so that our physical death has lost its sting and victory. Our physical death is to be seen rather as the necessary gateway into the final phase of our endless, eternal spiritual life in fellowship with God.

This new and endless eternal life begins here and now in this present world for those who seek it. We are born by natural means into our family of origin and we may marry into another earthly family. We have the privilege, through our relationship with Jesus, of this rebirth into God's family, the Church. In this family he adopts us as his sons and daughters to live with him, and with our earthly brothers and sisters, now and for all eternity. Our entry into membership of the Church is symbolised by the water of baptism (literally meaning 'plunged') that is the outward and visible sign and celebration of our new life and our acceptance into God's family. Baptism does not make us Christians but it symbolises the faith we have declared or, in the case of infant baptism, the faith and hope of our parents that we will one day wish to make that declaration for ourselves. We thereby become heirs with Christ of the inheritance that he has won for us – the joys of which we cannot even guess:

> 'No eye has seen,
>   no ear has heard,
>   no mind has conceived
>   what God has prepared for those who love him' -
>   But God has revealed it to us by his Spirit. (1 Cor 2:9,10)

This new spiritual life is subject to the same laws and principles as our physical life. These include the laws of growth and development and the need to be tended and nurtured, in this case by developing our relationship with Jesus in the fellowship of his Church. "Apart from me," he tells us in John 15:3, "you can do nothing," – any more than a plant can survive without water and the sun's warmth, and roots that go down into the soil from which it draws its nourishment. Scientifically speaking one of the chief characteristics of both physical and spiritual life is its correspondence with the environment. In the spiritual life it is correspondence with God who is our spiritual environment. Our correspondence with him is both conformity and communication. It is conformity through communication – through the prayer that is a natural outcome of our new life in him. The ideal result of this is that we become like him through our communion with him and through his transforming and regenerating spiritual influence. This eternal spiritual life involves a correspondence that can never be abolished because it is correspondence with an environment that can never cease to be. The sole ground of this confident hope and expectation is the Resurrection. Without this there is no evidence or guarantee of victory over death, no Gospel and no promise of eternal life with God.

JOHN CONTINUES IN CHAPTER 4

In his fourth chapter John tells the story of Jesus' meeting with the Samaritan woman at the well. For a man and a woman to meet alone was frowned on by the Jews and further than that this woman was a Samaritan, with whom Jews did not associate. Jesus broke all the rules and the resulting dialogue must surely be the most remarkable conversation ever recorded anywhere. He speaks to her not only about her five husbands and the man with whom she is now living who, as he tells her, is not her husband, but also about worship and about his being the Messiah. It demands to be read. Get a Bible and read it now! It is recorded that many Samaritans came to believe that 'this man really is the Saviour of the world' because of her testimony and Jesus' own subsequent teaching.

The following eight chapters are an extraordinary blend of teaching and miracles and reports of mounting opposition from the Jewish authorities. This opposition is countered by Jesus with sharp and withering challenges to them to read and interpret the Scriptures and to think clearly about their true meaning. Their determination to arrest and kill him and their attempts to do so are mentioned frequently, but they fail 'because his time had not yet come'. He is in control as John is at pains to emphasise everywhere.

In chapter 5 Jesus heals the sick man at the pool of Bethesda on the Sabbath – this again is recorded only recorded by John – and as a result, he is persecuted by the Jews. Because Jesus refers to God as his Father they 'tried all the harder to kill him' because he was 'making himself equal with God.' He explains to them that he only does what he sees his Father doing. The work that he is doing testifies that the Father has sent him, but because they fail to understand what Moses, who was their authority, wrote about him they cannot believe him. They are silenced by his detailed defence of his position.

In chapter 6 John records the feeding of the five thousand, as do the other Gospel writers. He follows it however, with Jesus' teaching of the greater truth that he is himself the 'bread of life', the 'true bread from heaven' that his Father gives them and that 'endures to eternal life.' The Jews question how the one they know as the son of Joseph can have come down from heaven and how he is able to give them the 'living bread' of his own flesh to eat, and we can sympathise with

Catching God at Work

them. The other Gospel writers refer to Jesus giving the disciples bread at the last supper that they are instructed to continue to use in remembrance of him as a symbol of this living bread. John goes on to tell us that on hearing this 'hard teaching ... many of his disciples turned back and no longer followed him.' To make things even more threatening Jesus knew that one of those who stayed was later to betray him.

He is surrounded by problems and they continue in chapter 7 when he purposely stays away from Judea because the Jews there are waiting to take his life. When he goes to Jerusalem, to the Feast of Tabernacles, the Jews are watching for him and when he asks them why they are trying to kill him the crowd accuse him of being demon-possessed. When he speaks to them of their not knowing the Father from whom he has come they try to seize him. Many put their trust in him, however, so that the people were divided because of him. To the fury of the Pharisees, the temple guards who are sent to arrest him return empty-handed saying that "No-one ever spoke the way this man does." Nicodemus advises them to find out what he is doing before condemning him. The battle continues to rage around him.

Chapter 8 begins with the story of the woman taken in adultery which must be read for its poignancy and its demonstration of Jesus' brilliance in resolving a dilemma that would have defeated all but the One who can himself forgive sins. He alone can be truly both pastoral and prophetic at one and the same time; who can both minister to her and forgive her – and tell her not to do it again. He next announces that he is the light of the world and is immediately challenged by the Pharisees for being his own witness, thus invalidating his testimony. This he counters by claiming the Father who sent him as his other witness. The argument continues and finally Jesus tells them that when they have 'lifted up the Son of Man' – that is, when they have crucified him – they will know that he is the one he claims to be. And again 'many put their faith in him.' Jesus says to those of them who hold to his teaching and are really his disciples: "Then you will know the truth, and the truth will set you free." This starts the Jews off once more, this time claiming that as descendants of Abraham they have never been slaves of anyone. Jesus makes it clear to them that they are not following Abraham's example, though they claim to be his children. After further heated dialogue he says to them: "I tell you the truth before Abraham was born, I am." This powerful and unequivocal statement, in which he clearly identifies himself with the God who revealed himself to Moses in Exodus 3:14, is the last straw and they try to stone him. But he hides himself and slips away. Some scholars have claimed that a first century Jewish carpenter could not have made this statement, as well as others that are attributed to him by John. But it would appear more reasonable to believe that he did than to suppose that the most sublime words of the One we worship needed to be made up for him by one of his followers.

In chapter 9 John describes at length the healing of the man born blind, another miracle that he alone records. It contains some wonderful dialogue involving Jesus, the blind man and his parents and neighbours, and the Pharisees, who are predictably incensed because, yet again, the healing happens on the Sabbath! They tell the man that Jesus is a sinner to which he tartly and courageously replies: "Whether he is a sinner or no, I don't know. One thing I do know. I was blind but now I see!" "How dare you lecture us", they say to him, and throw him out. Others as well as the man himself are also naturally impressed and once again this causes division.

In chapter 10 Jesus speaks once again in metaphor, describing himself as "the good shepherd who lays down his life for the sheep," who follow him because they know his voice. He also describes himself as the gate for the sheep so that "whoever enters through me will be saved." He speaks of having other sheep that are not of this sheep pen, which he must bring also so that there will be one flock and one shepherd. In speaking of these other sheep he is clearly referring to the Gentiles. Later Jesus is in Jerusalem once again and the Jews ask him: "How long will you keep us in suspense? If you are the Christ, tell us plainly." He tells them he has already made it plain, but they do not believe. "The miracles I do in my Father's name speak for me but you do not believe because you are not my sheep." His sheep have been given him by his Father who is greater than all and no-one can snatch them out of his hand. "I and my Father are one" he continues and again the Jews pick up stones to stone him – for blasphemy this time, "because you, a mere man, claim to be God." He argues with them decisively from their own scriptures and again they try to seize him, but he escapes their grasp.

Chapter 11 consists mainly of a description of the raising of Lazarus that is perhaps the most remarkable account in any of the gospels of Jesus' authority and power and love. It is followed by the usual and by now predictable division. Some believe, and the Pharisees call a meeting of the Sanhedrin. One of their number, Caiaphas, who was high priest that year speaks up and says that "it is better that one man die for the people than that the whole nation perish." John tells us that 'He did not say this on his own, but as high priest that year he prophesied that Jesus would die for the Jewish nation, and not only for that nation but also for the scattered children of God, to bring them together and make them one.' 'So from that day they plot to take his life.' What irony that Caiaphas should have been instrumental, more perhaps than any other, in helping to fulfil his own unwitting prophecy. For good measure the chief priests make plans to kill Lazarus as well because 'on account of him many of the Jews were putting their faith in Jesus'. The pace of opposition is accelerating.

Chapter 12, following a description of Jesus' triumphal entry into Jerusalem, returns to an account of the fury of the Pharisees at the publicity value of the raising of Lazarus. It also returns to the failure of the people to understand Jesus when he predicts his death. They had thought that the Christ would remain for ever but he urges them to "walk in the light just a little while longer before darkness overtakes you." He has made it as clear as he can but they are blinded, as foretold in Isaiah 6:10. Nevertheless, yet again, 'many, even among the leaders believed in him. But because of the Pharisees they would not confess their faith for fear they would be put out of the synagogue; for they loved praise from men more than praise from God.' We can understand their reluctance: they cannot know until after the resurrection and Pentecost how clearly Jesus and their faith in him will be vindicated. This passage helps us to understand Jesus' claim in Luke 10:57 that his coming will create division rather than peace.

In Chapter 13 where John records the last supper he does not mention Jesus giving the bread and wine of his body and blood to his disciples but describes Jesus 'showing the full extent of his love' by his washing of their feet. In a memorable verse he says, 'Jesus knew that the Father had put all things under his power, and that he had come from God and was returning to God; so he got up from the meal and began to wash his disciples' feet.' It would appear that his certainty of his origin and his destiny gives him the security and freedom to serve others. Jesus, above all, could say: 'In my beginning is my end.' What if we and all of his disciples nowadays also had something of this certainty and security in believing and we were also able to disregard our own pride and status and carry out Jesus' instruction to 'wash one another's feet'? – both literally and metaphorically. Paul speaks in 2 Cor 4:5 of 'Jesus Christ as Lord, and ourselves as your servants for Jesus' sake'. As Jesus tells us here, he is our model and example in this as in all else. It has been said that we seek him on the throne of grace and find him kneeling at our feet.

In chapters 14 to 17, before the account of his arrest in chapter 18, there is a record, in place of the story of his agony in the garden of Gethsemane, of a series of exchanges with his disciples. They take the form of sustained, profound spiritual teaching and of Jesus' prayers for himself and for his disciples and for all subsequent believers. These chapters contain some of the most wonderful and most-quoted things that Jesus is recorded as saying. He speaks of there being "many rooms" in his Father's house and of himself as being "the way and the truth and the life" and he says that "no-one comes to the Father except through me." He also makes the startling claim that "Anyone who has seen me has seen the Father," which they naturally cannot understand and is still almost equally hard for us to understand even now. Referring to his predictions of his death he tells them that "I have told you now before it happens, so that when it does happen you will believe." In this revealing explanation he spells out the vitally important function of prophecy as a means of increasing our faith and confidence in God's sovereignty.

In chapter 15 Jesus describes himself as the 'true vine' and his Father as the gardener. We are the branches and the gardener "cuts off every branch in me that bears no fruit, while every branch that does bear fruit he prunes so that it will be even more fruitful." He tells us that unless we remain in him we will bear no fruit and that "apart from me you can do nothing." He goes on to say "You are my friends if you do what I command" – if you "love each other." There is much of comfort but also of challenge and warning: "If they persecuted me, they will persecute you also."

In chapter 16 he tells his disciples that in the end and above all there is love and reassurance, "so that in me you may have peace." And there is the extraordinary promise: "I tell you the truth, my Father will give you whatever you ask in my name." Jesus promises that when the time comes for him to leave them he will ask the Father to send them another Counsellor, the Holy Spirit, to be with them for ever, so that they will not be orphans. The Spirit will guide them into all truth: he will remind them of everything that he has said, and tell them what is yet to come. Towards the end of the chapter Jesus tells the disciples: "I came from the Father and entered the world; now I am leaving the world and going back to the Father." They are words that lead the disciples to say to him: "Now you are speaking clearly and without figures of speech. Now we see that you know all things and that you do not even need to have anyone ask you questions. This makes us believe that you came from God." "You believe at last!" Jesus answers. "But a time is coming, and has come, when you will be scattered, each to his own home. In this world you will have trouble. I have told you these things, so that in me you may have peace. But take heart! I have overcome the world."

In chapter 17 there follows the great so-called high-priestly prayer in which Jesus prays for his disciples and "for all those who will believe in me through their message." He goes on to ask his Father that "the love you have for me may be in them and that I myself may be in them." Towards the very end of this passage is his prayer to his Father for us and for all believers that we may live in love and unity. He asks that "they may be in us so that the world may believe that you have sent me." Maybe John was able, alone of all the disciples, to record these intimate sayings of Jesus because he listened to him more carefully. Or maybe it was because he spent more time in private discussions with his Lord. In that this whole chapter is a prayer that Jesus addresses to his Father it may be that John, and possibly the other disciples, were present with him at the time and John was enabled to remember it.

John's account of Jesus' arrest, trial, crucifixion and resurrection in the next three chapters is very similar to that in the other Gospels. It has already been included, together with several additional details to which he alone refers, along with the synoptic accounts of these events. The description in chapter 21 of Jesus' post-resurrection appearance that includes the miraculous catch of fish and Jesus cooking the disciples' breakfast, and Peter's reinstatement, are again peculiar to John. These also have been described already in the section devoted to these appearances. John ends his gospel with the telling words that "Jesus did many other things as well. If every one of them were written down, I suppose that even the whole world

would not have room for the books that would be written." They
would have to describe the whole of creation!

LIGHT

Light is a recurring theme from one end of Scripture to the other. It
appears more frequently in St John's Gospel than in any other New
Testament book and for this reason it has been included here. At the
very beginning of the first chapter of Genesis God calls forth light and
he is himself frequently referred to, literally and metaphorically, as
light. He is in himself the eternal light of which the light of the sun
and all the stars of the universe is but a pale image and reflection. He
is the light that reveals all else for what it really is, as Paul tells us in
Eph 5:13. All else in turn, because it is an image and reflection of its
creator, casts light on him for us and on his 'invisible qualities – his
eternal power and divine nature.'. (Rom 1:20). He is the King of kings
and Lord of lords who lives in unapproachable light and who cannot
be seen with mortal eyes. (1 Tim 6:15,16). If we are unable to look at
the sun without being blinded how much less could we, in our present,
physical body, gaze on God and live. The Psalms and the Prophets
speak of him and of his Word in scripture as the everlasting light that
lights our path. (Is 60:19 and Ps 119:105).

In the first chapter of his Gospel John describes Jesus as 'the true
light that gives light to every man.' Later, in 8:12, he records Jesus
saying to the people: "I am the light of the world" – though the world
does not recognise him. In Luke 2:32 Simeon, who was 'waiting for
the consolation of Israel', when he saw the child Jesus, praised God
and described Jesus as "a light to lighten the Gentiles and for glory to
your people Israel." The light is not understood however and is often
purposely avoided because it shows up our evil deeds for what they
are, as Jesus tells us in Jn 3:20. The secret of human fellowship is that
we should walk together in God's light – and thereby ourselves be
light and salt to the world. (Mt 5:14).

In Revelation 21:23,24 there is a description of the heavenly city
where God will be all in all and dwell with men and there will be no
need of the sun and the moon 'for the glory of God gives it light and
the Lamb is its lamp. The nations will walk in its light, and the kings
of the earth will bring their splendour into it.' We can have no real
idea of the reality of this prophecy but the fact that anyone can be

given to write words as uplifting as these is arguably a strong reason for thinking that he is expressing spiritual truth. God himself is the ultimate source of light as he is of everything else.

ACTS

Luke set himself an almost impossible task when he attempted to give his friend and patron Theophilus an account of the most important events and personalities in the first thirty years of the Christian Church in only twenty eight short chapters. He was clearly inspired, like the writers of the Gospels, to be able to select his material and to condense and simplify it with such great care and skill. He cannot be expected to have given us a complete picture or to have enabled us to work out the precise timing of some of the events he describes. Many things must have happened during those thirty years that he could not have known about, let alone passed on to us. But Luke accompanied Paul on at least part of three of his four journeys and this giant among the early apostles is the central figure in Acts. Without this unique book, which provides the only record of the coming of the Spirit and the early years of the New Testament Church, we should have had no real understanding of the initial and enduring impact of Jesus Christ on the world. It reveals the way in which the Christian faith spread from Jerusalem, through Asia Minor and Greece, and on to Rome.

Luke begins his dramatic story where he ended his Gospel. He describes how on one occasion during the forty days of his post-resurrection appearances, Jesus commands his disciples: "Do not leave Jerusalem, but wait for the gift my Father promised ... you will receive power when the Holy Spirit comes on you; and you will be my witnesses in Jerusalem, and in all Judea and Samaria, and to the ends of the earth." 'After he said this he was taken up before their very eyes, and a cloud hid him from their sight.' Two men in white tell them that "this same Jesus, who has been taken from you into heaven, will come back in the same way you have seen him go into heaven."

After this final, decisive departure the disciples returned to Jerusalem where they spent their time in prayer, but as Jesus had told them they had no power to witness until the coming of the Holy Spirit. On the day of Pentecost, ten days after the Ascension, when the disciples were all together, 'suddenly a sound like the blowing of a violent wind came from heaven and filled the whole house where they were sitting. They saw what seemed to be tongues of fire that separated and came to rest on each of them. All of them were filled with the Holy Spirit and they began to speak in other tongues,' thus enabling visitors from many nations 'to hear the wonders of God in our own tongues.'

The people asked "What does this mean?" Peter at once stood up with unaccustomed courage and explained to them that this was the fulfilment of the prophecy in Joel 2:28:

> "In these last days, I will pour out my Spirit on all people. Your sons and daughters will prophesy, your young men will see visions, your old men will dream dreams."

It means that God, having made us in his own image, and been able, through this affinity, to appear to us in the likeness of man in Jesus, is now able to become embodied in us through his Holy Spirit. This unique event can be likened to a second 'Big Bang' in which God's Holy Spirit, who had previously only become embodied in certain privileged individuals in the Old Testament, is now available to all who would receive him, by virtue of their belief in Jesus. This could not have happened until he had appeared in order to provide us with a model and example; there would have been no image for the Spirit to make real to us in our own hearts. It is a perfect partnership, in which the Father is also made known to us.

When the Holy Spirit came upon the disciples at Pentecost they were changed men. Like the Old Testament prophets they had to be called and anointed by the Holy Spirit before they could speak for God. It was not what they made of the evidence of his resurrection but what God made of them that enabled them to be his courageous witnesses to it. After Jesus had ascended and left them on their own, the fact that they knew that he had risen and that they had seen him alive and touched him and eaten with him on a number of occasions was somehow not enough to enable them to share the Good News. Until he was alive in them through the power of the Holy Spirit the early disciples were not truly alive themselves. They did not have the courage and conviction to speak to others of his resurrection in a world that was hostile to the Gospel, as it still is today. Peter, the one who had so recently denied Jesus to a servant girl, could not otherwise have become fearless even though he had visited the empty tomb and seen his risen Lord. Only by waiting for the coming of power from on high was Peter given the authority, even the very words he needed, to preach the first sermon of the newborn Christian Church and to face opposition and persecution. The change that came about in the lives of these early disciples at Pentecost must surely be the most compelling evidence for the truth of the Gospel story.

It is only when truth becomes a part of us that we can communicate it with conviction. If the Holy Spirit had not come at Pentecost the Crucifixion and Resurrection would have been forgotten when those who had witnessed them had died because there would have been no power to enable them, or those who came after them, to proclaim the Good News. There would have been no Gospel and no Church, and no future generation would have taken up the baton. It had to be handed on by those who had seen Jesus crucified, seen the empty tomb, seen their risen Lord after his resurrection and above all been empowered by the Holy Spirit. Jesus the Son was necessarily limited by the brief span of his earthly life and the Father by his inevitable invisibility. We need God's agent to be with us and in us if we are to be effective witnesses. We cannot serve him in our own strength. Without the Comforter, God's Holy Spirit, whom Jesus asked the Father to send for us when he had ascended, his Church has no power.

When Peter had convinced the people at the close of his sermon that the One whom they had crucified was none other than the Christ, they were cut to the heart and asked him and the other disciples, "Brothers, what shall we do?" Peter replied, "Repent and be baptised, every one of you in the name of Jesus Christ for the forgiveness of your sins. And you will receive the gift of the Holy Spirit." He pleaded with them to "Save yourselves from this corrupt generation" and about three thousand of them accepted his message and were baptised and added to their number that day. Following this the believers 'devoted themselves to the apostles' teaching and to the fellowship, to the breaking of bread and to prayer. Everyone was filled with awe, and many wonders and miraculous signs were done by the apostles. All the believers were together and had everything in common. Selling their possessions and goods, they gave to anyone as he had need.' Naturally this extraordinary level of commitment could not be maintained as a permanent feature of Church life but in this remarkable series of events we can see evidence of the explosive beginning of God's programme. His plan was that the Holy Spirit, living in men, would bring into existence the New Israel of the Church that would continue the mission of demonstrating and proclaiming the kingdom of God that Christ came to bring to the world. Thereafter in Acts the Spirit is active, filling the apostles (4:8, 31), guiding, directing, even compelling them (16:7, 20:22, 21:4), warning them of danger (20:23) and on occasion enabling them to prophesy. (11:28).

The remainder of the Acts of the Apostles is about the growth of the new Church and the active resistance to it. Above all it is about the conversion of Saul, later known as Paul, about his remarkable ministry, his missionary journeys and his last years in Rome. The book of Acts must be read in order to appreciate the pace and excitement of the story it has to tell. Until his dramatic encounter with the risen Lord and his conversion on the road to Damascus Paul had been persecuting the Church and was present at the stoning of Stephen. He was 'giving approval to his death', even 'guarding the clothes of those who were killing him.' Stephen's death was followed by a great persecution of the Church that led to a scattering of all except the apostles throughout Judea and Samaria and those who had been scattered preached the word wherever they went. By his involvement in Stephen's death Paul was already contributing, albeit unintentionally, to this first wave of missionary activity, even before his conversion. How many more seemingly accidental events has God used in his strategy for spreading the Good News?

Paul might have seemed an unlikely choice but he must surely have been the only man alive at that time, or possibly at any other time, who could have done the job that God had for him to do. His calling was intensely dramatic. All the rules of engagement seem to have been broken. There was no cajoling as there was with Moses, no "Who will go for us?" as in the call of Isaiah and no opportunity to acquiesce as with Mary. Whilst on the road to Damascus to take members of the Church as prisoners to Jerusalem, Saul was suddenly surrounded by a light from heaven. He fell to the ground and heard a voice say to him, "Saul, Saul, why do you persecute me?" "Who are you Lord" he asked. "I am Jesus, whom you are persecuting. Now get up and go into the city, and you will be told what you must do." Everyone gets individual treatment: the masterful Saul had finally met his match and was issued with this curt instruction. He was blinded for three days by the brightness of the light of his vision until one of the disciples, Ananias, was sent to lay hands on him so that his sight could be restored and he could be filled with the Spirit.

He was at first naturally viewed with suspicion by the other apostles and believers but this was apparently overcome and he was soon preaching in the synagogues in Damascus that Jesus is the Son of God. What a transformation! He tells us himself in his letter to the Galatians that he had first spent a necessary time of preparation in the desert. It was not long before his preaching led the Jews to conspire to kill him but this was thwarted by his followers who took him by night and lowered him in a basket through an opening in the wall. There is never a dull moment from now on!

Luke writes next about the apostles' preaching and teaching with frequent references to the Old Testament prophets in order to convince their predominantly Jewish hearers that Jesus was the long-awaited Messiah. He also records two instances of raising the dead and numerous conversions. The three thousand on the day of Pentecost itself and the subsequent dispersion due to persecution had already led to the establishment of congregations in many towns and cities in Palestine, Asia Minor, Greece and Macedonia. It was these places that Paul later visited and it was to the new Christians in these places that he later wrote his epistles. A large part of Acts is taken up with a description of his three missionary journeys and his final journey to Rome and of the people who accompanied him. The most notable were Barnabas, Silas, John Mark and Timothy, amongst whom there were occasional disagreements: things did not always go smoothly, even in the early Church. There was opposition and active persecution from the Jews who objected to being held responsible for crucifying God's Messiah and the Sadducees who objected to the teaching about the resurrection. The Jewish Christians initially objected strongly to Gentile believers being included in the Church and to the lack of insistence on their obedience to the Jewish Law relating to circumcision and forbidden meats. The disciples were arrested, tried and imprisoned – and on several occasions were miraculously released.

If it had not been for Peter's vision described in chapter 10, in which he was clearly shown that previously forbidden meats were now acceptable food, it is hard to believe the early Church would ever have believed that things had changed and that God was serious about the mission to the Gentiles. Paul's conversion and Peter's vision and its consequences were necessarily, after Pentecost, the most important events in the history of the early Church, without which its worldwide spread would surely never have begun. In addition to this, Peter was led to baptise Cornelius, a Roman centurion, who was naturally a Gentile, and he was able to convince the believers that his vision had been authentic and that the baptism was God's will. It was eventually decided to insist only that the Gentile Christians should be told that they were to 'abstain from food sacrificed to idols, from blood, from the meat of strangled animals and from sexual immorality.' The Jews were not so enlightened and their objection to the inclusion of the Gentiles was the chief issue involved in their vicious opposition to Paul's missionary activity.

During a visit that Paul later made to Ephesus there was a riot on account of the threat posed by the Gospel to the business of the silversmiths who made silver shrines of Artemis, the Roman goddess Diana. Following this, things became more threatening, as they had done with Jesus' own ministry, and like Jesus he insisted on going to Jerusalem. "I am ready not only to be bound, but also to die in Jerusalem for the name of the Lord Jesus." On arrival he was warmly received but soon arrested yet again because the Jews claimed that he "teaches all men everywhere against our people and our law and besides, he brought Greeks into the temple area and defiled this place." He was saved by the commander of the Roman troops who arrested him and bound him with two chains and took him into the barracks, where the commander directed that he be flogged and questioned, in order to find out why the people were shouting at him. Following this he was brought before the Sanhedrin where he caused a dispute between the Pharisees and Sadducees by mentioning the resurrection. and the assembly was divided. A great uproar followed and Paul was returned to the barracks for his own safety. That night the Lord stood near him and said, "Take courage! As you have testified about me in Jerusalem, so you must also testify in Rome." The die was cast: there was now no going back.

From here on the story has the same inevitability as Jesus' last journey to Jerusalem but with the great difference that Paul was to become a martyr. The crucial death of Jesus had already taken place and Paul was ready to take on the world and to die for his Saviour. He was brought before the Roman governor, Felix, at Caesarea – but not before being saved from an ambush in which the Jews planned to kill him. After two whole further years in prison, he was brought before Festus who was the successor to Felix. The Jews 'brought many serious charges against him, which they could not prove' and Paul, doubting that he would receive justice from the court, and knowing he was destined for Rome, appealed to Caesar. Being a Roman citizen he was entitled to do this and Festus readily agreed to it. Being at a loss to know how to deal with the case, Festus then took the opportunity of discussing it with King Agrippa, the Jewish king whose kingdom included Caesarea, and Paul later appeared before him also. He was invited to speak and took the opportunity to defend his record and to preach the Gospel to him. The king's judgement was that "This man is not doing anything that deserves death or imprisonment ... and he could have been set free if he had not appealed to Caesar." God's hand is everywhere at work; his planning is perfect and he will allow nothing to stand in the way of the coming of his kingdom.

The last two chapters of Acts consist largely of a succinct and brilliant description of Paul's journey to Rome, during which they suffer a shipwreck on Malta in which the ship is broken up but no lives are lost, as Paul had promised. Acts ends with Paul as a prisoner for two whole years in Rome, awaiting trial before Caesar. He stayed there in his own rented house and welcomed all who came to see him, boldly and without hindrance preaching the kingdom of God and teaching about the Lord Jesus Christ. It is not difficult to understand why God was so insistent that Paul, a giant of the faith, and arguably the Church's greatest apostle, should come to Rome, the capital of the Roman Empire in which his preaching and teaching needed to be continued. If it had not been for Pentecost and for the courage and persistence of the original apostles and Christian disciples we should never have had the Good News two thousand years later, handed down to us through successive generations of faithful messengers. The early years of any enterprise are liable to be the most exciting but we are bound to wonder whether the Church would have ever got under way if the early believers had been as hesitant as we are in witnessing to our faith.

PAUL'S EPISTLES AND HIS MISSIONARY ACTIVITY

Those disciples who, like Peter and John and James, had known Jesus during his earthly ministry and had seen and touched him were clearly convinced that Jesus was the one and only incarnate Son of God and would one day return to earth. But it was Paul who was enabled to complement John's understanding of the incarnation and to whom Jesus' exalted status and cosmic significance was so clearly and progressively revealed. It was Paul, more than any other, who was given the task of preaching the Gospel to the Gentiles and thus beginning the worldwide growth of the Church. It is impossible to overestimate the greatness and unique significance of this outstanding apostle. His calling and subsequent ministry, his missionary work and journeys and his epistles are of crucial importance for the history of the Church and of the world.

His apparently random series of letters to the young church congregations, that together make up a third of the New Testament, continue to be one of our chief sources of orthodox Christian beliefs. It was left to subsequent generations of the Church, over succeeding years and even centuries, to organise these beliefs into creeds and into a body of teachings or doctrines. It was also left to them to decide finally on a canon of accepted Scriptures to act as an authoritative source of this orthodox belief. Christian theology is an organic body of knowledge, necessarily dependent on the limitations of words and language, not a rigid system of doctrines. The doctrines of the Christian Church are arguments from facts that we have good reason to accept as such rather than arguments or deductions from propositions. For this reason no logical proof of them is possible. Christianity is reasonable rather than essentially rational: it is not a philosophy but a faith. If it were to be purely rational it would have no warmth and would not gladden our hearts as well as enrich our minds.

We have to try to 'catch God at his work' rather than attempt to confine him in a straightjacket of dogmatic teaching. It is not the ultimate truth about God that Paul or any of the other Old or New Testament writers have captured in a form of words but only what it is possible to say about him. It has been said that all religious language is unsatisfactory, and appearances of absolute certainty in formulating spiritual truth are inevitably misleading. Words can take us only to the verge of spiritual truth: the reality of our experience of God, and of meeting and worshipping him, is discovered as an indescribable encounter. It is a sense of nothing, yet everything; of a vacuum, yet full to overflowing. Theology provides us with a framework within which we are able to exercise the spiritual freedom that God has given us.

The history of theology is the story of the continual re-examination and re-interpretation of Scripture in the light of tradition and reason and in relation to changing external circumstances. The truth it contains is made progressively richer for us by its continuing relevance to these changing circumstances. Scientific insights and discoveries are superseded by those of subsequent observers who build on the foundations laid by their predecessors. Works of philosophy, literature and art, other than the greatest of them, tend to be products of their time. But the core of the writings of Paul, along with the rest of Scripture, are of perpetual relevance and they have withstood continuing critical analysis and often venomous attack. We still return to these documents for inspiration and instruction. They continue to contribute to our Christian judgements about practical issues, as well as matters of fundamental Christian belief.

We have thirteen of Paul's epistles, though he no doubt wrote others that have not survived. The first and best-known of these, probably the most famous letter ever written, was to the Romans. It was in their city that he later spent two years preaching and teaching and it was here also, on a subsequent visit, that he was imprisoned, tried and suffered death at the hands of Nero in about 68AD. The remainder of his epistles were written to the churches in Corinth, Galatia, Ephesus, Philippi and Colossae. He also wrote several others to individuals such as Timothy. These letters were written mainly to address problems that had arisen in the young congregations and in their towns and cities – such as moral laxity and heresies – as well as to provide them with sound teaching.

Paul is considered by some to be obscure and difficult to understand, with a harshly legalistic approach and an undue insistence on our justification by faith, for which he was criticised by James in his epistle. Another easily misunderstood feature of his writings is his critical approach to human wisdom which has been argued to be in part responsible for the supposed conflict between Christian faith and Science. But Paul was expressing the same truth as Jesus himself when he spoke in Mt 11:25 of his Father's having hidden spiritual truths from the 'wise and learned and revealed them to little children'. Paul was acutely aware of the need to guard the young believers in the early Church against being unduly influenced by Greek philosophy, above all by gnosticism, a term derived from the Greek word gnosis meaning wisdom. This heresy involved the claim, amongst other erroneous beliefs, that salvation is escape from the body, which they regarded as evil, and achieved not by faith in Christ but by special knowledge. Paul clearly felt the need to speak strongly in order to counter this subtle and potentially damaging error.

The Greeks had made a massive contribution to the intellectual background and the expression of the Christian faith through their alphabet and language and the depth and range of their thinking. But Christianity is not a matter of human wisdom but of God's wisdom and their influence on the early formulation of its teachings was at risk of becoming too great. Paul had to use persuasive arguments in order to counter this tendency and to insist on the truth of the Gospel that had been revealed and entrusted to him. Again and again he uses the circular argument of which the general shape, however expressed, is God ... therefore we ... because God. Everything begins and ends in him. When his epistles are read carefully one of the most striking things about them is his obvious care and concern and Christian love for those to whom he addressed them. In 1Corinthians 13 he wrote about love in what is arguably the most sublime passage in the whole of literature. Each of his epistles begins with his credentials as an apostle of Jesus Christ and courteous Christian greetings of grace and peace from God and ends with warm personal messages, often to individual believers.

It must be remembered also that he had a difficult job to do. He had been accosted by the risen Christ and called to minister to the Gentiles. Jesus the Christ, who had come from a Jewish background, had to be made comprehensible to a Gentile audience who came from outside it. For this purpose he had to free the Gospel, the new covenant, from those parts of the old covenant that were unhelpful and unnecessary for its further spread to those who were unfamiliar with its Jewish origins. The Gospel that he had received 'by revelation from Jesus Christ' was that Jesus was the one and only Son of God who had been crucified and raised to life to redeem all who would come to him, both Jews and Gentiles. Paul was obliged to emphasise the fact that believers are accounted righteous before God or justified by faith, through his grace and not through their own merit. This was essential in order to dispel the error that we could earn our own salvation. His preferred emphasis was made very clear in Galatians 5:6 where he said that 'The only thing that counts is faith expressing itself through love.'

The central theme of Paul's teaching is that we are a new creation, destined to live a new life in Christ. We are born again into this living relationship with Christ, a mystical union that he described as being 'in Christ', a phrase that he uses many times in his epistles. In this rebirth we become related also to the Father, and it is through the Holy Spirit that we are able to know God as Father and Jesus as Lord. This relationship with Christ is not for our benefit only but for the benefit of others also and in it we are united with him in his suffering and in his ministry to the world. 'For we do not preach ourselves, but Jesus Christ as Lord and ourselves as your servants for Jesus' sake.' (2 Cor 4:5). This suffering is not to be compared, however, with the glory that will be revealed in those who share his resurrection life when he returns at the end of the age. In the meantime as Paul tells us in chapter 8 of Romans we and all creation groan and travail in expectation of this return to earth of the finally exalted, cosmic Christ. Then the sons of God will be revealed, the whole creation will be made new and the Kingdom of God will finally be established. It is no surprise that Paul, whose life involved so much suffering in the cause of the Gospel, should have written in this way about the suffering experienced throughout the whole of creation.

GRACE

Grace is a wonderfully rich word, especially when it is used in speaking of God and of the Good News of Jesus Christ and what he has done for us. It is therefore a very precious word for Christians. It appears a number of times in the Old Testament where it is used to speak of individuals finding favour with God, but not explicitly as an attribute of God. Grace has a much richer meaning in the New Testament as a translation of the Greek word 'charis' which denotes both the gracious giving of a gift and its grateful acceptance, thus implying relationship. It is related to the word for joy and gladness, and so suggests also the spontaneous wish to share the gift that has been received with others. It thus helps to convey the reality of how love works in enabling and sustaining our relationship with God and with our neighbour. It is used only four times in the Gospels: Jesus himself is not recorded as speaking of it but rather as bringing it. As God's love freely given to us, grace is on every page even when not specifically referred to as such. God loved us before Jesus came as so many Old Testament passages reveal but until he came we could have had no idea just how much. John tells us in his first chapter that 'the law was given through Moses; grace and truth came through Jesus Christ' whose coming heralded a totally new dispensation.

This short section devoted to grace is included here because Paul used the word grace more often than any other New Testament writer: it appears almost ninety times in his epistles and twenty times in the epistle to the Romans alone. He begins all his epistles without exception with the greeting: 'Grace and peace to you from God our Father and the Lord Jesus Christ' and in almost every case he commits them to God's grace again at the end. He ends his second epistle to the Corinthians with the well-known and well-loved prayer: 'May the grace of the Lord Jesus Christ, and the love of God and the fellowship of the Holy Spirit be with you all.' Paul tells us that we are called by grace, and that we are saved by grace solely through our faith in Christ, which alone gives us access to God's grace. He speaks in Ephesians of the 'incomparable riches of his grace' and of God's glorious grace as an 'abundant provision, given freely in the One he loves.' When he sought freedom from some unidentified 'thorn in my flesh' that afflicted him God said to him "My grace is sufficient for you, my power is made perfect in weakness." (2 Cor 12:9). He had to rely on God's strength, not his own.

It is apparent from these varied uses of the word grace that it is an attempt to convey the abundant, overflowing love of God that is above and beyond what we deserve and might therefore expect. It is goodness, mercy and love as only God can bestow it and as we receive it with gratitude from him. By somehow including our response to this gift of God, it adds a richness to the portrayal of our relationship with him. The word grace provides a beautiful addition to our terminology and gives an extra dimension to the word love that is so difficult even to describe, let alone define. Grace is a gift that cannot sensibly be rejected. In the words of a poster displayed outside a Methodist Church in Petersfield: Don't wait for four strong men to carry you to Church! The Church does not always look an attractive place but for better or for worse it is where Christians regularly meet together to worship God and seek his priceless gift of grace.

The words of the General Thanksgiving in the Book of Common Prayer express this sense of God's gifts graciously bestowed and gratefully received that is the essence of grace:

Almighty God, Father of all mercies, we thine unworthy servants do give thee most humble and hearty thanks for all thy goodness and loving-kindness to us, and to all men. We bless thee for our creation, preservation, and all the blessings of this life; but above all for thine inestimable love in the redemption of the world by our Lord Jesus Christ; for the means of grace, and for the hope of glory. And, we beseech thee, give us that due sense of all thy mercies, that our hearts may be unfeignedly thankful, and that we show forth thy praise, not only with our lips, but in our lives; by giving ourselves up to thy service, and by walking before thee in holiness and righteousness all our days; through Jesus Christ our Lord, to whom with thee and the Holy Ghost be all honour and glory, world without end. Amen.

This may sound to some old-fashioned language, even old-fashioned thinking, but it gives us an opportunity to wonder whether we have lost as well as gained in our recognition of God's greatness and in our expression of gratitude to him for his goodness to us.

ROMANS

Paul, introducing himself as the apostle appointed 'to call people from among the Gentiles', wrote his first epistle to the mainly Gentile Christians in Rome. It is complex and more of a general presentation of the Christian faith than a personal letter to the church in Rome. It was no doubt intended for a wider readership in other churches as well. Paul had not yet visited Rome but he prays for the Christians there and expresses his longing to be with them and to be able to encourage them and be encouraged by them. Romans is painted on a colossal canvas on which Paul depicts God's dealings with all mankind, both Jews and Gentiles. It gives an account of his programme for the redemption of his whole creation through Christ, which he had promised before-hand through his prophets. He also speaks of God's wrath against all the 'godlessness and wickedness of men, to whom his 'eternal power and divine nature' should have been apparent in his creation, so that they are 'without excuse'.

The people of Israel have been 'entrusted with the very words of God' but they cannot boast of this or rely for their righteousness on their circumcision, or on the law. The law can never make men righteous, but rather brings their sin to light and makes them conscious of it. The God who is himself righteous credits men with righteousness, as he made clear to Abraham, on the basis of their faith in him and in his promises. The righteousness of God, 'apart from the law', now comes through faith in Jesus Christ. There is no difference between Jew and Gentile for 'all have sinned and fall short of the glory of God', and are 'justified freely by his grace'. Therefore we have peace with God through Christ; but we have also been 'baptised into Christ's death and died with him' in order to be given his new life and to be one day united with him in his resurrection. This involves our suffering with him, in which we should also rejoice, because this suffering produces perseverance and character and hope. Having been set free from our slavery to sin we are in a real sense willing slaves to God. To experience a living relationship with him is to have eternal life. This life is not only everlasting but unique in quality; being close to God and therefore influenced by him, results in holiness. In spite of this Paul is still aware of a struggle with sin: 'When I want to do good, evil is right there with me.' 'Who will rescue me from the body of this death?' he asks; and in answer to his own question he says, 'Thanks be to God – through Jesus Christ our Lord.'

Then comes, at the start of Chapter 8, one of the most remarkable in all his epistles, his triumphant assertion: 'Therefore there is now no condemnation for those who are in Christ Jesus.' This is because we have been forgiven through his atoning death and the Holy Spirit has come to live in us to set us free and give us life and peace and the hope of eventual resurrection. 'Therefore brothers we have an obligation ... because those who are led by the Spirit of God are sons of God ... and by the Spirit of sonship we cry "Abba , Father". 'Now if we are children then we are heirs – heirs of God and co-heirs with Christ, if indeed we share in his sufferings in order that we may also share in his glory.' The Christian faith is not a bed of roses; the privileges carry responsibilities. Paul then continues with his conviction that 'our present sufferings are not worth comparing with the glory that will be revealed in us' and he then opens out the discussion to encompass the whole of creation which will one day be 'liberated from its bondage to decay.' This passage will be quoted more fully in the next section on Creation.

Paul goes on to say that as we wait patiently for our release from this bondage, not knowing what we ought to pray for, the Spirit helps us in our weakness and intercedes for us with 'groans that words cannot express'. 'And we know that in all things God works for the good of those who love him,' who have been called, as he purposed from eternity, 'to be conformed to the likeness of his Son, that he might be the firstborn among many brothers.' As Christ's brothers 'we are more than conquerors through him who loved us.' This launches Paul into an expression of joyful confidence:

'For I am convinced that neither death nor life, neither angels nor demons, neither the present nor the future, nor any powers, neither height nor depth, nor anything else in all creation, will be able to separate us from the love of God that is in Christ Jesus our Lord.'

In the next three chapters Paul expresses his sorrow and anguish for 'those of my own race, the people of Israel' who have received all the benefits that God could give them, including 'the patriarchs from whom is traced the human ancestry of Christ.' But not all of them are saved – as yet only a remnant. In 'seeking to establish their own righteousness' they 'stumbled over the 'stumbling-stone' of Christ by putting him to death. As a result they would be punished but God said through Isaiah, "All day long I have held out my hands to a disobedient people" and as Paul argues, 'God's gift and his call are irrevocable.' It is hard to recognise the Jews of present day Israel as God's chosen people but the truth is, Paul tells us, that 'Israel has experienced a hardening in part until the full number of the Gentiles has come in,' but then 'all Israel will be saved.' (11:25-26) Some of the branches have been broken off the olive tree, but if the wild olive branches of the Gentiles can be grafted into the tree, how much more can the natural branches be grafted once again into their own olive tree. We cannot know how God proposes to resolve this problem; how he proposes to fulfil his promises to his people Israel, dispersed throughout the world and throughout the centuries. This is a colossal and complicated argument. Paul's pleasure at the prospect of Israel's eventual salvation and the magnificence of God's plan of salvation that we can only dimly grasp, prompts one of his greatest outbursts of praise:

'Oh, the depth of the riches of the
  wisdom and knowledge of God!
How unsearchable his judgements,
and his paths beyond tracing out!
"Who has known the mind of the Lord?
Or who has been his counsellor?"
"Who has ever given to God
that God should repay him?"
For from him and through him and to
  him are all things.
To him be the glory for ever! Amen.'

'Therefore', Paul says, 'I urge you brothers, in view of God's mercy, to offer your bodies as living sacrifices.' He continues with a series of practical instructions. 'Be transformed by the renewing of your mind.' God accepts us as we are but he has no intention of letting us stay that way, if only we will let him change us. Be humble, he says, recognising the contributions of the other members of the body of Christ, and their different gifts. Be devoted to one another in brotherly love. Honour one another above yourselves. Practise hospitality. Bless those who persecute you; do not repay anyone evil for evil. If it is possible, as far as it depends on you, live at peace with everyone. If your enemy is hungry, feed him; do not be overcome by evil , but overcome evil with good. He goes on to talk of politics: 'Everyone must submit himself to the governing authorities,' and if you owe taxes pay them. He who loves his fellow-man has fulfilled the law; the commandments are summed up in this one rule: 'Love your neighbour as yourself.' This epistle is full of down-to-earth practical advice and encouragement to sound living as well as weighty teaching.

Paul closes by asking God to give the Roman Christians a spirit of unity so that they may glorify him. He goes on to ask that the God of hope will fill them with all joy and peace as they trust in him so that they may 'overflow with hope by the power of the Holy Spirit.' He tells them that he hopes to visit them when he has been to Jerusalem and urges them to join him in his struggle by praying to God for him. He then sends a series of personal greetings and a final, all-encompassing message of praise that is in keeping with the grand scale of the whole epistle:

'Now to him who is able to establish you by my gospel and the proclamation of Jesus Christ, according to the revelation of the mystery hidden for long ages past, but now revealed and made known through the prophetic writings by command of the eternal God, so that all nations might believe and obey him – to the only wise God be glory for ever through Jesus Christ! Amen'.

CREATION

In the beginning God created the heavens and the earth. In the beginning was the Word through whom 'all things were made' and who 'became flesh and made his dwelling among us'. The first words of Genesis in the Old Testament tell us that God has created the universe and the first chapter of St John's Gospel in the New Testament tells us he has come to earth in Jesus. Both the Old and the New Testaments are about the Maker of heaven and earth, about his concern for all that he has made and about the plans that he has for it. The fact that God created all things is taken for granted. What is also taken for granted is that the creation belongs to God. 'The earth is the Lord's, and everything in it, the world, and all who live in it.' Ps 24:1. This emphasis on the whole of creation as belonging to God and on our stewardship of the earth is, for the Christian, at the centre of the present-day discussions about climate change and the damage that we are doing to the environment.

Genesis goes on to give us an account of the stages of God's creation. The earth was initially formless and empty and dark and 'the Spirit of God was hovering over the waters'. First he created light in order to separate the day from the night and then he made the sky to separate the water above from the water below. This water below was then 'gathered to one place' in order to let ground appear, thus creating land and seas. Next God decreed that the land should produce vegetation; 'seed-bearing plants and trees on the land that bear fruit with seed in it, according to their various kinds'. 'And it was so.' He does not need to issue instructions that have then to be carried out. There is no delay – apart from the fact that, as we now know, some of his plans may take millions or even billions of years to mature! The present estimate of the age of the universe, from its beginning with the Big Bang, is said to be around 13,700 million years; that of the earth and solar system is around 4,500 million years, and the earliest evidence of life on earth is said to be 3,850 million years ago. Even a quite large percentage error either way could hardly affect the overall significance of these colossal figures.

Isaiah 45:18

For this is what the Lord says –
he who created the heavens,
  he is God;
he who fashioned and made the earth,
  he founded it;
he did not create it to be empty,
  but formed it to be inhabited –
he says:
"I am the Lord,
  and there is no other.

Psalm 95:3-7

For the Lord is the great God,
  the great king above all Gods.
In his hands are the depths of the earth,
  and the mountain peaks belong to him.
The sea is his, for he made it,
  and his hands formed the dry land.
Come, let us bow down in worship,
  Let us kneel before the lord our Maker;
for he is our God
  and we are the people of his pasture,
  and the flock under his care.

God then installed lights in the sky that would give light on the earth and separate the day from the night and also 'serve as signs to mark seasons and days and years.' The greater light was 'set in the expanse of the sky' to govern the day and the lesser light to govern the night, thus stating God's purpose in creating them and the function they would serve. The writer might have gone on to say that he gave instructions to the earth to revolve about its axis every twenty four hours so that there should everywhere be periods of light for work and recreation and periods of darkness for rest and sleep – though not so conveniently distributed at the poles! Then God said, "Let the water teem with living creatures, including the great creatures of the sea, and let birds fly above the earth across the expanse of the sky," and "Let the land produce living creatures according to their kinds: livestock; creatures that move along the ground, and wild animals."

Last of all God said: "Let us make man in our own image," both male and female. He blessed them and said to them, "Be fruitful and increase in number; fill the earth and subdue it. Rule over the fish of the sea and the birds of the air and over every living creature that moves on the ground." Then God said, "I give you every seed-bearing plant on the face of the whole earth and every tree that has fruit with seed in it. They will be yours for food." No mention of meat at this early point. 'God saw all that he had made and it was very good.' 'Thus the heavens and the earth were completed in all their vast array,' and 'on the seventh day he rested' – a principle that stands as a vital lesson and instruction for us of the need of a balance between work and rest.

What follows is the graphic description of the disobedience of Adam and Eve in the Garden of Eden with all its consequences that are evident throughout the Bible story and the rest of history. The 'vast array' of God's work in creation is also evident throughout the Bible story but is less central than its concern with his work of redemption, without which creation could never reach the destiny that he has prepared for it. So glorious is his creation, however, that in our inevitable ignorance of the full nature and power of God himself, it is the clearest indication and measure of his majesty. Paul tells us in Rom 1:20 that 'since the foundation of the world God's invisible qualities – his eternal power and divine nature – have been clearly seen, being understood from what has been made, so that men are without excuse.' Dante, writing 1300 years later, quite possibly prompted by this very passage, speaks in the Divine Comedy of 'the shape that makes the universe resemble God.'[14] If we are made in his image then all of nature that has preceded us in the history of evolution and to which we now recognise ourselves to be related, must bear some resemblance to him as well.

The writers of the Old Testament, especially in the Psalms, frequently expressed their praise and worship to God as the One who has made everything that is; as 'the Maker of heaven and earth'. In 2 Kings 19:15 king Hezekiah prayed to the Lord: "O Lord, God of Israel ... you alone are God over all the kingdoms of the earth. You have made heaven and earth." Jeremiah tells us in chapter 51:15 that 'He made the earth by his power; he founded the world by his wisdom and stretched out the heavens by his understanding.' And he has not finished yet, as he makes clear in Isaiah:

> "From now on I will tell you of new things,
> of hidden things unknown to you.
> They are created now, and not long ago;
> you have not heard of them before today.
> So you cannot say,
> 'Yes, I knew of them."   (Is 48:6,7).

God's role as Creator is further emphasised in Isaiah when he records him as claiming responsibility and credit for his creation. "Has not my hand made all these things?" (Is 66:12).

> "It is I who made the earth
> and created mankind upon it.
> My own hand stretched out the heavens."   (Is 45:12).

This recognition of God's greatness as Creator of all things led the Old Testament writers again and again to uninhibited praise and worship, especially in the Psalms:

> "Sing praises to God, sing praises;
> sing praises to our king, sing praises.
> For God is the king of all the earth;

---

[14] Paradiso 1 Line 105

sing to him a psalm of praise." (Ps 47:6,7).

Their worship is not only channelled through creation but also arises from their personal praise and gratitude to him. "I will sing to the Lord, for he has been good to me." (Ps 13:6). In even more lyrical vein: "I will sing and make music... I will awaken the dawn." (Ps 57:7,8) This appreciation of God's glory and majesty leads naturally to a desire to see him honoured throughout the whole of his universe: "Be exalted, O God, above the heavens; let your glory be over all the earth." (Ps 57:5) We can detect the same Spirit at work when Jesus teaches us to pray "your kingdom come, your will be done on earth as it is in heaven."

Not only do these Old Testament writers express their own praise to God but they rejoice in seeing, in their rich and inspired imagination, creation itself offering its own praise and giving glory to God by virtue of its very existence and its natural beauty. As the psalmist says in 19:1,4:

> 'The heavens declare the glory of God;
> the skies proclaim the work of his hands.
> Their voice goes out into all the earth,
> their words to the end of the world.'

It has been claimed that the heavens no longer act in this way for us; that they now maintain an impenetrable silence. Is it not rather that we are no longer receptive to the wave-length on which they broadcast their message to us? It is not that God is dead but that we are no longer alive to him and to his presence in his universe. Why is it so beautiful if not because of the creative energy of his love within it? Even the clouds, the vessels from which the earth is watered, are things of beauty. There are numerous other indications that the writers of the Psalms were very much alive to God and to his creation and rejoiced in seeing his world as singing its own praises to him.

> 'Shout with joy to God, all the earth!
> Sing the glory of his name;
> make his praise glorious.' (Ps 66:1,2).

'Let the sea resound, and everything in it
the world, and all who live in it,
Let the rivers clap their hands,
let the mountains sing together for joy.'   (Ps 98:7,8).

From these examples we can see that the Psalms provide us with a
positive kaleidoscope of praise to God, for his creation, and for his
greatness and his goodness to his people. How great is our need,
difficult though it may be in the severely technological, secular world
of today, to recover something of this spirit of joy and praise, and
gratitude to God. God`s creation is an important element in our
response to him that our generation has tended to neglect until we
have recently begun to focus on it once more.

It is clear that creation is not less than everything. It is everything
that God has made, both what is visible to us and what is invisible to
us, even with the most powerful telescopes and microscopes. It is also
everything that is impossible to see, other than through the eyes of
faith. In the words of the writer of Hebrews: 'By faith we understand
that the universe was formed at God's command, so that what is seen
was not made out of what was visible'. (11:3).

By a combination of faith and speculation we can also see that
creation includes everything that God has permitted and encouraged
us to do and to make with the materials he has provided, so that we
can offer them to him. "For everything on earth is yours" in the words
of David's prayer in 1 Chronicles 29. Everything that we use for food
and clothing and shelter, and for medicines and manufacturing, and
for travel. However the raw materials are obtained and in whatever
way they are processed and marketed, they are all of them gifts of
God in creation. Payment gives both buyer and seller the illusion of
ownership but in truth everything that we have is derived from his
creation and belongs in the end to God. He provides the water we
drink and wash and cook with, the plants and fish and meat that we
eat. The materials from which we build our houses and their contents
and the steel from which we build our ships and planes, are there for
us to gather and process. The coal and oil and gas and nuclear power
that we use for light and warmth, transport and industry are all of
them his gifts for us. The same is true of the animal kingdom that
gives us so much joy and the countryside and the mountains in which
we walk and climb and the earth that we explore and investigate

scientifically. The sea in which we swim and surf; the wind that fills our sails and the stars by which we navigate are also his provision. The same also applies to fire that man must have made use of in creation long before he learned how to kindle it himself.

It also applies to the materials from which we fashion our works of art. They may be stones for the Parthenon or St Paul's Cathedral; clay for the Terracotta Army or marble for Michelangelo's sculptures. Or timber for Nelson's ships or for violins to make music, another of the creative gifts that God has enabled us to develop. They may be ink and dyes for writing, or pigment for Rembrandt's paintings, or gold and silver and precious stones for coins and for jewellery. It is right that we should take pride in our achievements but not that we should take undue credit for the materials from which we construct them, however clever we have been to obtain them and fashion them. Our natural tendency is to take our heavenly Father's gifts for granted. The Psalmist says in 104:14,15:

'He makes grass grow for the cattle,
and plants for man to cultivate –
bringing forth food from the earth:
wine that gladdens the heart of man,
oil to make his face shine,
and bread that sustains his heart.'

Less obviously, but no less certainly, we need to recognise God as the source, not only of the earth and its resources and its beauty, but of everything in our own lives and in the whole of the society in which we live. This includes the people we cherish, to whom we relate in so many different ways, and our families and friends, communities and nations. It includes all that is involved in terms of culture, commerce, industry and science, as well as politics. They too are part of God's provision for us, in spite of all the efforts we ourselves and our forebears and contemporaries have had to contribute. What matters above all is the use that we make of God's gifts. Everyone and everything has the potential for being the material out of which God will build his everlasting kingdom.

But what of the troubled history of our world and what of its future and the future of creation itself? How are we to understand the dark periods we read of and those we have experienced in recent years –

two World Wars and the Holocaust; the dictatorships of Hitler and Stalin, and other more contemporary examples? What of the health of our planet earth about which there is so much anxious debate and what of the unimaginable suffering of so many of those with whom we share it? We cannot forget that many millions in the world today have no clean water, not enough food, only rudimentary medical treatment and inadequate shelter, clothing and heating. Many more millions throughout the course of history have suffered from drought and flooding, tornadoes and disease, thus highlighting the dangers of God's world that it seems we have to accept as inevitable accompaniments of its beauty. It is right that we should ask searching questions, but who are we to criticise the arrangements God has made? The challenge is rather to us to live as he has taught us and to share the earth's huge but limited resources with our neighbours. Paul was in no doubt of the nature of our dilemma and in the eighth chapter of Romans he gives us the only coherent response that has ever been offered. He writes:

'I consider that our present sufferings are not worth comparing with the glory that will be revealed in us. The creation waits in eager expectation for the sons of God to be revealed. For the creation was subjected to frustration, not by its own choice, but by the will of the one who subjected it, in hope that the creation itself will be liberated from its bondage to decay and brought into the glorious liberty of the children of God. We know that the whole creation has been groaning as in the pains of childbirth right up to the present time. Not only so, but we ourselves, who have the first fruits of the Spirit, groan inwardly as we wait eagerly for our adoption, the redemption of our bodies. For in this hope we were saved. But hope that is seen is no hope at all. Who hopes for what he already has? But if we hope for what we do not yet have, we wait for it patiently.'

Sometimes, we have to admit, our patience is exhausted by the extent of evil and of human suffering and the massive time-scale of God's programme that is too prolonged for us to comprehend. It is apparent that we cannot solve all the problems that confront us on our own but must rather co-operate with him for as long as we are given and leave the rest to him and to the day of our final redemption at his coming.

The biblical vision of creation's praise to God and its eventual consummation is continued in the remaining epistles and in Revelation, where its true, all-encompassing extent is finally recognised and expressed in its unique Christian imagery. In Revelation 4:11 the angels of heaven are joined in their praise to God by twenty four elders who say:

> "You are worthy, Our Lord and God,
> to receive glory and honour and power,
> for you created all things,
> and by your will they were created
> and have their being."

In the next chapter the writer speaks of 'many angels, numbering thousands upon thousands, and ten thousand times ten thousand' and goes on to extend the vision even further in the following verses: 'Then I heard every creature in heaven and on earth and under the earth and on the sea, and all that is in them, singing:'

> "To him who sits on the throne and to the Lamb
> be praise and honour and glory and power,
> for ever and ever!" (Rev 5:13).

This is, in the words of T.S Eliot, a 'high dream' that demands from us a high imagination. God had already spoken through the prophet Isaiah saying , "Behold, I will create new heavens and a new earth." (65:17). At the very end of Revelation in Chapter 21 we are given a fuller vision of the future fulfilment of this prophecy in the Holy City of God's kingdom:

> "Then I saw a new heaven and a new earth, for the first
> heaven and the first earth had passed away, and there was
> no longer any sea."

John hears a loud voice from the throne saying, "Now the dwelling of God is with men, and he will live with them. They will be his people, and God himself will be with them and be their God." He goes on to speak of the wiping away of all tears and the abolishing of death and mourning, crying and pain. This is another 'high dream'. Once again it is beyond us, even beyond the writer himself, to know the reality of which this vision speaks, but it cries out as an authentic conclusion to God's programme for the final redemption of his people and his whole creation. We can only embrace it as a precious element, surely the most precious of all, in the richness of our Christian hope.

It is argued by some that creation is so magnificent that it is preposterous to imagine that a creator, however great and powerful, could have conceived and brought it into existence. There is no real answer to this except to say that it is even more preposterous to imagine that it could have come about by chance. If the world does not always appear to us logical or intelligible this may be because we have no experience or even imagination of what is involved in constructing and maintaining a system as vast as the universe. It is possible that nothing less than all that we can see of creation, and all that is invisible to us also, is the minimum required to enable the whole gigantic system to function and to achieve the purpose for which God designed it. Either it could be less big and still work or it has to be as big as it is in order to work as it does. Scientists have now expressed the view that if it were not such a colossal size it would lack the necessary durability. The universe has already lasted for nearly 14 billion years and is not yet worn out. The only reason that we are able to explore and investigate it as we do is because, as we believe, our own minds are created in the image of the mind of the God who made it.

EVIL, THE DEVIL, AND HUMAN SIN

God has clearly given us free will, not merely to make our lives more interesting but because it is not in his nature to demand our slavish obedience and thus deny us the possibility of enjoying a voluntary, loving relationship with him. This is a freedom that he must have known we would use to disobey and reject him, and thus cut ourselves off from him. In the fifth chapter of Romans, from verses 12 to the end, and also briefly in 1Corinthians 15:22 there is a reference to the origin of human sin that is linked with Christ's part in overcoming it on our behalf. Adam, being the first man in the biblical account of creation, is described by Paul as the first to disobey God and to 'fall,' and thereby enter into sin, and 'die' spiritually. He is for this reason the one who is held responsible in both these passages for introducing the spiritual death that is the result of sin. Adam is described as setting our human sinfulness in motion by his disobedience but it would appear that sin was already present in the world in the guise of the serpent who symbolically encouraged Eve to disobey God's command. The tendency to sin would also appear to have been inherent in the freedom we were given and that each one of us descends into it individually by what might be thought of as the spiritual equivalent of gravity. It was maybe that Adam, like all of us, was born mortal rather than becoming mortal, and that we inherited the mortality that we share with the rest of nature, along with all our other human traits, from him. The story of the Fall is in a real sense the story of each one of us as we fall into the same trap – not once only, but over and over again – and with the devil's encouragement. It is hard to believe that man can be as evil as he so often is without some outside encouragement. However we may try to resolve the mystery, we can rejoice with Paul when he writes that in contrast to the first man Adam in whom we all 'die', Christ our Saviour is the One in whom we are once more made 'alive'. (1Cor 15:22).

It was in order to do justice to the sin of humanity and its contribution to the evil in the world that the doctrine of original sin was introduced. This was championed by St Augustine in the fifth Century in order to avoid minimising the part played by God's grace in our salvation and to emphasise that he alone can take the initiative in bringing it about. If our tendency to sin is an inevitable consequence of the freedom he has given us then only God can put things right. In sending his only Son to die for us in order to reconcile us to himself, he has taken the initiative in a definitive and decisive fashion. The trouble is that in its more extreme form the doctrine of original sin paints a somewhat depressing picture of our fallen human nature and our total inability to help ourselves that the Church in the West has wrestled with for most of its two thousand years. The Eastern Orthodox Church has not accepted this radical teaching. Any statements that we make in an attempt to resolve the problem of our sinful nature are inevitably unsatisfactory and involve the risk of falling into error one way or the other. The gift of freedom and the sin into which it leads us are two sides of the same coin. Paradoxically, sin is somehow of use; it is necessary to enable us to understand goodness as darkness is necessary to enable us to appreciate light. In the words given to Mother Julian of Norwich by Jesus in a vision: 'Sin was necessary – but it is all going to be all right; it is all going to be all right; everything is going to be all right.'[15]

Evil and our own sin and the related problem of suffering are mysteries that we experience every day, but no one has ever explained them and they can certainly never be captured in a form of words. Dostoyevsky, in his prophetic novel, 'The Devils', may have got as close as it is possible to get in exploring them. Sin and evil are ever-present realities and they have to be resisted rather than explained. Jung expressed the magnitude of the problem when he wrote: 'We stand face to face with the terrible question of evil and do not know what is before us, let alone what to pit against it.'[16] This is a compelling expression of our human feeling of helplessness but as Christians we can add our confident expectation of God's ultimate triumph over it in Christ. In the words of Solzhenitsyn 'the line between good and evil cuts through the heart of every human being' and we cannot therefore separate them ourselves. This does not prevent us from seeking an outside enemy to blame for our own failings. It is hard to understand how the God who is Love can bear to look on the evil that is done in the world and the suffering it causes. In view of the extent of human wickedness that has existed throughout history and that we see all around us today God must surely have again been 'grieved that he made man on the earth'– in spite of his promise to Noah never again to destroy the earth with a flood.

Jesus taught us to pray that we should be delivered from evil. He taught us also that it comes from within us, as evil thoughts coming out of our hearts. (Mt 9:4, 5:19, Mk 7:22) It is also present outside us in the person of Satan, our enemy and accuser who must have rebelled against God before we were created – "Better to reign in hell than serve in Heaven" as Milton has him say in Paradise Lost. We too like our own way, often whatever the cost. Satan was introduced figuratively as the serpent that tempted Eve in the Garden of Eden –

---

[15] Revelations of Divine Love. Ch 27.

[16] 'Memories, Dreams, Reflections' p 363

and referred to again as the 'ancient serpent' in Revelation – but he is mentioned only three times in the whole of the Old Testament. Evil on the other hand is referred to several hundred times.

In the New Testament, with the coming of Jesus, it would appear that the struggle is personalised. God comes out of hiding in Jesus and Satan, the real enemy, comes out of hiding as well. Satan, or the devil, is now referred to frequently – most notably in tempting Jesus in the desert. He is described as the ruler of this world in Jn 14:30, as the prince of the power of the air in Eph 2:2, and as capable of disguising himself as an angel of light in 2 Cor 11:14. He is hostile to God, to Jesus and his ministry and to the people of God but he will flee if we resist him. (James 4:7). It was he who tried to tempt Jesus through Peter in Mk 8:33 and entered into Judas before he betrayed Jesus in Lk 22:3. Jesus describes him as taking away the good seed sown in the parable of the Sower and Paul describes him as interfering with the mission of the church in 1Thess 2:18. He prowls around like a lion looking for someone to devour in 1Peter 5:8 and as Paul tells us in Eph 6:11 we need the whole armour of God to resist him.

In and through all this struggle the Christian hope is of eventual release and freedom from evil, from the devil and from our own sin and its consequences. One day there will be an end to all of them. Jesus came into the world to 'destroy the works of the devil' (1Jn 3:8, Heb 2:14) By his Cross and resurrection he has ensured the ultimate defeat of all evil, to be realised when he comes again in judgement to establish his completed kingdom at the end of the age. Satan will then be condemned (Mt 24:41, Jn 16:11, Rev 20:16) and driven out (Jn 12:31) and he and his angels will finally be deprived of their power to harm. This is the only hopeful news that we have anywhere that the terrible question of evil will ever be resolved and that its causes and consequences will eventually be eradicated.

1 CORINTHIANS

Paul had himself established the church in this important Greek city of Corinth, so he knew of the immorality and religious diversity of the city and the weaknesses and shortcomings of the young church. He had been informed of divisions among its members and had received a letter from them in which they asked for his advice on a number of issues including marriage, spiritual gifts and collections for God's people. Paul's teaching, like that of Jesus himself, was frequently a response to people's situations and to the questions that they asked him. After his usual greetings and his statement of his credentials as an apostle, he speaks to them about their divisions. These involved excessive and unhealthy loyalty to Paul himself or to one of the other spiritual leaders. Paul's response is to emphasise the superiority of Christ, the central importance of his Cross and the uselessness of man's wisdom, which is foolishness to God in whom alone we should boast. Paul, having the mind of Christ, is resolved to know nothing but Jesus Christ and him crucified and to speak of God's secret wisdom and in words taught by the Spirit. It is not the human servants who are of chief importance – neither he who plants nor he who waters is anything, but only God, who makes things grow.

After reminding them of the hardships that he and Apollos have endured for their sakes he goes on to censure a particularly serious case of sexual immorality. This risked infecting the whole church and could not therefore be tolerated in a Christian brother who for this reason must be expelled. He also criticises them for pursuing lawsuits against each other before the ungodly, which means that 'you have been completely defeated already,' rather than settling the matter within the fellowship of the Church. He then answers their question about marriage, advising couples to fulfil their duties to each other. They should not divorce and thereby give up the hope that they might save an unbelieving spouse. His preference for celibacy, where possible, was apparently due to a conviction that the Lord's return was imminent and they should ideally be free to please and serve him.

In chapter 10 he warns against complacency: If you think you are standing firm, be careful that you don't fall! But God is faithful and will enable us to stand up under temptation. This conviction appears to remind him of Christ's strength in making his selfless sacrifice for us and he asks: 'Is not the cup of thanksgiving for which we give thanks a participation in the blood of Christ? And is not the bread we break a participation in the body of Christ? Because there is one loaf, we who are many, are one body, for we all partake of the one loaf.' He goes on to tell them in the next chapter:

> The Lord Jesus, on the night that he was betrayed, took bread, and when he had given thanks, he broke it and said, "This is my body, which is for you; do this in remembrance of me." In the same way, after supper he took the cup, saying, "This cup is the new covenant in my blood; do this, whenever you drink it, in remembrance of me".

Paul goes on to say that 'whenever you eat this bread and drink this cup, you proclaim the Lord's death until he comes'. Without the regular enactment of this ritual to remind us of Christ's death for us we lack the encouragement to look back to his sacrifice and forward to his coming again. And without the presence of the Spirit of the risen Lord in our hearts this eucharistic ritual of thanksgiving cannot become alive in our experience.

In chapter 12 Paul continues to address their difficulties with regard to spiritual gifts. These consist of wisdom, knowledge and faith, gifts of healing, miraculous powers, prophecy, distinguishing between spirits, speaking in different kinds of tongues and the interpretation of tongues. All these are given by one and the same Spirit 'just as he determines'. These gifts are for the common good of the Church, which he likens to a body made up of many parts, all of which are different and all of which are essential and rejoice and suffer together. Within this body of Christ, his Church, of which all believers are a part, God has appointed 'first of all apostles, second prophets, third teachers, then workers of miracles, also those having gifts of healing, those able to help others, those with gifts of administration, and those speaking in different types of tongues.' In Ephesians 4:11 he includes also evangelists and pastors.

He goes on to explain in a detailed argument in Chapter 14 that tongues must be interpreted if they are to edify or strengthen the Church. He says to them: 'Now brothers, if I come to you and speak in tongues, what good will it be to you, unless I bring you some revelation or knowledge or prophecy or word of instruction?' He says in four earlier verses:

> 'Follow the way of love and eagerly desire spiritual gifts, especially the gift of prophecy. For anyone who speaks in a tongue does not speak to men but to God. Indeed no-one understands him; he utters mysteries with his spirit. But everyone who prophesies speaks to men for their strengthening, encouragement and comfort. He who speaks in a tongue edifies himself, but he who prophesies edifies the church. I would like every one of you to speak in tongues, but I would rather have you prophesy. He who prophesies is greater than one who speaks in tongues, unless he interprets, so that the church may be edified.'

Paul concludes in the last verse of this difficult chapter: 'Therefore, my brothers, be eager to prophesy, and do not forbid speaking in tongues. But everything should be done in a fitting and orderly way.' The whole of this chapter needs to be read rather than commented on in order to digest what Paul is really saying about this complex phenomenon, though it might also require explanation from an experienced and reliable adviser!

Not many Christians can expect to fulfil more than one of these roles or be granted more than one of the gifts but it would appear that Paul himself fulfilled all the roles and had been given all the gifts. He exhorts us to desire the greater gifts but warns us in his matchless Chapter 13 against relying exclusively on any of them. We should rather concentrate on seeking the 'most excellent way' of Love. This chapter is briefly introduced, and quoted in full, after two further sections on the Church, and on the Creeds that the early Church eventually produced as a summary of the Christian faith.

THE CHURCH

Paul speaks of the Church as the Body of Christ, its members being likened to limbs and organs. It is a body of people, whether it be the local or the universal Church who, by God's grace, believe in Jesus as Saviour and follow him as his disciples. It is also the body of all those who have lived on earth as God's people both before and since Jesus' coming, and are now with him in heaven, and by extension all those yet to be born who will become the members of the Church in the future. As Christ's body on earth they seek to co-operate with him in demonstrating and proclaiming his universal kingdom of love and obedience until he comes again. The Church is not itself the kingdom but has been given the task of witnessing to it and showing it in action in the world – sadly not always very successfully. It is made up, like the rest of society, of fallible human beings and has even been described on occasion as the greatest obstacle to belief in Christ.

The Church is given to do all that a body does. As with a physical body, every organ is important and ideally works for the good of the whole. It exists to provide love and encouragement and intelligence, eyes and ears and tongues and hands and feet, to enable it do God's work. The image of the body suggests that the members should look after one another, set a good example and teach and serve each other in warm Christian fellowship. The roles and functions ordained for this work and the Spirit-given gifts to help church members to perform it have been described already in the previous section. The wider mission of the Church is nowhere more graphically outlined than in the passage from Isaiah 61, quoted by Jesus in Luke 4:18,19. He records Jesus reading it from the scroll that was handed to him in the synagogue at Nazareth at the start of his ministry and telling those present: "Today this scripture is fulfilled in your hearing."

> "The Spirit of the Lord is on me,
>   because he has anointed me
>   to preach good news to the poor.
> He has sent me to proclaim freedom for the prisoners
>   and recovery of sight for the blind,
> to release the oppressed,
>   to proclaim the year of the Lord's favour."

It is this ministry of preaching, teaching, healing and serving, enabled by the same Holy Spirit, that has been continued by the Church ever since. In chapter 2 of his first epistle Peter uses images of the Church as a spiritual house to be built of the living human stones of God's people and as a chosen people belonging to God, a royal and holy priesthood and a holy nation. Paul refers in Ephesians 2:19 to the new Gentile Christians as 'fellow-citizens with God's people and members of God's household.' Other models of the Church such as servant, herald, society, family, institution, sacrament, mystical communion and community of disciples have also been used, each denomination and each generation tending to emphasise one or more of them at the expense of the others. It has also been described, in a more modern idiom, as a hospital, or place of healing, as a job-centre, and as a building site where the Body of Christ is being built up. It has also been described as a fishing boat that enables us to be the 'fishers of men' that Jesus promised he would make us. But the Church bursts the banks of each and every model and description, as a mystery of God's providence.

No community or denomination or generation of Christians can represent the Body of Christ in all its fullness. It is still in the process of formation – a process that has involved many painful times in its history. Its unity has from time to time been strained by disagreements and schisms, notably at the time of the Reformation and in the subsequent breakaway of numerous Protestant denominations. These fractures have inevitably led to confusion and competition and to problems with authority. Throughout the history of each church there has been a constant need to maintain the balance between the preaching of the Word, the right administration of the Sacraments and its works of charity and evangelism. There has also been a constant struggle with the relationship between Church and State.

Since the fourth century the Church has been recognised, in the words of the Nicene Creed, as one, holy, catholic and apostolic. In other words it was called out as one body, to be set apart for the service of God in an all-embracing, universal community dedicated to continuing the work that Jesus gave to his apostles. To be known and to witness as a member of the Christian Church can be very costly and many millions have been persecuted and many martyrs have died in the history of the Church. This persecution and martyrdom continues today in many parts of the world and could become even more frequent.

The preaching of the Word and the administration of the Sacraments and all the other activities involved in any church community made it necessary, from the earliest times, to have some specialists. When Peter refers to the whole body of believers as a 'holy priesthood' he indicates that each member should minister to others as a priest, that is as a mediator, representing God to man in service and witness, and man to God in prayer. As the Church grew, however, it required a degree of organisation for which different roles and levels of authority were necessary. This led to the appointment of bishops or overseers who inherited the mantle of the apostles, and presbyters or elders. Both of these were ordained by laying on of hands. They also appointed deacons or helpers for practical tasks, as described in Acts 6:1-4, though the categories often seem to have overlapped. The bishops appear to have had overall leadership and responsibility for more than one congregation and authority to ordain elders, and along with two others, to ordain fellow bishops. They either presided over the breaking of bread or Eucharist, or delegated the task to an elder. In the present day the Roman Catholics and Anglicans have ordained bishops and priests, the Baptists, Methodists and the URC have ordained ministers but no bishops and the 'Free' Churches have non-ordained elders or leaders. All of them have the equivalent of deacons, whatever they call them and whether they are ordained or lay.

Every human family needs to have shared meals and memories and rituals to ensure identity and cohesion and the Church is no exception. The shared meal of the Eucharist, literally giving of thanks, also known as the Lord's Supper, the Holy Communion and the Mass, is the chief of the two defining sacramental rituals of the Christian Church. The other is the initiating sacrament of Baptism. The Eucharist is the sacrament that represents and commemorates Christ's sacrificial death for us. In its celebration as a shared meal, it reminds believers of the nature of the fellowship to which they belong and binds them to God the Father, to Christ and to each other in the Spirit. This sacrament and that of Baptism, together with the faithful proclamation of the Word, are the essential elements that enable a fellowship of people to be recognised as a part of the universal Christian Church. Believers will not be true to their calling however, unless they reach out to others in welcoming mission and works of healing and charity, as Jesus commanded them to do. What follows in the section on the Creeds is a brief description of how the Church eventually came to reach agreement on a form of words in which to express its beliefs.

THE CREEDS

In Deuteronomy 6:4 Moses told the people: 'Hear O Israel: The Lord our God, the Lord is one'. Paul wrote in 1 Corinthians 8:6 that 'for us there is but one God, the Father, from whom all things came and for whom we live; and there is but one Lord, Jesus Christ, through whom all things came and through whom we live.' In 1Cor 15:3,4 he told us that 'Christ died for our sins according to the Scriptures, that he was buried, that he was raised on the third day according to the Scriptures.' There are also other short statements of faith in some of the other epistles. Apart from these early biblical statements of belief, and the numerous different versions of the apostles' teaching used by the early Church, it is a surprise to learn that it was nearly another four hundred years before what we now know as the Nicene Creed was finally formulated at Constantinople in 381 AD. Even then it seems that this came about largely as a result of imperial and political pressure, exerted in order to achieve unity and peace and political stability. This creed was produced by the Nicene Council in 325 and was amended in 381 by the addition of a fuller statement of the person and work of the Holy Spirit. What is equally surprising is that this version, as with the older and shorter Apostles' Creed, has not been subjected to any further modification, but only a clarification of the being of Jesus as both completely God and completely man. This was achieved in the form of an additional Definition at the Council of Chalcedon in 451.

There is still a lack of agreement between the Western and the Eastern Orthodox Church on the question of whether the Holy Spirit proceeds from the Father or from the Father and the Son, as the Western Church believes, and their respective versions of the Nicene Creed reflect this difference. This has to do with the precise relationships between the members of the Godhead which must of necessity be beyond our comprehension, and certainly beyond our ability to capture in a form of words, as the continuing discussions reveal.

A further surprising fact is that the Church actually needed a creed in order to encapsulate its faith and that it nevertheless found it so difficult to arrive at. This is surely because it had to struggle – and continues to struggle – to make sense of what the God of creation has revealed to us of himself in history and in our own experience. We need to find out what it is possible to say about this progressive revelation so that we can achieve the best available understanding of the Good News and be in a position to pass it on to others. The truth of the Gospel needs to be stated as clearly as we can manage; not only the historical facts involved in it, but our interpretation of it and our understanding of its significance for us and for the world. The earliest versions of the creeds were probably prepared for new converts coming for baptism so that they could be instructed in the essence of the Christian faith. They were required to recite them or assent to them in a question and answer form and this is still the case today.

THE NICENE CREED

We believe in one God, the Father, the almighty,
maker of heaven and earth,
of all that is, seen and unseen.

We believe in one Lord, Jesus Christ, the only Son of God,
eternally begotten of the Father, God from God, Light from Light,
true God from true God, begotten, not made,
of one Being with the Father.
Through him all things were made.
For us men and for our salvation
he came down from heaven;
by the power of the Holy Spirit
he became incarnate by the virgin Mary and was made man.
For our sake he was crucified under Pontius Pilate;
he suffered death and was buried.
On the third day he rose again
In accordance with the Scriptures;
He ascended into heaven
and is seated at the right hand of the Father.
He will come again in glory
to judge the living and the dead,
and his kingdom will have no end.

We believe in the Holy Spirit,
the Lord, the giver of life,
who proceeds from the Father and the Son.
With the Father and the Son he is worshipped and glorified.
He has spoken through the Prophets.

We believe in one holy catholic and apostolic Church.
We acknowledge one baptism for the forgiveness of sins.
We look for the resurrection of the dead,
and the life of the world to come. Amen. ?

The creeds naturally focused on God the Father, God the Son and God the Holy Spirit but the word Trinity was not mentioned. They were not doctrinal statements but rather confessions and affirmations of faith in God and in his Church. They were also used in offering praise and thanksgiving to God in worship as a part of the liturgy in the way that we continue to use the Creed today. The difficulty about doctrinal statements is that orthodoxy can get in the way by emphasising the letter rather than the spirit of truth and fostering the illusion that it can be stated with complete precision. This can easily lead to controversy and intolerance. Having said that, it is hard to see how the Nicene Creed and the older and shorter Apostles' Creed could be improved on. They are remarkable summaries of the facts and the spirit of the Good News that is revealed to us in Scripture and made real for us in our own experience. In the next section, continuing our review of 1Corinthians, we come to chapter 13 in which Paul writes about Love in a way that certainly cannot be improved on.

CHAPTER 13. PAUL WRITES ABOUT LOVE.

This glorious chapter, like some of the Psalms, needs to be savoured for the incomparable beauty of its language before we even begin to think more deeply about its meaning. Having said that it may be helpful to note that the word translated love is the Greek word agape, meaning to love dearly. It is for this reason the preferred word for love throughout the New Testament when referring to the love that we share with God and with our neighbour. This is a strong love that is as much to do with will and reason as with feeling and thus involves our whole personality. It is something we decide to do because we have been commanded to love and because we find it works. A saintly Catholic friend once said, though maybe he was not the first to say it: "You don't have to like everyone, but you can love them." Agape is equivalent to the Latin word caritas and the French charité and hence it is translated as charity in the Authorised Version of the Bible. The other word for love that is used on only a few occasions in the New Testament is philia meaning the love between friends. Eros, the Greek word for the love between man and woman including but not exclusively involving physical, sexual love, does not appear in the New Testament.

CHAPTER 13

"If I speak in the tongues of men and of angels, but have not love, I am only a resounding gong or a clanging cymbal. If I have the gift of prophecy and can fathom all mysteries and all knowledge, and if I have faith that can move mountains, but have not love, I am nothing. If I give all I possess to the poor and surrender my body to the flames, but have not love, I gain nothing.

Love is patient, love is kind. It does not envy, it does not boast, it is not proud. It is not rude, it is not self seeking, it is not easily angered, it keeps no record of wrongs. Love does not delight in evil but rejoices with the truth. It always protects, always trusts, always hopes, always perseveres.

Love never fails. But where there are prophecies, they will cease; where there are tongues, they will be stilled; where there is knowledge, it will pass away. For we know in part and we prophesy in part, but when perfection comes, the imperfect disappears. When I was a child, I talked like a child, I thought like a child, I reasoned like a child. When I became a man, I put childish ways behind me. Now we see but a poor reflection as in a mirror; then we shall see face to face. Now I know in part; then I shall know fully, even as I am fully known.

And now these three remain: faith, hope and love. But the greatest of these is love."

1 CORINTHIANS CONTINUES

In Chapter 15 Paul teaches about the resurrection of Christ, experienced by many witnesses, including himself, on which the promise of our own future resurrection depends. He emphasises this in a lengthy and powerful argument:

"If Christ has not been raised, your faith is futile; you are still in your sins, and if only for this life we have hope in Christ, we are to be pitied more than all men. But Christ has indeed been raised from the dead and those who belong to him will also be raised when he returns. Then the end will come, when he hands over the kingdom to God the Father after he has destroyed all dominion, authority and power. For he must reign until he has put all his enemies under his feet. The last enemy to be destroyed is death. To those who ask 'How are the dead raised?' he says; What you sow does not come to life unless it dies ... So will it be with the resurrection of the dead. The body that is sown is perishable, it is raised imperishable; it is sown a natural body, it is raised a spiritual body. Flesh and blood cannot inherit the kingdom of God ... Listen, I tell you a mystery: We will not all sleep, but we will all be changed – in a flash, in the twinkling of an eye, at the last trumpet ... and death will have been swallowed up in victory."

Therefore, says Paul, stand firm. Let nothing move you. Always give yourselves fully to the work of the Lord, because you know that your labour in the Lord is not in vain. Paul is in no doubt about the reality of Christ's resurrection and about our own eventual share in its reality. He speaks graphically of the new spiritual body in which we shall eventually be clothed as an 'eternal house in heaven' to replace our earthly tent. (2 Cor 5: 1,2)

In the final chapter, as a response to their very practical question about the collection for God's people, he gives the Corinthian Christians a wise and equally practical answer: 'On the first day of every week, each one of you should set aside a sum of money in keeping with his income, saving it up, so that when I come no collections will have to be made.' He closes with personal messages and greetings and ends with 'My love to all of you in Christ Jesus. Amen.'

2 CORINTHIANS

'Praise be to the God and Father of our Lord Jesus Christ, the Father of compassion and the God of all comfort, who comforts us in all our troubles, so that we can comfort those in any trouble with the comfort we have ourselves received from God.' 1:3,4.

The second letter begins with this expression of praise to God and encouragement to the believers in Corinth. It continues with an attempt to explain the delay in his visit to them and to address their loss of confidence in his reliability, which was due to false teachers who were questioning his integrity and authority. He makes a forceful but gracious defence of his ministry, writing 'not to grieve you but to let you know the depth of my love for you.' He reminds them of the surpassing glory of the new covenant of which he is a minister:

> 'For we do not preach ourselves, but Jesus Christ as Lord, and ourselves as your servants for Jesus' sake. For God, who said, "Let light shine out of darkness", made his light shine in our hearts to give us the light of the knowledge of the glory of God in the face of Jesus Christ.'

He goes on to tell them: 'We are therefore Christ's ambassadors, as though God were making an appeal through us. We implore you on Christ's behalf: Be reconciled to God.' Later, by way of explaining his methods, he says: 'The weapons we fight with are not the weapons of the world ... We demolish arguments and every pretension that sets itself up against the knowledge of God, and we take captive every thought to make it obedient to Christ.'

He speaks of being hard pressed on every side and suffering with Jesus 'so that the grace that is reaching more and more people may cause thanksgiving to overflow to the glory of God.' He goes on to emphasise once again the cost of this ministry to him and his fellow apostles and mentions beatings, imprisonments and riots, sleepless nights and hunger. 'Dying, and yet we live on; sorrowful, yet always rejoicing; poor, yet making many rich; having nothing, and yet possessing everything.' We are not withholding our affection from you, but you are withholding yours from us, he tells the Corinthians, and beseeches them to open wide their hearts. Even if I caused you sorrow by my letter, I do not regret it ... because your sorrow led to repentance. He talks to them of the generosity of the Macedonian churches and of the need for them to give also – to excel in this grace of giving. Each man should give what he has decided in his heart to give, not reluctantly or under compulsion, for God loves a cheerful giver.

This epistle is sometimes tortuous and somewhat repetitive – for which Paul has been frequently criticised – but everything here speaks of his love and concern for the Corinthian Christians and is a lesson to us in our relationships, in our fellowships and in our concern for those outside them. The strain of an itinerant ministry with all the hazards of travel as well as the opposition within the churches and persecution from without, must surely account for a number of the things he says. It is not surprising that he returns several times to his terrible hardships. He mentions imprisonments and beatings, several shipwrecks, lack of sleep, food and even water, and being exposed to death again and again. And besides everything else, he tells them 'I face the daily pressure of my concern for all the churches'.

Other saints throughout the history of the Church have endured appalling suffering but no others have combined it with producing these incomparable, now canonical, writings. They must have encouraged countless millions of Christians in their own hardships, and no doubt many others also down the ages. We cannot know how Paul's epistles were influenced by the visions and revelations that he refers to in chapter 12. He describes what was clearly his own experience of being 'caught up to the third heaven' or 'paradise', when he heard 'inexpressible things, things that man is not permitted to tell.' 'To keep me from becoming conceited because of these revelations, there was given me a thorn in my flesh, a messenger of Satan, to torment me.' Whatever its nature, Paul had pleaded with the Lord to take it away but he was told, "My grace is sufficient for you, for my power is made perfect in weakness." This he accepted gladly, 'for when I am weak, then am I strong.'

After telling them of the way that God has dealt with him, Paul continues with his expressions of pastoral concern and warnings for his flock in Corinth. 'Everything we do, dear friends, is for your strengthening.' He ends with the prayer that must have been repeated an uncountable number of times since he wrote it:

"May the grace of the Lord Jesus Christ, and the love of God, and the fellowship of the Holy Spirit be with you all." Amen.

GALATIANS

Galatia was an ancient ethnic kingdom in Asia Minor that later became a Roman province. This epistle would appear therefore to have been written to a number of churches, all of whom seem to have been influenced, even 'bewitched', by Judaisers who were trying to bind Gentile believers to Old Testament Jewish rites, such as circumcision. Even Peter was regarded as guilty of forcing Gentiles to follow Jewish customs. Paul begins therefore by defending his credentials as an apostle – 'sent not from man or by man' – and states firmly that the Gospel he preaches was 'received by revelation from Jesus Christ,' and 'not to be changed' under penalty of 'eternal condemnation'. It must be obvious that if there had not been this degree of clarity at the outset the Gospel could never have taken hold and developed, and the history of the Church would have been even more plagued by erroneous beliefs.

The single clear message of the epistle is that we are justified by faith in Jesus Christ and not by observing the law, or by our own works. It was this epistle, and in particular this teaching, that had such a great influence on Martin Luther, whose conviction helped to accelerate the Reformation. It is a truth that Paul confirms here, as he does in Romans, with reference to the experience of Abraham, whose faith was credited to him as righteousness. The law, Paul says, was put in charge to lead us to Christ and the only thing that counts is faith expressing itself through love. He also makes clear his love and concern for the Gentiles, addressing them as 'My dear children for whom I am again in pains of childbirth until Christ is formed in you.' Serve one another in love. The entire law is summed up in a single command: Love your neighbour as yourself. Those whose lives are sinful and contrary to the Spirit will not inherit the kingdom of God. But the fruit of the spirit is love, joy, peace, patience, kindness, goodness, faithfulness, gentleness and self-control. Let us keep in step with the Spirit and carry each other's burdens and do not become weary in doing good. Paul ends characteristically, The grace of our Lord Jesus Christ be with your spirit, brothers. Amen.

EPHESIANS

Romans is Paul's theological masterpiece, the pinnacle of his Christian theological teaching. Ephesians, also a miracle of creative writing, demonstrates the depth of his spiritual insight into the mystery of Christ. This was not made known to men in other generations but has now been made known to Paul by revelation 'as it has now been revealed by the Spirit to God's holy apostles and prophets.' Paul's writing in this epistle is of matchless quality that is made possible only by the inspiration of God's Holy Spirit. We are not in the foothills of the Christian faith with Ephesians but rather it speaks to us from the summit – or as near as anyone has ever approached it. This is inevitably obscured by clouds of mystery that no mind but only faith and love and worship can even begin to penetrate.

Paul is not addressing particular problems in the Ephesian church – though they had later to be called to repentance by the Lord himself in Revelation 2:4,5 for 'forsaking your first love'. The vision and focus of this epistle is mankind viewed as the family of God, the members of God's household who are themselves a dwelling in which God lives by his Spirit. He begins by describing the exalted status of the individual believers in contrast to their previous condition, as 'dead in your transgressions and sins'. He goes on to describe how 'God has raised us up with Christ and seated us with him in the heavenly realms in Christ Jesus', and given us his Holy Spirit as a 'deposit guaranteeing our inheritance'. 'For it is by grace you have been saved, through faith – and this not from yourselves, it is the gift of God – not of works, so that no-one can boast.'

He then goes on to speak of the mystery of the inclusion of the Gentiles, only now revealed, that was referred to in Isaiah 49:6 in particular and taken up by Simeon in Luke 2:32. It is to them that Paul has been made a minister, to preach to them 'the unsearchable riches of Christ'. They were 'without hope and without God in the world' and are now 'heirs together with Israel'. The two have been made one in Christ in the body of his Church, through which the 'manifold wisdom of God' is to be 'made known to the rulers and authorities in the heavenly realms, according to his eternal purpose.'

A Prayer for the Ephesians   Chapter 3:14-21

For this reason I kneel before the Father, from whom his whole family in heaven and earth derives its name. I pray that out of his glorious riches he may strengthen you with power through his Spirit in your inner being, so that Christ may dwell in your hearts by faith. And I pray that you, being rooted and established in love, may have power, together with all the saints, to grasp how wide and long and high and deep is the love of Christ, and to know this love that surpasses knowledge – that you may be filled with all the fullness of God.

Now to him who is able to do immeasurably more than all we ask or imagine, according to his power that is at work in us, to him be glory in the church and in Christ Jesus throughout all generations, for ever and ever. Amen.

The Whole Armour of God   Chapter 6:10-18

Finally, be strong in the Lord and in his mighty power. Put on the full armour of God so that you can take your stand against the devil's schemes. For our struggle is not against flesh and blood, but against the rulers, against the authorities, against the powers of this dark world and against the spiritual forces of evil in the heavenly realms. Therefore put on the full armour of God, so that when the day of evil comes, you may be able stand your ground, and after you have done everything, to stand. Stand firm then, with the belt of truth buckled round your waist, with the breastplate of righteousness in place, and with your feet fitted with the readiness that comes from the gospel of peace. In addition to all this, take up the shield of faith, with which you can extinguish all the flaming arrows of the evil one. Take the helmet of salvation and the sword of the Spirit, which is the word of God. And pray in the Spirit on all occasions, with all kinds of prayers and requests.

The only response that Paul can make to this revelation is worship. 'For this reason', as he tells us in the first passage opposite, 'I kneel before the Father...' He is overwhelmed by the sheer grandeur of God's plan for his people. After visiting the heights in this outburst of praise Paul returns to the plains to spell out, as usual, the inevitable practical implications of these glorious truths. The Ephesian Christians are to 'live a life worthy of the calling you have received. Be completely humble and gentle; be patient, bearing with one another in love.' 'To each one of us grace has been given as Christ apportioned it' and he has also given gifts: 'some to be apostles, some to be prophets, some to be evangelists, and some to be pastors and teachers, to prepare God's people for works of service.' This is 'so that the body of Christ may be built up until we all reach unity in the faith and in the knowledge of the Son of God and become mature, attaining to the whole measure of the fullness of Christ.' The Church is not always aware of the exalted nature of its calling.

Paul continues with lengthy, detailed instructions for Christian living, urging us, amongst other things, to 'forgive each other, just as in Christ God forgave you' and to 'sing and make music in your heart to the Lord.' He goes on to give advice about specific personal relationships, prefacing this with the principle that should govern all of them: 'Submit to one another out of reverence for Christ.' This applies especially to husbands and wives; husbands being instructed to 'love your wives, just as Christ loved the church and gave himself up for it.' Paul's remarkable teaching about marriage, likening it to the relationship between Christ as bridegroom and his Church as bride is a 'profound mystery', as he admits, and it moves the relationship between wives and husbands on to a new plane. Then follow instructions to children to 'obey your parents in the Lord' and to fathers not to 'exasperate your children' – a very interesting word of caution. Paul turns next to instruction about another important relationship in the wider community, that between slaves and masters. Surprisingly, this teaching can be readily transferred to our present-day commercial and industrial world equivalent of employers and employees. He exhorts slaves to be 'like slaves of Christ, and to serve wholeheartedly as if you were serving the Lord.' Masters are to remember that 'he who is both their master and yours is in heaven, and there is no favouritism with him.'

Paul ends this remarkable epistle with the second of the passages on page 252, in which he exhorts us to put on the whole armour of God to enable us to triumph in what is a spiritual battle. In this brilliant passage Paul makes use of symbols and metaphors that he borrows from Genesis, the Psalms and Isaiah, (Gen 15:1, Ps 7:10, 28:7, 119:11, Is 11:5, 59:17), and also some that he uses elsewhere in his own writings. (Rom 13:12, 1 Thess 5:8). He combines these symbols into a powerful composite image that was no doubt based on the Roman soldier with whom his readers would have been very familiar. His last words are, as usual, requests for prayers, in this case for courage in his preaching. He mentions Tychicus, his 'dear brother in the Lord' who will bring them news of him, and sends final greetings of peace, of love with faith, and grace.

MARRIAGE

The imagery of marriage is introduced at the very beginning of Genesis. God made man in his own image, as both male and female, with a powerful recognition that they belong together. 'For this reason a man will leave his father and mother and will be united to his wife and they will become one flesh.' This remarkable phrase conveys a sense of both physical and spiritual union and suggests the ideal of a faithful and exclusive monogamous relationship. There are no less than three examples of touching, tender husband and wife relationships in Genesis alone, Abraham and Sarah, Isaac and Rebekah, and Jacob and Rachel. Another example is that of Ruth and Boaz, whose story appears in the book of Ruth.

The importance of marriage is further emphasised, in the laws relating to sexual relationships, by their condemnation of both adultery (Ex 20:14) and divorce. "Do not break faith with the wife of your youth. I hate divorce," says the Lord God of Israel. (Mal 2:15,16). Jesus teaches us in Mathew 5:32 and 19:9 that divorce can be granted only for marital unfaithfulness, an exception not mentioned in Mark and Luke, where he simply states that a man who marries a divorced woman or who divorces his own wife and marries another woman commits adultery. (Mk 10:5, Lk 16:8). Jesus' response to those who reminded him that Moses had allowed men to issue a certificate of divorce to a wife who displeased them was that this was only 'because your hearts were hard'. This had not been the intention at the beginning when it was ordained that through the process of 'leaving and cleaving' they became 'one flesh' for life. "Therefore", Jesus says, "what God has joined together, let no man separate." (Mt 19:6, Mk 10:9). Gender, with its associated sexual aspect, is a paradox; it is that which separates in order to unite us, and it obliges us to share the decision to reproduce and encourages us to share the responsibility for the offspring. The only absolute end to a marriage comes with the death of one of the spouses. Only at the resurrection, Jesus tells us, will marriage itself come to an end; then people will "neither marry nor be given in marriage, they will be like the angels in heaven." (Matt 22:30). This surely does not mean that those who have been married will no longer know and love each other but that there will be no sexual union and no further offspring.

A further extension of the use of this imagery of marriage appears in the Old Testament where it is used to convey God's relationship to his people Israel. He is referred to in several passages, not only as Father, but also as 'husband' and 'bridegroom'. 'For your maker is your husband', (Is 54:5). 'Return faithless people for I am your husband.' (Jer 3:14). 'As a bridegroom rejoices over his bride, so will your God rejoice over you.' (Is 62:5) When we come to the New Testament Jesus refers to himself as the bridegroom on two separate occasions. (Mk 2:19, Matt 25:1). John records in the second chapter of his Gospel that he was a guest at a wedding at Cana in Galilee and played a very active part in the celebrations by turning water into wine.

Paul, in his epistle to the Ephesians attempts the almost impossible task of comparing the human marriage relationship with that between Christ and his bride the Church. Husbands are to love their wives 'just as Christ loved the Church and gave himself up for her' and wives should submit to their husbands as the Church submits to Christ. This is an exalted view of our human marriage relationship and Paul has to admit that he is dealing with a 'profound mystery'. He ends this passage by saying that 'each one of you also must love his wife as he loves himself, and the wife must respect her husband.' His overall exhortation is that we are all of us as Christians to 'submit to one another out of reverence for Christ.' We are all of us at the deepest level subject to Christ alone. Some may think that Paul's views on marriage are dated but has anyone ever, before or since, spoken of it in such profound and exalted terms and with a more accurate recognition of the reality of human relationships? The final word in Scripture on the theme of Christ and the Church comes in Revelation 19:7: 'Let us rejoice and be glad and give him the glory! For the wedding of the Lamb has come and the bride has made herself ready.' The Lamb is Jesus himself who has given his life as a sacrifice for his bride the Church.

It is no wonder, in view of all this, that the writer of Hebrews says that 'marriage should be honoured by all, and the marriage bed be kept pure.' The idea of the marriage relationship is clearly at the heart of God's kingdom but is it sufficiently honoured at the heart of our own society – and even by the Church itself? It is not merely that, in the words of the Preface of the Common Worship Anglican Marriage Service, marriage 'enriches society' and 'strengthens community' but that without marriage and the discipline that it provides, no recognisably ordered and civilised society and no coherent community would be even remotely possible. (See Appendix 1) Heterosexual relationships, especially where there is the intention to have children, must ideally involve long-term commitment and are never a purely private matter. This commitment needs to be recognised in the community and witnessed, celebrated and registered on behalf of the whole of society. This is for the benefit of the adults themselves, and above all for any children they may have, and for the order and stability of society in general, and of the nation.

Marriage stakes out the relationship of the couple not only to each other and to their children but to their families on both sides, to their friends and neighbours, to the community and to the rest of society. Nothing else can perform all these essential functions. For a number of reasons, however, marriage is not sought by everyone and it does not happen for all those who wish for it. But for the majority who seek heterosexual relationships it is a provision that cannot responsibly be neglected without a very good reason. It is also important that those who feel obliged to point out the importance of marriage do not ignore the feelings of those who do not have a spouse to share their lives, or have lost one, or for whatever reason are living on their own.

Marriage is the safest place we know, or can imagine, for adults to receive the mutual comfort and companionship and the exclusive sexual fulfilment that they need. It is also the safest place for children to be conceived and brought up, for women to be made secure and for men to become civilised and to play their own important part in the rearing and disciplining of children. God expressly says in Genesis 2:18 that 'It is not good for the man to be alone'. Stable families, with a family name in common that only marriage can ensure, are the best and safest places for children to be nurtured and taught by two parents, representing both the male and female elements in their make-up. It is becoming increasingly clear that fathers have a hugely important part to play in bringing up balanced children, especially in the case of boys. Where Christian marriages are concerned, the family is the chief place in which they can learn about the faith and come to know Jesus and in which the parents have the possibility of experiencing him as the ever-present third person in their relationship.

The more complex society becomes the greater is our need of order and therefore of our need of marriage. We have yet to discover the long term outcome of the alternative arrangements that are at present being explored for parenting and adoption. Rather than honouring marriage we are increasingly often neglecting it altogether in favour of less stable and satisfactory arrangements without any clear evidence of commitment. One of the practical reasons for this is that weddings have tended to become too lavish and expensive; another is that it is cheaper for young people to live together than separately. We are also dishonouring marriage in our dangerously high rate of marital breakdown and divorce, with the inevitable deterioration that it causes in our communal life. This is one of a number of ways in which we are seeing the vital ingredient of discipline being eroded in our society. In our selfish pursuit of individual fulfilment we are suffering from a failure of loving on an unprecedented scale.

Marriage is not honoured by government, whose responsibility is limited but vital in supporting marriage in every way possible, above all in the practical provision of tax benefits, as a recognition of the expense involved in bringing up the nation's children. Nor is it honoured by our people, who appear to be either unaware of what is happening to the very fabric of the society in which we live, or to lack the will to do anything about it. Many appear to think that the situation is so serious that there is nothing that we can do about it. Even the Church is finding it hard to speak about it with a clear voice.

There are numerous other important relationships in which we engage but if we neglect to honour marriage as a safeguard for families we cannot expect our society to continue to flourish. It has been said that so long as a society's first concern is for its homes it matters little what it seeks second and third.

The entire sweep of the biblical revelation of God's purpose for his people can be seen as the greatest love story of all time in which the Father is seeking a bride for his Son, through the activity of his Holy Spirit – and who can tell what further fruit may issue from this marriage both now and in the age to come? Marriage is thus the model for God's relationship with his people and his provision for the closest and most important relationship in which we can become involved as human beings.

PHILIPPIANS

Paul wrote this epistle from prison in Rome to the church in the city of Philippi, a Roman colony named after King Philip of Macedonia, the father of Alexander the Great. It is unusually thickly studded, even for Paul, with gems of instruction and encouragement, and the predominant note is one of joy. He gives his usual greeting of grace and peace to the saints, together with the overseers and deacons. He gives thanks for them, for their partnership in the gospel and for their gifts and their prayers and he tells them that he 'always prays for them with joy, that their love may abound more and more in knowledge and depth of insight.' His chains have served to advance the gospel by encouraging some others to speak the word of God more fearlessly. For Paul to live is Christ and to die is gain but for them 'it is more necessary that I remain in the body.' Whatever happens, conduct yourselves in a manner worthy of the gospel of Christ. Our Christian faith must make a difference to the way we live. It has been said that behaviour is more important than belief, as James argues in his epistle. Paul continues, in the second chapter, with a remarkable passage in which he writes about Christ's self-emptying and his subsequent exaltation:

Your attitude should be the same as that of Christ Jesus:
Who, being in very nature God,
did not consider equality with God something to be grasped,
but made himself nothing,
  taking the very nature of a servant,
  being made in human likeness.
And being found in appearance as a man, he humbled himself
  and became obedient to death – even death on a cross!
Therefore God exalted him to the highest place
  and gave him a name that is above every name,
that at the name of Jesus every knee should bow,
  in heaven and on earth and under the earth,
and every tongue confess that Jesus Christ is Lord,
  to the glory of God the Father. Phil 2:5-11

'Therefore, my dear friends', says Paul 'continue to work out your own salvation with fear and trembling, for it is God who works in you to will and to act according to his good purpose.' All this to the end that they may, through Paul's endeavours for them, be blameless on the day of Christ. The prospect of the return of Christ to earth should influence us in all we do and think. From this high point Paul returns to praise Timothy and Epaphroditus, both of whom work constantly for Christ and on behalf of others. He then warns, as he has already done in Galatians, about those over-zealous Jews who were trying to insist on out-dated customs and traditions and boasting of their Jewish nationality and status. We can recognise modern equivalents – not infrequently in ourselves. For himself, Paul says, 'I consider everything a loss compared to the surpassing greatness of knowing Christ Jesus my Lord, for whose sake I have lost all things.' It is Christ for whom he longs and all the treasure that resides in him alone. He talks of 'pressing on' and of 'winning the prize for which God has called me heavenward in Christ Jesus', who when he comes again, will 'transform our lowly bodies so that they will be like his glorious body.' Therefore stand firm in the Lord, dear friends. He exhorts them to agree together, to rejoice in the Lord always and to think positively:

'Do not be anxious about anything, but in everything, by prayer and petition, with thanksgiving, present your requests to God. And the peace of God, which transcends all understanding, will guard hour hearts and minds in Christ Jesus. Finally, brothers, whatever is true, whatever is noble, whatever is right, whatever is pure, whatever is lovely, whatever is admirable – if anything is excellent or praiseworthy – think about such things.'

Paul goes on to say that he has learned the secret of being content in every situation and that he can do everything 'through him who gives me strength'. Finally, he thanks them once again for their gifts to him, gives glory to God the Father and commends them to the grace of the Lord Jesus Christ. Paul's unvarying focus on God's glory and the good of his Christian brothers and sisters is a constant example.

COLOSSIANS

'Christ is the image of the invisible God, the firstborn over all creation. For by him all things were created: things in heaven and on earth, visible and invisible, whether thrones or rulers or authorities; all things were created by him and for him. He is before all things, and in him all things hold together. And he is the head of the body, the church; he is the firstborn from among the dead, so that in everything he might have the supremacy. For God was pleased to have all his fullness dwell in him, and through him to reconcile to himself all things, whether things on earth or things in heaven, by making peace through his blood, shed on the cross.' (1:15-20).

Paul wrote this rich epistle, also packed with jewels of instruction and inspiration, in order to emphasise the supremacy of Christ as the 'mystery of God'. He is God's 'very image in whom are hidden all the treasures of wisdom and knowledge', and who is, in us and for us, 'the hope of glory'. The Colossians were at risk of being led astray by fine-sounding arguments and regulations and of 'losing connection with the Head'. The problems faced by the Church today, in the West at least, are different – apathy and ignorance of God's truth, materialism, and numerous alternative ideologies – but they have the same effect of separating us from Christ. In the passage at the head of the chapter Paul describes the unique stature, divinity and supremacy of Christ in words that echo John's words at the start of his Gospel and a number of Jesus' own words about himself.

After his usual courteous greetings Paul tells the Colossians of his thanks to God for their faith in Christ Jesus and love for all the saints – the faith and love that spring from the hope that is stored up for them in heaven. He goes on to tell them in the third chapter:

'Since, then, you have been raised with Christ, set your hearts on things above, where Christ is seated at the right hand of God. Set your minds on things above, not on earthly things. For you died, and your life is now hidden with Christ in God. When Christ, who is your life, appears, then you also will appear with him in glory.'

Paul's teaching is as usual combined with his care and concern for them. His prayer is that 'God will fill them with the knowledge of his will through all spiritual wisdom and understanding' and that they may bear fruit in every good work. He goes on to speak of the commission he has been given to present to them the word of God in its fullness and the struggling and suffering that this causes him for the sake of the Church. The Gospel was fresh news to them but though it is now two thousand years old it is no less Good News for us today. In spite of this we somehow find it hard to speak of it in such glowing terms and to spread it with the same enthusiasm.

Paul ends, as usual, with personal messages and greetings from, amongst others, 'our dear friend Luke, the doctor' and finally his accustomed 'Grace be with you.'

1 AND 2 THESSALONIANS

These are two of Paul's earliest epistles, written mainly to Gentile Christians. His chief theme in both is the 'end things' – the return to earth of Jesus at the end of the age, for which we are still waiting. 'May God himself, the God of peace, sanctify you through and through. May your whole spirit, soul and body be kept blameless at the coming of our Lord Jesus Christ.' This event will come 'as a thief in the night' so let us be alert and self-controlled. The epistles are full of his love and concern for the believers, his prayers and his encouragement for them in their persecution, which will make them worthy of the kingdom of God.

In the first epistle Paul gives a description of the characteristics of a minister of the Gospel that he has demonstrated to them. He is entrusted with the gospel; he is to please God and not try to please men or flatter them; to be gentle and to care for his people as a mother and father care for their children. He is also to share not only the gospel but his own life as well, and to be holy, righteous and blameless. Paul has sometimes been portrayed as an obscure, dogmatic theologian but what comes across most strongly in his epistles is his devoted, unselfish pastoral care for those entrusted to him. He ends, as usual, with requests to the believers for prayer and with detailed instructions for living out their faith. Among them is his warning against sexual immorality and his warning to the idle, whom we 'command and urge in the Lord Jesus Christ to settle down and earn the bread they eat'. He urges them to 'stand firm and hold to the teachings we passed on to you.' His final greeting is a characteristic prayer: 'Now may the Lord of peace himself give you peace at all times and in every way. The grace of our Lord Jesus Christ be with you all.'

1 TIMOTHY

Paul writes this epistle as a personal letter to Timothy, 'my true son in the faith' and begins by warning him of the danger of false teachers who do not know what they are talking about. He gives thanks that, though previously a blasphemer and persecutor, he has been shown mercy 'because I acted in ignorance and unbelief'. The Lord Jesus Christ has 'appointed me to his service' and his grace was 'poured out on me abundantly'. This leads Paul into an outpouring of praise:

'Here is a trustworthy saying that deserves full acceptance: Christ Jesus came into the world to save sinners – of whom I am the worst. But for that very reason I was shown mercy so that in me, the worst of sinners, Christ might display his unlimited patience as an example for those who would believe on him and receive eternal life. Now to the king eternal, immortal, invisible, the only God, be honour and glory for ever and ever. Amen.'

He then urges Timothy to pray and give thanks for all in authority 'that we may live peaceful and quiet lives in all godliness and holiness. This is good, and pleases God our Saviour, who wants all men to be saved and to come to a knowledge of the truth.'

He goes on to describe the qualities required in an overseer or elder – including a sound family life. He follows this with further general advice to Timothy and tells him: 'Do not rebuke an older man harshly, but exhort him as if he were your father. Treat younger men as brothers, older women as mothers, and younger women as sisters, with absolute purity.' Some of this may sound strange to our ears but what a wonderful image it presents of the family of the Church, and what a challenge to our modern day culture. He goes on to give detailed, practical instructions for personal life and relationships including the treatment of widows, in a society in which there were no welfare benefits. He reminds Timothy that we brought nothing into the world and we can take nothing out of it and that the love of money is a root of all kinds of evil. This is a timely message for today.

'But you, man of God, flee from all this, and pursue righteousness, godliness, faith, love, endurance and gentleness. Fight the good fight of the faith. I charge you to keep this command without spot or blame until the appearing of our Lord Jesus Christ, which God will bring about in his own time – God, the blessed and only Ruler, the King of kings and Lord of lords, who alone is immortal and who lives in unapproachable light, whom no-one has seen or can see. To him be honour and might for ever. Amen.'

2 TIMOTHY

The second epistle to Timothy, Paul's last recorded letter, was written from prison in Rome, as were those to the Ephesians and the Philippians. This time however he was not under house arrest but 'chained like a criminal'. He was lonely – 'everyone in Asia has deserted me; only Luke is with me.' He was concerned about the welfare of the churches during the time of persecution under Nero and he was himself shortly to be tried and executed. Nevertheless he addresses Timothy with his usual courtesy as 'my dear son whom I constantly remember in my prayers, and long to see, so that I may be filled with joy.' It is a very moving letter and everywhere reveals a man who knows that he is nearing the end of a unique and remarkable life of ministry:

> 'So do not be ashamed to testify about our Lord, or be ashamed of me his prisoner. But join with me in suffering for the gospel, by the power of God, who has saved us and called us to a holy life – not because of anything we have done but because of his own purpose and grace. This grace was given us in Christ before the beginning of time, but it has now been revealed through the appearing of our Saviour, Christ Jesus, who has destroyed death and has brought life and immortality to light through the gospel. And of this gospel I was appointed a herald and an apostle and a teacher. That is why I am suffering as I am. Yet I am not ashamed, because I know whom I have believed, and am convinced that he is able to guard what I have entrusted to him for that day.'

What a testimony to be able to give at the end of a life of Christian ministry! He goes on to encourage his 'son' Timothy to keep what he has heard from him as the pattern of sound teaching and to entrust it to reliable men who will be qualified to teach others. The Gospel must be preached in every generation, as we are learning to our cost today. He tells him that 'there will be terrible times in the last days' and warns him that 'everyone who wants to live a godly life in Christ Jesus will be persecuted.' He reminds him how 'from infancy you have known the holy scriptures, which are able to make you wise for salvation through faith in Christ Jesus.'

Paul goes on to exhort Timothy to 'Preach the Word; be prepared in season and out of season; correct, rebuke and encourage – with great patience and careful instruction. For the time will come when men will not put up with sound doctrine.' He then tells him that 'the time has come for my departure. I have fought the good fight, I have finished the race, I have kept the faith.' and 'the Lord will bring me safely to his heavenly kingdom. To him be glory for ever and ever. Amen.' Finally, the last recorded words of the Church's most influential saint, always focusing on those to whom he was writing, in this case his favourite young colleague Timothy: 'The Lord be with your spirit. Grace be with you.'

SCRIPTURE

Following his reference to the holy Scriptures in 2 Timothy, Paul makes the striking statement that 'All Scripture is God-breathed and is useful for teaching, rebuking, correcting and training in righteousness, so that the man of God may be thoroughly equipped for every good work.' Scripture is God-breathed, not God-dictated. It is not the letter but the spirit of the truth that is imparted: not the very words themselves but the spiritual truths expressed through them. Scripture is thus a form of inspired creative writing. Unless the truth is directly dictated by God's Spirit, which few thinking Christians seriously believe, or is merely human wisdom which is an even more untenable notion, it must have been revealed to the writers who digested and internalised it, struggled to understand it and expressed it in their own words and styles. This flexibility is made possible because words are often stretchy, 'like woolly jumpers', sometimes with quite a wide range of related meanings, so that the same ideas can be expressed in different words and different ways by different writers. For the same reason these ideas can also be expressed in different translations of the original Hebrew and Greek words in the various versions of the Bible without altering their basic meaning.

The unique feature of the Scriptures, especially the books of the New Testament, is that although they are useful for sound teaching their real message is not a written word to be slavishly observed but a living Word to be embraced, a person to be trusted and loved and followed. The Bible would soon lose its credibility without the continuing, living witness of those who follow Jesus. It was the leaders of the early Church, aided by the Spirit, who established the canon of the New Testament Scriptures – that is the body of those books that they gradually recognised to be authoritative and therefore worthy of inclusion. We cannot add to the canon but its living, permanently relevant truths need to be freshly understood and applied in each generation because our circumstances are constantly changing. Scripture and the good news it has to tell are never out of date.

TITUS

Although this epistle comes after 2 Timothy, it was written several years earlier, as was his letter to Philemon that comes next. Paul writes this epistle to Titus, 'my true son in our common faith' and gives him, amongst other general guidance, some very practical instructions. These include teaching what is in accord with sound doctrine and providing specific, appropriate teaching for older men, older women, younger women in their relationships with their husbands and children and younger men, who are encouraged to be self-controlled. 'In everything set them an example by doing what is good. In your teaching show integrity, seriousness and soundness of speech that cannot be condemned, so that those who oppose you may be ashamed because they have nothing bad to say about us.'

> 'For the grace of God that brings salvation has appeared to all men. It teaches us to say "No" to ungodliness and worldly passions, and to live self-controlled lives in this present age, while we wait for the blessed hope – the glorious appearing of our great God and Saviour, Jesus Christ, who gave himself for us to redeem us from all

wickedness and to purify for himself a people that are his very own, eager to do what is good.'

'Everyone with me sends you greetings. Greet those who love us in the faith.' Finally he ends as always: 'Grace be with you all.'

PHILEMON

Paul wrote this short epistle, from prison in Rome, to Philemon, 'our dear friend and fellow-worker' who was a Christian but also a slave-owner. It is a tactful plea that he might take back, as a Christian brother, his one-time slave Onesimus who had apparently stolen from him and run away, but had since become a believer. 'Confident of your obedience, I write to you, knowing that you will do even more than I ask. And one thing more: prepare a guest room for me, because I hope to be restored to you in answer to your prayers.' It is a beautifully constructed letter that must surely have produced the positive response that Paul hoped for.

HEBREWS

Hebrews, whose author is not known, was written to the descendents of those to whom God had spoken through the prophets in the Old Testament. Its purpose was to make clear to them the absolute supremacy of Christ as 'superior to the angels' and as the One in whom all the Old Testament prophecies and promises are being fulfilled:

> 'In the past God spoke to our forefathers through the prophets at many times and in various ways, but in these last days he has spoken to us by his Son, whom he appointed heir of all things, and through whom he made the universe. The Son is the radiance of God's glory and the exact representation of his being, sustaining all things

by his powerful word. After he had provided purification for sins, he sat down at the right hand of the Majesty in heaven.' (1:1-3).

As the long-awaited Messiah he is, through his own death, the mediator of the new covenant, or testament, that was foretold by Jeremiah. (Heb 8:8-12, quoting Jer 31:31-34). He is both the High Priest who offers the sacrifice and also the Lamb who is himself the sacrifice. His once-for-all sacrificial death seals this new covenant and supersedes the oft-repeated, always inadequate sacrifices of the Old Testament. He is also the King, whose 'throne will last forever' in the words of Psalm 8. The model of his everlasting priesthood and his kingship was provided by Melchizedek, meaning 'king of righteousness' who 'brought out bread and wine' to Abraham and blessed him. He was not only 'priest of God Most High' but king of Salem, meaning 'king of peace'. He was an early intimation of Christ's perfect priesthood and kingship, anticipated in the Old Testament as early as the fourteenth chapter of Genesis.

Jesus is now crowned with glory and one day everything will be subject to him because he underwent suffering and death on our behalf, having identified with us in our humanity. In this way both he who makes us holy and we who are made holy become members of the same family so that he is not ashamed to call us brothers. In view of this extraordinary truth the author asks: 'How shall we escape if we ignore such a great salvation?' He goes on to say that 'since we have a great high priest over the house of God' we are to persevere, to draw near to God and hold to the hope that we profess, spurring each other to love and good deeds, not giving up meeting together and encouraging one another – 'all the more as you see the Day approaching'. In the meantime 'the righteous will live by faith.' But why faith and what is this faith by which Christians are to live?

There are numerous examples of the Old Testament giants of faith described in chapter 11 – Noah and Abraham, Moses, Samuel and David, amongst many others. They pleased God and were rewarded for trusting and obeying him, often through terrible hardships. They took the long view, being 'aliens and strangers' and 'looking forward to the city with foundations whose architect and builder is God.' It was this same sense of expectancy that prompted GK Chesterton to say: 'Now I know why I could feel homesick at home.' He too knew that he was on a journey to another country. Jung was describing the same experience of something missing when he said that 'a secret unrest gnaws at the roots of our being.'[17] The writer of Hebrews goes on to say: 'Yet none of them received what had been promised. God had planned something better for us so that only together with us would they be made perfect.' (11:39,40). This is a mystery but it appears that even heaven itself has not yet experienced the final destiny that God has for all his people. This is because it will involve the whole of God's creation, all of which must enjoy it together: no-one can enjoy it fully until Jesus returns at the end of this present age to bring the kingdom to its final fulfilment.

The last two chapters of Hebrews are full of wonderful insights and encouragements. 'Therefore, since we are surrounded by such a great cloud of witnesses, let us throw off everything that hinders and the sin that so easily entangles, and let us run with perseverance the race marked out for us.' The writer goes on with an uplifting exhortation: 'Let us fix our eyes on Jesus, the author and perfecter of our faith, who for the joy set before him endured the cross, scorning its shame, and sat down at the right hand of the throne of God.' Hebrews ends on a high note:

> 'May the God of peace, who through the blood of the eternal covenant brought back from the dead our Lord Jesus, that great Shepherd of the sheep, equip you with everything good for doing his will, and may he work in us what is pleasing to him, through Jesus Christ, to whom be glory for ever and ever. Amen.'

FAITH

Chapter 11 of Hebrews is concerned exclusively with faith. Its first verse is halfway between a description and a definition. 'Now faith is being sure of what we hope for and certain of what we do not see.' It presents faith as an experience of confidence in God and a foretaste and intimation of the good things that he has in store for us. Paul perfectly expresses the attitude of faith when he writes in 2 Cor 4:18

---

[17] Collected Works 9 pt 1, para. 50. Quoted in Archetype p 286

that 'we fix our eyes not on what is seen, but on what is unseen. For what is seen is temporary, but what is unseen is eternal.' There are numerous different translations of this first verse of Hebrews 11, all expressing the same truth and thus illustrating the complexity and elasticity of words. They render this certainty as the sign or the evidence and also as the assurance or the conviction and even the proof of what we do not see. Dante, speaks of it, in the Divine Comedy, as the argomento, [18] the argument for what is not seen. Iris Murdoch said that 'the Good is the unimaginable object of our desire.' The writer of Hebrews is saying , in effect, that faith is the confidence that this unimaginable object is a reality, albeit invisible. The Christian belief is that the 'unimaginable object of our desire' is God himself and that he has made himself imaginable in Jesus.

Faith involves the whole of our personality; it gives us a focus and purpose and liberates us from our obsession with ourselves. Our hearts are 'strangely warmed' by a growing confidence in the reality of the love for which we long and our minds are increasingly convinced by the evidence of the reality of what we cannot see. As a result our wills concur; we are increasingly drawn to what we recognise as right and true and are gradually led to a change not only in our belief but also, more importantly, in our behaviour. Our hearts and minds and wills are, at best, only partially satisfied in our various human relationships. They are only drawn together by faith and fully satisfied by being brought into their natural focus in our relationship with the God in whose image we are made. It is because he has shown us both the true and ultimate shape of love and perfect wisdom and because we also perceive him as holy and righteous, that we are drawn to him in worship. This worship is an activity in which we both give and receive and in which our whole personality is balanced and integrated by being directed towards the One who made us for himself.

Religious faith can relatively easily be made to appear ridiculous by those who do not experience it but we all of us exercise a form of faith every time we drive our car or fly in an aircraft. We have to believe that other drivers will stay on the correct side of the road and obey the traffic lights, and trust that the pilot will bring us safely to land. The rejection of faith has been described as the 'refusal of light

---

[18] ParadisoXX1V line 65

in humanity's darkness'. The opposite of faith in God is not simply lack of faith, though it is obviously that. More positively our rejection of the salvation that he offers arises in a real sense because we take offence at it. This is due to the fact that it is at variance with our preferred perception of the way things are. The Cross reveals God's estimate of how things are and this inevitably appears to put us in a bad light. We are unhappy at the thought that Jesus had to die to put us right with God but that is the uncomfortable truth that is revealed in Scripture.

But why all this emphasis on faith: why not just love? Because faith is our necessary lifeline, joining us with the One we cannot see. Faith is like the ropes hanging from the church bells that are hidden from the ringers in the chamber above them. The only way that we can love an invisible God, as he has commanded us to do, is by believing in him and in what he says and does, in other words by exercising faith. This is the way he deals with us and it is hard to see how else he could have arranged it. It is as though he says to us: "Do me the favour of believing what I have done and what I say and then we can get to know each other and begin to do business." If we do not believe him we are refusing his gift and making him a liar. If we say that we do not need this lifeline, if we think that we are safe without it, then Jesus died for nothing, which is unthinkable.

All we can and all we need to do to be justified, to be made righteous in God's sight, is to change our minds about him, to turn to him and believe in him and in his promises. We cannot receive his gift of love if we do not believe that he exists. He wants our hearts and if we give them to him he welcomes us into his family; he accepts and 'saves' us from ourselves and from his condemnation. Paul tells us in Ephesians: 'For it is by grace you have been saved, through faith – and this not of yourselves, it is the gift of God – not by works, so that no-one can boast.' We are saved not by what we do for God but, by his grace, through our trust and belief in what he has done for us. Our response to this should be to do good works: there can be no true faith without them. Paul tells us in Galatians that 'the only thing that counts is faith expressing itself through love.' We have to roll up our sleeves as well as offer up our prayers.

If we are understandably anxious about the dangers of misplaced faith and of too fervent a faith in anything, however wholesome, it is possible to take the argument a little further. If God is love, then love is the only appropriate response to him. If we believe and trust in God he will become increasingly real to us as Love. In the words of Austin Farrer 'God loves us into loving him.' The stronger our Christian faith becomes the more it will come to resemble the Love to which it is a response. But he remains invisible and a mystery; we still have to reach out to him in faith. St Augustine asked: 'What do I love when I love my God?' and he could find no answer. In the words of the anonymous author of the 'Cloud of Unknowing', we have to smite the cloud with a 'sharp dart of longing love'. This is what faith does and for now, in this life, we cannot do without it. Paul describes this in another way when he writes in Romans 8:24 that 'hope that is seen is no hope at all.' We cannot do without hope either and because both our faith and our hope are centred on God and what he reveals to us of himself and of his promises it is hard to distinguish between them. Our faith today is in the One who is our hope for the future. We yearn and pray for what is yet to be. Paul writes in 1 Corinthians 13:13: 'And now these three remain: faith, hope and love. But the greatest of these is love.'

JAMES

This epistle, written by James the brother of Jesus and Jude, is very different from Hebrews. It consists in the main of a series of beautifully expressed ideas and instructions, rather like Proverbs, with teaching evidently borrowed from the Sermon on the Mount. We are exhorted to pray in faith, to persevere under trial which will win us the crown of life, to be quick to listen and slow to speak and become angry and to get rid of all moral filth. We should not only hear but obey the word, and 'keep a tight rein on the tongue' that 'no man can tame'. With it 'we praise our Lord and Father, and with it we curse men, who have been made in God's likeness,' which should not be. We are to keep the whole law, to love our neighbour as ourselves, to be merciful and to look after orphans and widows and show no favouritism to the rich. In a well-known passage he emphasises the need to demonstrate our faith in practical ways. He says what has to some appeared to contradict Paul's insistence on justification by faith: 'Show me your faith without deeds, and I will show you my faith by what I do.' But Paul's whole remarkable life of toil and suffering for Christ revealed that deeds were a natural accompaniment and consequence of faith and the history of the Church has confirmed it. In order to persuade Wilberforce to remain in Parliament as opposed to entering the Church, William Pitt expressed the view that 'Christianity leads not to meditation only but to action.'

Do not 'harbour bitter envy and selfish ambition in your hearts and fight and quarrel,' James goes on to say but 'Submit yourselves to God. Resist the devil, and he will flee from you. Humble yourselves before the Lord, and he will lift you up.' 'Do not swear. Do not slander one another – who are you to judge your neighbour?' He warns the rich against hoarding wealth that will rot and corrode, and against failing to pay the workmen's wages. Finally he writes:

> 'Persevere, and be patient until the Lord's coming.' 'Is anyone of you in trouble? He should pray. Is anyone happy? Let him sing songs of praise. Is any one of you sick? He should call the elders of the church to pray over him and anoint him with oil in the name of the Lord. And the prayer offered in faith will make the sick person well; the Lord will raise him up. If he has sinned he will be forgiven. Therefore confess your sins to each other and pray for each other so that you may be healed. The prayer of a righteous man is powerful and effective, and whoever turns a sinner from the error of his way will save him from death and cover over a multitude of sins.'

For concentrated practical as well as spiritual instruction, this epistle has scarcely an equal.

1 AND 2 PETER

Peter begins both these letters with great courtesy by introducing himself as an apostle of Jesus Christ. He addresses them to those who are privileged to be believers, with the prayer that grace and peace may be theirs in abundance. He yearns to see them coming to a full knowledge of the truth and living it in love with others so that they miss nothing of what God has in store for them, even if they have to suffer for a while. Towards the end of his second letter Peter says 'I have written both of these letters as reminders to stimulate you to wholesome thinking.' He shows clearly what he means by this in a remarkable passage in his first epistle. He gives praise to 'God, the Father of our Lord Jesus Christ who in his mercy has given us new birth into a lively hope through the resurrection of Jesus Christ from the dead,' and also into an imperishable inheritance. This inheritance is kept for us who, through faith, are shielded by God's power until the coming of salvation that is ready to be revealed in the last time. This teaching is in line with what we find throughout the New Testament that God's kingdom has already arrived but will be completed only when Jesus comes again. We rejoice in this hope, he tells us, even though 'for a little while we have to suffer all kinds of trials' in order that our faith may be proved genuine and may result in praise, glory and honour when Jesus Christ is finally and fully revealed.

All this produces inexpressible and glorious joy because we are receiving the goal of our faith, the salvation of our souls. This is the salvation that the prophets eagerly awaited and to which the Spirit of Christ was pointing when he predicted through them 'the sufferings of Christ and the glories that would follow'. For this reason we must prepare our minds for action and be holy in all we do because we have been redeemed with the precious blood of Christ through whose resurrection we have faith and hope in God. Holiness involves 'loving our brothers deeply from the heart'. It also involves 'ridding ourselves of all malice', as we come to the living stone and are built into a spiritual house to be a holy priesthood, offering spiritual sacrifices to God through Jesus Christ. He is this living stone that the builders rejected but has become the capstone or cornerstone of the building.

Peter goes on to tell us that we are 'a chosen people, a royal priesthood, a holy nation, a people belonging to God'. Therefore as aliens and strangers we are to abstain from sinful desires and set a good example, which includes submitting ourselves to every authority instituted amongst men. His instructions are wide-ranging. We are to show proper respect to everyone, live in harmony, be compassionate and humble, serve others and offer hospitality. More specifically wives are to be submissive, husbands to be considerate and treat wives with respect, elders to be shepherds of the flock and young men to be submissive to those who are older. What we are to be and do follows from what God is and what he has done and is doing. Therefore we are to follow him, to obey his example and to accept suffering, because it is he who makes us strong and calls us to his eternal glory. He ends his letter, like Paul, with personal greetings by thanking Silas for his help with his letter, sending greetings from Mark and finally expressing 'Peace to all of you who are in Christ.'

In his second letter Peter issues many warnings about false teachers with cleverly invented stories and destructive heresies, who deny the Sovereign Lord and lead many people astray. He also warns against scoffers who ask: "Where is this coming that he promised?" He tells us, as Jesus did, that 'the day of the Lord will come like a thief' and that, echoing the words of Isaiah, we are looking forward to a new heaven and a new earth. He ends with a generous tribute to 'our dear brother Paul who wrote to you with the wisdom that God gave him' – even though 'his letters contain some things that are hard to understand.' Many will sympathise with this difficulty, but he goes on to say that 'ignorant and unstable people distort these hard things, as they do other scriptures, to their own destruction.'

But grow in the grace and knowledge of our Lord and Saviour Jesus Christ. To him be glory both now and forever! Amen.

1, 2 AND 3 JOHN

The first two verses of John's first epistle are an unmistakable reminder of the start of his Gospel. We have heard and seen and our hands have touched the Word of Life which was with the Father from the beginning and has appeared to us. This is a wonderfully succinct précis of his first chapter. 'We proclaim what we have seen and heard so that you also may have fellowship with us. And our fellowship is with the Father and with his Son Jesus Christ. We write this to make our joy complete.' How the Church of today needs to experience this joy in sharing the Good News.

The message of the first epistle is that God is Light and Love: if we love him it is because he first loved us. If we know God and love him we must show our love for him not only by our 'words or tongue but with actions and in truth' and by our obedience, and we must love our brother also. 'Any one who claims to be in the light but hates his brother is still in the darkness.' There have been times during the history of the Church when its members have killed people for disagreeing with them about their understanding of the Saviour who taught us to love even our enemies!

'Anyone who does not love his brother whom he has seen, cannot love God, whom he has not seen.' 'But if we walk in the light, as he is in the light, we have fellowship with one another, and the blood of Jesus, his Son, purifies us from all sin.' 'Anyone who does not believe God – and anyone who claims not to have sinned – has made him out to be a liar, because he has not believed the testimony God has given about his Son.' The real liar is 'the man who denies that Jesus is the Christ. Such a man is the antichrist – he denies the Father and the Son.'

He goes on to say that he is 'writing these things to you about those who are trying to lead you astray.' There were, and always have been, false prophets and teachers. Those to whom John refers in particular were the early Gnostics who taught that spirit is entirely good and matter is entirely evil and that salvation is escape from the body that is brought about not by faith in Christ but by special knowledge. There are still those today who attempt to bypass Christ in pursuit of truth and salvation. Earlier in the epistle he writes 'And now, dear children, continue in him, so that when he appears we may be confident and unashamed before him at his coming.' 'When he appears we shall be like him, for we shall see him as he is.'

He ends the third of his epistles with a personal message that is reminiscent of Paul. Having so much to say to his readers he is frustrated by having to write to them: 'I hope to see you soon, and we will talk face to face. Peace to you. The friends here send their greetings. Greet the friends there by name.' John's writing is, as usual, full of warmth and love.

JUDE

Jude introduces himself as a 'servant of Jesus Christ and a brother of James' – presumably too reticent to mention his and James' relationship, as half brothers to Jesus, though others refer to it. He writes a short letter in which he warns against 'grumblers and fault-finders' and 'shepherds who feed only themselves' and he predicts 'scoffers in the last times who will follow their own ungodly desires.' We are to 'build ourselves up in our most holy faith and pray in the Holy Spirit.' He ends with one of the most uplifting verses in Scripture:

'To him who is able to keep you from falling and to present you before his glorious presence without fault and with great joy – to the only God our Saviour be glory, majesty, power and authority, through Jesus Christ our Lord, before all ages, now and for evermore! Amen.'

What an extraordinary experience and privilege to be able to write such a tribute to a brother – albeit a half-brother!

REVELATION

It might seem that we have enough books in the New Testament already to convey the message of the Gospel, without adding another to the canon of Scripture. But each of them plays an essential part. Without the Gospels we would have no account of Jesus' coming and of his death and resurrection, without Acts no description of the consequences in the coming of the Holy Spirit and the growth of the early Church. Without the Epistles we would have no knowledge of how the early Christians were taught to understand Jesus and the new life that they had come to live in him. Without Revelation we would have no final vision of what God has planned as the destiny of his people and no final instructions about how Christians should prepare for it, above all the possibility that they might even have to lay down their lives.

Paul wrote in 1 Cor 2:9 that 'No eye has seen, no ear has heard, no mind has conceived what God has prepared for those who love him.' But the Spirit enabled John to attempt the near-impossible task of giving us a visionary, symbolic glimpse of God's completed kingdom, and of the spiritual battle involved in bringing it about. By its very nature we cannot in a real sense expect to understand it, but we need to have our appetite whetted to learn more of God's plans and to be spurred on by the hope that they give us. Without hope we cannot live a truly fruitful life. We also need to become aware of this spiritual battle that is raging and the monumental issues and the struggles and sacrifices that are involved in bringing the kingdom to fruition.

Revelation is nothing less than a picture painted on an enormous canvas of the destiny of all that is, the scheme of all schemes from which nothing in heaven and earth appears to be left out. It is a gigantic divinely inspired cosmic myth that is full of scriptural references and unusual images and symbols and saturated with God's glory. It has to be read, not once but many times, before we can begin to absorb its message. As always it is helpful to consult commentaries written by those who have immersed themselves in it, as long as we are prepared to find that they often disagree about the interpretation of a good deal of it. Revelation is written in complex typically Jewish

278

symbolic language, known as apocalyptic, with imagery similar to that in the book of Daniel and with frequent mention of numbers and their symbolic significance. Apocalyptic literally means revelation, with particular reference to 'end things' or eschatology, which is the study of these last things. It is characterised by the idea of a sovereign God who not only judges individuals at the end of their lives but will ultimately intervene dramatically to judge the nations at the end of history. In New Testament terms it is God finally ushering in his kingdom of righteousness and peace, which has been developing since Jesus came to inaugurate it. This accords with the teaching of Jesus himself who speaks of his own return as Son of Man at the end of the age to achieve this consummation. (Mt 24:27, Mk 13:26, Lk 21:27).

After a short explanatory introduction John tells us of his experience of being 'in the Spirit' on the Lord's day whilst on the island of Patmos and of the risen Lord appearing to him. 'His eyes were like blazing fire ... his voice was like rushing water ... and his face was like the sun shining in all its brilliance.' Even though John had been Jesus' closest friend during his earthly life he 'fell at his feet as though dead.' But Jesus says to him: "Do not be afraid. I am the First and the Last. I am the Living One; I was dead, and behold I am alive for ever and ever! I hold the keys of death and Hades." John is instructed to write individual messages of criticism, challenge and encouragement to the seven chief churches in Asia Minor. They are exhorted to wake up and obey and repent, to endure and to overcome. In each case he ends with "He who has an ear, let him hear what the Spirit says to the churches." The number seven is a symbol of completeness – as twelve is of perfection – and this strongly suggests that the messages addressed to each of these churches are also addressed to every other church, including our own, and to the whole Church throughout history.

In the fourth chapter John goes on to speak of his experience of 'a door standing open in heaven'. He is invited to "Come up here, and I will show you what must take place after this." What he speaks of seeing in this chapter and those that follow cannot be described. They are full of praise and worship. The work of Christ as our redeemer is emphasised in a striking passage in chapter 5 in which the 'Lion of the tribe Judah' (one of the Messiah's titles, from Gen 49:9-10) is seen by John as a Lamb 'looking as if it had been slain'. An uncountable multitude of angels sing his praise in a sublime act of worship. We

279

can imagine that our own sporadic worship and praise is added to the praise that is continually being offered to God in heaven:

"Worthy is the Lamb, who was slain
to receive power and wealth and
    wisdom and strength
and honour and glory and praise!"

Then I heard every creature in heaven and on earth and under the earth and on the sea, and all that is in them, singing :

"To him who sits on the throne and to
    the Lamb
be praise and honour and glory and
    power,
for ever and ever!"

John goes on to speak of the cosmic setting in which, as here on earth, the struggle is taking place between good and evil, between God and the devil and his allies. The earth is not the only theatre of operation in this struggle but it is here that Jesus lived and died and rose again and it is therefore crucial to the history of God's whole redemptive programme. Finally he speaks of the consummation to which God's programme of redemption is moving. It is not surprising that this book is frequently incomprehensible in that John is attempting to describe the realm that is completely hidden from our eyes in which God dwells with the hosts of heaven.

Commentators are not in agreement about whether the main body of Revelation relates to the history of the Roman Empire or is prophetic of the whole sweep of history until the return of Christ, or is the story of the end times before his return. There is also disagreement about the interpretation of prophecies relating to these end times. Neither is it clear how we are to understand the events following Christ's return. We are told to pray for God's kingdom to come on earth but it is not possible for us to understand or even imagine how this might be brought about. It must be enough that Jesus teaches us to ask for this above all else and that this is the vision that is progressively revealed to us throughout Scripture. We are also told that there will be a new heaven and a new earth and that the saints are 'co-heirs with Christ, if indeed we share in his sufferings' and 'will reign on the earth' with him. (Rom 8:17, Rev 5:10).

It is extraordinary and challenging teaching. The sense of the Greek is that heaven and earth will not be new, as completely new and different, but rather as the originals made new, in other words renewed. There will be continuity as well as discontinuity. Without the biblical records we know nothing about these last things and many other things as well and all we can do is to struggle to understand what they are telling us. It is not possible, even for God, to reveal to us the truth about them, bounded as we are by our restricted vision and by the limited historical context in which we live. We are obliged to be appropriately agnostic about how Christ's return will burst upon the world and precisely what will follow it but he gives us these tantalising clues. In the words of Ecclesiastes 3:11, 'God has set eternity in the hearts of men; yet they cannot fathom what he has done from beginning to end.' This need not diminish our interest in his coming or in what he tells us of his purposes in this astonishing book.

It is no doubt this inevitable obscurity that explains why some have questioned whether Revelation deserves to be included as part of the Scriptures. But it was accepted by most from early times as part of the canon and without it our eyes would not be sufficiently directed to the future that God has planned for us. The last three chapters describe the final battle and the defeat of Satan and the 'beast and the false prophet' and the judgement of all men before the great white throne, with the final end of evil and of death itself. The devil himself will be banished and deprived of the power to harm. In the imagery used in Revelation the dead will be judged 'according to what they have done as recorded in the books', and death and Hades and those whose names are not in the 'book of life' are thrown into 'the lake of fire' which is the 'second death'. Hades was the Greek word used for the unseen world of the dead. In the Authorised Version of the Bible this word is misleadingly translated as hell, as is sheol, the Old Testament Hebrew word for the unseen realm of the dead or the grave. In the New International Version and others the only word translated as hell or hell-fire is the New Testament word gehenna which was the rubbish dump outside Jerusalem where the fire never went out and also a place of punishment. Jesus used this word in his warnings about the consequences of our deliberate holding on to sin. (Matt 5:22-30 and Mk 9:43-47.) C.S. Lewis wrote of hell that 'There is no doctrine

281

which I would more willingly remove from Christianity than this doctrine. But it has the support ... of our Lord's own words.' [19]

We cannot possibly know, and do not need to know, the real meaning of this imagery of judgement and what follows from it. But it is a sobering revelation to us of our ultimate exposure to God who is described in a number of passages in the Bible as a 'refining' and 'consuming' fire. (Mal 3:2, Is 30:27, Heb 12:29). It is hard to imagine that even those of us who believe that we are saved by the grace of God in Christ will not be scorched by the burning truth when we see our sinful lives in the blinding light of divine perfection. (Mt 12:37, 1 Cor 3 13-15, 2 Cor 5:10). It is even harder to imagine that those who have deliberately rejected him and the voice of their own conscience will not be scorched even more surely without the benefit of the saving grace that they have continued to refuse. In Psalm 111:10 we are told that 'the fear of the Lord is the beginning of wisdom' and in Hebrews 10:31 that 'It is a dreadful thing to fall into the hands of the living God.' We cannot afford to remain oblivious to the power and holiness of God and the need for us to continue to point people to their Saviour. The challenge has been expressed in the haunting question: "What will you say when you finally stand before God, and the others are not with you?" The others to whom we have not known how to speak.

Only when we come to chapter 21 do we have a glimpse of the glorious finale of the symphony of all God's previous activity in creation and his plans for its redemption. All the themes we have been following from Genesis onwards during the course of this great biblical journey are finally and wonderfully fulfilled and brought together in a triumphant concluding coda. The devil finally defeated and all evil and suffering abolished, all prophecies and sacrifices at an end, God dwells at last and forever with his people in the fullness of his everlasting kingdom. It provides us with overwhelming evidence of the guiding hand of the divine Composer, Father, Son and Holy Spirit. If this is just a dream it is a very good one. For Christians it is the ultimate and irresistible hope. The only danger is that we may wait for it passively rather than using our talents and living with integrity in God's strength so that we are worthy of a place in his company.

---

[19] The Problem of Pain

This picture of God's ultimate triumph is painted in the words of Isaiah's vision of 'a new heaven and a new earth'. The majestic symbolic language here describes a picture of the Holy City, the new Jerusalem, coming down out of heaven from God, prepared as a bride beautifully dressed for her husband. The imagery of marriage suggests that the renewed heaven and earth will involve a new union in which the relationship between God and his people will be restored and perfected.

> 'Now the dwelling of God is with men, and he will live with them. They will be his people, and God himself will be their God. He will wipe away every tear from their eyes. There will be no more death or mourning or crying or pain, for the old order of things has passed away.'

By inference, there will be no more disease and hunger, no more poverty and injustice and exploitation, no more abuse of women and children, no more abuse of drugs and alcohol and no more crime and violence.

> "I am making everything new. It is done. I am the Alpha and the Omega, the Beginning and the End. To him who is thirsty I will give to drink without cost from the spring of the water of life. He who overcomes will inherit all this, and I will be his God and he will be my son."

It is a wonderfully comforting passage and it is no surprise that it is used in the funeral liturgy. It is also a terrifying passage because not all will be included. It appears that there will be those who will have excluded themselves by their persistent unbelief and by the lives that they have lived. What we cannot know is how God will continue to extend his mercy and to heal our relationship with him and with others.

This picture of the 'Holy City' is a vision of the glorious consummation of the Kingdom of God that was anticipated by the Old Testament prophets, by Jesus himself and by the writers of the epistles. It is made possible only by Jesus' death and resurrection and by the coming of the Holy Spirit. It will finally come about only when Jesus returns at the end of the age. The prophets are at long last vindicated. Their prophecies are finally fulfilled in the triumph of God who sits on the throne with the Lamb, his crucified and risen Son. Jesus is both our great High Priest and the sacrifice through whom the victory has been won. From the throne, down the middle of the great street of the city, there flows the river of the water of life with on either side the tree of life whose leaves are for the healing of the nations. What can this river symbolise but the Holy Spirit, who was described by Jesus in John 7:38 as the streams of living water that would flow from those who believed in him. The Spirit has been present always and everywhere since the second verse of Genesis where he was described as 'hovering over the waters'. He is pictured here as still active in creative, cleansing and healing activity. The three persons of the Trinity are seen at long last together, as the focus and centre of the heavenly city and of the whole universe. We are told that God's servants will – for the first time ever – 'see his face'. It is a majestic vision.

We are further told that 'There is no temple in the city, because the Lord God Almighty and the Lamb are its temple' and there is 'no sun or moon to shine on it, for the glory of God gives it light, and the Lamb is its lamp', as Isaiah foresaw in 60:19. 'The nations will walk in its light, and the kings of the earth will bring their splendour into it.' The splendour of Egypt, Babylon and Assyria, Persia, Greece and Rome and every civilisation before and since that time. 'The kingdom of the world has become the kingdom of our Lord and of his Christ, and he will reign for ever and ever.' (Rev 11:15). It is as though we are being told that all that withstands the fire of judgement and is worthy of being salvaged will be 'saved' as on some vast cosmic computer. It is tempting to envisage computing as a fertile, prophetic pointer to the hugely enhanced communications that will be possible in the age to come. There is continuity and discontinuity, as we have seen. We ourselves and the realities of the old earth and of its history will still be recognisable but all will have been transformed and made new. It will be, in T.S Eliot's words 'both a new world and the old made explicit'. [20]

Why else should the glorious art and literature and music and science and all other legitimate human achievements have been permitted and produced if the best of them at least are not destined to

[20] Four Quartets Burnt Norton II

survive? Maybe they will all be taken up into eternity to thrill us, as they have done here on earth, along with all the glory and wonder of God himself and of the heavenly realm. Unless we are obliged to read them in purely symbolic terms Paul's words in 1 Cor 3:12-15 are suggestive. And will not creativity continue? It may be that metaphorically speaking the 'Father's house' with its 'many rooms' will not be fully furnished and that we shall find that some of the earth's finest treasures will also be redeemed and somehow still be available for us to enjoy. It must surely be a legitimate exercise for us to use our God-given imagination in our response to these revelations as to all other passages in Scripture.

John ends his book with the warning that 'if anyone takes words away from this book of prophecy, God will take away from him his share in the tree of life and in the holy city, which are described in this book.'

He who testifies to these things says, "Yes I am coming soon."
Amen . Come, Lord Jesus.
The grace of the Lord Jesus be with God's people. Amen.

These are not only the last words of Revelation but the last words of Scripture. It might seem that 'coming soon' would suggest less than the two thousand years that have elapsed since his first coming. But not in God's reckoning, and it is important that in spite of the delay we are always ready for his reappearing. Jesus himself tells us earlier, in 16:15, "Behold, I come like a thief! Blessed is he who stays awake..." We might wish to know more than we have been told but what we are told must be an encouragement to us to remain faithful to him. It is he who overcomes who will inherit the kingdom. (Rev 21:10). This must be enough for us to know. In the words of Eliot again: 'The only wisdom we can hope to acquire is the wisdom of humility. Humility is endless.'[21]

---

[21] Four Quartets East Coker II

CONCLUDING COMMENTARY

From this final vantage point of our journey we can see the vast scale of God's monumental and unstoppable programme. It is not so much that the biblical story of this programme operates within history, though in one sense it does so, but that the history of our world and of the universe itself takes place within the framework of the story that the Bible tells. This story begins with the creation of the heavens and the earth and it ends with their envisaged consummation following Jesus' return to earth at the end of the age. There is no point in his coming once unless he comes again to claim the fruits of his victory. The Swiss theologian Oscar Cullmann likened Jesus' first coming to D-day and his second coming to VE-day, when the battle is finally won and the fruits of victory savoured.

Without Jesus' coming to earth again there is no conclusion to this present age, no judgement of the nations, no final judgement of all men from the great white throne and no possibility of our ultimate redemption or of a new heaven and a new earth. It is this all-inclusive scope of the Christian faith that enables the Church to be the focus for individuals and for whole communities and nations to celebrate and to give thanks, to mourn, to seek help at times of tragedy and to remember those who have given their lives in war. Christ's sacrificial death makes the Christian altar the unique table on which to place our prayers and offerings in times of joy and sorrow and remembrance.

The chief impression left on us by the journey we have made is the majestic stature of the central figure of the Biblical story, Jesus Christ, our 'shepherd, brother, friend, our prophet, priest and king.' He is our redeemer and our ruler. He is the Son of God, born of a virgin, who was crucified, and raised to new life. Everything that God the Father gives to his creation comes to us in and through him. Because of his massive saving work in his death on the Cross he has been 'exalted to the highest place' and been given 'a name that is above every name, that at the name of Jesus every knee should bow, in heaven and on earth and under the earth, and every tongue confess that Jesus Christ is Lord, to the glory of God the Father.' (Phil 2:8-13) This will include kings, emperors, presidents and dictators, elected and self-appointed, both before and since his coming to earth. Many of them will have already stumbled on the rock of his judgement in their earthly lives. It will include everyone else as well and people of every age, including our own. Having completed his work of defeating his enemy the devil and banishing all evil and gathering his body the Church from every nation, he will hand over the kingdom to his Father that he may be 'all in all'. (1Cor 15:24).

This is nothing less than a vision of the final destiny of our world and of the whole of God's creation to which there is no comparable alternative. Christians believe that this is the ultimate truth about the goal to which we are all of us moving. This goal is large enough to encompass the destiny of all who have ever lived or ever will live throughout the whole of history, whatever beliefs they may have held, or none. It is too good to be true; but it is. C.S Lewis said: 'I believe in Christianity as I believe in the rising sun, because I see it, and by it I see everything else as well.' It is the ultimate and only standpoint from which everything can be seen in its true perspective.

Those who hear of this vision of God's kingdom and will stay to try to come to terms with it and begin to understand it are faced with a challenge. They must either embrace it, become followers of Jesus and co-operate with him in bringing it about or risk the remorse of having declined the invitation to be involved. What more terrible experience could there be than to miss the feast of the Kingdom? The story of the rich man and Lazarus in Luke 16:19-31 is a terrifying warning. Jesus tells us in Matthew 8:12 that 'There will be weeping and gnashing of teeth.' What more does hell need to be than this experience of remorse and of the burning truth? What greater punishment than to see our lives in the light of God's blinding holiness and to find that life in his eternal kingdom is the only thing on offer and to recognise that we have declined his offer of a seat at the feast. If we don't like the sound of it, if God's best is not good enough for us we are at liberty to refuse it. We are not obliged to respond; there is freedom, not pressure, but in view of what we have seen of the programme we would surely be crazy not to do so. Even if it looks like interfering with our own plans.

POSTSCRIPT

The clear message of Scripture is that there are no limits to the relevance of the Christian faith to every department of our lives and to every part of God's creation. This faith has provided the supreme source of spiritual nourishment for Western civilisation and for all those who have embraced it during the past two thousand years and we need to rediscover its greatness for ourselves. We have inherited a major part of our culture and our notions of private and public morality from our roots in Greece and Rome, especially in Roman Law, and above all from Israel as the cradle of both the Mosaic Law and of the Christian faith. Our political institutions have been built on this Judeo-Christian foundation and our leaders have somehow to do justice to this fact. President Barack Obama is an admirer of President Lincoln and has written with approval of his practice of invoking God in his rhetoric. This is because, as Obama says: 'Scrub language of all religious content and we forfeit the imagery and terminology through which millions of Americans understand both their personal morality and social justice.'[22] The same is true of millions of people in our own country and throughout the rest of the world, but few leaders manage to find a way of handling this difficult problem effectively. Our own politicians in the United Kingdom find it difficult to mention his name: only the Queen appears to be able to enrich her language with religious content.

Jung wrote as long ago as 1933 that 'the various forms of religion no longer appear to modern man to come from within – to be an expression of his own psychic life.'[23] He went on to say that 'when religion can no longer embrace his life in all its fullness – then the psyche becomes something in its own right which cannot be dealt with by the measures of the Church alone.' In other words man feels that he has grown out of the Gospel. This means that the Gospel must, if possible, be made comprehensible in all its limitless relevance in order to satisfy our present-day needs and aspirations. It must be seen

---

[22] 'The Audacity of Hope' p214
[23] 'Modern Man in Search of a Soul' p237

as great enough to stretch across the whole breadth and depth of our expanding horizons. Jung also wrote more than thirty years later that the fault lies not in the truth as it is set down in the Scriptures 'but solely in us' who have not continued to live out its relevance for our own day.[24] Henry Drummond expressed this even more clearly when he wrote over a hundred years ago that 'What we require is no new revelation, but simply an adequate conception of the true essence of Christianity.' [25] Our failure is that we are not exploring and proclaiming the fullness of the Christian faith. Either that, or for several generations in the Western nations at least, we have been increasingly deafened by our multiple modern-day distractions. Both the Church and society appear to be to blame, if indeed they can be separated. We have lost our recognition of the 'grandeur of God' in the words of Gerard Manley Hopkins and of the mystery of his creation and of our place in it that the Old Testament writers so often refer to. We have thereby become diminished and our entire culture deprived of depth. The American philosopher William Barrett, writing in 1958 in 'Irrational Man', said that Protestantism achieved a 'heightening of the religious consciousness, but at the same time severed the consciousness from the deep unconscious life of our total human nature.' The Reformation involved a necessary return to the Word of Scripture and its availability to all believers. But it was also in danger of leading to a reduction in the rich and nourishing imagery and symbolism of the liturgy and hence in the mystery of the Eucharist and of the whole of the rest of our worship. The increased emphasis on Scripture led in its turn to a greater risk of disagreement about its teaching on matters such as church organisation and baptism and the importance of evangelism and of the Holy Spirit. As a result the Congregationalists and Baptists, the Quakers and later the Methodists, Brethren and Pentecostalists became separate denominations within the Protestant Church. The Charismatic Christians form a separate grouping across the denominational spectrum.

The Roman Catholic Church places more emphasis on tradition and its own handed-down apostolic authority and is more wary of believers exercising their own private judgement. They point out that

---

[24] 'Memories, Dreams, Reflections' p 364
[25] 'Natural Law in the Spiritual World' p 60

the early Church itself was responsible for the gradual collective discernment of those Scriptures that demonstrated the authority that made them evidently worthy of a place in the canon. They would further claim that the Catholic Church retains a unique authority in the essential task of interpreting it for today. The papal encyclicals are clearly not in the same category as the canonical apostolic epistles in the Bible but they nevertheless serve a somewhat similar function in providing authoritative theological reflections on current spiritual issues confronting the contemporary Church. This authority and the discipline that goes with it, though it is liable to abuse, has enabled them to avoid the numerous denominational schisms to which the Protestant Church is prone. It is interesting that Pentecostal and more recently Charismatic Christians have by and large been accepted and contained within the parent body of the Catholic Church. They have other difficulties, however, such as the obligatory celibacy of the priesthood and the sexual frustration that it frequently causes, and a number of their teachings are hard for Protestants to accept. But they have for the most part been able to avoid the fundamentalism that is proving to be such a serious issue today both inside and outside the Christian Church. Protestants may think that Catholics give too high a place to the Virgin Mary but her unique position as Jesus' mother and as his physical link with the material world has undoubtedly more to say to us than we are willing to recognise.

There are no doubt many different reasons why the Church in the West, regardless of denomination, is becoming less influential and its services less well attended. As salt and light, the role of Christians is to preserve and flavour what is good and provide illumination in a world of decay and darkness. There is a loss of richness in the whole of our lives that makes us less effective ambassadors for God's kingdom in both these ways. As a result of this increasing loss of the sense of a spiritual dimension to life in society in general, to quote Jung once again: 'Most people nowadays identify themselves almost exclusively with their consciousness, and imagine that they are only what they know about themselves.'[26] We need to know of our origin and destiny in God, of which the whole Bible speaks. We are paying a terrible price for our failure to take these fundamental realities into account and for our reluctance to read this Book with the attention it

---

[26]Memories Dreams and Reflections p330

deserves. We have to be allowed to make our own mistakes but we also need light by which to recognise them.

The true light is ultimately the Christ of the Gospels, and Christians believe that there is no comparable or credible alternative. Our plain duty as Christians is to trust and follow him and to learn more of him and of how our faith differs from all other prescriptions for our deepest needs. This should lead us to pass on the faith to our children and to spread the good news of the kingdom by the way we live our lives and by all we say and do. The words of Psalm 78 are a challenge to us: 'What we have heard and known, what our fathers have told us ... we will tell the next generation, the praiseworthy deeds of the Lord, his power, and the wonders he has done ... so that the next generation would know them, even the children yet to be born, and they in turn would tell their children'. There is no other way that they will come to know about them. It has been said that we have multiple opinions but not a common story. We have lost our Christian vision for the society in which we live and have nothing to put in its place. We have allowed the Christian foundation on which our culture has been built to become eroded and it is not possible for a multicultural society to be held together by secular values.

The world-wide Anglican Church in particular has lost its confidence and its leaders are obliged to attend to internal issues that are at risk of distracting it and tearing it apart. It has either to find the will to repent and to pray and to communicate the Good News of the Gospel with conviction or lose ground to other alternative versions of religious faith and spirituality. In fact this is already happening. These alternatives can make no such massive claims but nevertheless appear to be attracting a great deal of attention. The multicultural nature of society is one problem and its materialist, secular aspect is another, with an increasing number of people unfamiliar with even the basic essentials of the Christian faith. It has also become increasingly difficult to discern the relevance of the faith to the increasing number of ethical issues raised by rapid advances in technology, such as In Vitro Fertilisation and the freezing of sperms and embryos, stem-cell research and cloning. We also have to contend with the previously unheard of variety in child-bearing and rearing that they make possible. The growing confusion caused by these multiple moral choices was yet another difficulty that was recognised by Jung. He said that 'Nothing can spare us the torment of ethical decision.'

291

Science is exciting but it presents us with some agonising choices. It is no longer a simple question of what is clearly right, or best, but increasingly often a matter of making a choice between the lesser of two evils and we cannot always judge rightly. We have been given an extraordinary degree of freedom that is often too difficult for us to manage.

Jung was acutely aware of the presence of evil in the world, embodied for him at that time in Nazism and Russian Communism. He said, and these words have already been quoted in the section on evil: 'We stand face to face with the terrible question of evil ... empty-handed, bewildered and perplexed' not knowing 'what to pit against it'.[27] What would he have made of suicide bombers? As Christians we believe that all evil will one day be defeated but for the present we have to struggle with it, with our hearts and minds and wills and with all the spiritual and political resources at our disposal.

It is harder now, for all these reasons, to present the challenge of the Gospel but it has never been a simple matter. We cannot say that unless a man begins to follow Christ today that God will never accept him into his kingdom. Nor can we say for certain – though it may sound heretical to some – that he must consciously make a commitment in this life in order to live one day with God in heaven. If, as Paul argues in Romans, all Israel will one day be saved their salvation will have to be retrospective because the majority of them have been blinded and have not accepted their Saviour during their earthly lives. Jesus is recorded in John 3:18 as saying that those who do not believe 'in the name of God's one and only Son' are 'condemned already'. But can we fully understand the meaning of this condemnation and the application of his warning? Clearly some have never truly heard the truth about Jesus. And can we know how well others, whoever they may be and whatever other faith they hold, or none, have understood the truth they have been shown and fully recognised its challenge? Paul writes of this difficulty in an interesting passage on judgement in Romans 2:6-16 that needs careful study. We have to struggle with these questions, but even the light that God has given us cannot penetrate the mystery: only he himself can know precisely how he will judge us.

---

[27] Memories, Dreams, Reflections pp 363, 365

Although God has made us in his image and has appeared to us in Jesus, we have not yet seen him in his fullness and his glory. We cannot therefore fully comprehend him and his ultimate intentions for us. From the story of the prodigal son it seems that we have only to give him a hint of our intention to seek him and return to him, to repent and trust in him, and he will come to meet us. The Gospel must be proclaimed with all its terrifying challenge but maybe Austin Farrer is right when he says that 'If God threatens me with hell it is that he may give me heaven.'[28] There are irreconcilable contradictions that reason cannot unravel. In the end only love can truly understand. The anonymous writer of 'The Cloud of Unknowing' put it in another way when he said that 'God may well be loved but not thought. By love he may be held, but by thinking never.'

All we can and must do is to witness to the truth as far as we are able to understand it. As Christians there is one thing we believe that we can say with certainty. Unless God had sent his Son to die so that all men could have the opportunity to be reconciled to him, then not one single one of us could ever reach the goal for which he created us, to live with him in heaven for eternity. "No-one comes to the Father except through me." Jn 14:6. If this is not so then the sacrifice that God made in Jesus was for some at least irrelevant, which is unthinkable. If there had been any other alternative to the Cross of Christ as a means of redeeming his creation then God would surely have chosen it. The Christian conviction is that no-one who has really heard and understood the truth about the challenge of the Cross can afford to ignore it with impunity. If there are those we know who have not heard and understood then maybe we shall one day be asked why we did not tell them. If we are tempted to resent the fact that some will inherit the kingdom without struggling as Christians in this life we need to be aware of the lesson of the parable of the hired workers who objected to the fact that they were paid no more than those who started work late in the day. The pay that the workers were awarded was a knowledge of God and he has nothing greater to give us than himself, whenever we come to know him.

Christ's coming, as a sovereign act of God, was both in and out of time and his death must be decisive whatever our circumstances, and whether we happen to live our lives before or since he came to earth.

---

[28] The Essential Sermons -'Predestination'

For all sorts of reasons it was not possible for God to reveal himself to us in Jesus before many thousands of years had passed, during which men and women were obliged to search for him in their own ways and to found their own religions. It was no doubt important, amongst other things, to give them time to establish their own ideas and insights, to make their own experiments and to formulate the questions to which he alone could provide the answers. However much God reveals to us we still have to do some thinking for ourselves in order to understand the truth we have been shown and to make it our own.

Such is the freedom he has given us that it still remains possible for humanity to continue its own search for truth in a multitude of different ways in spite of what we believe to be his definitive revelation to us in Christ. There is a discussion of this massive freedom that we have been given and the problems that it causes in an extraordinary story entitled 'The Grand Inquisitor' that is told by Ivan, one of the brothers in Dostoyevsky's novel 'The Brothers Karamazov'. This story is explored by Rowan Williams in his book 'Dostoevsky'. He sees the Grand Inquisitor as a 'perennially haunting figure in that his voice is clearly audible on both sides of the current global conflict.' His successors can be seen not only in those who oversee the stifling of human freedom and the diminishing of the human soul in the almost exclusive concern with material prosperity in the West, but also in the violent enforcers of 'a system beyond dialogue and change' in the East. (p237). All forms of human government and all human institutions are subject to the limitations imposed by our ignorance and sinfulness and to the ultimate exposure of these limitations.

All other attempts to reach God can none of them, in themselves, provide salvation in the Christian sense; in truth they do not claim to do so in the same specific way. It has been said that 'Anyone who honestly and passionately searches for truth is on the way to Christ.'[29] This would appear to be another way of expressing Jesus' own statement in John 6:45 that 'Everyone who listens to the Father and learns from him comes to me.' The recognition of the requisite insights and experiences for overcoming our shortcomings and achieving self-knowledge and 'salvation' are one thing; the infinitely costly God-given provision for our true salvation, as reconciliation to

---

[29] Edith Stein, quoted by Pope Benedict in 'Jesus of Nazareth' p 91.

him, is quite another. Our God is 'a consuming fire' (Heb 12:29) and only Christ's work on our behalf can equip us with the fire-proof suiting of the spiritual bodies that we shall one day be given to enable us to live in his presence.

There is a mystery and a contradiction here, as elsewhere in God's work, that we cannot fathom or reconcile. The paradox arises from a combination of his endless love and wisdom and our inevitable ignorance that will be resolved only by his grace. There are certain things that for the present we cannot and do not need to know. Austin Farrer asks, rhetorically, in the same sermon: 'How do I know that God will not prevail at length with all? How do I know what means he may devise here or in other worlds hereafter to warm cold hearts or reconcile rebellious wills?' Whatever road we're on we shall all bump into the same God one day. Christians believe that the Gospel of God's incarnation in Christ is the definitive, authentic revelation of the God that we shall all of us eventually bump into, but we shall no doubt all have some big surprises, Christian believers included. It is as though God says to us: "Try whatever means you will, but in the end you will find that it is only through Christ and through his death for you that you can come to me." It would appear that there will be many who will be amazed that they have reached him in this way.

The judgement of the nations in Matthew 25 describes the coming of the Son of Man in his glory and his separation of their people into sheep and goats. The sheep who are invited to enter the kingdom prepared for them since the creation of the world, on the basis of their having given him food and water and clothing and invited him in as a stranger, express surprise and claim that they are unaware of ever having done so. They appear to know nothing of serving him in their serving of his brothers and Jesus surely cannot therefore be referring to Christians. But he says to them: "I tell you the truth, whatever you did for one of the least of these brothers of mine, you did for me." The goats are told the exact opposite and the story ends: "Then they will go away to eternal punishment, but the righteous to eternal life." This passage is bound to fill us with fear and trembling as well as with astonishment and joy. The Church, and the kingdom of God that it is given to demonstrate and proclaim, is not a haven in this world and in eternity only for those who have the privilege of believing in the Gospel and trusting in Jesus during this earthly life. It must surely be that Christian believers are the first-fruits of God's harvest and his servants and map-readers in pointing others to their true destination in his kingdom. (Jer 2:3, James 1:18). Not all are equipped to try to understand where they are heading in the mysterious journey of their lives. God is concerned not only with his servants but also with those they serve and who in turn serve them and thereby Jesus himself. There are no limits to the relevance of the Christian faith because there are no limits to the kingdom of God that is its central message. We can have no more than a glimpse of its magnificence. 'Thy Kingdom come…..'

CHRISTIANITY AND COMMUNITY AND FAMILY LIFE

The history of the Christian faith provides abundant examples of the part it has played in every aspect of human thought and behaviour. It has shaped the lives of individuals and families and nations and its waning influence today in our own country and elsewhere can be seen as one of the causes, in truth the chief cause, of the increasing chaos in our families and hence in our society. Contracts and accountability abound in employment, in business negotiations and in the insurance of goods. But we are in too great numbers either ignoring or breaking the commitment of marriage that is designed to help safeguard our closest and most important human relationship. This commitment is even more vitally necessary where children are involved. We now have an unprecedented incidence of divorce and of cohabitation and of births outside marriage. In certain parts of the UK more than 50 percent of children are now born to unmarried mothers. This has resulted in huge costs not only in terms of finance and the need for extra housing but even more importantly in terms of human unhappiness, especially for children. The unmet needs of so many of them are giving rise to anger, frustration and violence and to a high incidence of mental illness. Angry young people increasingly find a sense of belonging in their peer groups rather than their families and there is a more sinister pattern of adolescent crime than we have previously experienced. One of our problems is that we are no longer ashamed of our behaviour.

We also have record levels of sexually transmitted diseases, teenage pregnancies and abortions, in spite of the availability of contraceptives. We are now destroying around 200,000 foetuses a year. There is an epidemic of drug and alcohol abuse and obesity, all of which are, in the end, symptoms of spiritual deprivation and are leading to increased levels of ill-health and unhappiness. The cult of greed and instant gratification is leading to a high incidence of excessive private debt fuelled by unwise levels of borrowing and spending and a massive increase in gambling. These have already got us into serious trouble. They are all of them, at the deepest level, problems that reveal our severance from our spiritual roots. They arise from our lack of a belief in judgement and a recognition of our responsibility for ourselves and others. We do not have an adequate sense of what we owe to each other as God's children. These problems are not normal or sustainable phenomena as familiarity might lead us to suppose: they all of them carry a high price in human misery that we cannot endlessly afford.

Christian belief and practice has given rise to the greatest outpouring of unselfish service to mankind that the world has seen and we must somehow recapture a concern for people; for family, neighbours and community – and above all for God. There has never been a golden age but each generation has to recognise its own particular ills to which the faith needs to be seen as relevant and to which appropriate responses need to be made. Sadly, like all else in human affairs, the faith has not always been associated with integrity, all too often giving rise to internal and external conflict and to persecution, for which repentance and requests for forgiveness have been required. It seems that the more wonderful the gifts we are given the more of a mess we make of them. Blind, intolerant faith, in whatever deity or ideology it is placed, can distract us from the here and now and separate us from our neighbours. It has also been a pernicious cause of fanaticism and violence and bloodshed throughout history and continues to be so today. Jesus taught us to pray to the Father that his name might be glorified, his kingdom might come and his will be done. It remains our privilege and our priority to seek the coming of his kingdom above all else in our own lives and in our communities, as far as we can come to understand what that means for us.

CHRISTIANITY AND THE ARTS

The Christian faith has been a massive influence in art and drama and literature but this influence has been gradually eroded by the fragmentation of human knowledge and the rapid advance of secular values. As already noted, when the authorities in Communist Russia banned the Bible they omitted also to ban the works of Tolstoy and Dostoyevsky both of whom, though in very different ways, bore powerful witness to the Christian faith. In his novel 'Resurrection' Tolstoy wrote in graphic terms of Nekhlyudov's reading of Scripture: 'Like a sponge soaking up water he drank in all the vital, important and joyous news the book revealed to him.' Great literature can express spiritual experience with colossal power and authenticity. Another example is the passage in 'Agnes Grey' by Anne Bronte in which Nancy, an old, half-blind and dispirited cottager is visited by the new curate, Mr Weston. She later tells Miss Grey, the governess: "An' then he took that Bible an' read bits here and there, an' explained 'em as clear as day: and it seemed like a new light broke in on my soul; an' I felt fair a glow about my heart, an' only wished poor Bill an' all the world could ha' been there, an heard it all, and rejoiced wi' me." A more recent outstanding example of influential fiction inspired by Christian faith is The Chronicles of Narnia by CS Lewis. A more recent example still is the unusual and powerful book, 'The Shack' by Wm Paul Young that challenges our conventional ideas of God.

In each of the three areas of art and drama and literature there has been an obvious loss of direction, with a concentration on the body; on the physical and often crudely sexual, rather than the wholeness of body, mind and spirit. This is especially the case in the media. In the visual arts we have increasingly chosen rather to mimic the ugly and sordid in life rather than to attempt to redeem it by creating objects of beauty. In part, no doubt, our discomfiture with all this is that it mirrors something of the failings that we recognise within ourselves – to which, as secular prophets, our modern artists are calling attention. It is hard to make moral comments of this or almost any kind without being inconveniently reminded of the poignant question asked by Sir Toby Belch in Shakespeare's 'Twelfth Night': 'Dost thou think, because thou art virtuous, there shall be no more cakes and ale?' We can share our own experience but we cannot prescribe what others should do.

Most things are paradoxical rather than straightforward; the colour is provided by those who, like the prodigal son, experiment outside the prescribed limits, though they have to prove that they can get away with it and end up facing in the right direction. King David in the Old Testament is a good example. Most if not all serious literature is concerned in some way with the conflict between good and evil. Fine poetry and prose arise more often from sadness than happiness and out of questioning rather than faith. Writers and artists tend to be the most acute observers of life and to see our human failings and their implications more clearly and quickly than the rest of us. They are likely to identify the issues that Christians need to consider before they have recognised them. Outstanding perceptive works of this kind in the last century were 'The Waste Land' by T.S Eliot (1922), 'Guernica', a painting by Picasso prompted by the Nazi bombing of its people in 1937 during the Spanish Civil War and George Orwell's 'Animal Farm' and his '1984' that he wrote in 1949. There have been many others before and since.

However great our confidence and however strong our faith we all have to 'work out our own salvation with fear and trembling' whether or not we are aware of God's presence with us. (Phil 2:12). Our lives remain a struggle with or without faith. Even Jesus in his final agony uttered the cry of all who feel abandoned: "My God my God, why have you forsaken me?" (Mt 27:46, Mk 15:34). Faith or no faith we have to work out our own answers to the questions life poses to us, but faith provides us with a foundation and a guide.

PHILOSOPHY AND POLITICS

Philosophy is also involved in the same process of fragmentation and estrangement. It has tended to become detached from the concerns of ordinary people; from the way we live our lives and from our spiritual roots. The Existentialists attempted to address this estrangement, but only, in most cases, with the tools of the 'wise and learned' from whom Jesus tells us in Matthew 11:25 the real truth is hidden. In politics, there is continuing evidence of the corruption, arrogance and inefficiency that power seems almost always to bring with it. We cannot do without leaders but the temptations that power inevitably brings are too great for most of them to resist. This is accentuated by the apparently increasing failure to recognise the reality and inevitability of judgement. It is hard to see how anything less than a repentant, faithful and obedient Church and a sufficient sense of God's presence in the rest of society can even begin to curb the decay that we are experiencing. To quote T.S Eliot again: 'The world is trying the experiment of attempting to form a civilised but non-Christian mentality.'[30] We have to co-operate with those of all other creeds and none, but he predicted that the experiment will fail. There is no other power we can invoke and no other goal to which we can aspire but the coming of God's inclusive kingdom for which, as Christians, we should be constantly praying and working.

THE RELATIONSHIP OF FAITH AND SCIENCE

For hundreds of years the biblical account of an ordered creation has been a stimulus to scientific enquiry. At the same time, ignorance and a lack of humility and tolerance on both sides have frequently contributed to friction and to a perceived conflict between faith and science. Galileo and Charles Darwin were initially seen by some as a threat to the faith and to the Church and to the privileged position of the earth and of Man's place in it. Galileo was imprisoned for supporting the Copernican theory that the sun was the centre of the solar system and that the earth went round the sun, rather than the reverse. In the Church's conflict with Darwin and his theory of Evolution it took a long while for it to be recognised, as Cardinal Newman and others recognised from the start, that whatever was known by revelation, properly understood, could never be at odds with what was discovered by science, properly interpreted.

The perceived conflict between religion and science persists however and is starkly exemplified by 'DNA The Secret of Life' by James Watson in which he claims that 'Life, we now know, is nothing

---

[30] 'Thoughts after Lambeth' 1930, in Selected Essays p387

but a vast array of co-ordinated chemical reactions.' Watson is not alone in believing that science will one day advance to a point where there will be no room for revelation, that is for the God of creation to make himself known to us. E.O. Wilson claims that 'preferring a search for objective reality over revelation is another way of satisfying religious hunger'.[31] This involves a confusion of categories that needs disentangling before dialogue can begin.

There is an interesting discussion of the complex relationship between science and religion in the second chapter of 'Faith and Speculation' by Austin Farrer. The evidence of the seen and the unseen clearly have to be obtained by the use of different methods and there is the question of whether and to what extent faith can be in any real sense described as scientific. It would seem that the rigorous examination of evidence of any kind can be described as a scientific process. In the third chapter of his book Austin Farrer asked the suggestive question: 'When shall we substitute a scientific for a mythical account of the forces on which religion has always known how to draw?' His question was prompted by Henry Drummond's 'Natural Law in the Spiritual World' written in 1899 and Farrer commented, writing sixty years later, that 'the line of investigation so suggested is still waiting to be properly taken up.'

Since that time this has been remedied and there has been a great deal written in an attempt to bridge the gap between faith and science. A notable example is John Polkinghorne's book 'Quantum Physics and Theology', written in 2002, in which he states: 'The purpose of this book is to pursue further the analogies between the scientific investigation of the physical world and theological exploration of the nature of God.' Confusion still exists in both camps, however, and there is often an unwillingness to try to dispel it. What is needed is for scientists, philosophers and men of faith to engage together in honest and detailed discussion. Each side needs to set out its wares and all parties need to agree on rules of engagement. What we require is not polemic in which we trade exaggerated statements but an attempt to form a reasoned assessment of each others' arguments and their implications. There is so much that each side can learn from the other but faith is a premise that is not shared by both parties and this is a fact that inevitably stands in the way of progress. Faith can inhibit

---

[31] Concilience p5

scientific objectivity and the lack of it is a barrier to spiritual understanding.

James Watson, later in his book, expresses the view that 'DNA, the instruction book of human creation, may well come to rival religious scripture as the keeper of the truth.' It would be truer to say that DNA is the 'instruction book', if it can be called such, not of creation but of reproduction and it does not therefore explain life itself but only helps us to understand the means by which its replication is achieved. Pope Gregory 1 said of the philosophers of his time, in the sixth century, that they were 'so concerned with finding the immediate causes of things that they were blind to the ultimate cause, which was the will of God'. "Has not my hand made all these things, and so they came into being?" the Lord asks in Is 66:2. DNA, as a chemical substance, is in a separate category from spiritual truth and if it were possible to give it the personal-sounding role of keeper, it would be keeping a different kind of truth.

Both Watson and Wilson are, in the instances quoted, misusing words and language, apparently in an effort to evade accepting the reality of an unseen, spiritual dimension. This evasion involves an inevitable distortion of their thinking. Francis Bacon pointed out that confusion occurs wherever argument or inference passes from one world of experience to another. T.S Eliot was more controversial when he referred to the 'disintegration of the intellect which is a concomitant of the decay of religious belief'. This proposition would require a particularly good-tempered debate! In discussions about science and faith and the relationship between them there is a need to use words with unusual precision in order to avoid complicating if not eliminating communication altogether. Scientists and theologians have to find the desire and the time that is required to enable them to understand what the other is trying to say. There is a need for humility and honesty and for civilised, non-confrontational dialogue.

When Darwin wished to describe the mechanism of the origin of species he used the term natural 'selection', a word suggesting intelligent choice. James Lovelock, in his book 'The Revenge of Gaia' speaks of the earth system to which he has given this name of Gaia, the earth goddess, as 'appearing to have the unconscious goal of regulating the climate and the chemistry at a comfortable state for life.' (p15). This is surely to deprive the word goal of its more usual meaning of conscious aspiration. This 'goal' looks to be more like a function that it has been designed to perform, thus implying the notion of a creative, delegating being. He also speaks of Gaia as having 'authority' and 'obligations', both of which imply consciousness and responsibility, which it cannot properly be said to possess, and both of which would also have to be similarly conferred by the One who created it.

Richard Dawkins has said that 'faith is a kind of mental illness' and that all supernatural faiths 'miserably fail to do justice to the sublime grandeur of the real world.' He is using a word that is suggestive of awe and almost of worship, in order to dismiss religious aspirations. It is, incidentally, a severe rebuke to Christians that a scientist without faith in God is more excited about the natural world than we are about the God whose handiwork we believe it to be. However this may be, those who believe that God has raised his Son Jesus from death, which it has been found impossible to disprove, would argue that he is quite capable of creating both life, and the universe, however sublime, in which this life has arisen. But this is perceived by faith rather than by reason: miracles are credible only to those who trust in a God they believe to be capable of performing them.

It is also interesting that Dawkins, using his own intelligence to enjoy and to investigate the real world, can deny that a supernatural intelligence must have been involved in bringing it all, including himself, into existence. His own experience of anything worthwhile that he undertakes himself must surely be that it requires careful thought and intelligent planning and needs to have a purpose and be provided with a meaning. It is hard to see how the world in which he lives and does his thinking and planning can have come about without similar careful thought and planning. Unless the universe has been created by a supernaturally intelligent being for a purpose and therefore have a meaning, however obscure it is to us, then nothing in our own lives or elsewhere can possibly have purpose or meaning either. It is our experience that we can give our own actions meaning by the purpose we have in performing them. But what if we ourselves have no meaning, if there was no purpose in creating us? Meaning has to be provided; nothing and no-one can provide it for themselves. It is provided by the purpose for which they are intended by the One who brought them into being. If the world we live in is not conceived with intelligence there can be no intelligence anywhere in it and we cannot presume to think and act intelligently ourselves.

Dawkins claims in his book 'The God Delusion' that 'Natural selection not only explains the whole of life; it also raises our consciousness to the power of science to explain how organised complexity can emerge from simple beginnings without any deliberate guidance.'[32] The arrival of the long march of natural selection up the gradual slope of the mountain, as he describes it, has somehow resulted in the possibility of our emerging with the intelligence with which we can presume to look back from the top of the mountain and explain what has been going on during the ascent. Whence comes the material from which the selection is made? Natural selection, as a means whereby the more robust and resilient forms of life survive in the course of evolution rather than the less robust and resilient, cannot of necessity explain its own beginnings, as Darwin himself recognised. Rather than being opposed to creation all credible theories of evolution begin by assuming it. Dr Denis Alexander writes that 'There is nothing intrinsically materialist, anti-religious, or religious about evolution … but evolutionary history is perfectly consistent with the creator God who has intentions and purposes for the world, including us'. [33]

Can we reasonably maintain that the infinitely complex development of living things, taking place over a period of three or four billion years and beginning in a universe that had already been in existence for around ten billion years, really required no deliberate guidance to set it in motion? And Dawkins does not regard natural selection as an explanation of the inorganic matter of the universe. Where does he think that came from? Henry Drummond wrote of the specialist: 'His limitation is his strength. But when he proceeds to reconstruct the universe from his little corner of it, and especially from his level of it, he not only injures science and philosophy, but may fatally mislead his neighbours.'[34] We cannot leave God out of our reckoning. Nietzsche, who is given credit for the idea that 'God is dead', demonstrated conclusively by all he wrote and all he tried to be that we cannot solve the riddle of life and save ourselves without him.

---

[32] The God Delusion p116
[33] 'Creation or Evolution. Do We have to Choose?' p351
[34] The Ascent of Man p 14

Nietzsche pitted his brilliant intellect against God but his lone quest to overcome the dark side of his nature without him was a failure. He lost the battle, and his sanity, which makes him a parable and a prophet for our time.

Evolution and the mechanism of natural selection and the associated sexual selection by means of which populations either thrive or die out may not appear to some to be guided by intelligence. But for all the apparent anomalies and the brutality and waste and destruction, the world in which they have operated has worked, with a highly efficient system of maintenance, for several billion years. And what better and more intelligent way could be devised for ensuring both variation and development through inheritance over time, and the survival of the finest and best adapted specimens, in a constantly changing and often dangerous environment? This apparently haphazard but highly successful method of operation must surely have been devised with intelligence. Building sites always look a mess.

Dawkins has nevertheless attempted to hijack Darwin for the cause of atheism. This is in spite of the fact that Darwin wrote in a letter in 1879, only three years before his death, that 'In my most extreme fluctuations I have never been an atheist in the sense of denying the existence of a God.' Those who talk of the 'intelligent design' of the universe, many of whom also believe in Darwin's theory of evolution, are on the other hand, accused in the United States of hijacking religion and of trying to smuggle it, along with their theory, into the science curriculum in schools. There is naturally a real difficulty about teaching the two different disciplines of science and theology in the same context. It is no doubt unwise to try to do so but closed minds on both sides make this a tough issue to resolve. Another complication is that a number of believers in intelligent design use the term in a very restricted sense. They use it not for the whole creative process but solely with reference to what they call 'irreducibly complex' phenomena in nature that they do not believe can be accounted for by Darwin's theory of evolution. This wing of the intelligent design lobby is hard to distinguish from creationism and its underlying fundamentalism which leaves no room for evolution. The different views are firmly held and it is no wonder that there is so much confusion and antagonism.

It is clear that although Darwin saw natural selection as the mechanism of the evolution of species, he did not see it as the origin and explanation of creation itself. At the end of the final chapter of his 'Origin of Species' he wrote:

> 'There is a grandeur in this view of life, with its several powers, having been originally breathed by the Creator into a few forms or into one; and that, from so simple a beginning endless forms most beautiful and most wonderful have been, and are being, evolved.'

He may have had difficulties with his Christian faith and his discoveries undoubtedly modified his religious beliefs but he was evidently at this point not an atheist. His battle with faith is described by Nick Spencer in his book: 'Darwin and God'. He makes it very clear that Darwin gradually lost what little real faith he had and later became an agnostic rather than an atheist. This change was evidently due to a combination of the need for a severe scientific rigour in everything he encountered and to the suffering he saw in nature and that he experienced personally in his loss of three of his ten children. Freud was another scientific genius who had a struggle with faith throughout his life, complicated in his case by his unhappy relations with his father and by his natural revulsion at the prevailing antisemitism of the Catholic Church in Austria.

It would appear from a poignant letter from his wife written in 1839, and the anguished comments that he added to it, that Darwin's loss of faith was at first a great sadness to them both. But his faith had never been deep and nearly forty years later in 1876 he wrote in his autobiography that 'I felt no distress when disbelief crept over me.' Perhaps his difficulty with faith is revealed most clearly by his candid admission in another letter that his theology was a 'simple muddle'. It was not his forte and we can well understand his muddle; he was after all a scientist and not a theologian. His need to insist on hard evidence in his scientific studies made faith difficult for him, as it does for so many scientists. He was muddled by the evident coincidence of order in the big picture suggesting design by an intelligent being and the apparent chaos and brutality in the details of nature suggesting the opposite. In his concentration on the struggle for life and the adaptation necessary for survival he failed to see the concurrent struggle for the life of others. This unselfish and often costly struggle is revealed in the gradually emerging, evolutionary development of the mammalian mother's care of her offspring and of the related but deeper human love and of the family.

In another passage in his autobiography he wrote revealingly of his extraordinary life of scientific exploration having led to a lack of balance that many others must also have experienced. 'My mind seems to have become a kind of machine for grinding general laws out of a large collection of facts, but why this should have caused the atrophy of that part of the brain alone, on which the higher tastes depend, I cannot conceive.' He did not have the advantage of our modern understanding of the different functions of the right and left halves of the brain. In another revealing personal comment in 1878 he said that 'Reason may not be the only instrument for ascertaining truth' and he could no longer be sure that he could trust his mind. His life is yet another parable to us of the cost of the pursuit of all forms of extreme specialisation, and a lesson for all who do not manage to develop a balance between head and heart. He may not have got everything right but he was nevertheless a giant, albeit aided in certain respects by other giants of science in the Victorian era. Chief among these were the geologist Sir Charles Lyell and Darwin's staunchest supporter, Thomas Huxley, who incidentally coined the term agnostic to describe his own position. He too was far from being an atheist.

Rather surprisingly, considering his difficulties with faith, Darwin wrote in a letter in 1878, 'I hardly see how religion and science can be kept distinct.' He went on to say that 'there is no reason why the disciples of either school should attack each other with such bitterness.' We are nevertheless confronted with the continuing need to marry up the insights of science resulting from observation and experiment with the spiritual insights and experiences given to faith by means of revelation. They have this at least in common that they are both of them part of the evidence that we make use of in the exercise of living our lives and both are in their different ways open to continual re-examination. There are no startling 'radical theory changes' in theology as there can be in science but what has been revealed requires constant re-interpretation in our individual experience and throughout history. There is a difficulty about looking at the Gospel as an assumption about how things are, about how God sees them and what he has done about them, as one of our starting points for open-minded enquiry. The Christian faith involves our accepting the awkward message of the Cross that we are sinners in need of salvation. This is an assumption that is, for many, too difficult or too painful to accept. But what if the Cross is the definitive and truly scientific solution to the problem of sin and evil that is otherwise insoluble?

If the Gospel really does provide us with the truth about how things are with us it means that the unbelieving investigator is hampered in this area of thinking by his neglect of some of the evidence. There are many eminent scientists however, including John Barrow and John Polkinghorne who, like Newton before them, are able to accept this challenge and reconcile their scientific knowledge with their faith. There is also the eminent theologian Alister McGrath who started out as a scientist and a convinced atheist but became a Christian in the course of his scientific studies. He has written numerous books, including a critique of Dawkins' arguments for his atheism in 'The Dawkins Delusion?'. John Polkinghorne says of science in his book 'The God of Hope and the End of the World': 'Its questions are framed in terms of efficient causes and not in terms of meaning and purpose. Its official discourse deals with measurement and not with values. It is because both science and theology are telling us about the reality within which we live, that they are capable of fruitful interaction.' (p44). Science on its own does not tell us all we need to know about the world in which we live: it cannot provide us with the reason for its existence. If it is not to prove ultimately pointless, as some suppose it to be, the meaning of the world must come from outside itself and therefore be beyond the reach of science. John Polkinghorne goes on to say that individual Christians and the Christian Church, with a belief in the faithfulness of God, should not lose their nerve in witnessing to our generation about the eschatological hope that we believe to exist beyond the ultimate ending in cosmic futility that scientists predict for our world. 'God is the God of hope because he is the God of past, present and future. This eschatological hope is that nothing of good will ever be lost in the Lord. It assures us that our strivings for the attainment of good within the course of history are never wasted but will bear everlasting fruit.' (p101-2).

Einstein wrote in his book 'The World as I See It' of the majority of the profounder sort of scientific minds having a 'peculiar cosmic religious feeling' of their own. This religious feeling takes the form of a 'rapturous amazement at the harmony of the natural law, which

308

reveals an intelligence of such superiority that, compared with it, all the systematic thinking and acting of human beings is an utterly insignificant reflection. It is beyond question closely akin to that which has possessed the religious geniuses of all ages.' (p29). It is interesting that in spite of this religious feeling Einstein, like so many scientists, apparently found it impossible to believe in a personal God. What he did not recognise, for all his genius, was that an intelligent mind can exist only as part of a greater whole, as part of personality. Our ability to think has to be powered by will and love. The thinking that we do has to be motivated and enjoyed: it cannot take place in a vacuum. What he also failed to recognise was that God, of his very nature, seeks to communicate with us. But how encouraging these words of Einstein's are and what a valuable contribution to the continuing dialogue between science and theology.

Julian of Norwich wrote in 'Revelations of the Divine Love': 'Before ever he made us God loved us. Our beginning was when we were made, but the love in which he made us never had beginning. In it we had our beginning.' If as we are now told we were fashioned from the dust of dying stars then God was in a real sense in the dust. There is more to chemistry than meets the eye. There is the element of sublime grandeur; the mystery that defies our total understanding of whatever we observe. We see the natural world also only 'in part' – it does not disclose its meaning to us: it too is a mystery that has yet to be fully revealed. In his 'Hymn of the Universe', Teilhard de Chardin spoke of Christ as 'the divine influence active in the depths of matter'. John Constable the painter wrote from his native Suffolk to a friend: 'Every step I take and on whatever I turn my eye, that sublime expression in the Scripture, "I am the resurrection and the life", seems verified about me.' With God the Father and the Holy Spirit, Jesus inhabits the heavens as his eternal dwelling place, and in his cosmic dimension he inhabits the entire universe with the energy of his creative love. He inhabited an earthly body in order to reveal the Father, and through his sacrifice on the Cross, to refashion and redeem everything that has been made. By the Holy Spirit he inhabits all who respond to the call to follow him in the fellowship of his Church so that they may continue his work in the world. In this fourfold inhabitation we see something of the all-encompassing majesty of his divine nature and of his part in the programme of redemption.

Only by thinking of Jesus in these multidimensional terms can our imagination begin to work at the very edges of his colossal, ubiquitous being. St Paul speaks of him in Colossians 1:15 as 'the image of the invisible God in whom all his fullness dwells.' He reveals to us the definitive shape of love; as crucified redeemer, and as a world in which we see the creative energy of divine love displayed. In the words of Teilhard de Chardin again: 'Christ is known as a person; he compels recognition as a world.' We have to struggle in order to reconcile the eternal Son who is a member of the Godhead, the Jesus of history we read of in the Gospels, the Jesus we experience in our own hearts by his Spirit and the cosmic Christ in whom 'all things hold together'. (Col 1:17). If another name were to be needed for this book it could be given the sub-title 'Homage to Christ', as he is made known to us in all these ways.

This might appear to some to be a form of obscure, unhelpful mysticism. An alternative view would be that it is a recognition of the necessary, logical implication of the nature of the creative process and of the Christian revelation and that an exercise of imagination of this sort is a valid way of approaching the mystery of God and of his creation. If we can allow the notion of a creator, he has of necessity to invest his world with his own creative energy. This energy is love, and mass by virtue of its multiple physical properties, is how we see and experience it. It is this mass, visible to us in all its forms and throughout the whole of creation, that gave rise to Einstein's rapturous amazement. The astonishing relationship between energy and mass is revealed by his deceptively simple equation $E = mc^2$, where c is the speed of light. God is not to be confused with his creation but his is the presiding power and presence in it. Paul wrote in Eph 4:6 that 'There is one Father who is over all and through all and in all.' If you make something out of existing materials you can walk away from it; if you create something out of nothing, which is the orthodox Christian view of creation, then its continued existence depends on your perpetual, sustaining power. God cannot walk away from his creation without it ceasing to exist. And if the power required to bring it into being, and to sustain it, resides in him alone, what does this begin to tell us about God himself?

If we can accept that God is the Creator of the universe and that it is his creative energy that continues to drive it, then he is the only possible end of the scientists' search for the theory that explains

310

everything. As the originator he is the only possible vantage point from which all things can be explained and understood. It follows that until we are enabled, in the age to come, to 'know fully, even as we are fully known' in Paul's words in 1Cor 13:12, we cannot fully know and understand the physical universe, let alone the God who made it. This means that we shall not achieve what Stephen Hawking refers to at the close of his 'Brief History of Time' as the 'ultimate triumph of human reason' which would be 'to know the mind of God'. No science can penetrate the spiritual realm that he inhabits. It cannot resolve the paradoxical mystery of the incarnation in which, as Christians believe, the God who created the endlessly vast universe that science investigates was able to reveal himself in Jesus. This is only possible because Paul is able to write of Jesus in Col 1:17, in Weymouth's translation, that 'HE IS before all things and in and through him the universe is a harmonious whole.' He is the Logos, the creative Word made flesh as John presents him in the first chapter of his Gospel. But the mystery remains: no human mind can comprehend it and no words can cope with what is required of them in expressing this extraordinary paradoxical truth. Einstein said of his scientific investigations that 'The state of mind that enables a man to do this kind of work ... is akin to that of the religious worshipper or the lover.' If what we have said about God's continued active involvement in his universe is true, then Einstein could well speak of 'trying to catch God at his work' and it is no wonder that he experienced his work as worship!

If the God we worship as Christians is truly such an exalted being how then can we really speak, in Jung's words, of 'the inability of religion any longer to embrace man's life in all its fullness' – or claim, with Dawkins, that this Christian faith 'miserably fails to do justice to the sublime grandeur of the real world'? The Gospel is like a prisoner waiting to be released. To quote Henry Drummond's words again: 'What we require is no new revelation, but simply an adequate conception of the essence of Christianity.' Faith is required, of course, but how can we decline to accept so great a gift and share in so great a vision without a thorough investigation of the biblical evidence? This process of investigation is a necessary element in the discovery of truth in the realm of faith as well as in science, albeit the evidence is of things that are not seen.

GOD'S UNFINISHED SYMPHONY

All that has been written in the previous chapters has been an attempt to reshape the data of the biblical revelation by painting a picture worthy of its gigantic canvas, with a view to clarifying its message. It is apparent throughout that this unique biblical story, like the world in which it has unfolded, is profoundly evolutionary, and that the story has not yet come to an end. To return to the metaphor with which we began, the great symphony of God's creative activity is still unfinished and its themes have yet to be fully developed and brought to their final conclusion.

The fossilised remains, and more recently also the genetic records, of our plant and animal ancestors bear witness to physical evolution. The recorded deeds of man in history bear witness to changes, if not always progress, in the social and political aspects of a huge variety of different peoples and cultures. Only in science and technology, for all the inevitable errors, do we see evidence of man's continuing progress. The biblical record of God's revelation of himself to man and man's response to him in history bear witness in their turn to the turbulent story of our spiritual life. Evolution did not come to an end with the development of the purely physical aspects of the natural world. 'First that which is natural, then that which is spiritual', as Paul tells us in 1 Cor 15:44. Properly understood, evolution was never concerned only with the struggle for life that Darwin saw so clearly. From a very early stage it was concerned also with the 'struggle for the life of others', a term coined by Henry Drummond in his 'Ascent of Man', written in 1894, to describe this even more important element in the story.

Alongside the selfish, competitive search for food involved in nutrition there has been, in both the plant and animal world, the more costly, 'unselfish' drive to ensure the continuation of each individual species involved in reproduction. Jesus, speaking in John 12:24 of his own death, says that "unless a seed falls into the ground and dies, it remains only a single seed. But if it dies, it produces many seeds." With the arrival of the Mammals in the course of evolution there has come the emergence of mothering and later of fathering. Mothers and fathers co-operate to provide their essential sacrificial contribution to the care of their offspring, with all the advantages that this brings with it to make their survival more likely.

The highest achievement of evolution was the eventual emergence on earth of love and of the family, above all of the human family. The working together in caring for their young and the making of a 'home' that it increasingly necessitated led to parents becoming gradually more aware of each other and to their slowly developing sympathy and sociability, over thousands of years. The crowning glory has been the ultimate emergence of the family of God, the first-fruits of his new creation, of which, through Christ's redeeming work, he makes us members by adoption. To the eye of faith, redemption is the final stage of the entire, manifestly evolutionary creative process and will one day bring about the consummation of all things. In the words of Henry Drummond once again: 'There is nothing in Christianity that is not in germ in nature ... It is the main stream of history and of science, and the only current set from eternity for the progress of the world and the perfecting of a human race.'[35] It provides us in a unique way with the key to our understanding of the natural world in which we live, of the entire historical process of which we are a part, and of our destiny in the One who made us.

What is easily forgotten is the importance of the environment without which none of these developments could ever have taken place. Our physical environment is perfectly attuned to the needs of life on earth, to an almost unbelievable degree of accuracy, by means of what has been termed the 'anthropic principle'. Stephen Hawking writes that on a certain reading of the Big Bang model of creation 'It would be very difficult to explain why the universe should have begun in just this way, except as the act of a God who intended to create beings like us.'[36] Our spiritual environment is God himself, the One in whom we 'live and move and have our being'. (Acts 17:28). He created us in his own image and he is the only One in whom we can ever be totally fulfilled. He is the One in whom alone we experience the abundant life that he has already given us and that will be even more abundant in the age to come. 'Now the dwelling of God is with men, and he will live with them.' (Rev 21:3). The anthropic principle

---

[35] The Ascent of Man p 441
[36] A Brief History of Time p140

of the ideal, perfectly attuned environment operates not only in the physical but even more richly in the spiritual realm.

If we ourselves and the whole of God's creation are to be made new – as he will ensure in order to eradicate the stain of evil and imperfection – how glorious we must imagine the age to come will be. If there were a better life to lead, a finer creed to live by, a greater God to worship and a grander project to work for than his kingdom then we should have to abandon all of this and go for that instead. But there isn't. There cannot be. 'In our beginning is our end.'

APPENDICES

These appendices might seem to be a somewhat arbitrary series of essays on a wide range of completely separate topics. The reason for their inclusion is that all of them are forms of exploration within the theme of catching God at work and are not therefore as separate as they might appear. They are an attempt to explore God and his creation, the disciplines or methods we use to conduct these explorations and how we speak and write about them. They endeavour to reveal the remarkably close relationship between several seemingly separate disciplines whose followers often seem to have no knowledge of what their colleagues in other fields are talking about and often no real interest in finding out. The reason for including secularisation is that it has to do with the ways in which we attempt to negotiate our dual relationship with God and with his world. The final article on music is an investigation of a glorious and mysterious phenomenon that has associations with nature, with our response to God and with almost every area of human study and activity. Of necessity each of these appendices will be of more interest to some readers than others.

APPENDIX 1

HOW ARE WE TO UNDERSTAND GENDER?

If, as we read in Genesis, God created us in his own image he cannot be other than 'personal' in some sense. An affinity and a relationship is clearly implied but there is even more clearly a massive and immeasurable discrepancy involved as well. His true nature must be an ineffable mystery. Our experience of persons can only be in terms of gender so that our reference to God is bound to be similarly restricted and determined. We are created as both male and female in his image and he himself must have a single, not a dual nature. He can be neither male nor female, but is the greater reality from which they both proceed and from which they both derive their nature and significance. He is above and beyond gender as we know it. If in begetting his Son Jesus from eternity we need to call God the Father a parent then he is a unique, single parent, but the term is not applicable. He is the Creator. The justification for calling God Father must be fundamentally both relational and semantic, in that fathering means also being the author and initiator. When Jesus describes himself as the bridegroom and Paul speaks in Ephesians 5 of his relationship with his Church in the context of a passage about marriage, it would appear that we are all of us, both men and women, in some sense 'female' in relation to God's 'maleness'. Paul describes this as a 'profound mystery'.

Man, as father, the sower of the seed, can also be seen as the initiator in the reproductive process. He plays only a supporting role during the pregnancy, and becomes involved, ideally, in helping to care for the child when it is born. The mother has a different, arguably even more important role, that of bearing and normally playing the major part in looking after the children. Neither male nor female can do without a mate; at the very least a contribution from a donor 'mate' for the purpose of procreation, and ideally a permanent mate for support in the nurturing of the children. Where God is concerned the case is not comparable and the distinction is therefore not valid. He creates, not procreates, and looks after, and sustains, as well. He is a producer, not a reproducer.

Unless we change the meaning of the words we use it can be argued that we shall always have a sufficient reason for referring to God as Father. This is so in spite of the fact that in order to do justice to his loving care of his people we are at liberty to think of him acting also as a mother, as is the case in Psalm 131:2 and Isaiah 66:13, and arguably just two or three other Old Testament verses. These are Scripture's only references to God as revealing maternal qualities – which he is bound to do as One who created us in his image as both male and female, each possessing an element of the other. We cannot speak of him as possessing feminine gender. To do this would be to create confusion. Neither can we speak of him as possessing exclusively masculine gender. He is himself everything it means to be both male and female, mother and father, and in his being as love he loves us as no human parent can ever do.

When God planned the incarnation as the means whereby he would achieve our salvation through Jesus, man, in Joseph, was by-passed and Mary, as a young, obedient virgin, was given the indescribably great privilege of bearing the Saviour in her own body. If the Saviour was thus born of a woman – and how else could the incarnation have been brought about? – then her offspring had of necessity to be male. Man would otherwise have been by-passed, not only in the conception but also in the outcome. He would not have been represented and would thus not only have been excluded from any part in the redemptive process of the incarnation but also by the same token from the salvation that it was designed to accomplish. The redeemer had therefore of necessity to be a man. Caiaphas the High Priest was speaking prophetically, albeit without true understanding, when he said, as recorded in John 11:50, that there was "a need for one man to die for the people." If this argument is accepted it may explain in part the reluctance of some in the Church, with or without justification, to accept women in the role of priests.

To speak of God as Father and of his only-begotten as a Son is less easy to describe as exclusive language when Mary's role is included, as the one in whom God entered his world in Jesus. In spite of this these terms are maybe understandably difficult for some women in particular, in an age in which the issues of gender and roles are still being negotiated. There is a further practical difficulty in that children with unhappy experiences of fathers and women with unhappy relationships with men are naturally inhibited in their worship of an apparently male God. But both men and women can have unhappy experiences of women also, so that we cannot seek a solution in that direction. In neither case is God himself to blame; it is up to us to try to heal the wounds by showing the love that they have previously been denied, with his help. We are constrained by the way in which we have developed language for our own purposes and the way in which we have used it to describe our experience of the mystery of God's being as he reveals himself to us. Our understanding must be increased by an exploration within these dual limitations. To attempt to ignore them is to interfere with history and to risk creating confusion and sacrificing the possibility of a coherent statement of the Christian faith.

In the end God's nature and being – and the existence of gender – is a mystery that is beyond us to penetrate; we can only say what seems to be possible to say and see how it sounds. Parts of what I have tried to say may sound to some to be nonsense, but it is an attempt to think constructively about the issue. Others can no doubt make a better job of it.

THE SOCIOLOGY OF MARRIAGE

This short essay is an argument for the indispensability of marriage as a safeguard for the family, both adults and children. It is also a defence of the contention in the section on marriage that without it no recognisable community and society would be possible. It must be said at once that for a number of reasons marriage is not for everyone and that no-one should be obliged to remain in a marriage that has become truly intolerable. What also needs to be emphasised is that it is a gift of God in creation and has been found in virtually all societies studied to be a requirement for those couples who intend to live together and have children. For this purpose men and women are each of them incomplete and cannot do without a mate, (or at least a donated egg or sperm, though this may involve ethical issues). Their vulnerable relationship, and the children that depend on it, require protection. For this reason marriage needs to be defended, especially when it is being neglected, as is the case today. But there are possible pitfalls, in that too great an emphasis on it can appear to be divisive and to isolate those who are divorced, or unmarried single parents or simply, for whatever reason, living on their own. Those who champion marriage need to be aware of these pitfalls but should not be inhibited in their defence of it on this account.

Marriage stakes out, in a way that nothing else can do, not only the relationship of the couple to each other and to their children but to their families on both sides; to their friends and neighbours; to their community, and to society as a whole. Moreover it continues to stake out the relationships of succeeding generations of grandchildren and great-grandchildren and the whole of both sides of the increasingly extended families in the networks of the communities in which they live. It also serves a number of other vitally important functions, all of which would be lost to society if couples no longer decided to marry, or if the institution of marriage was no longer available:

1) Men and women would no longer have an effective means of announcing their life-long commitment that only their decision to marry enables them to do. If present figures persisted, and there is no reason to assume that they would improve, their cohabiting relationship would last on average around three years rather than around ten years in the case of marriage. This would bring about even more misery for adults, and above all for children, than we are already experiencing. It needs to be recognised that the nuclear family, even with the benefit of marriage, is extremely vulnerable and needs the support of the extended family and neighbours. There is a poignant African saying that it takes a couple to produce a child but a village to bring it up. On visit to a school in Islington Michelle Obama told the pupils: "I am an example of what is possible when girls from the very beginning of their lives are loved and nurtured by people around them."

2) They would cease, as cohabiting couples already tend to do, to inform their families and friends of their intentions and to provide evidence in the wearing of a ring. When a man and a woman decide to live together in an exclusive sexual relationship, with the likelihood of having children, it is never a purely private matter. There needs to be a public recognition of this exclusive physical relationship. Their intention needs to be communicated to the rest of society as a matter of courtesy at the very least.

3) There would be no opportunity to celebrate in public with relatives and friends who care about them and wish them well in their future life together and to have their union witnessed and recorded. Nor would they be able, without the possibility of a religious ceremony, to make public promises before God as well as before those present, or expect their family and friends to pray for their relationship.

4) In the absence of a marriage certificate any children born to the couple do not have the same name as both their parents to show that they come from a known stable, with all the benefits that this provides for them. Marriage also provides benefits for all those who encounter them, in whatever

capacity, and are thereby able to identify them as part of a single family unit. There are outstanding examples of happy so-called common-law marriages but they could never be a model for all. In addition the lack of a marriage certificate would make future genealogical studies difficult, if not impossible. These studies would be reliant in such cases, as indeed they already are, on birth certificates that are not always signed by both parents. It is also worth noting that as the law stands if an unmarried couple with a child separate and the father has not signed the birth certificate he does not have joint parental responsibility. Should the mother try to deny him access to the children the only way in which he can attempt to achieve it is through the courts in the same way as a married father and it may or may not be harder for him to do so.

5) If the above arguments are valid it is apparent that the absence of marriage would lead to social chaos in which both adults, and more importantly children, would suffer even more than they do at present. The resulting situation would make our modern-day damaged society look like paradise. Without the commitment that only marriage can truly indicate, and the discipline that it provides, adult relationships are more fragile and children are less safe. Terrible things can happen to adults and to children in their families and needless to say this can be so in spite of the benefit of marriage. Sadly they can happen even where there are all the appearances of Christian faith. There has never been a golden age but we are failing, in too great numbers, to recognise the unique importance of marriage as the best and only safeguard that we have for families and an institution that alone makes any meaningful community and society possible. Without the communication, celebration and witnessing of the union and the proper records that marriage alone provides, each individual community and society as a whole would lack ingredients that are vital to their very existence in any recognisable form. It is hard to imagine that they would be places in which anyone would wish to live.

APPENDIX 2

PHILOSOPHY, SCIENCE AND THEOLOGY

Both philosophy and science are terms that have had a wide range of usages over time and both have a number of different branches. They are therefore difficult to define or describe accurately without risk of oversimplification. One important branch of philosophy is metaphysics, a somewhat daunting discipline that deals with the first principles of things, such as being, substance, essence, time, space, cause, identity and immortality and is therefore of particular relevance to theology. Philosophy has developed over the years but cannot be said to have progressed in a cumulative fashion, whereas scientific knowledge and the technology that arises from it have been advancing at an ever-increasing rate. The story of Christian theology is of our growing into the revelation of God in Christ that has been delivered in Scripture. It also involves our continual re-examination and re-interpretation of this revelation in response to our changing circumstances, including advances in science.

Philosophy, literally love of wisdom, is an older term than science and originally included the investigation of the natural world. This is now the concern of science, a term that was not used for this sphere of investigation exclusively until the middle of the nineteenth century. Philosophy involves asking important questions and attempting to find answers by means of reasoning and argument. It explores what it is possible to say in the realm of concepts and propositions without losing our way or being shot down in flames. The abstractions with which philosophy deals are slippery customers. Philosophy is of great importance in teaching us how to think but it can sometimes look like an exercise in intellectual gymnastics in isolation from our other human faculties and from the lives and experiences of the majority of ordinary people. It can appear to lead to heated argument rather than to light.

Philosophy does not routinely include knowledge obtained by revelation but where that is available and relevant to the area of discussion it would seem to be unwise to ignore it. T.S. Eliot has argued that: 'Ultimately, apart from revelation there would appear to be no criterion of philosophic credibility.'[37] This is because each philosopher starts his thinking in a different place, with a different set of premises. This is due to the inherent bias of his personality, his beliefs, and his individual experience of life and it naturally affects the nature of his conclusions. It could be argued that without Christ there is ultimately no mooring for the mind. As the Logos, the eternal Word made flesh of John's Gospel, Jesus is the unique divine proposition, God's given premise from which alone we can truly begin to make a fruitful investigation of the natural and above all of the spiritual world. St Augustine said that we have to believe in order to know as well as to know in order to believe. Jesus is not only where we begin however; he is also where we make an end: he is also our conclusion. "I am the Alpha and the Omega, the First and the Last, the Beginning and the End" he tells us in his final words in Rev 22:12. In John 14:6 he amplifies this when he says "I am the way and the truth and the life." He is the path we tread and the place where we arrive and he gives us the strength to make the journey. When Jesus makes the even more extravagant claim in John 15:5 that "Apart from me you can do nothing," it is no mere rhetoric. We have already slipped without difficulty into the realm of theology, to which we shall return in a moment.

Science involves the acquiring of knowledge of the natural world by observation and the use of experiments and frequently the expression of their results in the form of mathematical equations and with the use of statistical analysis. In the words of Galileo 'the Book of Nature is written in mathematical characters.' The so-called empirical, scientific method normally also involves the complex processes of weighing evidence and making inferences and of confirming or disproving provisional hypotheses and theories. On occasion it realises its ultimate goal of formulating scientific laws that appear to be of invariable application in their own particular spheres. These provisional ideas may initially come from what Einstein called 'thought experiments' and they are often subsequently confirmed or disproved experimentally by others. Perhaps surprisingly, imagination plays almost as large a part in science as it does in philosophy and art

---

[37] The Idea of a Christian Society & other writings 'Revelation' p189

and is a close companion of experimentation. For further reference to the scientific method see under Hypothesis, Theory and Law.

Theology is the study or science that investigates God and what he has done in order to reveal something of himself and of his purposes to us. It also examines his relationship with us and with his universe, and what it is possible for us to say about his nature. Christian theology can be seen as the investigation of the greatest story in the world. This is the huge and endless story of God and of his unique revelation of himself and of his programme for the redemption of his whole creation through the death and resurrection of his Son Jesus Christ. This investigation involves the use of imaginative philosophical reasoning and argument and also a disciplined, scientific approach to all the relevant evidence. It includes studying the earliest available biblical texts and the languages in which they were written, looking into the history and archaeology of the period, and more recently using an increasing variety of different methods of biblical criticism.

Christian theology is also concerned with the doctrines and creeds formulated by the early Church from their experience of God and from their interpretation of those Scriptures that they came to recognise as authoritative and that therefore became part of the canon. Chief among the doctrines are the Incarnation and the Trinity. Another of its concerns is the impact of the revelation on those individuals and communities who came to believe in it and experience it and what they have traditionally said and written about it over the past two thousand years. In our attempt to understand theology we cannot afford to neglect psychology. We need to understand ourselves as the ones who exercise faith as well as the God in whom we put our trust. Numerous gifted theologians have shed light on Christian truth for their own generation and for those who come after them. The fundamentals of the faith have not changed but the focus and emphasis have changed in a number of areas of truth over the years in response to changing needs and circumstances and are still doing so. An example is the need to use methods of mission and evangelism that keep abreast of social and cultural changes.

Some of what has been said and written is heresy, or unorthodox belief, but this is an inevitable aspect of investigating the mystery of God and of the dialogue from which truth is forged. He is too big to be captured in a form of words and we have continually to listen to him and to each other in order to avoid being satisfied with a superficial understanding. If the God of the Christian Gospel is in some indefinable sense everywhere present throughout his creation then theology can have no limits and can still be the unifying Queen of Sciences. God himself is the one true centre of all things and as Paul tells us in Romans 1:20 there is nothing in all creation that does not tell us something about the One who brought it into being.

SCIENCE AND THEOLOGY COMPARED AND CONTRASTED

This section contains a number of ideas that have already appeared in various forms elsewhere but a degree of repetition can arguably be justified by the importance of the relationship between these two disciplines. The whole of this book is about God and about what he has done and is continuing to do in his creation, and in the redemption of his creation, and about how we catch him at his work. These twin studies are the concern of science and of theology and because they explore a coherent and dependable cosmos on the one hand and its Creator on the other they have considerable similarities, as well as obvious and inevitable differences. Perhaps the chief difference is that science addresses the question how – how the natural world works – and theology encompasses also the question why, in other words the related spiritual questions of meaning and purpose. This added spiritual dimension means that the theological study of God's being and actions must be approached in a spirit of prayer, without which a real understanding of spiritual truth is not possible.

Both disciplines involve painstaking and rigorous investigation of valid evidence and sound reasoning in drawing their conclusions, which arguably gives theology the right to be regarded as a science. Both are subject to development. As scientific knowledge is provisional and subject to further observation and to reassessment and modification, so biblical truth must always be open to fuller interpretation and understanding of what has already been revealed. In science we grow out of provisional truths and into a fuller truth; in theology we grow into the spiritual truth already revealed in Scripture and in the Church.

While science focuses on the physical world the concern of theology is the nature and activities of the invisible, supernatural being who is the creator of this physical world. Henry Drummond, in the introduction to his 'Natural Law in the Spiritual World', described the natural world as a 'working model of the spiritual', whose phenomena are analogous and whose laws are identical. Science and theology are complementary disciplines therefore but the difference in their subject matter clearly demands different methods of enquiry. These include the use of intrusive experimentation in science and of biblical study and interpretation in theology, and differences in their methods of expressing their findings. Science is often able to make use of the precise language of mathematics as a means of expressing its physical findings. Theology is less precise because it has to make do with words to express its ideas and relies on the discipline of philosophy for the construction of its arguments and conclusions. Both use hypotheses and models and pictures and both make use of bottom-up, empirical investigation to provide a worm's eye view from below and top-down thinking to make a coherent assessment of the results of observation and to provide an overall conceptual bird's eye view from above. This is what John Polkinghorne describes as a 'creative interaction ... between stubborn experimental findings and imaginative theoretical exploration.'[38] This is an interactive process that never ceases as long as we continue to investigate the world in which we live. It is this dual process that enables us to discover truth and to provide explanations and formulate theories and laws in science. It also enabled the early Church to express its experience of God in the creeds and doctrines of Christian theology. In this latter case the evidence is not the phenomena of the natural world but above all God's coming to earth in Jesus, the Cross and Resurrection and the pouring out of the Holy Spirit at Pentecost. These, unlike the continual progress of science, are unique foundational events but it took the Church several hundred years to struggle with the stubborn truths of the revelation and to find a satisfactory form of words for the formulation of these Christian creeds and doctrines. We still struggle

---

[38] 'Quantum Physics and Theology' p26

to understand these truths and their meaning for us as we work out how our faith continues to make sense in a changing world.

There are numerous examples in science also of the need to struggle over long periods of time with irreconcilable paradoxes and unanswered questions before they are resolved. The dual nature of light as both wave and particle was an unsolved puzzle for many years. This has now been explained but the conflict between Quantum Physics and General Relativity remains, as described in the section below. Comparable unresolved paradoxes are encountered in theology. Examples of these are the Incarnation and the Trinity. It is impossible for us to understand how God can be revealed in human flesh and how Jesus can be both God and man. It is similarly impossible to understand how God can be One and yet be also three interrelated persons – Father, Son and Holy Spirit. Perhaps the final paradox, spanning the sphere of both science and theology is the fact that, as we believe by faith, the One who began his earthly life as a baby in Bethlehem is not only a member of the Trinity of the Godhead but also the co-creator of the universe into which he was born. If we are looking, as the scientists do, for a theory of everything it is hard to see how it can be less than the Logos, the divine Word made flesh of St John's Gospel. It has already been argued in the Postscript that the creator whose originating energy is essential for the sustaining of his universe is the One in whom alone the working and the meaning and purpose of all things can be explained.

THE SCIENTIFIC METHOD
– HYPOTHESIS, THEORY AND LAW

A hypothesis is an initial assumption that, in the scientific setting, is an attempt to explain known facts and is a starting point for further observation and experiment as opposed to purely rational investigation, as in philosophy.

A theory can be regarded as a hypothesis that has stood the test of preliminary experimentation and appears to be a reasonable explanation of known facts and phenomena, eg Einstein's theory of relativity. It can be useful not only in explaining observations already made but can also enable scientists to make predictions about what they might expect to observe subsequently if it is correct. Awkward facts that do not fit with the theory should never be ignored! The scientific approach, the so-called empirical scientific method, thus involves, in general, the process of testing these hypotheses and theories by means of further observation and experiment and ultimately, where it is relevant, of establishing scientific laws. More simply, the observing and experiencing of things around us leads to reflection and to provisional explanations. These in turn prompt further observation and experiment in order to confirm or refute them and this process goes on endlessly throughout the history of science.

A law is a theory that is found to apply in every case within its sphere of operation. Laws have frequently to be expressed in mathematical equations, some of which are beyond the comprehension of the scientists themselves, not all of whom are also brilliant mathematicians. One of the most famous and most exquisitely beautiful equation of all – Einstein's $E = mc^2$ – has the added benefit of apparent simplicity. This element of beauty is highly prized in science as well as in art and it is one of the intriguing truths of engineering that what looks right also works.

The method of arguing by inference from particular experimental findings to more general principles or theories, and thence to laws, is known as induction. This is in contrast to deduction which consists essentially of arguing logically from general principles to particular instances, though both types of reasoning are likely to be involved, in varying degrees, in solving any particular scientific problem. Induction is inevitably a less water-tight form of argument in that it involves the assumption that the findings will always be repeatable. This confident assumption that scientists need to make is an exercise of faith of which they are not always aware and which they might be reluctant to recognise!

The scientific method of investigation is used in many different ways in a huge variety of different disciplines and is inevitably highly complex. Numerous devices may have to be used, such as 'controls', mathematical equations and statistical analysis in order to try to avoid erroneous interpretations, to express experimental results and to ensure their validity. For this reason there are various explanatory models of the scientific method, each of which does justice to one or other aspect of its complexity. The need to take account of the context of a scientific investigation and of the method of arriving at initial hypotheses are further factors for consideration. The process of scientific induction in its various guises, and in its disputed relevance to theology, is for all these reasons very difficult to describe. It is one thing to define the terms at our disposal; it is quite another to use them in an attempt to give an exhaustive general description of the principles involved and how they apply in a myriad of different situations. It is easy to get lost in a philosophical discussion of science!

What looks like good luck can sometimes play a part in scientific discoveries. A famous instance was the apparently chance discovery by Alexander Fleming in 1928 of a destructive mould on his cultures of bacteria whose active agent turned out to be penicillin. Discoveries can also fortuitously result from findings that are made in the course of a search for something quite different, though it is notoriously easy to ignore findings, however obvious and significant, that we are not actually looking for. Scientists may also on occasion engage, as mentioned in the section above, in 'thought experiments' in order to investigate the nature of reality and may have the intuitive genius that enables them to see further than they or anyone else have seen before. These penetrating insights tend to come about only as a result of relentless hard work and profound, imaginative perception of how the world works, often owing a huge debt to the preparatory work of others. True 'Eureka' moments are rare. The outstanding example of this need for patience and persistence is Newton who said that he had come upon gravity by 'thinking on it continuously'. Almost equally remarkable examples are Einstein's theories of special and general relativity. These theories did not result initially from experimental work but from inspirational thinking carried out over many years, in his case mainly at his desk in the Patent Office in Bern. They were only later confirmed, as with Newton's discoveries, by numerous observations and experiments carried out by others.

The full implications of Einstein's theories are still being struggled with a hundred years later. This also true of their awkward failure to fit with quantum mechanics for which the string theory, or its most recent modification, is at present thought to be a possible resolution. The theories that account for the behaviour of the very large and the very small in physics, whilst applying perfectly in their own fields, have yet to be reconciled. They are discussed briefly in the section below.

Scientific Laws are modes of operation discovered to be governing the phenomena of nature and as such are of invariable application in their particular sphere of operation, as described above. They could be said to be theories to which no exception has as yet been found. Newton's law of gravity is an example, though Einstein's theory of Relativity replaced it in terms of its mechanism of action. Natural laws can in some instances also be seen to apply in the spiritual realm, due to the correspondence between these apparently separate spheres. Examples are the laws of growth and development that govern the behaviour of living things.

RELATIVITY, QUANTUM MECHANICS AND STRING THEORY

General relativity, Einstein's theory of gravity, expresses our understanding of the predictability of the large-scale behaviour of matter. It has been elegantly if over-simply expressed by saying that 'matter tells space-time how to curve, and curved space tells matter how to move', thus emphasising their majestic reciprocal relationship. It has also been said that general relativity 'provides the choreography for an entwined cosmic dance of space, time, matter and energy'. Quantum theory, on the other hand, expresses the unpredictability of the behaviour of matter when we reach the smallest, sub-atomic level of its ultimate, most minute particles – the so-called 'uncertainty' or 'indeterminacy' principle. This is an indication of our inability to measure both the position of a particle and its velocity due to the inevitable limitations of our experimental observations.

Each of these explanations works in its own sphere but they do not appear to agree together – they are 'contradictory theories'. The present favoured means of resolving the disagreement, though its proposed elements are far too small for experimental investigation, is the so-called 'string theory' or a modification of it. This suggests that the ultimate elements of matter are not particles but vibrating 'strings' and that, according to one explanation, 'the mass of an elementary particle is determined by the energy of the vibrational pattern of its internal string'. This is in line with the fact that the volume of a sound is determined by the energy of vibration of the string or whatever it is that gives rise to it.

There would appear to be a parallel to the scientific paradox in the relative predictability of the behaviour of large numbers of human beings and the largely unpredictable nature of the behaviour of each individual. Like elementary particles we are hard to pin down. It may also be justifiable to fancy a parallel with the scientific model in the variation of the energy of these individual human beings and the power and influence they exert. Paradoxically, it would seem to be necessary that in any natural system the predictable and reliable behaviour of the whole is achieved only by a myriad of unpredictable, interacting and counterbalancing activities of the individual elements of which it is composed. It is perhaps a predictable finding. This combination might appear to be the only possible way of constructing an apparently dense and coherent world that holds together but is yet vibrant and recyclable rather than immobile and inflexible, as though set in concrete. It must be possible for the elements that once inhabited the dinosaurs, and even earlier species, to be available for incorporation in our own and other bodies now.

It is understandable that one of Darwin's problems with faith was this co-existence of order in the big picture and apparent chaos in the details. The two different aspects of matter and of the world of nature, the very large and the infinitely small, are perhaps irreconcilable in the same way that we cannot unaided see two sides of a coin at the same time: the necessary viewpoint is denied us by our inevitable limitations. Only the creator himself can resolve the ultimate paradox that lies at the heart of matter and of the life of all that he has brought into being. As Stephen Hawking expressed it in his 'Short History of Time', only God can observe his creation without disturbing it with his experimental intervention.

APPENDIX 3

MYTH AND HISTORY

Myth is a certain sort of traditional story, most frequently associated with ancient Greece, whose myths were especially rich and enduring, but common, in some form, to all cultures. Myths present deep truths about life in stories and by means of ritual rather than in statements. The stories are not told by individual storytellers but by a people, from the depths of their human experience. They are particular to each tribe and culture but also varying expressions of primitive archetypal images common to Man's primordial collective unconscious. They arise out of their need to make sense of the mystery of their origins and of life and death and of their relationship to the supernatural and to divinity and to their perception of another invisible world that exists in parallel to our own. They are also concerned with their relationship to the visible world and to their fellow human beings and thence with right behaviour. Myths thereby come to embody and perpetuate their understanding of themselves and of their culture and for this reason have provided a rich source of material not only for anthropologists but also for the disciplines of psychology and sociology. To be effective in maintaining the integrity of a culture, whether it is simple or sophisticated, myths have to be kept alive by their commemoration in some form of ritual enactment. They are naturally modified over time, however, as they are developed by succeeding generations in order to maintain their relevance. They need to be distinguished from fable and pure fiction in that real people and events may have formed the basis of some of the stories and from legend which is popularly regarded as history but may or may not be, eg King Arthur. In some tales two or more of these forms can exist together in combination.

Myth, like all good story-telling, is a rich source of nourishing truth and subject to constant repetition, but its basically fictional nature can make it sound somehow inferior. It can be regarded as a derogatory term of dismissal, as when certain vital elements of the Christian faith, such as the incarnation and resurrection are seen by some as 'merely myth'. In Jung's words 'it is not that God is a myth, but that myth is a revelation of the divine in man.'[39] This misuse of the term makes it important to distinguish between myth and the historical nature of the fundamental truths of the Christian Faith. The powerful myth of God coming down to earth is rendered more powerful still by being acted out in history. We should not be surprised that he has implanted in us the expectation of what he intends to do. The life and crucifixion of Jesus are accepted as historical facts and the resurrection has defied all efforts to disprove it. Tacitus, the great Roman historian tells us (in his Annals (15.4) that Jesus was crucified under Pontius Pilate and there are references to Jesus and his followers in the Lives of the Caesars by Suetonius (Life of Claudius 25) and in the Letters of Pliny the Younger. (10.96) A further independent record of these events is to be found in Book 18 of 'Jewish Antiquities' by the first century Jewish historian Josephus, where he writes:

> 'Now there was about this time Jesus, a wise man, if it be lawful to call him a man; for he was a doer of wonderful works, a teacher of such men as receive the truth with pleasure. He drew over to him both many of the Jews, and many of the Gentiles. He was the Christ. And when Pilate, at the suggestion of the principal men among us, had condemned him to the cross, those that loved him at the first did not forsake him; for he appeared to them alive again the third day; as the divine prophets had foretold.'

If man, in his imaginative creation of myths, anticipated some of the things that God was later to do in Christ it does not mean that we are entitled to regard these things as part of this same mythical tradition, and hence non-historical. It must also be said that the Bible itself contains elements of what can be described as myth, especially in its description of the origins of creation in the early chapters of Genesis and of its destiny in Revelation. The biblical myths revealed to the prophets are rich and endlessly nourishing truth that can often speak to us in a more powerful and enduring way than practical explanations or particular events in history.

---

[39] Memories, Dreams, Reflections p 373

There is thus a difference that needs to be appreciated between story and history, even if it is not always absolutely clear-cut. The origin of myth is mysterious but myths are men's stories, albeit often involving gods. The Gospel, on the other hand is believed by Christians to be the account of how the one true God has himself become involved in history and could thus be said to have given us the true, enacted myth that makes sense of our lives and of everything else as well. This true, enacted Christian myth reveals to us our origin and destiny in God, our relationship with him and with creation and provides us with teaching about love and how we should treat each other. It thus gives us the definitive resolution of the questions that myth was designed to address, albeit still retaining the element of mystery.

The Greek myths clearly began as an oral tradition and appear to have originated from pictorial images and enacted ritual and drama and only later to have been written down. They were followed by the more organised mythological writings attributed to Homer, chiefly the Iliad and Odyssey, written in the eighth or ninth century BC. In the next few centuries the mythos, or story, tended to be replaced by the logos or word, and the ancient myths were subjected to investigation in the dramatic presentations of Greek Tragedy. Poetry then began to be replaced by prose, notably by Plato, and these changes paved the way for the use of reason and of philosophy, as well as a form of early, rudimentary scientific investigation of the natural world. It is interesting that over the next few hundred years these changes started to happen elsewhere also. At the end of the sixth and the beginning of the fifth century BC two very important contemporaries began their teaching in the East. These were Confucius, the hugely influential philosopher and social reformer in China, and Buddha, the equally influential religious leader and psychologist, in India. It was Confucius who first taught his followers: 'Do not do unto others as you would not have done to you.'

Thus myth, by virtue of its broad scope, whilst remaining of continuing interest as creative story-telling, tended to be increasingly replaced, not only by the organised thinking of philosophy and religious teaching but by the observational method of science and also by history. There is a risk in this gradual replacement however in that people need to maintain their own myths and stories in order to sustain the integrity of their cultures.

In the middle of the fifth century, Herodotus and Thucydides, the pioneers of modern-day secular **history**, made the first serious attempts to give reliable accounts of events, though still with a large mythical content. It must be said that myth can be created consciously or unconsciously in what purports to be accurate and authentic history nowadays. A form of myth, in its sense of fiction or fantasy, is often consciously used as a wilful distortion of the truth by unscrupulous leaders to publicise and exaggerate their achievements. An example is the propaganda employed in wartime. It can be what people come to believe or are led to believe rather than the true, maybe rather unpalatable facts about themselves, their country and their great men and women. Secular history naturally differs from Jewish Old Testament religious history in having no recognition of God's involvement in it.

In the following one and a half centuries Greek philosophy reached its highest point of development with Socrates and Plato and Aristotle, who together spanned the years between 470 and 322 BC. It was during this period of the flowering of Greek secular history writing and philosophy that the later history of the Jewish people was being written following their return from exile in Babylon. This was a continuation of the tradition of the written history of the people of Israel and the writings of the prophets that began hundreds of years before this. It is this early date that makes the Old Testament such a unique document. There were a number of much earlier, remarkably advanced and cultured eastern and middle-eastern peoples with whom God's people Israel came into contact. At the time of Abraham, probably around 2000 BC, the Egyptians, Babylonians and Assyrians were already established or emerging civilisations with distinctive political, intellectual and artistic achievements. But none of these, including the later even more influential Greeks, with their massive contributions in terms of alphabet and language and philosophy, produced a coherent, continually developing body of literature and history to compare with the Judaeo-Christian Scriptures.

These Scriptures came to fruition with the good news of the coming of God into his world in Christ and its early spread throughout the Roman Empire. They have continued to provide not only intellectual, artistic and political influence, but above all a nourishing spiritual influence over an ever increasing area of the world during the past two thousand years. The Church that attempts to live by them has often committed terrible sins. It has also been responsible for preaching the Gospel of God's love revealed in Jesus and providing the greatest sustained outpouring of impartial charitable works and giving that the world has seen. This has included the provision of food, shelter and clothing, medicine and education to the poor and needy of the world, regardless of colour, race and creed. People do wonderful things for their neighbours without any particular, conscious motivation but the Christian Church, through the activity of its members in all manner of organisations and none, is unequalled in its provision of impartial charity. These works of charity provide some of the most powerful evidence of the coming of God's Kingdom on earth for which Christians are commanded to pray.

The plans that God has laid are made to endure and will one day come to fruition. Scripture teaches that his inclusive kingdom will encompass every other kingdom and nation of people and everything else as well throughout the entire sweep of world history. God's kingdom has already been inaugurated and will one day be fully established when Jesus comes again and history as we know it will be at an end. The whole of this history thus takes place within the compass of the vast Judaeo-Christian myth of all myths, the story of God's programme for his universe that the Bible relates, from creation in Genesis to the new heaven and the new earth in Revelation.

APPENDIX 4

SIMILE, METAPHOR, SYMBOL, PARABLE AND ALLEGORY

These linguistic devices and forms of thinking are considered together because they are closely linked and some of them are difficult to describe, let alone to define, in isolation. Treating them as a group may help to build up a picture of their complex relationship and of what each of them contributes to language and to our understanding of the world. Apart from **similes** where one thing is directly likened to another for clarification eg "The kingdom of heaven is like a pearl of great price;" and metaphor, in those cases where it involves a direct identification, eg "I am the good shepherd," it is often difficult to see what is happening. **Metaphor** comes from the Greek word meaning a transference and refers to the use of words in other than their literal sense, for instance pressing home an argument or knocking a rumour on the head. It has been described as a 'fundamental mode of knowledge' on account of the universal importance of relationships. It consists in literally 'carrying across' a name or a term usually from something relatively simple that resembles it in some important and helpful way, to something more complex that needs clarification or embellishment. We need to bring together parallel objects and ideas to highlight the interesting and illuminating relationships in our experiences of the world and to add colour and interest to our speaking and writing. This can aspire to what has been beautifully expressed as making 'magical connections'.

There are many examples of metaphor in the Bible, especially in the Psalms and the Prophets and in Jesus' teaching. A striking example is when he tells Nicodemus he must be born again in order to enter the kingdom. The transfer of a natural term into the spiritual sphere brings out the close, analogous relationship involved and casts light on the nature of the more complex spiritual issue at stake.

Metaphor depends on this correspondence between two things that are often seemingly quite different in the coherent whole of creation. It is a measure of the difficulty of the term metaphor that it includes both of these things, the primary subject or idea and also what it is fancied as resembling in a certain way or ways. The two together, in their area of overlap and similarity, form what has been called the 'ground of the metaphor' but their dissimilar features also add to the surprise and interest that results from bringing them together. Jesus' description of the kingdom of heaven as yeast is a somewhat surprising metaphorical allusion. We all of us make use of metaphor, consciously or unconsciously, every day of our lives in the subtle and complex activity of talking and writing whenever we use words in other than their literal sense. This is not always easy to distinguish in that, for instance, a wooden leg is both literal and metaphorical! Care needs to be taken in using metaphor if we are to avoid various pitfalls. One example is mixing one metaphor with another and thereby causing a confusion in thinking. Professor I.A Richards says of this highly complex phenomenon of metaphor: 'Our skill with metaphor, with thought, is one thing – prodigious and inexplicable; our reflective awareness of that skill is quite another – very incomplete, distorted, fallacious, and over-simplifying.'[40]

A **symbol** stands for something else, as a 'clear visual image', usually something concrete representing something more complex, but not involving an analogous relationship. Examples are the forbidden fruit in the garden of Eden, standing for the knowledge of good and evil, a crown as a symbol of royalty and the cross as the definitive symbol of the Christian faith. The cross can also be used metaphorically as when Jesus speaks in Matt 10:38 of our denying ourselves and taking up our cross daily as a condition of becoming his followers. When the mark of the cross is made on the forehead in baptism it is used as a sign of the faith that makes the believer a Christian and a member of the Church.

A **sign** is a less powerful image that indicates or points to something or somewhere and may name it, as is the case with a signpost, but does not symbolise it. A wedding ring, as a complete circle, made of gold or some other valuable metal, acts as both a symbol and a sign. It symbolises the precious, enduring love and faithfulness of the couple and is also a sign of their married state.

When we come to **parable** and **allegory**, there is no absolutely clear, generally accepted distinction. Parable comes from the Greek word meaning literally 'putting things side by side', and hence inviting comparison. As used by Jesus it is a story or illustration that is designed to convey a moral or spiritual lesson and to offer a challenge and a stimulus to thought and imagination on the part of his hearers. The interpretation of a typical parable is not spelled out, leaving the hearers to think about its meaning for themselves. The mystery of God can only be gradually revealed and is hidden until they begin to understand the spiritual truth at issue.

An allegory, literally 'speaking otherwise,' is a story used to cast light on something complex by the use of other simpler terms that act as symbols for what we wish to speak about and clarify. Both are explanatory stories, parables being normally the shorter and particularly used by Jesus when he was addressing the crowds. If there is a real difference it might be said that a parable involves the

---

[40] The Philosophy of Rhetoric

use of metaphor and an allegory the use of symbols. A well-known example of allegory is Bunyan's 'Pilgrim's Progress'.

It has been said that metaphor and allegory are usually best kept separate, presumably to avoid a confusion between two different methods of expression. But Jesus' parables, in the unique form in which he used them, can involve simile, metaphor, and allegory as well. In his parable of the sower in Matthew 13 where the seed is the Word of God, and as such a metaphor, its reception by the hearers is depicted in terms of the nature of the ground on which it falls. The path, the rocky places, the thorns and the good soil, whose meaning Jesus later explained to his disciples, are figures of speech providing examples of both metaphor and symbol that cast light on the different ways in which people respond to the message of the kingdom. We can therefore argue that allegory is also involved in the parable and we are provided with further evidence of the subtlety of Jesus' teaching.

There is an interesting indication of the difference between speaking metaphorically and literally in John 16:25 where Jesus says to his disciples: "Though I have been speaking figuratively, a time is coming when I will no longer use this kind of language, but will tell you plainly about my Father." He then tells them that "I came from the Father and entered the world; now I am leaving the world and going back to the Father and they say to him: "Now you are speaking clearly and without figures of speech." There were few things he was able to teach them in literal terms and that were as easy for them to understand as this simple truth. It is no wonder, in view of the mysterious nature of the truths that he had to tell them that even the disciples, let alone the crowds, found it difficult to understand him.

The synoptic Gospels record a number of Jesus' parables in which he teaches about the kingdom of heaven with the use of metaphors. John records Jesus teaching the same truths in a different way. His metaphors refer to himself, as light and bread, and to our relationship with him as sheep to the shepherd, rather than to the kingdom in which we live with him and our neighbours.

IMAGINATION

Imagination is the means by which we perceive what is absent as though it were present and what is not seen as though it were, as in the exercise of faith. It is the means by which we are enabled to be inventive and creative. It also encompasses the harnessing and focusing of all our faculties for the investigation of whatever aspect of reality it may be, in science or literature or any other field of human exploration. It can be seen as a rich mixture of observation, thought and intuition, and of pondering and wondering. When it is used in a spiritual setting it plays an important part in perceiving the truths of divine revelation, and it also plays a vital part in communicating them to others.

Because we all have different gifts and interests we think the world that we encounter is fragmented, not a seamless whole. The part played by observation and thought and above all imagination is what makes the seemingly totally separate pursuits of art and literature, philosophy and theology and the sciences seem less separate after all. Einstein has been quoted as saying that 'You can recognise truth by its beauty and simplicity. I am enough of an artist to draw freely on my imagination.' It is just that the observing and thinking and imagining are employed in appropriately different ways in the different disciplines. In each case there is the same creative striving after truth and beauty and the same joy in their discovery. In order to make full use of this faculty of imagination we have to try to be, in the words of Henry James, 'one of those people on whom nothing is lost'.

It has been said that children want to see the laws of the physical universe turned topsy-turvy for purposes of imaginative exploration, but not those of the moral universe. Right and wrong are not negotiable: evil cannot be allowed to triumph in the end, even in fiction, without doing violence to the hope and confidence that are central to our humanity. We cannot truly live without hope. The trustworthiness of relationships has ultimately to be respected and affirmed.

Finally, imagination needs to be distinguished from fantasy which is at its worst an exercise in undisciplined and fanciful self-indulgent escapism. Imagination on the other hand is at its best a source of nourishment to the mind and spirit and helpful in increasing our understanding of the reality of the natural world as well as embellishing it in the creation of fiction.

APPENDIX 5

SECULAR, SECULARISATION AND SECULARISM

Secular literally means of the present age, or temporal, and hence pertaining to the visible, physical world as opposed to the unseen, eternal world. It thus speaks of a material in contrast to a religious or spiritual attitude; of the worldly as opposed to the sacred. For this reason it can appear to those with a religious faith as a purely negative term, but not all that it stands for should be seen in this way. We are bound to see a positive aspect to the secular in the need for a separation of our loyalties to God and to the State that Jesus emphasised in Matt 22:21 when he told the Pharisees to "Give to Caesar what is Caesar's, and to God what is God's." Christians live not only in this world but through faith are, in Paul's words in Eph 2:19, 'members of God's household' and like Abraham are 'looking forward to the city with foundations whose architect and builder is God.' (Heb 11:10). Our primary loyalty is to God but we owe an obedience to the law of the land and a loyalty also to the government that is provided for our benefit and Jesus is teaching us here that we should honour both, albeit in different ways. Both faith on the one hand, and law and politics on the other, must of necessity develop throughout history and for this purpose they need to be sufficiently separate to enable them to develop with a sufficient degree of independence.

There is a tension and a need for balance, in the individual life and in the community, between the secular and the spiritual, between being full and responsible citizens of this material world and also recognising our even more important obligations to God. These loyalties not infrequently clash and lead to conflict as we are all too aware in today's world. There have also been, and continue to be, innumerable instances of religion itself being misinterpreted and given too great prominence and leading to bloodshed, not only between rival faiths but even more tragically between rival factions of a single faith. The widespread presence of religious fundamentalism in the present day in both East and West is no doubt in part people's response to the materialism and the instability and uncertainty that they are experiencing. Once strongly held essentially non-rational religious beliefs are in contention, and especially where national governments are relatively weak, conflict is inevitably harder to resolve. On the other hand, in the twentieth century, unbridled atheism, in the form of Nazism in Germany and Communism in Russia, gave rise to the two most horrific instances of bloodshed in history.

Secularisation, as we now understand and use this somewhat slippery abstract term, is a process that could be said to have begun, though not under that name, with the Old Testament and with the Greeks. At that time it involved the gradual erosion of superstition and the slow process of shedding false gods and provisional explanatory myths. These gods and myths were the means by which the people of the nations surrounding Israel attempted to explain their origins and their relationship to nature, to each other and to the unseen world and thereby give meaning to their lives. There was the constant risk that Israel itself would succumb to the temptation of taking the easy path that they offered rather than following the one true God and accepting the demands he made on them. These false gods and myths, many of them of great and enduring interest as stories, were gradually replaced by the true explanatory myths of God's revelation of himself and his involvement in history. The supreme example is his coming to earth in Jesus. This coming enables us to understand the truth of our relationship not only to the world and to each other but above all our relationship to God as our creator and redeemer.

What Jesus achieved in his brilliant teaching about our dual loyalty to God and to Caesar, that is to the social and political world of the state, was to clarify our need to try to live on these two interdependent levels. It is not only our primary loyalty to God and our relationship with him that are important but also our life in the world. This is because this earthly life too is the material from which God's spiritual kingdom is being fashioned by the transforming and purifying process of redemption. No single individual and no society in history, has ever managed to live with complete success on these two levels. Only

Jesus himself was able to do this because he was both God and man and belonged in heaven and, for a brief period of thirty years, on the earth. As human beings we are both of this present age, that is secular, and also spiritual beings destined for the age to come. We do not belong forever in this world. We are therefore, as we read in Heb 11:13-15, 'aliens and strangers on the earth' and 'looking for a better country'. We are in truth a people in transition from one stage of our development to another, much as adolescents are children on their way to becoming adults. Hence Paul talks in Ephesians 4:13-15 of our 'becoming mature' of our 'growing up' and eventually 'attaining to the whole measure of the fullness of Christ'.

As we make this journey we are constantly obliged, both individually and collectively, to renegotiate the relationship between our maturing spiritual hopes and expectations and our experience of the unfolding, rapidly developing world in which we live. This will always be the case until the physical, secular world is taken up into the spiritual realm in which it originated, when God will be all in all. Only then will our hopes and expectations be fulfilled in the perfect government of God's everlasting kingdom. It will then be possible to say in the prophetic words of Rev 11:15: 'The kingdom of the world has become the kingdom of our Lord and of his Christ, and he will reign for ever and ever.' There would appear to be no other possible alternative destiny for any part of God's creation but we cannot be given more than hints of its true nature. The danger is that nowadays, in the West at least, the process of secularisation is taking the form of the neglect of the truth of the Christian Gospel. The Good News of the Gospel is becoming submerged beneath the growing body of complex scientific, cultural and political developments that characterise our modern-day, materialistic society. It is also coming to be seen as one of a number of religious options, with their own very different explanatory stories and practices, in a society that is increasingly experienced as not only multicultural but also multi-faith.

The resolution of the tension between sacred and secular has had to be constantly renegotiated throughout history in every culture and in respect of all the world religions. This is true both in the United States where church and state are intended to be kept separate at one end of the scale, and in Islam where religion and law and politics now tend to be seen as indivisible, at the other. In both situations there is a need for constructive dialogue and co-operation in order to achieve a balance. The Holy Roman Empire and the rise of Christendom was the most obvious example of the Christian Church becoming too powerful politically and thereby compromising its true mission.

In the last hundred years we have seen dramatic changes in this balance in the Islamic world. The social and political influence of Islam was severely curbed by the Turkish military hero Mustafa Kemal Ataturk in the 1920's but this was naturally unpopular with many and Islamic faith and politics continue to be intertwined in what is still classed as a secular state. A change in the opposite direction was made in 1979 in what was then Persia when the Shah, who was put back on the throne by Britain and America and for this reason bitterly resented, was deposed in favour of a radical Islamic supreme leader in the shape of Ayatollah Khomeini. Only thirty years later there is evident dissatisfaction with his successor and the hard line Iranian Islamic president recently re-elected in a flawed ballot, and some are looking once again for a return to a more secular and democratic state. There is an interesting discussion of the uneasy, constantly-changing relationships between the various forms of faith, fundamentalism and atheism in the continuing struggle between the sacred and the secular, and its frequently political implications, in the final chapter of 'The Case for God' by Karen Armstrong. She offers an explanation of the origins of fundamentalism as in part a perception of the threat to faith from science and liberal theology, and of atheism as frequently a response to an inadequate understanding of faith or to the failures of the faithful.

There were brutal attempts to suppress and even to eradicate the influence of Christianity under the godless secular regimes of National Socialism in Nazi Germany and of Communism in Russia and Eastern Europe. In both these countries a new balance has since been negotiated between religion and the state but a degree of tension is inevitable. In China where Communism now exists alongside European style Capitalism there is considerable tension but the Church is flourishing nevertheless, in spite of attempts to promote a secularised model.

More recently, maybe in part as a reaction to the obvious failure of these atheistic ideologies and as a positive outcome of the persecution involved, there has been for both good and ill a return of religious influence of various kinds in many parts of the world. Christianity is growing at a remarkable rate in a large number of countries but not in

343

those of Western Europe. There is also a widespread resurgence of an unprecedentedly militant form of Islam that is now arguably the greatest threat to world peace, but also a challenge to our western decadence. Christianity is in a competitive market and there is an increasing need for the Church to seek forgiveness for its failings and look for opportunities to witness to the truth that is in Jesus. It also has a duty, in obedience to its God-given prophetic calling, to critique both society and government in the light of the truth of the Gospel. These are of course not the only ways in which it plays its part in restoring the balance between the spiritual and the secular on which the health of every individual and every society and nation depends. It is easy to forget the numerous ways in which the Church continues to minister to the physical, mental and spiritual welfare of those in need as a major part of its mission.

In that secularisation is the process of reducing or attempting to remove the religious influence in society in a number of different ways, it tends to be associated somewhat naturally with a reduction in the number of people engaging in public worship. The history of the parish church of St John the Baptist in Yeovil, and no doubt many others also, illustrates elements of both of these two aspects of secularisation over the past 600 years. When it was built in around 1400, the Church was the political as well as the spiritual centre of the town. The Rector was the Lord of the Manor of the Borough, with jurisdiction over the administration of local government, including the law, and commerce in the form of the markets. The Church was also the prime mover in education and in the provision of medical care, welfare and shelter for the sick and needy of all ages. As society developed and became more complex those responsibilities that the Church could no longer undertake were gradually taken over by other agencies, through this inevitable and necessary process of secularisation. These agencies included the Mayor and Corporation in the case of local government; the law courts including lay magistrates; independent commercial companies in the case of the markets, and local and central government in the case of education, health care and welfare. When, after a prolonged and often bitter struggle, the town of Yeovil became a self-governing municipal borough in 1854 the Mayor and Corporation retained the Rector's Seal with the Lamb of God symbol of St John the Baptist, thus doing justice to its history and the important, continuing relationship between the sacred and the secular.

The Church records show that in 1548, the year before the introduction of Archbishop Cranmer's first English Prayer Book, there were 822 'partakers of the Lord's Supper' though we have no way of knowing how often they attended. What we do know is that on the day of the ecclesiastical census of 1851 there were 400 people in St John's Church in the morning and 600 in the evening, though no doubt many of them worshipped both morning and evening. There were also 500 people in the daughter Church of Holy Trinity that had been consecrated only five years earlier in 1846 in order to cater for the worshippers for whom there was not enough room in St John's, in spite of the addition of galleries. There were no doubt also hundreds more worshipping in the various Nonconformist Churches and this was at a time when the total population of the town was less than 8000. There are now some 200 worshippers on a Sunday morning at St John's, with a population of around 40,000.

These facts and figures give us a clear picture of secularisation as both the necessary decline of the political power of the Church and the less satisfactory decline in the number of those involved in public worship. This long drawn out process of change has naturally led to a declining interest in the message of the Christian Gospel that inspired men and women to introduce the public services in the first place. Without these services to provide for people's physical, mental and spiritual welfare, society would be a very different place for everyone, especially the poor, as many other cultures reveal. Without the continuing presence of a sufficient number of people holding on to faith and giving their unselfish voluntary help to supplement these services, society will become a much less happy place for everyone, both rich and poor. In fact the decrease in this voluntary contribution is already obvious in our own communities. We are living on spiritual capital that can be drawn only from the source from which it originally came. If this is so we need to see an increasing number of people inspired by this same vision of the kingdom of God that helped to produce the civilised society that we have enjoyed. It is not too much to say that our society is now disintegrating and this disintegration is a challenge to the Church and to the conscience of the nation. The revival of our fortunes will not happen by itself. This is a message that the Church must believe and preach. The world is crying out for hope that only a knowledge of our origin and destiny in God can satisfy.

Any brief account of a phenomenon as complex as secularisation is bound to appear simplistic and there is a need to take more account, amongst other things, of the part played by the unusual movement of peoples with their different faiths and cultures in the present day. We also have to take account of the huge variety of ways in which individual men and women attempt to find answers to their deepest needs, other than in organised religion; for example in a return to superstition and horoscopes and various new age cults and man-made philosophical systems. We are busy nowadays making our own idols and fashioning new false gods and myths, or more often describing the old ones in new terms. The issue of human rights, for example, has been elevated almost to the status of a religious dogma, without sufficient emphasis on the need also for responsibility. This is giving rise to distortions in our relationships and can interfere with the dispensing of justice. Secularisation is an umbrella under which all manner of issues can legitimately be discussed, amongst others the relation of faith to science as it affects our view of the world in which we live. Some adopt a spiritual approach and see the world as created by God and belonging to him, with all that implies, and others a severely secular approach that has no place for him at all.

Secularism is the school of thought that denies the importance of any spiritual element in our lives and takes the view that morality should be based on what is good for men and women in this material world, without reference to a belief in God or in an after-life. Terrible things have been done in the name of religion but many more good things. Secularism is equivalent to atheistic humanism which has a very bad record.

APPENDIX 6

MUSIC

Music as we know it, though present in many fascinating rudimentary forms in the natural world, is a highly complex art form. It developed over the centuries, from its origins in folk music, as one of the products of evolving human culture and creativity. Any attempt to explain it must of necessity explore the extraordinary ability of sounds of varying frequency or 'pitch' and of a certain quality, arranged usually in rhythmic form through time, to engage both our minds and our emotions. Music speaks to us, like mathematics, in ways that we often cannot even begin to understand in any other terms. Its effect may be to enlighten us, to soothe or excite us, give rise to joy or sadness or carry us to heights and depths of experience that can only be described as spiritual. This is so whether the sounds are embodied and enriched by the human voice or by one of the numerous types of musical instrument. The individual musical notes may succeed each other in the form of a simple melody or a more complicated arrangement, or be combined and blended with other notes in chords or even more extensively in harmony. The shape or 'form' of a musical composition, of whatever length, is provided by the repetition and variation of its basic ideas or 'themes', and the element of change and contrast that is necessary to give it balance and interest. The majority of music has tended to end in the same musical place or key in which it began, wherever it goes in between. We all of us like to come across old friends as well as meeting new ones.

The mood or spirit of music is influenced by the performer and the instruments employed and its speed or 'tempo'. It is even more fundamentally influenced by its composition, in which the frequency of recurring accented notes or 'beats' that determine its 'time' plays a major part. There must surely be a relationship between these accented beats and the systolic or active contraction phase of our heart beats, and no doubt other bodily rhythms. There is no satisfactory explanation of the power of music to produce a response in us and to affect us in so many different ways. The varying frequency of vibration of the individual musical notes is a function of numbers, with their almost infinite variety of relationships. The distribution of these definitive notes in time, that together constitute the essence of music, must surely have to be an acoustic expression of the intrinsic mystery and beauty of mathematics. Hence music can be seen as the beauty of numbers artistically arranged and expressed in an audible dance. There is a similar beauty in the rhythm of language and especially in the cadence of all great oratory.

The vibration of the waves set in motion by musical sounds of whatever kind, in activating the sensory strings of our auditory apparatus, must thereby in some way gain access to the very centre of our being – body, mind and spirit. This explains why we can sometimes experience music as a kind of glorious, healing massage for all these areas. It is no surprise to learn that the various elements of music are processed and integrated in many different areas and at many different levels of the brain. It is for this reason that damage to each of these areas can selectively interfere with the perception of either rhythm, melody, harmony or pitch but not with all of them. It is no surprise either, to learn that the foetus in the mother's womb can be respond to the rhythm of music.

Such is the healing and integrating power of music that many people who have intractable problems with speech and movement can find release in singing and playing music and in dancing. Even patients with severe dementia can retain their ability to respond to music and to play and sing pieces they remember long after other forms of memory have disappeared. They are also able to sing with others long after they have ceased to make any other contact with them. Sadly these benefits persist only as long as the music lasts, or for a short time afterwards, and there is no progressive therapeutic effect.

No two people are affected by music in the same way. The rhythms and styles of music to which we naturally respond are dependent on age, ethnic and cultural differences, and the development of music over time. Needless to say, regardless of our taste in music, there is a huge variation in our ability to appreciate it, or to perform it in any way, and even more obviously in our ability to compose it. It is given only to a very few, as in all art forms, to be possessed of genius and startling originality and to produce works that continue to provide nourishment and enjoyment for millions. It is part of the mystery of music that individual composers can stamp their unmistakable signature on what they write and can often express not only their own spirit but that of their people or their age. The giants among them can seem, at times, to transcend all these limitations and to enter a realm that is beyond time.

Music is able to enhance almost every form of human activity, from meditation to marching into battle. In its various forms it appears to have an almost unique, universal appeal, especially for the blind, for whom it somewhat naturally tends to be an especially rich and beneficial experience. It has been described as a 'part of being human' and is a fundamental element in every known culture, though there are people for whom it appears to have little or no appeal or even to be irksome. The instinctive urge to make and listen to music and frequently to move and dance to it is possibly built into our genes, and into the dance-like configuration of the double helix of our DNA, if not even more deeply into the matter of which we and all other things are made. Stephen Hawking tells us that at the level of its ultimate and most minute particles 'the universe is like a crazy dance of waves tangoing to a myriad beats.'

If string theory should prove to be the resolution of the discrepancy between relativity and quantum mechanics and to be therefore the so-called 'theory of everything', or 'quantum gravity' in Hawking's terminology, it would fit well with this colourful image. According to one description of string theory the mass of the smallest elementary particle of matter is determined by the 'energy of the vibrational pattern of its internal string'. This resembles the dependence of the volume of a musical note on the amplitude, or energy of vibration of the violin string or whatever gives rise to the sound wave through which we perceive it. The influence of these 'myriad beats' and our instinctive, subconscious sensitivity and response to nature's dance within us might provide us with a clue in our attempt to understand the phenomenon of music. Maybe we can see how this potential for rhythm already present in our physical make-up might lead us to 'tango' to the patterns of notes that we recognise as music so that we are moved not only to dance but provided with other profounder experiences also.

It is a measure of the marvel and mystery of music that these notes, enriched by voices and instruments of a certain quality and maybe enhanced by the atmosphere and acoustic excellence of a cathedral or concert hall, are able to affect us in so many different ways. It is interesting that the female voice is, on average, an octave higher than the male, which helps to explain the extraordinary harmony of the two singing together. It is one of the greatest joys of music that it can be performed and listened to with others and it is one of the most powerful means of bringing people together. It is the nearest thing we have to a universal language, and especially for those who compose and perform it, is a life-changing experience.

It is perhaps no wonder that as human beings made in the image of God we respond to the dance at the heart of his creation and engage in the uniquely human activity of composing, performing and enjoying music. It is no wonder either that music plays such a large part in our worship. "Come, let us sing for joy to the Lord" the Psalmist exhorts us in 95:1, and Paul, in Eph 5:19, bids us "Sing and make music in your hearts to the Lord." We naturally praise him in the exercise of one of the very greatest gifts he has given us, just as we join with him as co-creators in our making of gardens and in a multitude of other pursuits. It is no surprise either that the Psalms and the book of Isaiah are full of singing and that in Revelation 'ten thousand times ten thousand' angels and 'every creature in heaven and on earth' are described as singing a 'new song'.

GLOSSARY OF WORDS AND TERMS

DEFINITIONS AND DESCRIPTIONS

It has been said that all 'all religious language is unsatisfactory'. Words 'strain and crack' and nowhere more so than in speaking of the things of God. This in part due to the ultimate mystery of his being and in part to the fact that the words we employ for this purpose have almost always to be borrowed from secular usage, albeit invested with a new and more exalted meaning. The Church has rarely needed to invent new words and there is no separate dictionary of exclusively spiritual terms. We need to attempt the greatest possible degree of precision in the meaning of the words we use and the list of definitions below is provided with this in mind. Due to the elasticity and subtle shades of the meaning of words, the original Hebrew and Greek words of Scripture are often translated differently in the numerous different versions of the Bible. This only rarely affects the true meaning of what we read but it is all too easy to fall into the trap of dogmatic interpretation of a verse without recognising this and comparing the various renderings – or better still, if possible, learning Hebrew and Greek!

The task of expressing any truth in language is highlighted by T.S Eliot when he writes, in an essay on Ezra Pound, that 'Words are perhaps the hardest of all material of art: for they must be used to express both visual beauty and beauty of sound, as well as communicate a grammatical statement.' There is plenty of evidence of all these three ingredients in Scripture in which certain passages exert a powerful, constructive and healing influence on our hearts and minds. This influence is explained in some measure by Professor I.A Richards when he says that 'Words are not a medium in which to copy life. Their true work is to restore life itself to order.'[41] Remarkable examples of this function have been Churchill's wartime speeches and President Kennedy's inaugural address in 1961 in which he said to the people of America: "Ask not what your country will do for you. Ask what you can do for your country." In both cases the

---

[41] The Philosophy of Rhetoric

words focused the minds of millions on what was required of them, as do the words of Scripture.

Some words cannot be accurately defined, only variously described by different authorities in their sometimes disparate uses and their particular meaning can often be determined only by the context in which they are used. It can be difficult on occasion to clarify the precise distinctions between certain words. In several cases below a number of them are for this reason taken together in an attempt to clarify their relationships as well as their individual meanings.

Allegory: See **Parable** below and Appendix 4.

Analogy: A likeness or correspondence between two things in terms of some of their attributes that enables us to make clarifying or colourful comparisons. These comparisons can take the form of similes or metaphors. See Appendix 4 and **Myth** below.

Angel: A messenger of God and minister to man; a holy and uncorrupted spirit, yet endowed with free will, therefore not necessarily impervious to temptation and sin.

Apocalypse/apocalyptic: The Greek word apocalypse means literally uncovering, or revelation. Apocalyptic refers to a particular style of visionary Jewish writing and its content which was largely in terms of eschatology or the end times and envisaged direct divine intervention, judgement and the transforming of the whole creation. Daniel is the chief example in the Old Testament and he and other apocalyptic writers, as interpreters of prophecy, were an enormous encouragement to the Jews in the period of persecution between the Testaments. In the New Testament the idea of the end times reappears specifically in Jesus' teaching about his return at the end of the age and Revelation, in envisaging the last things, is full of visions and colourful images typical of apocalyptic writing.

Apologetics: The use of argument in supporting and defending the Christian faith.

Apostle: Literally 'one sent, a messenger' and applied to Jesus himself in Heb 3;1. The term usually applies to the twelve witnesses that Jesus sent out to preach the gospel and later Barnabas and Paul, the Apostle of the Gentiles, and others who played a leading role in the early Church.

Atonement: Literally at-one-ment or making at one, hence bringing those who are estranged into unity. More specifically the work of Christ in dealing with the problem of sin and thereby bringing sinners into a right relation with God.

Baptism: John's baptism was with water, denoting repentance and cleansing in anticipation of the One who was to come. Christian baptism in the name of Jesus also signifies repentance but in addition faith in him and by inference the forgiveness of sins that goes with that commitment. This is a baptism with the Holy Spirit and with fire and was from the first the sacramental rite of entry and acceptance into the body of believers and of identification with Jesus. Where infant baptism is practised the parents and God-parents and the Church are expressing the hope and prayer that the child will one day wish to make the promise to follow Jesus on his or her own account.

Canon: Gr: kanon, rule or standard. Used since the fourth century to denote the authoritative list of books belonging to the OT and NT which the Church acknowledged as inspired scripture and normative for faith and practice.

Covenant: See separate article listed in Contents.

Creed: A brief summary of the main points of Christian doctrine. See separate article.

Deacon: lit 'one who serves' in order to enable the elders or overseers to give their full attention to prayer and the ministry of the word. See Elder below, and article on the Church.

Disciple: literally pupil or learner. Used of followers of various teachers, including John the Baptist, but chiefly of followers of Jesus during his lifetime, especially the original twelve, and all who have followed him since that time as members of his Church. The need to put the claims of Jesus first gives the word a sense of a costliness in following him.

Doctrine: literally something taught; more specifically a set of religious beliefs.

Dogma: a belief that is authoritatively stated or even, in a pejorative sense, aggressively stated and insisted on.

Elder: The duties of an elder in the early Church were to teach and preach, to direct the affairs of the church, to shepherd the flock of God and to guard the church from error. See separate article on the Church.

Enthusiasm: lit. en-theos or God-inspired, supernatural inspiration; hence intensity of feeling and interest expressed in a belief or cause.

353

Eschatology: lit. end or last things, the goal of God's purpose in history, depicted in the Bible as involving the return of Christ, the final judgement and the completion and perfecting of God's already inaugurated kingdom.

Eucharist: See **Sacrament.**

Evangelist: literally announcer of news; more specifically a preacher of the Gospel; one of the gifts of the Spirit to the Church, (Eph 4:11), and a term later used of the writers of the gospels.

Evidence: Something that gives grounds for belief.

Faith: 'Faith means that we are confident of what we hope for and convinced of what we do not see'. (Heb 11:1 Moffatt) See separate article in section on Hebrews.

Gentile: literally nation, but came to be a term of scorn used by Israelites to describe other nations whose religious practices would contaminate their own and had therefore to be shunned. In spite of this they had a place in the prophetic messianic promises notably in Isaiah, and they were later accepted by the Church as equals with the Jews as inheritors of God's Kingdom, especially through Paul's ministry.

Gnosticism: A term derived from the Greek word gnosis or knowledge. It refers to a system of belief, of unknown origin, whose central, dualist teaching was that spirit is entirely good and that matter and the whole created world is entirely evil. This led to harsh treatment of the body and to disregard of God's law. The only escape from the body and from the world was through the enlightenment of a secret knowledge or gnosis. This is at variance with the orthodox teaching of salvation that is achieved for us only through Christ's sacrificial death.

Grace: The gift of God's unmerited love to us in Christ, and in this sense, not known in the Old Testament. Our word grace is derived and developed from an ancient word that has given us also gracious, graceful, grateful and gratitude and the related Greek word charis embraces joy and gladness and the notion of receiving as well as giving. Grace, in the Biblical sense, is thus not truly grace until the welcome gift of God's love is recognised and gladly and joyfully received and experienced and shared with others so that we live and move in it together. It is essentially and intensely relational. The good news of the Gospel cannot simply be stated and conveyed as truth about God but has to be internalised and ministered to others as his reconciling love, in thought and word and deed. See separate article before chapter on Romans.

Heathen/Pagan: Unbelievers, non-worshippers.

Heaven: Where God dwells with the heavenly hosts and where he has made it possible for us to one day dwell with him.

HEBREWS, ISRAEL AND JEWS

Hebrews: The seed of Abraham, later to become known as the Israelites or the children of Israel. The name Israel was given by God to Jacob (Gen 35;10) who fathered the children who gave their names to the twelve tribes of Israel. **Israel** means literally 'one who struggles and overcomes'. The name is applied in the New Testament to all true believers, the Church being referred to as the 'New Israel'. The word Israel, in its various meanings, appears over 2000 times in Scripture. The term **Jew,** a term derived from Judah, was the name that was given not only to the people of the tribe of Judah but also to the remnant of the two southern tribes of Israel, Judah and Benjamin, together with some Levites, who were allowed by Cyrus the Persian to return to Jerusalem from Babylon when he defeated the Babylonians in 538 BC. The term is still used to describe their descendents today.

Heresy: An opinion or teaching that is a departure from what is generally accepted as orthodox belief. Paradoxically, conflicting views are essential for the dialogue from which truth emerges. The gradual development of Christian doctrine and the creeds in the early church is an example of this process of distinguishing truth from error.

HOLINESS, RIGHTEOUSNESS AND SANCTIFICATION

Holiness: lit. being set apart. God is set apart; among other ways, in his moral perfection. We in our turn are set apart for worshipping and serving him. By virtue of our fellowship with him and through the work of his Holy Spirit in our lives, we ideally become more like him. This comes about by the process of **sanctification** which literally means 'making holy'. **Righteousness**: A characteristic of God as holy; also used of a right relationship with him, established above all by his grace, and our commitment to him in faith. It should also ideally lead to right relations with each other, and hence to justice and peace.

Incarnation: Lit embodiment, or enfleshment. The Christian use of this term is primarily to highlight the seemingly scandalous belief that God himself was 'made in human likeness' in Jesus. John tells us at the start of his Gospel that God's eternal Word or Logos was made flesh or embodied in him. The incarnation is one of the central doctrines of the Christian faith.

Israel: See under **Hebrews** above.

Jews: See under **Hebrews** above.

JUSTIFICATION, REDEMPTION AND SALVATION

Justification: A legal term meaning acquittal as opposed to condemnation and punishment. To be justified is to declared righteous, or rightly related to God, and hence saved, by his grace and through our faith in him. Good works should naturally follow from this new relationship of eternal life with God. **Redemption** involves delivering from some evil by payment of a price or ransom eg. buying and freeing a slave in the market. The value of this term is that it emphasises the costly nature of Christ our redeemer's work in achieving our salvation and our entry into his kingdom. The risk is that the application of the idea involved can be pursued in ways that interfere with our attempts to fathom the overwhelming, incomprehensible love of Jesus in his voluntary, sacrificial giving of himself on the Cross in accordance with his Father's will. We are told that the Father sent him but they must have been of one mind in their determination to seek and save the lost. **Salvation**: The original meaning of the Hebrew word that is translated as save is literally to 'bring into a spacious environment,' 'a place of abundance' and to 'free from limitations'. Other faiths speak of various modes of salvation but for the Christian it denotes God's deliverance from our state of sinfulness and its consequences and our restoration to a right relationship with him. This is achieved by his grace and through our faith in Christ's work for us on the Cross and our following him as his disciples. We cannot do it for ourselves.

Legend: A story, based on truth, often fancifully embroidered, popularly regarded as historical but quite possibly not. As opposed to a Folk Tale, that is told simply to amuse.

Metaphor: See Appendix 4 and also **Myth** below.

Myth: See Appendix 3. It may be that Myth and metaphor are at risk of being confused. Myth is a certain sort of traditional story. Metaphor is a universal feature of language in which colour and interest and clarification are achieved in speech and writing by bringing together objects or ideas that share one or more illuminating and helpful similarities. These similarities or analogies are a reflection of the correspondence of phenomena that are often seemingly quite different in the rich and infinite variety of creation.

Natural theology: a theology based on human reason, apart from revelation.

Oracle: Gr: logia. In NT meaning divine utterances, generally referring to whole OT or some specific part of it. Now effectively all inspired scriptures which adequately proclaim and define apostolic doctrine and are considered fit for public reading in divine worship.

Parable: Lit: putting things side by side; a comparison. A story told to illustrate and convey moral or spiritual truth; an 'earthly story with a heavenly meaning'. Because creation is a coherent whole there are multiple similarities and correspondences. This gives rise to the need for both similes that are straight comparisons and metaphors that involve identification by means of analogous resemblance. If it is possible to make a distinction between a parable and an allegory it might be that where stories are told in which metaphorical analogies are used, eg the far country in the Prodigal Son, we call them parables; where symbolic allusions are involved, eg the apple in the Garden of Eden, we call them allegories. The beauty of both is that they demand thought and interpretation from the hearer. See Appendix 4.

Paradise: a word from ancient Iranian meaning literally a garden with a wall. The Greek equivalent occurs three times in the New Testament; once where Paul describes in 2 Cor :4 being 'caught up to paradise' where he 'heard inexpressible things' and above all where Jesus tells the penitent thief on the Cross in Lk 23:43 "I tell you the truth, today you will be with me in paradise." The third occasion is in Rev 2:7 where the Spirit, speaking to the churches says "To him who overcomes, I will give the right to eat from the tree of life, which is in the paradise of God." The walled garden, reminiscent of the picture of the original garden of Eden, clearly symbolises the glorious experience of being in the presence of God himself.

Parousia: lit to be present, to arrive. Used to describe Jesus' second coming.

Passion: The Greek word 'pascho' meaning suffering is used several times in the New Testament by Jesus himself, by Luke, by Paul in

Acts, and once by the writer of Hebrews, in speaking of Jesus' need to suffer in carrying out his work of redemption. The word is still used to refer to Jesus' suffering and death.

Patriarchs: Abraham, Isaac and Jacob, especially, as father figures and forerunners of God's new universal family, bound to him in a covenant relationship, and inheritors of the promised land.

Pentateuch: lit from Gk pentateuchos, five-volumed book, and referring to the first five books of the Old Testament, Genesis to Deuteronomy.

PHARISEES, SADDUCEES AND SCRIBES

Pharisees: lit. separate ones. A Jewish sect who were teachers in the synagogue and self-appointed guardians of the Law and its proper observance. They considered interpretations and regulations handed down through tradition to be virtually as authoritative as Scripture. According to them God's grace and favour extended only to those who adhered rigidly to the Law and this legalism involved them in hypocrisy that Jesus so vehemently condemned. They made the administration of the Temple their primary interest and initially held the large majority of seats in the **Sanhedrin.** This was the supreme Jewish council, a legislative and executive assembly exercising control and authority over political, judicial and religious matters. It was this body, meeting as a court, that judged Jesus worthy of death and sent him to Pilate, the Roman governor, who was the only one who could sentence him to death. **The Sadducees** were a wealthier, more worldly and politically-minded and religiously unorthodox sect who did not believe in the resurrection, personal mission or angels. They accepted only the Pentateuch, the first five books of the Old Testament Scriptures, flatly denying the oral tradition, or Talmud, and they hated the Pharisees. **The Scribes** were Jewish lawyers and scholars, mainly Pharisees, sometimes also priests, who studied, interpreted, preserved and taught the Law, both oral and written, and acted as judges in the Sanhedrin.

Phenomenon: simply means a thing observed, chiefly a fact or an occurrence eg a volcano or a volcanic eruption.

Priest: A mediator, one who performs sacrifices and other religious rituals on behalf of others, as did the Old Testament priests, who offered animal sacrifices as thanksgiving and as reminders of God's holiness and the people's need of cleansing from their sins. The New Testament Christian priest, is ordained – that is 'called', and ceremonially appointed – and amongst other duties, his most precious is presiding over the sacrament of the Eucharist. This sacrament is an enacted reminder, through the symbols of bread and wine, of the once-for-all saving death of Christ that brings forgiveness and cleansing from sin in a way that animal sacrifices could never do. Non-ordained, lay Christian believers are referred to in 1 Pet 2:9 as a 'holy priesthood'. This means that they too are ministers to others, that is they act as mediators, representing God to man in service and witness, and man to God in prayer.

Revelation: Something not previously known about God or about his future plans that we cannot discover for ourselves but that he has to disclose to us by supernatural means.

Righteousness: See above under Holiness.

Sacrament: An outward and visible sign of an inward, invisible blessing. The term is normally used only of Baptism and the Eucharist, also known as the Lord's Supper, Holy Communion and Mass. Water and bread and wine are the earthly elements, with their clear symbolic significance, through which grace is channelled in these traditional Christian rituals.

Sadducees: see above under Pharisees.

Sanctification: See under Holiness.

Sanhedrin: The highest tribunal or council of the Jews. See under Pharisees above.

Scribes: see above under Pharisees above.

Secular: see Appendix 5.

Son of Man: This is not an easy term to understand. It originated in the Old Testament and appears to have had both human and divine connotation: See Dan 8;17 and 7;13. It was Jesus' preferred way of referring to himself as explained in Jesus the Towering Central Figure.

Symbol: See Appendix 4.

Synoptic: Of the nature of a synopsis, or providing a condensed, overall view. The literal Greek meaning is 'viewing together'. Hence its specific biblical application to the first three Gospels, Matthew, Mark and Luke who all describe the life of Christ from a similar point of view.

Tax Collectors: Jewish agents who collected taxes on behalf of the pagan Romans. They often defrauded their own people and were therefore hated. Matthew and Zacchaeus were included in their number and both became disciples of Jesus, Matthew being one of the original twelve and Zacchaeus a later follower.

Theme: The chief idea or subject or consistent thread of an essay, a speech or a sermon, or of a piece of musical composition, usually subject to development with both repetition and variations.

BIBLIOGRAPHY

I am more aware of the numerous potentially valuable and relevant books that I cannot possibly have read, or even heard of, rather than the few that I have. The following is an incomplete list of the small number that I have read, or partly read or scanned for treasures, over the past fifty years. I have quoted or taken facts and ideas from a number of them, sometimes with attribution and sometimes without. In the latter case it is usually because the ideas I have 'stolen' are differently expressed rather than being verbatim quotations. It will have been apparent that I have found T.S Eliot a particularly rich source of ideas and I have quoted on numerous occasions from several of his works, especially his Four Quartets. Where there are unattributed phrases in quotes they are likely to have been borrowed from him. I am grateful to all the authors I have read, even if I have presumed to disagree with them, with or without adequate reason. Truth is arrived at by experiment and discussion. Amongst the most valuable reference books of all, apart from the Concordance and various commentaries, have been the dictionaries. If there is one thing that is more vital than any other in writing of whatever kind it is to understand the meaning of the words we use.

Alcorn, R. *Heaven.* Tyndale House Publishers, 2004.

Alexander, D. *Creation or Evolution. Do We Have to Choose?,* Monarch Books, 2008.

Anon. *The Cloud of Unknowing and Other Works.* Penguin Classics, 1978.

Armstrong, K. *A Short History of Myth.* Canongate, 2005.

Armstrong, K. *The Case for God.* Vintage Books, 2009.

Barrett, W. *Irrational Man.* Doubleday, 1958.
Benedict XVI. *Deus Caritas Es.* 2005.
Benedict XVI. *Spe Salvi.* 2007.
Benedict XVI. *Jesus of Nazareth.* Bloomsbury Publishing, 2007.
Bettelheim, B. *The Informed Heart.* Penguin Books, 1986.
Bible in Transmission. The Bible Society, *Perspectives on Secularisation.* 2007.
Boardman, J. et al. *The Oxford History of the Classical World.* OUP, 1991.
Bonhoeffer, D. *Letters and Papers from Prison.* Fontana Books, 1965.
Bragg, M. *Twelve Books that Changed the World.* Hodder and Stoughton, 2006.
Bryson, B. *A Short History of Nearly Everything.* Doubleday, 2003.
Bullock, A. and Stallybrass, O. *The Fontana Dictionary of Modern Thought.*
Bunyan, J. *Pilgrim's Progress.*
Britannica Online Encyc. *The Gorbachev Era: perestroika and glasnost.*
Butterfield, H. *Christianity and History.* Bell, 1949.
Chadwick, S. *The Way to Pentecost.* Hodder and Stoughton, 1966.
Combined Dictionary Thesaurus. Chambers, 1995.
The New Testament in Four Versions. Collins, 1967.
Cox, H. *The Secular City.* Pelican Books, 1968.
Cullmann, O. *Christ and Time.* SCM Press, 1951.
Cullmann, O. *The Early Church.* SCM Press, 1956.
Dante. *The Divine Comedy.* The Worlds Classics, OUP, 1993.
Engineering and Technology 16-30 January 2009 pp 34 and 42.
Darwin, C. *The Origin of Species.* The World`s Classics, 1947.
Darwin, C. *The Descent of Man.* John Murray, 1901.
Darwin, C. and Huxley, T. H. *Autobiographies.* Oxford University Press, 1974.
Dawkins, R. *The God Delusion.* Transworld Publishers (Bantam Press), 2006.
Dodd, C. H. *The Parables of the Kingdom.* Fontana Books, 1967.
Dostoyevsky, F. *The Brothers Karamazov.* The Penguin Classics, 1958.
Dostoyevsky, F. *The Devils.* Penguin Classics, 1971.
Drummond, H. *Natural Law in the Spiritual World.* Hodder and Stoughton, 1899.

Drummond, H. *The Ascent of Man.* Hodder and Stoughton, 1894.
Dulles, A. *Models of the Church.* Gill and Macmillan, 1987.
Einstein, A. *Relativity, The Special and General Theory.* Crown Publishers, New York, 1931.
Einstein, A. *The World as I see it.* Citadel Press, 1984.
Eliot, T.S. *Selected Essays.* Faber and Faber, 1932.
Eliot, T.S. *The Use of Poetry.* Faber and Faber, 1933.
Eliot, T.S. *The Idea of a Christian Society.* Faber and Faber, 1939.
Eliot, T.S. *Four Quartets.* Faber and Faber, 1944.
Eliot, T.S. *Towards a Definition of Culture.* Faber and Faber, 1948.
Eliot, T.S. *The Idea of a Christian Society and other writings.* Faber and Faber, 1982.
Farrer, A. *Faith and Speculation.* T. and T. Clark, 1988.
Farrer, A. *The Essential Sermons.* SPCK, 1991.
Farrington, B. *What Darwin Really Said.* Sphere Books Ltd., 1969.
Fowler, H.W. and F.G. *The King's English.* Oxford University Press, 1951.
Fowler, H.W. *Modern English Usage.* Oxford University Press, 1952.
Freeman, J. *The Closing of the Western Mind.* Heinemann, 2002.
Frutiger, A. *Signs and Symbols, Their Design and Meaning.* Ebury Press, 1998.
Graves, R. *The Greek Myths.* Penguin Books, 1960.
Green, M. *Lies, Lies, Lies!* Inter-Varsity Press, 2009.
Greene, B. *The Elegant Universe.* Vintage Books, 1999.
Isaacson, W. *Einstein, His Life and Universe.* Simon and Schuster, 2007.
Hawking, S. *A Brief History of Time.* Bantam Books, 1997.
Homer. *The Iliad.* Penguin Classics, 1981.
Homer. *The Odyssey.* Penguin Classics, 1981.
Hopkins, G.M . *Poems and Prose.* Penguin Books, 1978.
Houghton, J. *The Search for God: Can Science Help?* John Ray Institute, 2007.
Josephus, F. *Antiquities of the Jews.* Whittingham, London, 1822.
Julian of Norwich. *Revelations of Divine Love.* Penguin Classics 1966.
Jung, C.J. *Memories, Dreams, Reflections.* Fontana Press, 1995.
Jung, C.J. *Answer to Job.* Ark Paperbacks, 1987.
Jung, C.J. *Modern Man in Search of a Soul.* Routledge and Kegan Paul, 1970.

Kitchen, K.A. *On the Reliability of the Old Testament.* Eerdmans, 2004.
Kung, H. *Christianity and the World's Religions.* SCM Press, 1986.
Larkin, P. *Collected Poems.* Faber and Faber, 1988.
Lawrence, D.H. *Selected Poems.* Penguin Books, 1972.
Levi-Strauss, C. *Daily Telegraph Obituary,* November 4 2009.
Lewis, C.S. *The Four Loves.* Collins, 1986.
Lewis, C.S. *The Problem of Pain.* The Centenary Press, 1941.
Lewis, C.S. *Fern-seed and Elephants.* Collins, Fount Paperbacks, 1989.
Lichterman, B. *Obituary: Mark Edelman* BMJ, 28/11/09.
Liddell and Scott. *Greek-English Lexicon.* Oxford.
Lincoln, A. *Gettysburg Address.* 1863.
Lloyd-Jones, M. *Authority.* IVF, 1966.
Lovelock, J. *The Revenge of Gaia.* Penguin Books, 2006.
MacArthur, B. *Historic Speeches.* Penguin Books, 1996.
Macquarrie, J. *Mary for All Christians.* Collins, 1990.
Magee, B. *The Great Philosophers.* Oxford University Press, 1987.
May, R. *The Evolution of Cooperation.* Pres. Address, BSA, 2009.
McGrath, A.E. *Christian Theology.* Blackwell, 1995.
McGrath, A.E. *The Dawkin's Delusion?* SPCK, 2007.
McGrath, A.E. *Christianity's Dangerous Idea.* SPCK, 2007.
McGrath, A.E. *The Open Secret.* Blackwell Publishing, 2008.
Morison, F. *Who Moved the Stone?* Faber and Faber, 1966.
Murdoch, I. *Existentialists and Mystics* Chatto and Windus, 1997.
National Geographic Magazine. *'What Darwin Didn't Know'.* Feb. 2009.
New Bible Dictionary. Inter Varsity Press, 1982.
New International Version Study Bible. Hodder and Stoughton, 1991.
Nicholi, A.M. *The Question of God.* Simon and Schuster, 2003.
Norman E. *Secularisation.* Continuum 2002
Obama, B. *The Audacity of Hope.* Canongate, 2007.
Orr-Ewing, A. *Can We Trust the Bible?* IVP, 2005.
Orwell, G. *1984.* Penguin Books, 1949.
Orwell, G. *Animal Farm.* Secker and Warburg Ltd., 1995.
Oxford English Dictionary. Clarendon Press, 1983.
Partridge, E. *Usage and Abusage.* Penguin Books, 1947.
Pascal, B. *Pensees.* Penguin Books, 1966.

Peake, A.S. *A Commentary on the Bible*. Thomas Nelson and Sons Ltd.
Plato. *The Republic*. Oxford University Press, 1966.
Polkinghorne, J. *The God of Hope and the End of the World*. SPCK, 2002.
Polkinghorne, J. *Quantum Physics: A Very Short Introduction*. OUP, 2002.
Polkinghorne, J. *Quantum Physics and Theology*. SPCK, 2007.
Richards, I.A. *The Philosophy of Rhetoric*. Oxford University Press, 1976.
Rohl, D. *A Test of Time*. Century, 1995.
Sacks, O. *Musicophilia*. Picador, 2007.
Sanders, E.P. *Paul*. Oxford University Press, 1992.
Sargent, T. *The Sacred Anointing, The Preaching of Dr M Lloyd-Jones*. Hodder and Stoughton, 1994.
Scholes, P.A. *The Oxford Companion to Music*. Oxford University Press, 1970.
Scruton, R. *The Need for Nations*. Civitas, 2004.
Singh, S. *Big Bang*. Fourth Estate, 2002.
Spencer, N. & White, R. *Christianity, Climate Change & Sustainable Living*. SPCK, 2007.
Spencer, N. *Darwin and God*. SPCK, 2008.
St John of the Cross. *The Dark Night of the Soul*. James Clarke, Cambridge, 1973.
Stanton, G.N. *The Gospels and Jesus*. Oxford University Press, 1992.
Stevens, A. *Archetype, A Natural History of the Self*. Routledge, 1982.
Stevens, A. *On Jung*. Penguin Books, 1990.
Studdert-Kennedy. *The Best of Studdert-Kennedy*. Hodder and Stoughton, 1947.
Teilhard de Chardin, P. *Le Milieu Divin*. Fontana Books, 1960.
Teilhard de Chardin, P. *Hymn of the Universe*. Collins, 1966.
Teilhard de Chardin, P. *The Phenomenon of Man*. Fontana, 1967.
Tolstoy, L. *Resurrection*. Penguin Classics, 1966.
Truss, L. *Eats, Shoots and Leaves*. Profile Books, 2003.
Vanstone, W.H. *Fare Well in Christ*. Darton, Longman and Todd, 1998
Virgil. *The Aeneid*. Penguin Classics, 1966.

Walsh, W. *The Use of Imagination.* Chatto and Windus, 1959.
Ward, K. *What The Bible Really Teaches.* SPCK, 2004.
Ward, K. *Christianity, A Guide for the Perplexed.* SPCK, 2007.
Watson, J. .D *The Secret of Life.* Weidenfield and Nicholson, 1968.
Westrup, J. & Harrison, F.L. *Collins Encyc. of Music.* Chancellor Press, 1985.
Williams, R. *Open to Judgement.* Darton, Longman and Todd, 1994.
Williams, R. *Grace and Necessity.* Morehouse, 2005.
Williams, R. *Dostoevsky.* Continuum, 2008.
Wilson, E.O. *Consilience – The Unity of Knowledge.* Little Brown, 1998.
Wright, T. *The Lord and His Prayer.* Triangle, SPCK, 1996.
Wright, T. *Simply Christian.* SPCK, 2006.
Wurmbrand, R. *In God's Underground.* W.H. Allen, 1968.
Wurmbrand, R. *Sermons in Solitary Confinement.* Hodder and Stoughton, 1969.
Young, F. *The Making of the Creeds.* SCM Press, 1991.
Young, R. *Analytical Concordance to the Holy Bible.* Religious Tract Society.
Young, Wm. Paul. *The Shack.* Hodder and Stoughton Ltd., 2007.

Since completing my book I have read *England: Before and After Wesley* by J.W. Bready (Hodder and Stoughton, 1938). It describes the spiritual and social depths to which the country had fallen and the massive influence of the Evangelical Revival, both here and in America. It involved the conversion of thousands of working people and many men of influence and power in all walks of life. It led to the abolition of slavery, the opening of schools and the reform of prisons and the penal code. It also gave rise to Foreign Missions, Factory Legislation and to the Trade Union and Labour movements. Social services were a further outcome, notably voluntary medical services and charitable foundations including Dr Barnardo's Homes, The Salvation Army, Scouts and Guides and the NSPCC. Bready writes on p273: 'Without the sobriety, the discipline, the joyous fellowship, the love of knowledge, the training in co-operation and the new consciousness of human dignity and divine purpose, which the revival brought to countless numbers of humble folk, the vigorous Self-Help and Social Reform movements... could never have been born.'

MAPS

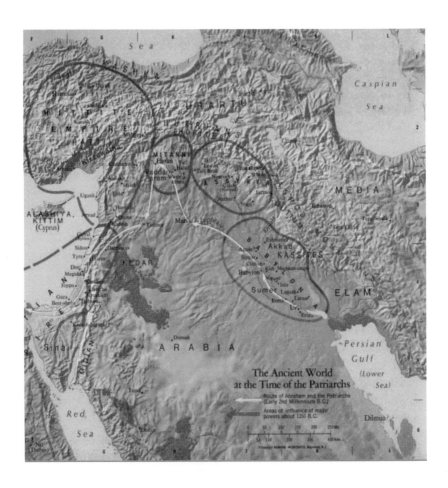

These maps are reproduced courtesy of
the Hammond World Atlas Incorporated.

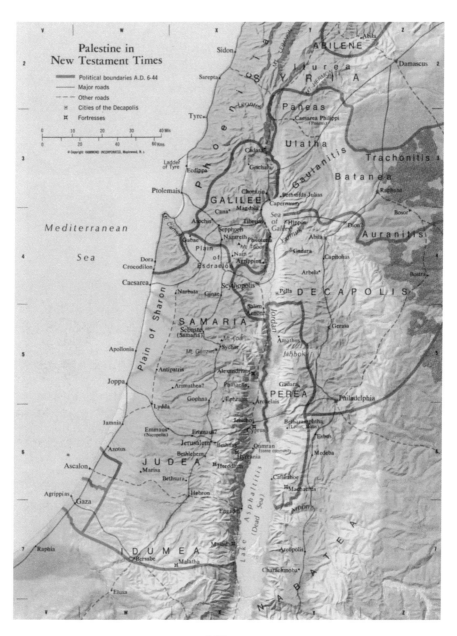

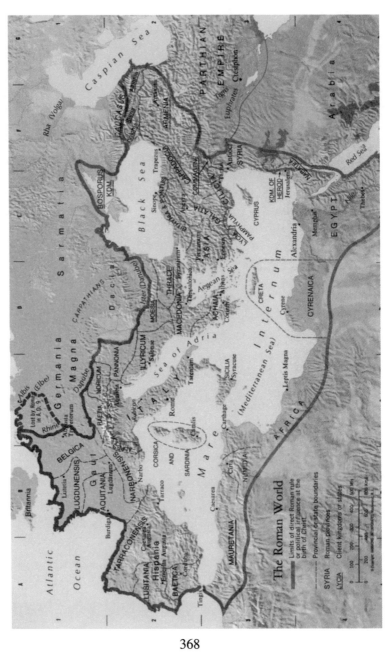